MICHAEL PORTILLO

The Future of the Right

MICHAEL PORTILLO

The Future of the Right

MICHAEL GOVE

FOURTH ESTATE · *London*

To Ernest and Christine Gove

First published in Great Britain in 1995 by
Fourth Estate Limited
6 Salem Road
London, W2 4BU
Copyright © 1995 by Michael Gove

The right of Michael Gove to be identified as the author of this
work has been asserted by him in accordance with the Copyright,
Designs and Patents Act 1988.

A catalogue record for this book is available from the British Library.

ISBN 1−85702−335−8

Typset by Rowland Phototypesetting Ltd, Bury St Edmunds, Suffolk
Printed in Great Britain by Clays Ltd, Bungay, Suffolk

Contents

Introduction

This book would not have been possible without Tony Blair.

It is, as I have had cause to realise over the last nine months, difficult to write about politicians while they are still alive, let alone still in Parliament. However, the appearance of two biographies of Mr Blair in the past year inclines me to believe that there is an interest in the background, beliefs and influences of active and ambitious politicians which this book can go some way to satisfy.

Both main political parties have shifted to the Right in the nineties, and during this decade no serving politician has come to be so closely identified with efforts to wrench Britain further to the Right as Michael Portillo.

The story of the son of a Spanish Republican refugee who has become the most punchily populist minister in a Conservative Cabinet would be interesting in itself. But Portillo's progress over the last twenty years also tells us something about the way Britain has changed, and our rulers have adapted. Portillo has been at the heart of power – as adviser, acolyte and player – for the past two decades, and his influence on the shape of the Tory party has grown throughout that period. I have attempted to tell something of that story, and I hope that my efforts make it a little easier to understand how we have been governed and how we might be governed.

This is an unauthorised biography. I have not had the benefit of access either to Michael Portillo's private correspondence or to hours of tape-recorded reminiscence. Portillo has, however, put no visible impediments in my path and has not sought to prevent me talking to friends, relatives, colleagues and teachers. I am grateful to him for his forbearance. Additionally, while writing this book I have encountered him on a number of occasions in my capacity as a reporter with the BBC. On all those occasions he has shown courtesy without undue curiosity, and I am indebted to him for his straightforwardness.

While I was conducting the research for this book, a great many people agreed to speak to me. Many of their names appear in the text, either quoted directly or referred to as authorities for this or that anecdote or insight, and I should like to thank them all for their kindness in agreeing to see me, their candour under questioning and their patience with my impertinence.

Several people agreed to talk to me in confidence. Their names, obviously, do not appear in the text, but I should like to record here my gratitude to all those who took the time to help me build up a picture of a politician notoriously shy of personal publicity.

In addition to those mentioned, I should also like to thank Edward Vaizey, Gary Gibbon, Matthew D'Ancona, John Antcliffe, Marcus Kiggell, Frank Johnson, Dean Godson, Andrew Roberts, Lawrence Donegan, Russel Newmark, Sinclair McKay and Paul Goodman for their encouragement, advice and insights.

My publishers, Fourth Estate, have shown rare patience and kindness. I should like, particularly, to thank my editor, Clive Priddle, for his innumerable nuggets of good advice and his wise guiding hand, and Bob Davenport, my copy-editor, for transforming a patchwork text with rare speed and grace. I am also grateful to my agent, Andrew Lownie, for his encouragement and professionalism.

My employers at the BBC have been indulgent, particularly Roger Mosey, editor of *Today*, and Francis Halewood, Richard Clark, Rod Liddle and Andrew Hawken. Writing this book would have been impossible without their support. In addition, all my colleagues on *Today* have been generous with help and attentive to any morsel of information that might make this story easier to tell.

The BBC's News Information Library and Political Research Unit has been invaluable, in particular the PRU's Robbie Gibb.

The staff of the London Library, Salamanca University, the Spanish Civil War Archive in Madrid, Kirkcaldy Art Gallery, the British Library and the Newspaper Archive at Colindale have rendered much valuable assistance.

Writing this book at such speed would not have been possible without the research help given by Gurutze Aguirre in Spain and

Sean O'Grady in London. Sean has given up long hours to plough through *Hansard* and correct my initial drafts. I am indebted to him for his knowledge, verbal felicity and unfailing good humour throughout.

I am grateful to Simone Kubes for her persistence in prodding me into writing this text, and am deeply in debt to Amanda Foreman for innumerable acts of kindness which ensured I could finish it.

All the above, and many more, have made this book possible, but any mistakes of fact, errors of judgement or unsupportable opinions are my responsibility alone.

There are no footnotes in this book: the sources of all quotations and all references, where possible and relevant, are cited in the text. In doing so I have followed journalistic rather than academic practice. This is a biographical essay not a textbook, and I hope my decision makes for a clearer, and less interrupted, read.

Michael Gove
London
August 1995

CHAPTER ONE

Prologue

To be conservative then is to prefer the familiar to the
unknown, to prefer the tried to the untried, fact to mystery,
the actual to the possible, the limited to the unbounded, the
near to the distant, the sufficient to the superabundant, the
convenient to the perfect, present laughter to utopian bliss.
                    Michael Oakeshott, *On Being Conservative*

No change equals no chance.
                    John Redwood leadership campaign leaflet

It had been a gamble. At a time when his party was in turmoil,
its leadership unresolved, its direction uncertain, he had ignored
advice, taken risks and trusted to his instincts. He had been loyal
to his principles, and his friends, and had seen some of that loyalty
returned. Would it be enough?

He was at his desk, in his office, when Sir Marcus Fox, the
chairman of the 1922 Committee, announced the result: 'John
Major 218 votes; John Redwood 89 votes.'

He heard the pundits and politicians first to the microphone
make their instant judgements and establish the conventional wisdom – a clear-cut victory, a decisive end to the destabilising gossip
about the leadership. But he was not so sure. The man he had
voted for had been victorious, but, as Michael Portillo prepared
to go outside, greet the cameras, and express his pleasure that his
candidate had won, he knew that it was not all over – far from it.
He knew the party had avoided the contest it could have had –
the battle between him and Michael Heseltine which could have
decided the party's direction and replaced a pastel premier with
a leader in a bolder blue.

As he left his office to face the cameras, Portillo could allow
himself some satisfaction. In a straight choice between Major and
Redwood, he had his reasons for taking pleasure in the Major
victory. He knew Major's virtues, and knew too that the Conservative Party rarely elected the assassin to succeed a recently deposed

leader. And, best of all, Portillo lived to fight again. He was still the most prominent Euro-sceptic in the Cabinet, still the most charismatic standard-bearer the rising Right had, and he had seen his rival for the prince's crown defeated.

Michael Portillo had taken a risk by refusing to resign his office and join the leadership contest. He had argued that principle and pragmatism united to make resignation impossible, and he had suffered a temporary eclipse on the Right for his refusal to break out of the lock of Cabinet loyalty. But the realities remained. Throughout the contest between the two Johns there had been a yearning in the press, and among politicians, for a bigger battle: Michael versus Michael – Heseltine versus Portillo.

For five years, following Margaret Thatcher's fall, John Major had struggled to unite a party riven by a struggle for its soul. On one side were the old 'wets' and their successors. Once instinctive interventionists, they were now more market-driven, but they were still unhappy with the direction 'their' party had taken in the eighties. They wanted to drag it back to the centre, back into the heart of Europe and back into dialogue with the groups that Thatcher had shut out. On the other side were the Right. From desiccated economic 'dries' to old-fashioned English nationalists, they were the inheritors of Thatcher's legacy and wanted a Britain strong, proud and free – united at home, respected abroad. Most MPs were not completely in either camp. They inhabited the vast dead centre of the party, loyal to whichever leader would save their seats and provide the party with a new narrative to justify the latest policy twist.

Despite five years of leadership from the centre, the two wings of the party had grown stronger and more restive. They had sniped at each other relentlessly, and caught Major in their cross-fire.

By early 1995 the need for a resolution of this struggle seemed overwhelming. Eight MPs had had the party whip withdrawn following an unprecedented breakdown of party discipline. Could the party continue to be led?

Many thought the party was ungovernable – just as Britain had seemed in 1974 and 1979, when union leaders had defied elected governments. What was needed was a man prepared to lead, rather than manage: a prince, not a committee chairman.

The two men in the party who had the necessary princely air

about them, the two whose entry into a room attracted the gaze of every uncommitted eye, were the unofficial champions of Left and Right – old wet and young Thatcherite: Michael Heseltine and Michael Portillo.

Portillo was, in the words of the *Independent*'s political commentator Andrew Marr, 'the candidate with sex appeal. The Prince Rupert of the Right.'

Tipped for the Cabinet when he was only thirty-one, he made it in eight years, in 1992. For all those who in the eighties had been attracted to the Tories by the sense that politics was again an adventure, with dragons to be slain, ideals to be defended, principled battles to be fought and maidens – one above all – to be cherished, he was the natural candidate.

He was the candidate of the Romantic Right, but he was also an intriguing, enigmatic professional politician who had impressed many, and enraged more. The son of a Spaniard and a Scot, his attachment to Britain and its institutions had won him the support of Tory activists tired of apologising. The last-ditch defender of the poll tax and then architect of its replacement, he had impressed a series of senior ministers with his cool dispatch of the difficult business of government. The practised charmer and loyal friend, his charisma and fidelity made him the guest of choice at a lunch with a Labour MP or a dinner for Tory activists in Aldershot.

In his mix of dash, colour, excitement and political presence his natural rival was Michael Heseltine – the Great Pretender. A minister when Portillo was still at school, darling of the party conference for fifteen years, a dangerous, reckless, mace-swinging, flakjacket-wearing, Maggie-mauling, mane-waving, intervening, barn-storming politician, he had planned his ascent to the top in his twenties, and in his sixties he still had the gleam of ambition in his eye.

During the ten days in the summer of 1995 that the Tories were leaderless, these two natural leaders circled each other warily – waiting to strike. There was a sense throughout the leadership crisis that the real leaders would have to emerge.

The battle between the prime minister – persistently underestimated but to many Tories still second choice – and John Redwood – the Welsh secretary who saw his chance to shine – did not inspire or excite in the same way as the struggle between Heseltine and Portillo promised to. After years of Majorite managerialism, was it enough just to be offered another merchant banker called John? Should one cricket-loving son of the suburbs with a dry delivery, schoolboy parting and Home Counties ordinariness replace another? If no change meant no chance, as Redwood insisted, was it wise to choose a new leader who offered the mixture as before but with added ideology and taxes taken out?

Redwood's leadership campaign and his actions thereafter certainly enhanced his reputation in the eyes of many on the Right – Portillo's apparent equivocation and the nocturnal activities of certain BT engineers cast a shadow over the golden boy. But the long lead Portillo had built up has never been tested. In the end, Tory MPs shrank from making any change at all, but throughout the election manœuvring there had been furious calculations about how to finesse events to allow the men the *Sun* called 'the Gladiatories' to slug it out.

After Major's victory he emerged strengthened, having again defied the doubters with his capacity to convince a sullen electorate to give him another chance. But there was about the whole battle a sense of the decision deferred. As the dust cleared on the day after the contest, the opposition, eyes focused on the far horizon, calculations uncluttered with factional obsessions, could see who the long-term winner was. As the political editor of the *Daily Mirror* explained:

Michael Portillo was last night appointed the Tory heir-apparent, the Conservatives' leader-in-waiting. That is the real significance of what happened in Committee Room 12 yesterday, not the survival of John Major. Heseltine is finished and John Redwood has failed in his audacious bid for the leadership of the Tory Right. The Tory Right has given Major such a fright for the past fortnight that Portillo must now be placated.

It was a potentially powerful position, an impressive accumulation of political capital. How had Portillo, at that point still the youngest member of the Cabinet, come to inherit it? How had he been able to prevent, albeit at considerable cost, seeing his position overtaken by an outsider? How would he make use of his situation? And what sort of Britain would it be if he, or those who have looked to him, were to wield the power they have prepared for?

CHAPTER TWO

Roots

I'm always surprised that someone who's half-Spanish finds it
so difficult to come to terms with Europe.

Edwina Currie MP

I want to be prime minister, but I never will because my name
is Portillo.

Michael Portillo, in conversation with a schoolfriend

An exotic background has never been a barrier to success in the
Tory party. Although it is supposedly the party of patriots, and of
the family, the leaders it has selected include a Jew, a bachelor, a
woman, a Canadian, an American and a clutch of unsuitable Scots.

Of its historic hierarchy of influences and great names, Burke
was in origin an Irish Whig, Disraeli a Jewish adventurer,
Churchill half-American and wholly promiscuous in his party
allegiance, Bonar Law and Macmillan were both of colonial stock,
Heath was the unmarried son of a Broadstairs builder, Thatcher
a grocer's daughter, and married to a divorcee, and John Major
the son of a circus trapeze artist who faced financial ruin, and
whose forebears lived in America. They may all have had hearts
of oak but none was a prototypical John Bull.

However, even by the standards of Tory politicians past,
Michael Portillo's background is unusual. His father was not
merely Spanish, but a Castilian intellectual of breeding and
refinement. His mother is Scottish, but from a merchant family
with a proud philanthropic and artistic tradition. Brought up in
Betjeman's Metroland, the settled suburbia that represented the
idealised location of semi-detached Tory virtue, Portillo was heir
to a rich mix of influences which helped build his character.

Michael's father, Luis Gabriel Portillo, was born in 1907, in the
village of Gimialcón, near Ávila, on the high Castilian plain, in
the centre of Spain. His father, Michael's grandfather, Justino,
was a doctor, from solid professional stock, and Luis was one of
ten children: seven boys and three girls. Two years after Luis's

birth Justino moved to become the general practitioner in the picturesque medieval village of Madrigal de las Altas Torres, a little
further west, near the Castilian university town of Salamanca.

Madrigal has been home to Portillos since 1578. The family once
owned most of the property in the village, which nestles, as the
name implies, at the foot of mountains. Madrigal was the birth-
place of Isabella, consort of Ferdinand, mother of modern Spain
and sponsor of Christopher Columbus. The convent where Isabella
was born still survives, unchanged since the sixteenth century.
Michael Portillo visited it as a boy, walking through streets barely
changed since his father's own boyhood.

Castile is Spain's heartland, and Madrigal lies at the heart of
Old Castile. Castile is also the most traditional part of Spain,
the area where the Spanish is most perfect. Catalonia, Galicia,
Granada and the Basque country all have their own flavour, smoth-
ered to an extent under Franco's centralised state and now
flourishing under federalism, but it is in Castile that the older
virtues of the essential Spain survive most strongly.

The Castilians are Spain's Prussians, epitomising virtues, and
vices, that permeate all their countrymen to a lesser extent. Like
Prussians the people of Castile have a nobility that can manifest
itself as hauteur. Chris Patten, now governor of Hong Kong, who
was to employ Michael Portillo at the Conservative Research
Department, recognised this strain in the young demi-Spaniard's
character and dubbed him 'the Castilian'. The name stuck, and
is used still by some older acquaintances.

Tristan Garel-Jones is a mutual friend of Patten and Portillo.
MP for Watford, he has been both a Foreign Office minister and
a deputy chief whip – posts in which his liberal views and taste
for intrigue did him no harm. Originally from Llangennech, near
Llanelli in Carmarthenshire, when he was young his family moved
to Madrid and founded a successful language school. He reads
Spanish poetry for relaxation, collects Spanish art, and keeps a
second home in Spain where the Majors have holidayed.

Most Englishmen find it difficult to trust the Welsh, and Garel-
Jones, Cambrian by birth, makes it more difficult in his case by
being Castilian by adoption. His sins in the eyes of the pure-bred
Englishmen of the Euro-sceptic hard core are compounded by his
part in the passage of the Maastricht Treaty through the Commons

in 1992–3. His persistence in trying to make Britain's membership of the European Community more 'constructive' has earned him the nicknames 'the Prince of Darkness' and 'the member for Madrid Central' from the sceptics. However, he and Portillo are good, and old, friends. He believes Patten's nickname accurately identified a trait in Portillo's personality that makes him sometimes slightly foreign to an English audience. 'This may sound harsh, but then I'm married to a Castilian and I adore the Castilians. The characteristics of these people? Proud, intelligent, dignified, anarchic, cold, honourable, tough. There's nothing gentle about a Castilian.

'And if you were to say, "What does Michael inherit?" Highly ambitious; highly intelligent; emotional, although it doesn't show. That again is a very Spanish characteristic. Spanish music and art are essentially austere. The Spaniard isn't like other Latins – effervescent, jolly. The Castilian is austere – in his personal habits, in his judgement of himself and others – and I think Michael has a certain amount of that dignified, personal austerity.'

Michael Portillo's grandfather, Dr Justino Portillo, was, apparently, douce, dignified and thoroughly middle-class in his behaviour, but far from wealthy. Luis, as the eldest son, often had to make sacrifices to see the other nine children provided for. He went without shoes to save money, but the one thing he never gave up was his books. Michael Portillo's earliest memories of his father are of him reading. The oldest picture of Luis in the family collection shows him clutching a book, and relatives remember he never had his nose out of a book as a child. It was no surprise, given Luis's love of learning, that he went on to the University of Salamanca. The only question was, what to study?

Luis toyed with the idea of a career in medicine, following his father, but he did not want to be a burden on his family. He decided to pursue a profession which would allow him to qualify as quickly as possible and start making his own way: law.

After a brilliant undergraduate career, Luis went to Madrid in the late twenties to study for his doctorate. Spain was enjoying a cultural renaissance, and Luis mixed in the 'generation of 1927' with metropolitan artists and intellectuals like the surrealist film-maker Luis Buñuel and the playwright Federico García Lorca. Michael's mother, Cora, remembers her husband reminiscing about those days with Lorca: 'I always understood that he had strolled through the night with Federico, hearing the nightingales and talking of his poetry. Luis asked him the meaning of some of his more obscure metaphors.'

In 1933 Luis returned to Salamanca to take up a post as an auxiliary professor teaching civil law. Madrid had its charm but Salamanca was home, and he was a great admirer of the university rector, Miguel de Unamuno, a liberal administrator and scholar who had done much to safeguard and improve the university's reputation.

Luis had three happy years as a young academic, but the shadow of the Civil War soon fell over every area of Spanish life and even the sequestered academic community of Salamanca was transformed by the struggle.

The war, between the legitimate Republican government of the Left and the Nationalist insurgents of the Right, led by Franco, supported by Fascists, royalists and the Church, lasted for three years and foreshadowed in its ideology and ferocity the horrors to follow in the Second World War. Fascist Italy and Nazi Germany tested the tactics of total war through the legions of 'volunteers' they sent to support Franco. Bolshevik Russia sent *matériel* to its proxies on the Republican side. Genuine volunteers from the Western democracies – many of them trade unionists – joined the Republicans. A flavour of the bravery, desperation and political confusion of their struggle is captured in George Orwell's account of his own campaign in *Homage to Catalonia*.

The Western powers stayed, officially, aloof, unwilling to exert themselves to prop up democracy in Spain. It was more apathy than appeasement, but the victory of Fascists in a European civil war sent a clear message to other opportunist aggressors across the Continent. The fate of pluralist Spain at the hands of nationalist insurgents has uncomfortable parallels with the crisis in Bosnia today – a point perhaps not lost on defence secretary Michael Portillo.

The impact of the first stages of the war on Salamanca, as the Nationalists attempted to claim the heart of Old Castile, was subsequently caught by Luis Portillo in an article he wrote for the wartime magazine *Horizon* when he was in exile in London. Entitled 'Unamuno's Last Lecture', it is a dramatic and moving account of the confrontation in October 1936 in the university's Ceremonial Hall between Miguel de Unamuno, the representative of liberal learning, and General Millán Astray, the crippled advocate of conflict and intolerance.

Millán Astray, whose battle-cry was *'Viva la Muerte'* – Long Live Death – had chosen to deliver an address at the opening ceremony of the new university term, to show that the new Spain of the Fascist Falange held sway even in what had previously been the home of toleration. Luis Portillo, a witness to Millán Astray's extraordinary speech, sets the scene gradually, detailing minutely the stately ceremonial of the old Spanish seat of learning before quoting the general's purist nationalist rhetoric to great effect:

'Catalonia and the Basque country – the Basque country and Catalonia – are two cancers in the body of the nation. Fascism, which is Spain's health-bringer, will know how to exterminate them both, cutting into the live, healthy flesh like a resolute surgeon free from false sentimentality. And since the healthy flesh is the soil, the diseased flesh the people who dwell on it, Fascism and the Army will eradicate the people and restore the soil to the sacred national realm.'

Luis Portillo then caught the power of the simple sloganising of the Fascists with his own staccato rendition of the Falangist chant:

'Spain!'
Mechanically, the crowd responded: 'One!'
'Spain!' he repeated.
'Great,' chorused the obedient public.
'Spain,' the Blue Shirt insisted, implacably.
'Free!' they all replied, cowed.

In contrast to the unthinking power of the Falangist rabble-rousing, Luis Portillo shows the quiet dignity of Unamuno and quotes his elegant reply to the war-wounded General Millán Astray:

General Millán Astray would like to create Spain anew – a negative creation – in his own image and likeness. And for that reason he wishes to see Spain crippled, as he unwittingly made clear.

'You will win, but you will not convince. You will win because you possess more than enough brute force, but you will not convince, because to convince means to persuade. And, in order to persuade you would

need what you lack – reason and right in the struggle. I consider it futile
to exhort you to think of Spain. I have finished.'

After his magnificent rejection of Millán Astray's twisted ideology, Unamuno was placed under house arrest. He died two months
later, of a stroke. His young disciple, who had so faithfully recorded
his principled stand, had by then put himself in the forefront of
the struggle against Fascism.

Luis fled to Madrid and enlisted in the Republican army, but
he declined to bear arms, as his widow, Cora, explained: 'Because
five of his six brothers were on the "Nationalist" side – one an
officer, others enlisted – he refused to fire a shot.' Instead he was
appointed, in Cora's words, 'as a sort of political commissar', reading extracts from newspapers to illiterate soldiers, educating them
and explaining politics. The notion of Michael Portillo's father
keeping a Communist-backed army in ideological line has its
ironies, but there is a certain continuity at least in the son following
his father as a party propagandist.

One of Luis Portillo's friends in exile, Martínez Nadal, a former
lecturer at King's College, London, remembers that Luis was certainly politically active, but never as an extremist and certainly
not as a card-carrying Communist: 'He was always a moderate
socialist – almost a Liberal.' Nevertheless, Luis was responsible
for keeping the troops at an appropriate pitch of ideological fervour,
and was a member of a Popular Front body, the Alliance of Anti-
Fascist Intellectuals for the Defence of the Culture. He was their
247th recruit when he joined in October 1936.

Luis Portillo's front-line experience was brought to a halt at the
Battle of the Ebro. Deployed in the thick of the fighting as a courier,
he fell ill with severe inflammation of the kidneys while carrying
messages up and down the mountains. He was invalided out of
the army and found a desk job in Madrid. His legal knowledge,
and Christian faith, recommended him to the minister of justice,
Manuel de Irujo, a Basque.

Luis was a devout Catholic. All four of his sons have been
brought up in the faith. One of his sisters was a nun, and several
of his cousins were priests. Don Alvar Portillo, the head of Opus
Dei, the conservative Catholic order for priesthood and laity, was
a distant relative. While at the Ministry of Justice, it was Luis's

job to review the sentence of death passed on enemy prisoners. As a Catholic, he felt he could not happily acquiesce in the cold taking of a life. His widow recalls, 'Both he and Irujo were fervent Christians and commuted as many death sentences as possible.' Again, it is perhaps ironic that forty-four years after Luis was commuting death sentences his son was in the streets of Birmingham campaigning for their restoration.

It is certainly cruelly ironic that Luis Portillo was extending such clemency to the enemy. As a politically active former serving soldier and Republican *apparatchik*, he would have been a prime target for Franco's revenge. As his widow recalls, 'Franco shot more civilians after the war than the total casualties in the fighting. Luis would have been shot.'

At Irujo's urging, Luis Portillo fled Madrid in the first weeks of 1939. Madrid fell to Franco in March, but by then Luis was on his way across the Pyrenees with a party of Basques to whom he had been introduced by Irujo. They trudged across the mountains on foot through bitter winter weather, Luis still suffering from his diseased kidneys, until they reached temporary safety in the hands of the Basques of South-West France.

Luis then made for England, where he was attached, as a tutor, to a colony of émigré Basque children in London. Male émigrés from the Civil War had to have a British sponsor, and Luis was sponsored by the Labour MP for Mansfield. If it had not been for the sense of international solidarity amongst thirties socialists, Michael Portillo would never have been conceived.

Luis met the woman who was to become his wife, and Michael's mother, in the autumn of 1939. Cora Waldegrave Blyth had gone up to St Hilda's College, Oxford, in October 1937. A modern-linguist studying Spanish, soon after arriving she had volunteered to help out with a colony of Basque exiles at Aston Bampton, near Witney, just outside Oxford. It was to this colony, just before the declaration of the Second World War, that Luis was sent with seven of his hurriedly evacuated charges.

Cora, a natural linguist with an open, attractive and winning manner, had been moved by the desire to do good in a practical way while honing her Spanish. But it was more than charity and curiosity that drew Cora to Luis – the dignified young professor with his halting English and soulful eyes. She was still an undergraduate; he was a man without prospects, family or anything more than the clothes he stood up in. But he had formidable charm, and for a girl from small-town Scotland he was an intensely romantic figure.

Cora came from a well-to-do middle-class Episcopalian Scottish family. Her father, John Waldegrave Blyth, who died in 1962, was a wealthy linen manufacturer in the Fife town of Kirkcaldy. The family was from rural Fife, but Cora's great-grandfather had moved to Kirkcaldy in the early 1830s and set up a small cottage weaving business. His son moved to Lincolnshire in the 1850s, and found an English wife, Elizabeth Waldegrave. Then, after a few years in the south, he returned to Kirkcaldy with his wife and rejoined the family firm. John W. Blyth, Cora's father, was his eldest son. Born in 1873, he was educated at Kirkcaldy High School, leaving at eighteen to make his fortune in the firm.

Starting as a travelling salesman, he helped expand the firm by exploiting the growing demand for linen created by wars across the empire. The firm's prosperity was at a peak during the First World War, but after the 1930s the factory at Hawklymuir, just outside the town, settled into slow decline. It eventually closed in the sixties, but not before it had made Blyth a wealthy man, giving him the money to indulge his passion for painting.

He had married in 1908, and, like his father, took an English bride, Alice May Lowe, from Manchester. A year later he acquired a handsome new home, Wilby House, in a fashionable area of Kirkcaldy, and began to build up a superb collection of modern, mainly Scottish, art.

John Blyth had no formal artistic training, although he was musical. He played the organ and piano, and his wife the violin. There was, however, a vogue for collecting among Scots businessmen of the time; the most successful of them, William Burrell, bequeathed his magnificent collection to the City of Glasgow. Blyth was a collector on a much smaller scale than Burrell, but within his limits he was a connoisseur. He specialised in works by contemporary painters, mainly Scots, all of whom have gone on to enjoy deserved celebrity. He collected from three artists in particular, hanging McTaggarts in his dining-room, Sickerts in his drawing-room, and the works of the colourist S. J. Peploe in each of the four bedrooms.

Blyth's daughter Margaret, Michael Portillo's aunt, remembers her father as a strongly emotional man, easily moved by music or art: 'He was very Scottish – he would weep at a touch.' But the emotional side of his character was matched by another, more traditional, Scots trait: meanness. Margaret Blyth remembers that 'He used to groan heavily when he had to write a cheque.'

The capacity to be moved by art but remain completely unmoved by appeals for money survives as strongly in Blyth's grandson as ever in the man himself. Michael Portillo's enthusiasm for the arts – in particular music – is exceeded only by his reputation for keeping tight control of the public purse.

Blyth bought his paintings on regular trips to Glasgow, Edinburgh and London. He never visited the Continent, and his collection of foreign works was tiny, but it was economy, not insularity, that dictated the shape of his collection. His appetite for new works was huge, and soon every space on the walls was festooned with pictures – much to his wife's annoyance. Yet still he bought. His daughter Cora recalls, 'He used to smuggle his latest acquisition into the house, and hide it in the spare bedroom for a while. The factory was nearby, so he came home to lunch. He used to sit up in his bedroom before going back, contemplating the pictures.'

Eventually the collection grew too big for one house and Blyth donated a selection of his works to the town council, to form the core of their art gallery's collection. Blyth was appointed convenor of the gallery committee in thanks, and used to visit the building every Monday. On his death his collection was sold, and broken up, but much of it still remains in Kirkcaldy Art Gallery.

When Michael Portillo visited Fife in 1994, to speak to the local Conservative association, he made a point of visiting the gallery and talking to the curator about his grandfather. A Sickert and a McTaggart formerly belonging to his grandfather had adorned the walls of his parents' suburban semi in Stanmore, and he was anxious to see for himself some more of the divided collection.

Blyth did not spend all of his money on art. He ensured his three daughters were well educated. They had a governess for their early years, before being sent to St Leonard's School for Girls. Although local, St Leonard's was an expensive choice. Scotland's poshest girls' school, it considers itself the Celtic cousin of English establishments like Wycombe Abbey and St Mary's, Ascot. Cora was a pupil there in the thirties. Her main memory is of the biting cold. Piano practice took place with windows wide open, and the breeze blew straight in from Siberia over the freezing North Sea. Baths were taken in the same icy waters. It may not have been an ideal education for refined young ladies, but it instilled a toughness that was to help in the war years to come.

Cora was a model pupil and easily secured a place at Oxford to read modern languages. She was only too happy to brush up her Spanish at the Aston Bampton colony, and, coming from a relatively sheltered background, she was fascinated to learn about the Civil War. The horrors of the conflict were brought home to her on the day Britain itself joined the fight against Fascism. She remembers it vividly: 'On Sunday 3 September we heard the declaration of war. A quarter of an hour later the sirens went off. The children all screamed – they had not forgotten Bilbao.'

With the declaration of war came the dispersal of many of the émigré colonies, but Cora was anxious not to lose touch with the handsome, dark-eyed and courtly Spanish intellectual she had met just a few months before. She contrived to keep Luis near at hand, and it was arranged that he and two other Spaniards should be given board and lodging by a friendly don, a Professor Duffey.

Luis, a professor and poet, with experience as a government administrator and a political organiser, tried to find suitable work. Despite his formidable education he spoke little English, and opportunities to harness his talents were not immediately available. His first job was simply sweeping snow, then he found work peeling potatoes for eleven hours a day, before taking up a labouring job digging an aerodrome at Swindon. Technically he was still an alien, and after a few weeks working on the aerodrome he lost his job because the RAF could not risk having a foreigner form too firm a grasp of its layout.

At the same time Luis tried to improve his English, by listening to the wireless, reading newspapers, and talking to friends like Cora. Life was far from easy as he, an alien from a nominally Fascist country, struggled to make ends meet in wartime Britain. But, despite the difficulties, his relationship with Cora developed. She recalls, 'He used to be smuggled into St Hilda's for baths. My friends thought it was all so romantic!'

As his English improved, Luis found work with Reuters, as a

translator, and moved to London. His first lodgings were a large flat in Courtfield Road, South Kensington, nominally the property of another émigré, but this time a refugee from Communism – the white Russian, Count Tolstoy. Tolstoy had let the flat to a wealthy young English Communist, Alec Wainwright, whose mother had met Luis Portillo when she invited the members of the Basque colony to tea at her home in Wickham Market. Wainwright did not use the flat himself but let it in turn to adult refugees from oppression.

Cora Portillo remembers visiting the flat while she was still at Oxford and seeing a bowler-hatted Wainwright – like her, a talented linguist – set off for an interview with the Foreign Office. He was eventually turned down because of his politics. Given that men like Philby, Burgess and Maclean were being recruited at the time, Wainwright must have been either extremely unlucky or just unluckily extreme.

At Reuters, Luis found himself translating political speeches. Speed was vital for the agency, and he would sometimes see the top of his page of type torn off as he wrote.

After six months of separation Cora also found a job in the capital, thanks to the good offices of her tutor, Helen Grant. She joined the London Transcription Service, which was subsequently taken over by the BBC.

Wartime London was a dangerous place, and the Courtfield Road flat was damaged by a bomb. Luis determined to move out. And there was also a greater reason to find a new home – Cora. Their affection, which had survived separation and transcended background, had grown in London into a lifetime commitment. Luis was determined to marry the woman with whom he had fallen in love and who had supported him for the last eighteen months. He and Cora married, in a Roman Catholic church in south London, on 17 March 1941. Cora's parents were not overjoyed that their expensively educated daughter was marrying a penniless refugee, but there was a small dowry.

Luis and Cora's first home was a flat in Woburn Square, in Bloomsbury. They chose it because it had a reinforced concrete floor and a bomb shelter. Their first son, Charles, was born on 1 July 1942. Cora left her job and they moved to another rented flat, in Wallington, Surrey. Their second son, Justin, was born on 21

September 1943, by which time they had moved to Stanmore, where the family were to settle, and where Michael was born. Their first house was bought with the help of money from Cora's father.

By this time Luis had moved from Reuters to work for the BBC. He wrote and directed material for the BBC's Latin American service, but his voice was thought unsuitable for broadcasting. He commissioned work from other émigrés, and even his rejection notes show a Castilian courtesy that survives in his son's formal good manners, taking the trouble to include suggestions for writers who might wish to resubmit. He also wrote short stories for the Spanish service and secured a commission for his wife to write a talk for Woman's Hour. Her words were never broadcast, however – the talk was cancelled to make way for an obituary.

It was while Luis was at the BBC that his wife fell pregnant for the fifth time. A third son, Denzil, had died in infancy, but a fourth, Jolyon, had been born fit and healthy in 1949. Their fifth son was born in Bushey on 26 May 1953. Originally registered as 'Denzil Xavier', after their third boy, 'Michael' was added a few weeks later. 'Denzil' had a certain sentimental value, but, fortunately for the future minister, 'Michael' was also a name with special associations – Miguel de Unamuno was Luis's hero.

Michael was born just a week before the coronation of Queen Elizabeth II. Winston Churchill was prime minister, and Britain was still an imperial power. But, behind the impressive façade of a nation led by its wartime saviour, preparing to embark on a new Elizabethan era, the dry rot of decline had done its work. As Suez would soon show, and the sixties confirm, Britain was adjusting painfully from its former greatness to a lesser role. Michael Portillo grew up acquainted with the reality of decline and came to maturity realising that decline could be reversed, but at his birth he was simply the son of parents grateful that their child was growing up in a land that was peaceful and progressive.

Born in the security of an NHS hospital to a socialist father employed in the public sector and a liberal mother supplementing their income with teaching, Michael Portillo was a child of the Welfare State. But, as with John Major, and Margaret Thatcher, economic insecurity was to upset the stable family background at an early age. Portillo grew up knowing that basic comforts, particularly in a big family, depend on hard work.

In 1954 Luis was made redundant by the BBC. As a resident alien, he was among the first to lose his job. Those were the days of full, but not necessarily fulfilling, employment and he eventually found another job, more menial but still stable, as a translator at the Central Office of Information. When, forty years later, cuts were again contemplated in the BBC World Service, the final decision rested with Michael Portillo as chief secretary to the Treasury. The leftish Tory Peter Temple-Morris believes his invocation of Portillo senior's record in the Latin American service, during a meeting with Michael, may have resulted in axes being swung with less gusto than they might have been.

Luis did not greatly enjoy the COI work, and the pay was not much for a man with a growing family. He supplemented his income by lecturing on Spanish literature at King's College, London, examining A-level Spanish papers, and acting as London correspondent for the Mexican newspaper *Excelsior*, as well as doing freelance translating for the Foreign Office and the Federation of Business and Professional Women. It was a remarkable array of work for one man, but with four boys to feed and clothe money was at a premium. Cora Portillo contributed to the family coffers by teaching Spanish part-time at Harrow Technical College and Borehamwood Grammar, as well as working as a tourist guide. All four Portillo boys enjoyed a grammar-school education and a secure home life, but, even though Cora came from a comfortable background, the family was never wealthy.

Despite all the work he took on, Luis found time to write for himself. Commuting to work at the COI, on the long, dull journey from Stanmore to the Elephant and Castle, he would write poetry on scraps of paper, even the backs of cigarette packets. According to Cora, 'He wrote mostly sonnets – an excellent discipline for his exuberant style. But there are longer pieces too – one an incredibly vivid evocation of a bullfight.'

The poems were published in Barcelona in 1989, under the title *Ruisenor del destierro* – 'Nightingale in Exile' – and were well received. Tristan Garel-Jones has read them in the original: 'They're beautifully written, and they have all that dignified, austere, unforgiving, cold sadness which typifies that generation.'

Michael remembers one moment when he realised the weight of sadness his father always carried with him – a vignette he has mentioned to friends. Luis was instilling in him the importance of saying his prayers every night, and explained whom he should pray for, before adding, 'I also pray for my enemies. You don't need to, because you don't have any.' There was sorrow in his father's eyes as he recalled who his enemy was: Franco, the man who had driven him into exile.

Because of Franco, Luis could not visit Spain for nineteen years after he left, and he was unhappy about doing so while the Caudillo was still alive. His wife and children went most years to visit relatives, but they had to be careful. All Luis's sons had been registered as Spanish citizens at the London consulate, so they were theoretically liable for military service.

In the fifties and sixties the Portillo family had a small flat in Campello, Alicante, where they went on bucket-and-spade holidays. It slept ten, and was often used to entertain friends and fiancées. Michael's first trip to Spain was by ship. It was an unhappy first brush with abroad: he caught chickenpox, and refused to eat any of the food offered. He first travelled abroad on his own at only eight, when he was dispatched by air to Medina. A misunderstanding meant his uncles were not there to greet him, and he was nearly sent home, but his self-possession and precocious Spanish allowed him to order a taxi to his destination.

Luis's relatives were not the only family members favoured with holiday visits. Although Cora's parents had been far from enthusiastic about her marriage, they were generous enough to entertain the growing Portillo family on several trips north. Michael enjoyed the opportunity to explore the Blyths' home, Wilby House, built on a much more lavish scale than the family's Stanmore semi. The Blyths lived in considerable comfort and right up to the end of the fifties kept a uniformed chauffeur, Tom, who was dispatched to Kirkcaldy station, boots gleaming, to collect the Portillos on their visits.

Humbler holidays were also spent in other parts of the UK, and several summers were spent on the beach at Ventnor in the Isle of Wight.

As Michael grew up and his brothers left home, the family ventured further abroad. In 1969 they visited Yugoslavia, holidaying on the Adriatic coast and even managing to spend a day on a strictly controlled tourist trip to Albania. At that point Albania was still in the grip of the Maoist dictator Enver Hoxha, and Portillo, then a secondary school boy, was struck by the drabness of the towns, enlivened only by bizarre slogans incorporating Chinese characters and massive posters of Hoxha, designed to encourage his cult of personality.

While Albania imprinted itself on Portillo's consciousness, Yugoslavia made a profound impact on his mother. She loved the country and its people, taking the trouble to learn Serbo-Croat. More recently, she has taken a keen interest in the human consequences of its break-up since 1991. Through her membership of Amnesty International she has befriended and worked with refugees from the former Yugoslavia, including Serbs, Croats and Bosnian Muslims.

The war in the former Yugoslavia has been the most immediate problem Michael Portillo has faced as defence secretary. Many observers, including Robin Harris, an aide to Lady Thatcher who worked with Portillo at the Conservative Research Department, assumed Portillo's attitude to the conflict would be the cold *realpolitik* of a follower of Enoch Powell, disdainful of foreign entanglements. However, writing in the *Spectator* on 12 August 1995, Harris detected a 'quiver of moral indignation' in an interview Portillo had given to the BBC's *World at One* in which he denounced the Croat invasion of the Krajina and the subsequent ethnic cleansing.

Harris found it 'unnerving', but an appreciation of Michael Portillo's family background makes his sympathy easier to understand. His father was a refugee, and his mother still devotes much of her free time to helping victims of foreign wars. Keenly aware of the human consequences of civil wars, it is not surprising that a politician normally as cool as Portillo should permit a touch of fellow-feeling for the civilian victims of a war to permeate his assessment of its strategic consequences for Britain.

The memories of the Spanish Civil War influenced Luis Portillo's life throughout his long exile but did not dominate it. Michael's father maintained a detached interest in émigré Republican affairs. During the forties members of the various pre-war parties had met in London in the flat of the author and poet José Antonio Balbontín. There was immense disappointment that

Franco survived the collapse of the other Fascist dictators in 1945, but the spirit of solidarity survived, and Cora Portillo ruefully remembers that 'Every 14 April, the date of the election of the Republic in '36, there was a gathering of all parties and much "eloquence".'

Luis Portillo's moderation and dignity won him respect among all the émigrés, and, in recognition of his stature, on 24 November 1972 Fernando Valera, minister of state of the Spanish Republic in Exile, which was based in Paris, made him head of the official diplomatic delegation of the Spanish Republic in England.

In 1975 Franco died, and Luis could then return, happily, to the land of his birth. The flat in Alicante had been sold, and a holiday home was bought in Salamanca. It brought him great joy to return home for some of his declining years.

Luis himself died on 19 October 1993. An illness related to Alzheimer's disease had not made his last years easy, but he had remained dignified to the end.

That December the rector of Salamanca University organised a commemoration of the life of one of its brave and honoured sons. Mrs Portillo and her four sons were invited. In a simple ceremony in the ancient library, the family were presented with books to mark their father's life; then they were shown round the house of Unamuno, now a museum, which Cora Portillo remembers was 'kept exactly as it was, in its stark simplicity, as if he still lived there'. Town joined gown in paying tribute to Don Luis. At another ceremony the Chamber of Commerce also presented a set of commemorative books, and a memorial mass was held in the university chapel.

In all, fifty-six members of the Portillo family attended the ceremonies, and after the solemn marks of respect had been paid they enjoyed lunch together in a university restaurant. Although it was a massive gathering, it was far from comprehensive – Mrs Portillo calculates that she has over 108 family still alive, scattered across Spain and England.

Of her immediate family, Michael's eldest brother, Charles, works near Heathrow for British Airways, having joined their predecessor, BEA, from school. He and his wife, Linda, have two daughters, aged twenty-four and twenty-two. The second eldest, Justin, is a modern-languages teacher. Now based near Newcastle, he used to teach at Dr Challoner's School for Girls, in Buckingham-shire. The third brother, Jolyon, known as Jo, lives in Harrow, where he works as a committee clerk for the borough council. The brothers remain close, seeing each other regularly and keeping in touch with each other through their mother.

Mrs Portillo retired formally from teaching in 1984, but she still works with refugees at the Windmill Project in Clapham Common. A keen Liberal all her life, she sports a yellow Lib-Dem poster in her window come election time, and has not yet been persuaded to change her allegiance by her son.

Michael may be unable to influence her, but the influences of both parents run strongly through his veins. The attachment to potentially unpopular beliefs come what may, a reverence for argu-ment, and a love of language all come to Michael Portillo from his father. From further back in the Portillo bloodline comes that mixture of pride and principle that is the mark of the Castilian. From his mother he inherits a hardiness and humour as well as a spirited loyalty. From her Blyth ancestry comes a sensitivity to art, an entrepreneurial flair and a carefulness with cash that are all, in their own way, very Scottish. And from his family's shared experiences Portillo carries the knowledge of how difficult it is to maintain genteel habits and civilised standards when money is tight. He knows the warmth and security family life can bring to children, having grown up with and remaining close to three brothers. He also knows something of the pain of exile, the nagging loss felt by his father and the idealised patriotism that sustained him.

But, while all these influences exist, they are far from being the dominant strains in Portillo's character. Easily as influential, especially on his politics and philosophy, have been the three insti-tutions in which he grew to manhood – school, college and party.

CHAPTER THREE

A Harrow Boyhood

We must above all remind ourselves that we in the grammar schools are in the forefront of the struggle for western civilization, its justification and its survival.

Dr A. R. Simpson, headmaster,
Harrow County School for Boys

During the last long period of Tory hegemony, from 1951 to 1964, the pre-eminent qualification for advancement was a 'good war'. The two most influential figures in the Conservative Party at the end of that era, Edward Heath and Enoch Powell, had both benefited from the erosion of social barriers and a more meritocratic temper in wartime Britain. The war gave them both a chance to transcend a petit-bourgeois background and fit more comfortably into the Tory party, buttressed by the sense that their administrative skills and willing service fitted them to take their place in shaping the nation's affairs.

When the Tory party next enjoyed a long lease on the government benches, in the eighties, the surest passport to power for any MP was a grammar-school education. From John Biffen to John Major, Kenneth Clarke to Michael Howard, having passed the eleven-plus ensured the same warmth from both leader and activists once secured by a brigade tie and a mention in dispatches. However, the traditional grammar school – the state-funded selective-entry ladder of opportunity – all but disappeared in the seventies. Ideologically objectionable to Labour and an affront to middle-class Tory voters whose less gifted children were elbowed out of the best schools by the clever children of poorer homes, they either became comprehensives or retreated into the private sector.

One of many grammar schools which turned comprehensive was Harrow County School for Boys. The first attempt to end its selective status came in 1965, with the Wilson government's Circular 10/65 which asked local authorities to submit their plans for the reorganisation of schools along comprehensive lines. The same

year that Harold Wilson started the process that was to see Harrow
County lose its grammar-school status, Michael Portillo arrived
there. It was to be ten years before HCSB finally did become a
comprehensive, consigned to that fate by a Tory council, but before
that it had secured places at Oxford and Cambridge for one of the
most talented generations to emerge from any state school.

The boys who entered the handsome Edwardian building in
Gayton Road in autumn 1965 included a group of around ten who
were to become firm friends and whose subsequent success would
be commendable if they had been starting a little further up the
hill at Harrow, but whose achievements to date are all the more
remarkable given the modest reputation of their own secondary
school. Starting at the same time as Michael Portillo were Clive
Anderson, the TV chat-show host; Geoffrey Perkins, one of the
creators of *Spitting Image* and now the BBC's head of comedy;
Matthew Francis, director of the Greenwich Theatre, London's
finest outside the West End; Nigel Sheinwald, the precocious young
head of the News Department at the Foreign Office, tipped for his
own ambassadorship, and a clutch of others now straddling the
City, law and the media.

Portillo, Perkins and Anderson all entered after passing the
eleven-plus while at Stanburn Primary School, in Stanmore. It
was at Stanburn that Portillo acquired his first nickname – Polly,
a variant of his elder brother Jolyon's nickname, Jolly – and a
taste for private enterprise: in his final year he was put in charge
of the school tuckshop.

The headmaster at Stanburn, Mr Morgan, was ambitious for
his boys and coached the cleverest to prepare them for the eleven-
plus, and grammar school beyond. Portillo has told friends that it
was in his final years at Stanburn that he had an inkling he might
be quite clever, as he would need to be to flourish at Harrow
County, a school that put academic achievement above everything.

When Portillo and his classmates arrived at HCSB it still bore
the imprint of the headmaster who was just retiring – and who
had run it for the previous twenty years – Dr A. R. Simpson. A
Scot who had distinguished himself as a scholar and athlete in his
youth, Simpson had created an environment where expectations
were high and standards exacting. An élitist in an age of thoroughgoing egalitarianism, the tone he set was outlined in his address

at the second school speech day of his long tenure, in July 1948. Praising Victorian virtues, he contrasted them with the mood of the moment: 'This present tendency to replace sound learning, to an inordinate degree, by free self-chosen interests, work by ease, modesty by forwardness, and earnestness by frivolity, is clearly the downward path to individual and to national ruin, and with it, very rapidly, to the demise of what was best in the Western civilization.'

This Spartan manifesto was complemented by a regime of rigorous competition of the kind invoked by Conservative ministers when attacking the folly of progressive educational theory. Pupils were streamed on entry, and to find yourself in classes C or D was, in the words of one former pupil, 'to cross a social as well as an educational Styx'. The system was designed to encourage hard work through competition or, as it was described in the school prospectus of 1961, 'timely promotion and relegation'.

As a further incentive to achievement, Dr Simpson adopted a practice revived in 1993 by John Patten when he was education secretary – full disclosure of unrefined exam results. He argued, 'Complete public examination returns, i.e. possibles, presentations and percentage results, in so important and costly a public matter should, in equity, not only be available, but published in detail.'

The exam results in which Dr Simpson was most interested were the Oxbridge awards his sixth-formers secured, and he increasingly bent his efforts to pushing the school up the league table of scholarships and exhibitions published in the *Times Educational Supplement*. To that end he reorganised the school's year structure, encouraging the most able to sit O-levels at the end of their fourth form, allowing them to bypass their fifth and sit their A-levels one year early, provided they stayed for a third year, the scholarship sixth, to get into Oxbridge. The regime worked, and in the year Michael Portillo arrived Harrow County was the leading state grammar school in Britain for Oxbridge awards, securing twelve awards and six 'ordinary' places.

It was into this intensely academic atmosphere that Portillo and his peers arrived. A new headmaster, Roy Avery, was taking over at the same time, but masters who worked with both him and Dr Simpson claim it was the austere Scot's influence that prevailed in the ethos of the school.

Dr Simpson had sought to develop more than just the minds of his charges: character was built too, but not by competitive sports – instead, boys were encouraged to join the army cadet force. In the sixties the Harrow County CCF was the largest of any British state school. The school was known as 'Little Sandhurst', and those who declined to join the CCF were regarded by the headmaster as 'non-conformists, saboteurs and cynics'.

Michael Portillo did not join. His father had refused to bear arms during the Spanish Civil War, and his son was no more militaristic. When Michael went up to Harrow County he shared his father's idealistic leftism and, despite his enthusiasm, bordering on zeal, for involvement in every other area of school life, he stayed resolutely aloof from the parade-ground. It may have cost him the chance to be head boy, but he had pacifist connections and refused to be cowed into conforming. It revealed a strong streak of stubbornness in Portillo's character and a principled opposition to 'playing soldiers'. Rather than join the CCF, Portillo opted for the Scouts.

Malcolm Rifkind was the first Tory defence secretary never to have served in any of the armed forces, even as a conscript. Michael Portillo may well be the first former conscientious objector to be placed in charge of the nation's defences by a Tory government.

It may raise eyebrows in the upper echelons of the armed services now, but Portillo's playground pacifism did not affect his academic progress at Harrow County. When he arrived he was placed in the A stream, and throughout his career he was never in any danger of relegation. He sailed through the first four years, securing straight As at O-level, two articles in the school magazine and his second nickname: 'Polygrit'.

One of his first friends at HCSB, Matthew Francis, remembers meeting Portillo on the very first day and being instantly struck by the self-assurance and intelligence of a boy who was 'easily the cleverest I'd ever met'. Not that Francis was altogether impressed: he told his parents, 'I've met this extraordinary boy called Portobello, with a terrible Oxford accent.' Despite the barriers, they soon became friends. Both were keen collaborators in the range of more cerebral and creative extracurricular activities the school encouraged.

The magazine, *The Gaytonian*, was one of the areas of school life modernised by Roy Avery. Far more than a compendium of notes

from the chess clubs and grainy photos of rugby heroes, its mixture
of poetry, humour, essays and stylish artwork won the 1966 issue
the accolade of best in the country from the National Association
of School Magazines. That issue, edited by his English master,
Jim Golland, contained Michael Portillo's first venture into print.

Portillo's contributions reveal an adolescent with a talent for the
telling phrase, a skill at combining straight reportage with stray
comment, a liberal world view and an ambivalent approach to his
mixed Hispanic and British heritage, all apparent in his first
article, on a subject on which his father, Luis, had also written: a
bullfight.

With a maturity and assurance that belies his age, the thirteen-
year-old Portillo recalls the spectacle from his previous summer's
holiday with the extended family of cousins in Salamanca. His
even-handedness aside – 'I have always had mixed feelings about
bull-fighting, being English by birth but having more Spanish
blood in my veins than anything else' – an early partiality for
risk-taking is apparent in his praise for the *banderillero*:

This valiant individual, armed only with a pair of banderillas (or small
swords), charged at the bull. If done properly he must lean right over
the bull's horns to insert these. I had a feeling here of equal odds. My
admiration goes to anyone who dares take his life into his hands this
way.

A year later Jim Golland encouraged Portillo to exploit his exotic
background once more. The fourteen-year-old Portillo's article
'Inside Spain' again displays a sophistication well beyond what
one would expect in a 'What I did in my holidays' essay. It begins
with a delicately sketched vignette of Easter Day in Malaga, blend-
ing the themes of religion and repression which run through the
essay.

Portillo describes the youth movement 'La Oje', with their
'black, paratrooper berets and their goose-step', and detects the
menace in the display of even civilian authority in a dictatorship,
noting the threat in the number of ' "traffic" policemen by the side
of the road [who] adjust the straps on their machine guns and
re-light their cigarettes'.

Conscious of his own father's difficulties in returning to Spain
while Franco remained in power, Portillo ruefully remarks, 'The

Civil War is not forgotten, though some people cannot even remember the dates . . . booklets tell you how the war was a religious crusade on the part of Franco and he only wanted to protect Spain from Communism.'

The prominence of religion in the life of Spain clearly made an impression. Portillo describes a country still overwhelmingly Catholic. 'On every corner there is a church, and on every other one a priest or a nun. You can make a fortune in Spain selling Bibles, rosaries and black dresses.'

Portillo's interest in religion is second only to his fascination with politics. A relish for argument is apparent in his description of Spanish café life, where the disputes are 'better than Speakers' Corner, the House of Commons and the Shop Stewards' AGM put together', and he finishes his essay with a dig at Spain's backwardness in embracing British socialist advances. Tellingly, he cites Spanish society's defects: 'There is no welfare state in Spain. If you are ill you pay for your doctor, hospital and medicines, and if you go to school, again you must pay. The only way to gain a "free" education is to win scholarships, usually just about enough to buy a few text books.' While the adult Portillo might approve of this minimal state encouraging a thrifty self-reliance in its people's approach to social spending, the teenage Portillo is majestically scathing in his assessment of Spain, commenting, 'She still has a long way to go before she is thought of as anything other than a place to go for holidays.'

The magazine was one of several outlets for Portillo's talents that Jim Golland encouraged him to exploit. Golland harnessed Portillo's nascent administrative skills by appointing him to run the 'bookroom', a library-cum-study for sixth-formers taking English. Golland remembers Portillo taking on all the unattractive drudgery of administering books, accounts, fixtures and fittings. One contemporary believes the bookroom became the bolthole for the 'in' crowd of sixth-formers to which Portillo was so keen to belong. Matthew Francis certainly remembers long hours spent there shooting the breeze and plotting in a sort of mini-Bloomsbury where the wittiest and most talented boys would bounce ideas off each other and enjoy a taste of the autonomy which university would bring. Friends recall that Portillo may not have been the most sparkling figure, but he was already the natural leader – and keen to remain so.

Figures like Francis, Anderson and Perkins set themselves a little apart from the rest of the school with their interest in drama, and, even though he was not a natural actor, Michael Portillo was determined to be a part of what was the centre of school life for the most interesting boys. He had been drawn early to the limelight, auditioning for several roles as a child actor and winning a place as the boy in the Ribena ads. Portillo's cherubic features and blond thatch were the perfect advertisement for the blackcurrant drink that promised to make you 'every day, a little stronger', but a string of other attempts to secure better roles came to naught.

Despite his failure as a child actor, Portillo persevered at school. He was cast as the corpse in Tom Stoppard's *The Real Inspector Hound*, and was also selected for a role requiring a little more animation: Friar Lawrence in a production of *Romeo and Juliet*. But it was in neither acting nor dry admin that Portillo flourished most, but in ventures that required a mixture of organisation and inspiration.

He acted as business manager for a school production of *Hamlet*, with Matthew Francis in the title role and Nigel Sheinwald directing. He was given a budget of £900 to play with – nearer £9,000 in today's money. It was a huge sum to be entrusted to the care of a sixteen-year-old, but according to Francis it seemed natural: 'Michael just had a very real sense of what it was to organise and run and be in charge of things. Of course he made a profit.'

Following the success of *Hamlet*, and with encouragement from Golland, Portillo attempted to make a full-length feature film of a school production of *Macbeth*. The play was produced with the help of the County School for Girls, where Diane Abbott, now Labour MP for Hackney North and Stoke Newington, was then a pupil. Competition for the female roles was hotly contested, and Portillo cast Abbott as Lady Macduff – a role which requires extravagant displays of grief and shroud-waving.

Portillo threw himself into the project, setting up jumble sales and the like to raise cash. He acquired a camera, and cine film. Footage was shot, and one of his contemporaries, Matthew de Lange, now with City accountants Price Waterhouse, remembers

Portillo being 'like a young Roman Polanski – the consummate director'.

Unfortunately, however, the money required to produce a full-length feature could not be found. Portillo tried to cut costs by planning to shoot the picture in modern dress, and he wrote to several stately homes asking if they would provide a scenic back-drop for free, but all his effort was in vain. The film was never finished. It was the first but not the last occasion when effort would be expended into making a film for Portillo only for it all to come to nothing.

Macbeth was not the only production with which Portillo involved himself. He and his friends had formed their own artistic circle, called 'Convergence', which discussed literature and put on its own little plays. The club had two aims: to foster the creative talents of its members and to allow them to meet girls. As the name implied, it was designed to allow the talent of the brother and sister schools to be pooled. Typical of their efforts was a revue they staged in December 1970, written and produced by Clive Anderson and Geoffrey Perkins, called *Happy Poison, or How we Conquered the Blue Peril*. A series of sketches and musical numbers which poked fun at teachers, pupils and public figures, it was an appropriate early venture on to the stage for the future producer of *Spitting Image* and the host of improvised television comedy. Matthew Francis, one of the performers, describes it as a mix of goonish humour and psychedelic references.

Portillo was one of the supporting cast, but he made his presence felt: he had himself put in charge of the programme, and ensured his name appeared more often than anyone else's – even crediting himself as supplier of the internal refreshments.

His flair for publicity, not least self-publicity, and organisational zeal meant Jim Golland gave him more and more responsibility for school productions. His talent as a producer was to be tested further at university but, despite the hiccup with *Macbeth*, every-thing else – from the meanest revue to the biggest Shakespeare – was a financial success. Golland recalls, 'He was remarkable for his ability to make a profit on any school dramatic activity.'

It was not just the school that benefited from Portillo's enter-prise. When he was eleven he was given a mini-meteorologists' kit as a birthday present. He set up a weather station in his back garden and then issued weather forecasts to his neighbours – for a fee. Matthew Francis recalls neighbours indulging the pre-teen tycoon by doling out a few coppers for the sheets.

A little later, his friends benefited from his infant entrepreneurialism. One summer the builders Trollope & Colls were engaged on some work at Northwick Park Hospital, and Portillo arranged for his mates to spend their vacation cross-checking accounts and filing. He even found work for two girls he had his eye on. He never revealed how he was able to swing the jobs. According to Matthew de Lange, 'He was just like the gaffer on *Auf Wiedersehn, Pet.* He got us the work and we didn't ask questions.' Long before Tory trade-union reforms, before the social chapter was even a twinkle in Jacques Delors's eye, the future employment secretary was already convincing his friends of the value of a flexible and deregulated labour market.

Michael Portillo's persuasive powers were not new to his friends. Several remember the young machiavel twisting them around their fingers during weekend sessions of their favourite board game, Diplomacy – a game which allows each of the seven players to assume the role of leader of one of the great powers on the eve of the First World War. It places a premium on strategic thought, subtle manipulation of allies and timely back-stabbing. The goal is world domination. Portillo was a master. He would often invite his friends over early on a Saturday morning, and they would still be playing late that night, fortified by home-made tortilla and cakes brought in by Mrs Portillo.

The manipulative streak that Diplomacy allowed Portillo to indulge made itself apparent to his friends in all sorts of other, less obvious, ways. One of his closest friends at school recalls both a wonderful and also a darker side to the way Portillo 'managed' his friendships, making him the natural choreographer of their circle: 'He had a visceral capacity for the social manœuvres within a group of people that impacted on everything else. He was, and is still, enormously interested in having a good time – he loved the idea of a social gathering. He was never very good at telling jokes, but he was very good at reacting to others' sense of humour in a warm, sensual way that wasn't toadying. He was good at stoking up a good time – never the jester, always the patron.'

His social skills were at their most acute one-to-one. In Matthew

Francis's words, 'He made friendship seem rich – when you're with him, you feel that the six feet around you are illuminated. He had it when he was twelve, and used it then. He broke the barriers of what you could talk about – there was a real quality of liberation with him. We talked in great detail about the relationships between people, the exact interplay between our friends and what made them tick.'

But this capacity to create an intensity and intimacy of friendship was matched by an ability to withhold it. Another friend recognised that 'He could withdraw favours in a moment, and the rest of us did all we could to get back in his good books. He was interested in control and power. I remember him on the bus one day looking out of the window. A friend asked what he was thinking, and he replied, "I'm considering who I'm going to have a campaign against."'

Desperate efforts would be made to win back his approval by those who had incurred his displeasure. No one recalls Portillo ever having to try to win another back, but one contemporary does remember that Portillo's rare moments of loss of composure were due to a feeling that he might be excluded. He had to be on the inside – preferably at the heart of things. The need to be on the inside track, the sense that where the interest was was where he wanted to be, was one of the factors friends identify as fuelling Portillo's early interest in politics.

Michael Portillo has mentioned in the past that this interest was first aroused at the time of the Profumo affair, in 1963. Portillo was nine when Harold Macmillan's administration, weakened by resignation and running out of steam, had had its amateurish inadequacies cruelly encapsulated by a scandal that was thought to embody many of the vices of an out-of-touch and hypocritical government.

Michael's early heroes were on the Left: JFK and Harold Wilson, young technocrats with a whiff of the outsider, who were trying to build meritocracies and shake up stuffy establishments. Most of Portillo's friends at school were also on the Left, if they had any interest in politics at all. Portillo's form master in his sixth form, Bernard Marchant, believes Portillo was far from alone in his support for Labour: 'All the school's young intellectuals looked up to Harold Wilson in the sixties.'

The intensity of Portillo's interest was, however, of a wholly different pitch. At the age of only eleven he acted as a teller during the 1964 general election. He stood outside polling-booths, marking off the names of Labour supporters on his canvass card and arguing with the Tory representative. On the night of the election he was so excited he was allowed to stay up until eleven. Even when he was sent to bed he could not sleep, and he still remembers lying awake and hearing the roar from below when Watford went Labour.

Having made his mark early, in the 1966 election, he graduated to running Labour's committee rooms in Stanburn School, collating canvass returns and mobilising party workers – at just thirteen. The precocious involvement was matched, however, with a typically teenage, almost fan-like, approach to the great game.

Portillo's closest friend at this point was Matthew Francis, who shared his interest in the personalities of politics but who was a Young Liberal, both more moderate in his views and less passionate in his beliefs than Portillo. Francis recalls both of them writing off to their respective party headquarters for information, posters, stickers and rosettes – much in the manner of fans writing to pop-stars or football teams. He also recalls their shared delight when bundles of propaganda arrived from headquarters to fire the enthusiasm of young zealots. 'I was sent leaflets, stickers and a magnificent poster of Jo Grimond. Michael was sent a poster of Harold Wilson. We stuck the posters on our bedroom walls at home. I know he liked Wilson, but it wasn't hero-worship: it was just another facet of teenage boys pursuing an enthusiasm by collecting things.'

Francis certainly believes politics was Portillo's passion, but he is keen to stress that they were both just curious kids, anxious to amass information about the world around them. He recalls Saturday afternoon trips to London's embassies, where the two boys would pester staff for maps, posters and leaflets with information on other countries.

Portillo's interest in politics, and his nascent pride in British parliamentary democracy, were reflected in 1966 when Spanish cousins came to visit: he took them straight to Downing Street to show off how unpretentious Britain's leaders were. As if on cue, Harold Wilson walked out while they were there, and Portillo was able to draw a favourable comparison between the Britain that had elected this man of the people and a Spain still suffering under a dictatorship.

As Portillo matured, so his enthusiasm for politics grew. He used to dominate school debates and carried the Labour cause into the playground, even as a prefect. One friend remembers him sporting a red rosette around school during the 1970 general elections. Matthew de Lange says that, of their generation, there was no doubt he was 'the political activist – he felt passionately about politics'.

The headmaster, Roy Avery, recognised at the time that Portillo was deeply interested in current affairs, although he did not imagine he would necessarily go into politics. Aware of that interest, he chose Portillo as the school's representative for a National Council for Education and World Citizenship 'Youth Parliament' in New York. This was Michael Portillo's first experience of being an elected parliamentary representative (even though there was only one voter – his headmaster), and it was also his first trip to America. He adored it.

He stayed with a Jewish family on the twenty-third floor of a Brooklyn apartment block, in an ordinary home in Saddlebrook, New Jersey, and with a wealthy East Coast family, the Balls, who had houses in Massachusetts and Long Island. Portillo was very taken with the Balls' daughter, Jamie, whom he was to meet again, much later. He was free to wander round Manhattan, meet fellow sixth-formers from around the world, and attend seminars arranged to allow the students to talk to senators and members of the National Security Council. It was an intoxicating time.

According to Roy Avery, Portillo enjoyed the trip but was not impressed by one aspect of what he saw in Manhattan: 'Michael was shocked by the desolation in one New York high school. He was particularly surprised by the drug scene.' It was not priggishness but simple social concern – a feeling that had been inculcated in the Portillo family home, where a sense of political commitment had been underpinned by faith.

Portillo's religion set him apart from his peers. In an overwhelmingly Anglican school, he was taught as a Catholic. All four Portillo sons had been raised in the Roman faith and took their first communion at a local Catholic church in Stanmore. Portillo attended his in 1960. Instead of attending the regular C of E school assembly, Portillo would go to a special service of prayers for Catholic boys taken by the Catholic classics master, Bernard Marchant. Portillo's father was particularly devout, and nearly refused to allow Michael to go on a scout trip to Scotland one summer, because he feared the Highland route would not allow his son to attend mass on the Sunday. It was only when the school secured from the bishop of Argyll a twenty-four-hour exemption from the obligation to attend that Portillo was allowed to go.

After a spell of near-atheism in his twenties, Portillo now chooses to describe himself as a 'bad' Catholic rather than a lapsed one. It may be a distinction worthy of Graham Greene, but Portillo feels more sympathy for two other Catholic novelists – G. K. Chesterton and Evelyn Waugh. He has told friends that he inclines to agree with both authors that, as a baptised Catholic, he will one day feel 'the twitch upon the thread' which will take him back to Mother Church. In the meantime, he retains a loose faith in the existence of God and a firm belief in Christian morality.

The Catholic character of the Portillo family home, the traditional nature of Harrow County and Michael's own interest in 'grown-up' hobbies such as politics and making money suggest a very serious teenager, but friends say the young Portillo could unbend as easily as any sixties sixteen-year-old. Several adolescent evenings were spent listening to favourite pop singers and earnestly discussing their rival merits.

Portillo had been brought up on a diet of classical music. His mother loved Sibelius, and they went to their first opera together when he was fourteen, visiting Covent Garden to see Puccini's *Tosca*. However, he was quickly converted by his contemporaries to more modern sounds. He became a keen fan of The Doors; Leonard Cohen; Crosby, Stills, Nash and Young; Joan Baez; Simon and Garfunkel and the Beatles. They were, for the most part, the typical enthusiasms of an intelligent, and self-conscious, teenager.

Portillo was also developing his own tastes in classical music, particularly opera, using his pocket money to start his own gramophone collection of Beethoven, Puccini and Verdi. As he has matured, Portillo's love of opera has deepened, but he remains fond of pop music – in particular Katrina and the Waves and the

Pet Shop Boys. According to his constituency agent, his favourite Pet Shop Boys song is 'Money'. The brazen eighties hustler entrepreneurialism of the chorus may appeal: it runs, 'You've got the looks, I've got the brains, let's make lots of money.'

The memories that Michael Portillo left in the minds of his old teachers and former schoolmates vary, but certain themes resonate: his intelligence, charm, interest in politics and, above all, desire to be at the centre, but not necessarily in the forefront. One other quality is mentioned by every teacher, as it is by almost every professional with whom Portillo has had contact throughout his career: his politeness. He possesses a manner that suggests an air of old-world courtesy inherited from his father. The figure he cut in the eyes of the masters was always composed. To a man – and they were all men – they remember a studious, talented and, above all, impeccably polite pupil.

Modern-languages teacher Don Wilkey recalls a 'tremendously polite lad, who was very engaging'. History teacher Harry Mees thinks Portillo was 'always impeccably behaved'. Bernard Marchant believed Portillo had perfect manners, and thought him an archetypal English gentleman. His suavity also impressed Roy Avery, who believed he had natural diplomatic skills and who also valued his 'exceptional loyalty at a time of chopping and changing'.

Despite such fond memories, Portillo did not behave well in every class. One classmate remembers his having in a high degree the schoolboy's ability to scent, and exploit, weakness in a master. According to his classmate, in his early teens Portillo singled out one teacher for sly sarcasm, cheek and ribbing. The teacher in question was pushed to breaking-point on a couple of occasions and had to bawl Portillo out – even, once, taking a slipper to his behind in front of the rest of the class. Whether because of Portillo or a deeper sense of having made the wrong career choice, he abandoned teaching soon after and left to become a rabbi in Paris.

Paris was also the scene of Portillo's only other major schoolboy misdemeanour. He and several of his pals, including Nigel Sheinwald and Matthew de Lange, spent a week on holiday there during an Easter vacation in their sixth form.

The holiday got off to a chaotic start when Portillo, taking the lead, decided that, after making their way to France by different routes, they should meet in the middle of the Place de la Concorde.

Not the easiest of meeting-spots in the city, it took hours for them to assemble. The friends spent the week experimenting with grown-up food and drink, visiting the Eiffel Tower, Fontainebleau and Versailles, and generally fooling around. It was all relatively innocent but, because they were enjoying themselves so much, Portillo decided they should defy the school and stay off for a few extra days before returning. One of those involved does not remember being disciplined but does recall a dim view being taken of Portillo's flexitime approach to his schooling.

These minor acts of rebellion did not prevent Portillo being appointed a senior prefect. At HCSB ordinary prefects were gowned like mini-masters; senior prefects had white bands, worn round the neck in the manner of the measuring-tape worn by floor-walkers in old-fashioned department stores. Selection as a prefect was far from automatic for senior sixth-formers and was viewed as a clear recognition of worth. In return for taking the register for classes and peace-keeping duties around the school, prefects were assigned their own safe haven, a room set apart from the main school buildings, at the top of a spiral staircase. A simple privilege, it became the object of lurid speculation for the excluded, and one master remembers the school caretaker muttering darkly about 'orgies' taking place there.

Whatever the calls on Portillo's spare time, his schooling did not suffer. Grade As in his English and history A-levels and a B in French were the launching-pad for securing an open scholarship to read history at Cambridge, and in between learning he also taught one of his colleagues Spanish. The schoolmate remembers the young Portillo running through conjugation in a quiet corner of the playground more used to harbouring furtive smokers than Hispanic scholars.

He was academically distinguished, but not unusually so in a very clever year. He had a talent for drama, but was easily eclipsed by Matthew Francis, Geoffrey Perkins and Clive Anderson. He was a charmer, but only one of several in a class that would boast, in Nigel Sheinwald, one of the most talented diplomats of his generation. He was an asset to the school, but not obviously *the* asset of his year. However, even then his English master, Jim Golland, recognised that Portillo, although not head boy, had a quality that placed him just ahead of his peers – he had leadership. Writing in the last issue of the school magazine before Portillo and his class left, Golland said:

Though his natural reticence would demur, Michael Portillo has long been the leader of this wild bunch of entrepreneurs, aesthetes, clowns and committee men. He too has dabbled in acting – as a corpse last year among other parts – but apart from his complete re-organisation of the Bookroom and his mammoth feat in typing the whole of last year's Jubilee Magazine, he was also remarkable for his complete inability to score anything less than a Grade A in the GCE.

The warmth of the compliment, to Portillo and his contemporaries, was handsomely returned on the day they left. At Portillo's inspiration, he and his friends organised a 'thank-you' dinner for their teachers. The school dining-room was commandeered, mothers were pressed into action as cooks, pansies were stuffed into wine bottles as table decorations, and a few daring flasks of Chianti were prised from the grip of reluctant dads. Some of those who helped organise it cringe now, but the masters present then were touched.

Two decades later, when the golden generation were on the verge of fulfilling their promise, Portillo returned the compliment again. He organised a 'twenty-years-on' dinner for the surviving masters and the friends with whom he was still in touch. A House of Commons dining-room was booked. Sherry and Commons claret replaced the seventies plonk. Instead of the home-baking of the original, there was melon, followed by Aylesbury duckling, Ice-Cream Soufflé Westminster and coffee with petits fours.

The two most prominent successes, Anderson and Portillo, proposed toasts to the Queen and the masters respectively. Jim Golland replied on behalf of the masters. Bernard Marchant remembers Anderson joking that he had thought Portillo would be a chat-show host and he the politician, then forecasting a glittering future for his schoolmate – as leader of the Opposition. Another master recalls good-natured ribbing of Portillo's recently remodelled hairstyle from former masters and pupils.

The evening would not be to everyone's taste. Some might consider such devotion to one's school cloying in a grown man, but those present believe the gathering was not in the least embarrassing. One saw it as evidence of loyalty and genuine gratitude. The gratitude is understandable: Harrow County had taken the young Portillo and equipped him with all the skills – social and intellectual – he would need to survive in Cambridge. It had prepared him for the next stage of his journey to the heart of England's establishment.

It wasn't a stage he would travel altogether alone. Before leaving Harrow County, Portillo acquired a steady girlfriend as well as a clutch of qualifications.

Carolyn Eadie was older, posher and more sought-after than Portillo, but there was something about the bearing of the young man that impressed her. Like Portillo and many of his friends, she lived in Stanmore, a short walk from the Portillo home, but she went not to Harrow County's sister school but to the subtly more prestigious North London Collegiate in Canons Park. Her father was a civil engineer and, like Portillo's mother, an Anglo-Scot. Matthew de Lange remembers her parents' home in the Ridgeway, Stanmore's snootiest quarter, as 'slightly grander' than his schoolmate's.

De Lange believes Portillo was introduced to Carolyn by Geoffrey Perkins at a teenage party thrown by Clive Anderson. Perkins was already an old flame, and Anderson was pursuing her sister Alison. A third sister, Irene, also had her admirers. At school Portillo was not remembered as one of the more aggressive girl-chasers, but he and Carolyn clearly hit it off. They started seeing each other regularly, and the relationship carried on when Carolyn went to St Anne's College, Oxford, to read geography and her boyfriend to Cambridge. The relationship was to be placed under some strain by the temptations strewn in Portillo's path at university, but when he left Harrow in 1972 he was innocently entwined with a girl who was subsequently to show him the loyalty he regards as the highest human virtue.

CHAPTER FOUR

Peterhouse Man

Nothing you do before the age of twenty-five should ever be
held against you in politics.
                                        Michael Portillo to research assistant

Small, malicious and very right-wing – Peterhouse and
Maurice Cowling were made for each other.
                                        Cambridge graduate

Most of her graduates remember her with affection, but Cambridge's oldest college had a decided character which is not to
everyone's taste. Most of his former pupils remember him with
admiration, but Peterhouse's modern-history tutor has never been
an easy man. Michael Portillo, however, looks back with affection
and admiration to both Peterhouse and Maurice Cowling – the
scene and the guide for his journey from Left to Right as an undergraduate.

When Portillo went up to Peterhouse in the autumn of 1972, on
an open scholarship in history, the college had not developed the
notoriety in political circles it was later to earn. But, even if
Michael Portillo had never walked through its courts, Peterhouse
would deserve a privileged place in the political history of the last
twenty years, for during the eighties the college was identified
as one of the sources of intellectual underpinning for Margaret
Thatcher's political programme.

The Tory dominance in that decade was held, by party theorists,
to be more than a happy accident or consequence of a divided
Left. Responsibility rested partly with the quality of Thatcher's
leadership, but also with the coherence of her doctrine. Her ideological self-confidence was attributed to the vigour and fecundity
in the seventies of a group of thinkers known as the 'New Right'
– an umbrella title for a collection of repentant ex-socialists, unrepentant Powellites and others emerging from the decaying postwar
institutions erected by social democracy. The New Right has been

tracked down to several lairs, but one of the darkest was Peterhouse.

Although one of the smallest, and most secretive, colleges in Cambridge, Peterhouse produced a number of figures whose public influence shaped the Toryism of the Thatcher years. Apart from Maurice Cowling, a whole *galère* of right-wing thinkers and journalists passed through the college as undergraduates or research students. They include Professor Roger Scruton, who upheld traditional Toryism through the columns of *The Times* and the *Salisbury Review*; Professor John Vincent, who straddled with rare skill a chair in history at Bristol University and a column on the *Sun*; Dr David Watkin, who led the counter-attack against the architectural modernism of the sixties; Dr Edward Norman, who fought a similar battle against the abandonment of ancient wisdom in the Anglican Church; and Peter Fuller, who deserted the ranks of the Marxists and modernists in the field of the visual arts to conduct a campaign against the errors of progressivism no less spirited and reactionary than that of Drs Norman and Watkin.

In Fleet Street, Patrick Cosgrave, the first official biographer of Enoch Powell; Peregrine Worsthorne and Colin Welch, the keepers of the *Telegraph*'s conscience; George Gale, the pungently anti-Heathite editor of the *Spectator* in the seventies; and that magazine's most perceptive political columnist of the eighties, Noel Malcom, had all studied at Peterhouse.

What united these writers, beyond their affinity for their old college, was not so much a detailed analysis as an attitude, close to but subtly different from that of other thinkers on the Right who attracted attention in the eighties. The members of the New Right saw themselves fighting against a set of assumptions that had become the received wisdom among the intelligentsia but which they felt were deeply corrupting of the nation's health and traditions. But whereas the most obvious battles fought by the New Right in the eighties were economic, the struggle dearest to the hearts of the Peterhouse Right was cultural. They believed in an unsentimental Toryism – traditional, but not in the manner of Harold Macmillan, whose 'Middle Way' moderation they despised. They were radically Right, but scornful of monetary manipulation and fiscal fiddling as the main object of political activity.

Cowling himself sought to characterise the Peterhouse Right in the preface to the second edition of his *Mill and Liberalism*. This had first been published in 1963, when, to its author's delight, the *Philosophical Quarterly* described it as 'dangerous and unpleasant'. It was reissued in 1990 by publishers shrewdly aware of the interest felt in the apparent dominance of the New Right on political thought.

Cowling argued that the Peterhouse Right's common prejudices were 'against the higher liberalism and all sorts of liberal rhetoric, including ecclesiastical liberal rhetoric, and in favour of irony, geniality and malice as solvents of enthusiasm, virtue and political elevation'. He went into the Peterhouse Right's position in as much detail as he dared: 'They wish elites and establishments to eschew guilt and self-doubt, to perform the duties of their stations, and to avoid unrealistic claims about their rectitude.'

Alongside this elegant hymn of hate against the conventional pieties of postwar democratic politicians was a sideswipe against any economics obsessives who might think that the free-market provides the most effective antidote to collectivism and liberalism. Cowling argued that the Peterhouse Right believe that 'government and politics have dignities, languages and reasons of their own, that these require illusionless re-furbishing in every generation, and that they should not be subordinated even to the most compatible of economic doctrines'.

The dominance of economic doctrine – albeit one intimately compatible with Cowling's prejudices – marked Margaret Thatcher's first years in power, and so one might be tempted to conclude that the Peterhouse Right's rhetorical assault was a histrionic sideshow to the main event in Whitehall and Westminster. However, the moral energy that animated Thatcher and the cultural climate that allowed her to operate were, to an extent, the product of those from the Peterhouse Right who had undermined the liberal legacy of the sixties and seventies.

Thatcher's early opponents – the 'wets': Jim Prior, Sir Ian Gilmour, Peter Walker, Francis Pym, Christopher Soames and even Peter Carrington – were inheritors of a whole raft of liberal assumptions but they focused their opposition on her economic policy, accusing her of an attachment to crude 'monetarism', arguing that she had substituted an ideological fixation with measurement of the money supply for a more balanced – i.e. interventionist – economic policy.

In taking them on, Thatcher certainly relied on the nuts-and-bolts number-crunching of professional economists like Ralph Harris, Arthur Seldon, Milton Friedman and Alan Walters, but the struggle between wet and dry was more than a dispute about the theological arcana of monetary statistics: it was a gut contest between a prime minister determined to break the collectivist consensus that she believed had stifled Britain for too long and ministers who feared that her radicalism would unleash forces that could fracture the kingdom and accelerate the gentle decline over which they were happy to preside.

Thatcher was convinced that the economic battle had to be won before advances could be conducted on any other front, so in her first Cabinet she concentrated those most loyal to her in the economic portfolios – Sir Geoffrey Howe at the Treasury with John Biffen, Keith Joseph at Industry, and John Nott at Trade with Cecil Parkinson. In other areas where the pre-1979 consensus might have been challenged, such as foreign policy or education, open conflict was avoided. That avoidance was tactical: only by winning the economic argument, Thatcher believed, would she have the strength to transfer her government's energies to attacking collectivism in other areas.

But in order to win the economic battle, and to prepare the ground for further advance, the claims of collectivism had to be submitted to scrutiny and found wanting. This the Peterhouse Right, and its allies in journalism and the academy, did with gusto. By laying into the liberals and setting out to drag every socialist sacred cow they could find straight to the knacker's yard, the Peterhouse Right and their allies prepared the ground for the first Thatcher administration.

Maurice Cowling's polemical style is vigorously bloody, but when it comes to accepting the victor's palm he exhibits an almost arch diffidence. In the preface to the second edition of *Mill and Liberalism* he deliberately underplayed the influence of his coterie, stating that the 'Peterhouse Right is an academic Right – a set of monastic, or country, cousins who have some journalistic connections and weak political connections'. But the power of that single disclaimer should be put in context. It occurs halfway through thirty-four pages devoted to an analysis of the influence of the New Right which places the Peterhouse Right at the centre of several overlapping networks, and positions Cowling himself lurking at the heart of the web of connections.

While the fellows of Peterhouse might not be able to produce a pamphlet listing the legislative changes which had sprung from their fertile minds, as the gentlemen of the Adam Smith Institute did, they can take credit for playing a profound part in reshaping the attitude and temper of the British political élite. But their hegemony was still in the future when Michael Portillo arrived as an undergraduate. At that time the idea of Peterhouse's fellows influencing anyone beyond Cambridge – and beyond inducing a twitch of distaste – would have been considered laughable. Peterhouse was seen by the rest of the university as marginal and eccentric, and Peterhouse saw the rest of the university much as Lot and his wife viewed the cities of the plain – with a shiver of disgust.

As well as being smaller and older than the other Cambridge colleges, Peterhouse is also, of those founded before the late nineteenth century, the furthest from the town centre. Its distance from the rest of the university has been more than just geographical. Cambridge has always held itself aloof from the rest of the country and its convulsions, but even those metropolitan fads that did make it up the A11 never got past the Peterhouse gatepost.

In the eighties it was the penultimate college to accept women, and the site of the bloodiest battle to prevent their admission. The same fellows who resisted coeducation for so long celebrated the college's seven hundredth anniversary in suitably antique fashion – with the erection of a sundial. In the seventies, when the rest of the university's undergraduate body was agitating for the Students' Union to be given a central site – preferably the premises of the élitist debating society confusingly known as the Cambridge Union – Peterhouse stood in its most familiar, and comfortable, posture: alone. The only political agitation in Peterhouse was to keep the college out of the university-wide Students' Union, in splendid isolation.

Seventies Peterhouse men did not involve themselves in university politics. The hacks who sought election to the committees of the Union or the Conservative Association were despised; the careerism of the generation of Kenneth Clarke, John Gummer and Michael Howard a decade earlier was considered an object of humorous pity rather than worthy of emulation. Those undergraduates who did consider themselves political and Conservative almost delighted in the antique irrelevance of their views.

One student there in the seventies remembers that those who were Tories were almost disconcerted by the pendulum swing to the Right during the decade. He remembers his friends preparing for a world doomed to become ever more progressive and hopeful that, as the years passed, their Conservatism would fossilise into a reactionary stance delightfully unintelligible to the modern world.

But while Peterhouse held itself apart, it did not fall prey to the Cambridge sin of puritan exclusivism. Simon Marquis, a columnist with *Marketing* magazine who read history at the same time as Portillo, describes the atmosphere as 'self-contained but not monastic'. Another seventies student remembers years of 'controlled outrageousness – food, drink and fellowship all pursued with a certain style'. It was an environment which supplied practically everything that Marquis and his friends required: 'I think I can count on the fingers of one hand the times we ventured outside. We were all very much at Peterhouse, not Cambridge.' On the rare occasions when their circle did venture out, it was not into town but further afield, to outlying villages like Trumpington or Newton, where the Queen's Head pub was a favourite resort.

Michael Portillo found himself at Peterhouse more or less by chance: it was the choice of his headmaster, on no basis other than the establishment of a Harrow County bridgehead over the years. The school had sent a succession of undergraduates into Peterhouse in the late sixties and early seventies to read history, including one old friend of Portillo's, Bill Davies, now an editor with the Cambridge University Press, who had found favour with the history tutors. Portillo was directed towards Peterhouse in the hope of consolidating that bridgehead, rather than for any reasons of personal compatibility.

However, when he went up, even though he was still a grammar-school-educated socialist, he very quickly found himself at home in the reactionary and traditional environment of Peterhouse. The college had a public-school feel, but it was neither as oppressively hearty as Trinity nor as preciously self-regarding as King's. It sought to preserve the feel of an establishment designed for gentlemen with a taste for learning rather than a shelter for sportsmen or an academic factory, and Portillo soon settled in.

There was something a little self-conscious about the college's traditionalism. Two of the dons with the biggest influence on the undergraduates – Maurice Cowling and Edward Norman – were, like Portillo, the products of suburban London grammar schools. In their precision of speech, antiquity of dress and loathing of progress, some contemporaries detected a whiff of affectation. But for most of those who have passed through Peterhouse the impression of Cowling, Norman and others who formed the character of the college in the seventies is of men with entertaining and individual views, and real style, who helped give the place a distinct and cherishable personality.

That personality, according to a former research student there during the seventies, was 'rich, gamy and louche. We worked hard during the day, but only to allow ourselves more time in the evening to enjoy ourselves.' There was certainly rich scope for such enjoyment. The college had a number of traditions and societies designed to allow debauchery to take place within prescribed, but elastic, limits. Four societies provided a focus for organised merriment: the Perne, the Cousin Club, Ratsoc and the Grafton.

The Perne was named after an ancient benefactor who is also commemorated in the college library. Originally a debating society, its intellectual justification had long since withered away by the time Portillo was up, and it survived only as an excuse for several black-tie dinners a term. One of Portillo's contemporaries, Bill Baker, now a wine merchant in the West Country but at that time a Falstaffian right-winger at the centre of most revelry, recollects only one guest speaker addressing the club during his time. His main memories are the relatively palatable quality of the college food, the disappointing nature of most of the wine (supplied by a Communist steward called Goodwin) and, notwithstanding its quality, the quantity drunk by most of his fellow members. Membership was by invitation but almost self-selecting: after the scientists, prudes and prigs had been excluded, the candidates were obvious.

The Cousin was practically indistinguishable from the Perne – a black-tie dining society named after a figure venerated in college history but unknown to most of the students who drank his health. It met once a term in the college's combination room, and a sprinkling of dons encouraged a more stately progress to dissolution. Maurice Cowling often attended, as did the mathematics tutor Adrian Matthias.

The Ratsoc was dedicated simply to gluttony. Each term, a ten-course dinner was punctuated, between the fowl and meat courses, with a champagne sorbet. All this indulgence was on offer for ten pounds a time, inclusive of wines.

The Grafton was a little different. A breakfast, rather than a dining, society, it was named after the only Peterhouse man to become prime minister, the third duke of Grafton, premier from 1766 to 1770, and it met on the last Friday of term. Its members wore morning dress, ate bacon and eggs, and drank champagne until they, or the bottles, were completely drained.

Bill Baker remembers Portillo as an early joiner and enthusiastic attender of all four societies, but already his behaviour was marked by the restraint touched with just a hint of hauteur that all but his closest friends remark on. 'He certainly joined in and drank with the best of us, but I never saw him riotously or embarrassingly drunk. He always held himself in check.' The most embarrassing thing about Portillo's behaviour that Baker recalls is a taste for Engelbert Humperdinck-style frilly dress-shirts.

Another contemporary, Ian Docherty, now a businessman in Ulster, considers the circle that he and Portillo moved in to have been sybaritic even for Peterhouse, but he recalls a disciplined edge to Portillo's self-indulgence, agreeing with Baker that he never lost control and seldom allowed the evening's excesses to keep him too long from his desk in the library the next morning.

That restraint was apparent also in his dress and carriage. Although his full lips and generous mop gave him the look of a young Mick Jagger, at a time when most students were happiest in denim and cheesecloth the undergraduate Portillo was usually smartly, even punctiliously, dressed – generally in flannels and sports jacket or blazer, and seldom without a tie. But the bourgeois respectability of his dress did not extend totally to his attitude towards the most distinctly public-school aspects of life at Peterhouse.

The Perne, Cousin, Ratsoc and Grafton may have had a Bright

Young Thing air about them, but there was none of the riotous vandalism associated with pure public-school societies such as Oxford's Assassins or the Bullingdon, no baying for breaking glass. However, the strong public-school strain in Peterhouse did find expression in elaborate pranks. The contents of rooms were removed and rearranged on college courts; undergraduates found themselves victims of 'Colditz' – nailed into their rooms for the amusement of their peers. Slightly subtler methods were deployed to torment dons. Bachelor tutors – David 'Wendy' Watkin a particular favourite – were sent Valentine cards purporting to be from other members of the senior common room. Portillo is remembered as a willing victim, and perpetrator, of several such stunts. Whether these schoolboy jokes actually amused the young Portillo as much as they did some of his contemporaries is unlikely. Friends says his sense of humour, though broad, is not cruel, and suspect he may have collaborated only to avoid the charge of priggishness – social death at Peterhouse.

He himself was the victim of one particularly elaborate practical joke. After a weekend away from Cambridge he received a note from one tutor, Bill Hinton, who claimed to have heard 'tittle-tattle' about his absence – reports of behaviour he considered 'cavalier and ungentlemanly'. Portillo, who had been in hot romantic pursuit over the weekend, was terrified of upsetting the crustily formal don and immediately penned an apology. Fortunately for him, the apology was never sent. The initial letter was a forgery, cooked up by his fellow historian Trevor Woolley, now a civil servant at the Ministry of Defence. Woolley confessed all when he saw a clearly distraught Portillo explain that he had written a full apology. Woolley begged him to intercept it, and was immensely relieved to discover that it had been written but not yet sent. If it had been, Woolley would have been grievously embarrassed – but not as embarrassed as Portillo, having to explain his private life to a Peterhouse fellow.

One old schoolfriend who kept up with Portillo at Cambridge suspects that Portillo had a deeper motivation than simple amusement for joining in with the practical jokes and attending the black-tie dinners: his determination to be 'on the inside', to be travelling with the in crowd.

Peterhouse's aloofness from Cambridge, and the exclusivity of the set that dominated the dining clubs within college, would have appealed to the undergraduate Portillo's taste for participation in an élite. The traditions, and the exquisitely reactionary politics of the presiding geniuses, would have made the mix all the more intoxicating. A premium was placed on wit and on an arch evocation of reactionary chic. There was a deeply complicit feel, at once flattering and frivolous, to being expected to outbid each other in the danger of the views advanced. As an intelligent and sensitive soul, Portillo was a natural for admission to this precious aristocracy of talent. The sense of being set apart provided by the close friendships and peculiar politics of Peterhouse provided what Portillo had been looking for all his life and framed his attitude to others ever after, for Portillo is an élitist not only in the sense of wanting excellence, but also in the sense of being thrilled to have others recognise that he is in the élite.

The intensity of life at Peterhouse may have been intoxicating, but it also had a hothouse side which was not to everyone's taste. An acquaintance of Portillo's at Peterhouse in the seventies stresses one element in the mix of traits that gave the college its 'gamy' flavour: a style — camp in some, decidedly homosexual in others — which owed something to the sexually liberated atmosphere of the early seventies and something to the insularity of the all-male college. Fellows and undergraduates were given girls' names; parties were organised in meadows a little out of town, and cross-dressing was encouraged. A brittle bitchiness of manner and favouritism towards certain students from some fellows was apparent even to those outside Peterhouse.

Michael Portillo's looks and bearing brought him to the notice of some of the more *outré* members of college. Handsome and self-possessed, he was the object of attention; but, while he appreciated aspects of the atmosphere, he was emphatically one of the more fastidious members of college.

Portillo disappointed some by his refusal to join in with the loucher aspects of college life, but he was not a party-pooper, as his university life outside Peterhouse showed. His interest in the stage, so carefully nurtured at school, led him to become involved in the ADC, the Amateur Dramatic Club, the university's oldest theatrical society. This rivalled Footlights, the revue group that first gave the young Clive Anderson's satirical talents full vent, as the most prestigious nursery of talent, but tended to attract a less obviously ambitious, more conspicuously cultured crowd.

Student actors in the early seventies were drawn to the experimental, in every sphere. Some Cambridge figures remember undergraduate drama hacks trying to demonstrate their bohemian rejection of middle-class morality with plays, and lifestyles, they thought daringly avant-garde. During the early seventies the Amateur Dramatic Club was known as the AC/DC and, although it was as advanced in its way as Peterhouse was reactionary, there was a similar clannish intensity about both institutions.

Portillo was not a central figure in the drama scene. Although he rose up the ADC committee ladder to become junior treasurer, he was not one of those determined to push back barriers – artistic or personal – but contented himself with proving an able administrator. Others, such as the novelist Michael Arditti, who was a director at the time, combined administration with occasional performances, but Portillo stuck to what he knew he could do – fixing financing and leaving the flamboyance to others. Arditti, whose novel *The Celibate* was published to critical acclaim in 1993, remembers Portillo as 'always charming – even when he was cutting budgets'. But, tight budgeting notwithstanding, Arditti confesses himself amazed that the engaging undergraduate he knew is now the hard man of the Tory Right.

Portillo enjoyed the atmosphere of the ADC and is still a keen theatre-goer, with a number of friends who are involved in drama or entertainment, but his fascination with the theatre is now overlaid with a passion for opera – the more demanding and Teutonic the better.

Portillo's time at Peterhouse and in the ADC has convinced the malicious that there must be some dark secret. Like Bill Clinton's dalliance with marijuana at Oxford, there has to be a damaging, or at least embarrassing, recollection that will return to haunt the golden boy. But, while few of Portillo's contemporaries would describe him as a model undergraduate, none recalls anything much more embarrassing than drunkenness or a taste for practical jokes. His dressing up for ten-course dinners, rehearsing his reactionary views at champagne breakfasts and lining his room with champagne bottles while the country faced a three-day-week may not be to everyone's taste, but they were not wildly out of the run of Cambridge life in the early seventies.

Portillo's extracurricular activities occupied a good deal of his time in his first two years, but he never neglected his studies. Ian Docherty, himself a keen historian, remembers Portillo as one of the college's most assiduous scholars. Another contemporary who was one of his partners for supervisions – the weekly reading of an essay to one's tutor, followed by its slow, painful dissection – remembers Portillo holding his own with all of them, including the most caustic critic of them all, inevitably, Maurice Cowling. When Portillo read out his first essay, Cowling's opening remark was 'You write with a pickaxe.' Cowling affected to believe Portillo's English was so bad because he was an imperfectly naturalised Latin, happier speaking Spanish.

Cowling was not Portillo's only tutor but he was perhaps the principal. Owen Chadwick, then master of Selwyn, taught him for one paper, England and the Papacy 1859–74, dealing with the conversion of Cardinals Newman and Manning and the activities of Odo Russell, the nephew of the Whig premier Lord John Russell, while ambassador to the Holy See. Portillo was, apparently, particularly interested in this narrow slice of history, perhaps moved by the intellectual pilgrimages the two men made in search of certainty, and maybe already appreciating the mastery of intrigue required of a diplomat in a closed world like the Vatican.

Edward Norman also taught him, and his asperity was much to Portillo's taste. Even though Norman was politically well-disposed towards Edward Heath, his attitudes were not those of a conventional admirer. One contemporary remembers him verbally laying about the reforms of the sixties, wrought by a 'guilty, moralising middle-class'. Norman believed the prevailing attitudes towards poverty and punishment of the politicians who supported the liberal stance of successive home secretaries such as Labour's Roy Jenkins or the Conservatives' Robert Carr were the product of guilt at a privileged upbringing instead of the result of rigorous thought.

Both Chadwick and Norman enjoyed Portillo's admiration, but it was Cowling to whom he was closest. They remain close. Portillo was the host in January 1994 at the launch party for a collection of essays written to mark Cowling's retirement from the college. It was at that party that Portillo revealed Cowling's final words to him at Peterhouse. Portillo explained that after his exams he had made a final pilgrimage to Cowling's rooms in Fenn Court, expecting a blessing and words of wisdom with which to face the world, only to be given the simple benediction 'Now bugger off!'

Despite this brusque farewell, the two men still meet and talk regularly. During the 1995 leadership crisis Cowling appeared on BBC *Newsnight* as a spectral figure on a screen from the Swansea studio to plead his pupil's case against advocates of Heseltine, Redwood and Major. After the election was over, Cowling took the trouble to write to *The Times*, praising Redwood for his challenge, but praising Portillo more for his wisdom in avoiding a contest which could have handed victory to Michael Heseltine.

Like Portillo, Cowling was brought up in the world of London's respectable lower middle classes. In the preface to the first volume of his most substantial work, *Religion and Public Doctrine in Modern England*, which he himself describes as a journey round 'the contours of a narrow mind', he sketches in something of his background. Piecing those sketches together with the recollections of friends and pupils, a picture emerges of a bookish boy, happy at his studies at Battersea Grammar School in the thirties, unathletic, clever and religious, tipped by his headmaster as a future archbishop of Canterbury. With a view to a clerical career he went up to Jesus College, Cambridge, his early inclinations to ordination disappeared. A period in the Indian Army at the end of the War excited an interest in the empire just as it began its melancholy, long, withdrawing roar, but, after a year studying in the subcontinent, Cambridge claimed him again.

He returned not to God but to Jesus. However, he did not settle. A short stay at the Foreign Office, periods as a leader-writer – including one with the *Manchester Guardian* – and selection as Tory candidate for the safe Labour seat of Bassetlaw, in 1959, all preceded his eventual arrival as a fellow at Peterhouse. He has assured friends that this restlessness was merely a precursor to settling to what he always enjoyed most: reading with as little interruption as possible, and thinking in as much free time as possible. Some, however, detect an itch to have performed on a more public stage, even after nearly forty years as a don.

His teaching style, common-room conversation, and high-table banter all betray a man acutely aware of the theatrical – the effect

of a conversational grenade tossed into polite college chit-chat carefully calculated, the provocation to a tiresome liberal colleague
delicately timed and beautifully delivered. But the style of the
performance should not detract from the seriousness of the purpose. Cowling has been exercised by the decline he has witnessed
in Britain's position during his adult life – a moral, or religious,
decline which has seen a people guided by Christian principle
lapse into apostasy, and a political decline which has seen Britain's
governing élite lapse into liberal error.

It was in the hope that those trends could be reversed, or at
least arrested, that he published a collection of essays in 1979.
Conservative Essays grew out of the conversations of the Salisbury
Group, a dining society which allowed academics, journalists and
politicians on the old Right, many with connections, or at least
affinities, with Peterhouse, to meet with the blessing, and occasionally under the roof of, the Marquess of Salisbury, the dynastic
inheritor of High Tory tradition.

Cowling's own contribution, 'The Present Position', exemplified
many of his rhetorical traits: a dense style, the enunciation of truths
through the exposure of error and inconsistency, and frequent discursive diversions that eventually buttress the central case. That
central case was the need for reasserting Christian and Conservative principles. Couched in a manner both scripturally evocative
and rhetorically forceful, the question he asked was: 'What should
be said that will make citizens feel that they are citizens of no
mean city?' That question and the arguments in the essay for the
need of élites to reassert leadership bear a similarity to the themes
developed in Portillo's speeches from 1993 to 1995, where he has
outlined the need for politicians to defend traditional values and
institutions and play their part in restoring national pride.

The influence of the whole Peterhouse Right on British politics
has been noted by Cowling himself, but his own, very individual,
influence on the current political scene is far broader, and more
subtle, than one can discern from simply listening for echoes on
public platforms. His careful cultivation of the talented and
ambitious suggests a keener eye for power than he might readily
admit. He is every bit as successful a head-hunter as Carolyn
Portillo.

Two of his younger, but particularly influential, protégés are chancellor of the exchequer Kenneth Clarke's main adviser David Ruffley and John Redwood's senior aide Hywel Williams. Although serving very different masters, both display the distrust of mandarin pieties, the relish for intrigue, the cool, sceptical intelligence and civilised taste for grown-up relaxations that mark out Cowling's pupils. In all those respects they differ little from Portillo. That all three found their way into Tory politics is not so much a matter of planning or coincidence but the consequence of carrying away from Cambridge the imprint of an attitude.

That attitude was conveyed most forcefully not in Cowling's writing but in his teaching. 'Frightening' is how Ian Docherty remembers it. 'Intellectually demanding and rigorous' is how another contemporary describes it. One student characterised Cowling's teaching method as 'vampiric' – partly because he preferred to take supervisions at night, but mainly because he so enjoyed drawing blood. Bill Baker, more a drinker than a thinker as a student, found his hours with Cowling 'tough and bruising'.

Simon Marquis remembers the encounters vividly, but with more affection. 'His first question would always be: "Is what you've written clever?" He was far more interested in our being clever than having read all the books. He was a wonderful tutor. He had an awesome intellect – dispassionate, with a touch of cynicism – and he encouraged detachment from the subject-matter. The one thing he could not abide was bullshit.'

Cowling taught modern political history and the history of political thought, but it was more the style than the subject that mattered. All those who remember him warmly point to the rigour he imbued their thought with, the respect for evidence, the appreciation of originality in insight, the need to challenge all assumptions, and the scorn for the cosy compromise. They acknowledge a bullying edge with those who did not give of their best, but also point to a generosity towards those who tried to match his exacting standards, with glasses of whisky, or even champagne, often poured towards the end of a particularly productive hour.

Those who shared supervisions with Michael Portillo believe he was initially attracted by Cowling's intellectual rigour, scrupulous testing of arguments and impatience with the incoherent or intellectually lazy. It was an attitude congenial to the cast of his own mind. The style of Cowling's supervisions sprang from a view of teaching that was deeply political. As well as inculcating a method of thinking, Cowling also initiated his best students into, in his own words, a 'bloody' and 'illusionless' ideological position.

Cowling never sought to do anything as crude as indoctrinate his pupils, even those thirsty for it. For much of his academic career he was profoundly sceptical of how relevant his professional work could be in framing a response to current political concerns. Although revered by some dons, like Norman Stone and Niall Ferguson, who use their academic eminence as a licence to comment on current affairs, Cowling was for much of his career leery of doing any more as a history don than trying to understand the world retrospectively rather than forecast it prospectively. However, Michael Portillo's arrival in 1972 coincided with a shift in Cowling's thinking, identified by Dr Peter Ghosh of St Anne's College, Oxford, who contributed a study of Maurice Cowling's thought to *Public and Private Doctrine*. Ghosh believes Cowling 'came increasingly to understand that the contrast between political and academic is academic, that dons play a part, however obscurely, in the development of the public mind, and that the way they do this is through teaching and writing, by informing teaching and writing with a tone and a posture'.

The tone and posture Cowling adopted during the time when Michael Portillo arrived at Peterhouse would have been, literally, shocking for the student socialist. The enthusiasm of Portillo's generation for Harold Wilson was fading, but the leftish assumptions that had been nurtured at home and encouraged at school were still in place when he went up. For a man whose father had fought Fascism and been driven into exile by a Nazi-sponsored dictator to be taught modern history by a man who argued that Germany was to be opposed only in so far as she threatened Britain's independence and her empire was, at the very least, bracing.

In an age where politics was held to be about discerning and enacting the popular will, it was challenging to be taught by a tutor who argued that politics was about the power play within élites which were only dimly concerned with the 'people' and then only in so far as the people's consent could be manufactured or manipulated in pursuit of power.

It was particularly provocative to be confronted with such

thinking at a time when the electorate's main preoccupations – immigration and Europe – were not the subject of violent dispute between the two main ideological enemies in Parliament but the preserve of 'fringe' figures, attacked for their shameful flirting with populism.

The piece of Cowling's writing which Portillo acknowledges as having had the greatest influence on his view of politics is the preface to *The Impact of Labour*, and its analysis of 'high politics'.

High politics was primarily a matter of rhetoric and manœuvre . . . The political system consisted of fifty or sixty politicians in conscious tension with one another whose accepted authority constituted political leadership.

It was from these politicians that almost all initiative came. The language they used, the images they formed, the myths they left had a profound effect on the objectives other politicians assumed could be achieved through the political system.

It is a view that would have appealed to someone whose instincts in favour of élites had been encouraged by Peterhouse, and whose taste for manœuvre had been there from his schoolboy initiation in back-stabbing around the Diplomacy board.

Cowling's positions are hardly fashionable stances now, but for a student socialist in the early seventies they were so eccentric as to be perverse. However, they were far from being the quixotic prejudices of a mind seeking to provoke for provocation's sake: they were a coherent riposte to many of the lazy assumptions that governed political thought on Left and Right, and had a deep effect on the formation of Portillo's own principles.

As *Religion and Public Doctrine* makes clear, Cowling's analyses sprang from a political position which, writing in 1981, the *Daily Telegraph* columnist T. E. Utley characterised as 'a brand of English Conservatism which now seems almost extinct among the articulate but, in those days [before 1945] represented the unstated assumptions of many generations'. The book is a 'history of opinion', concentrating on the thinkers who played a part in shaping Cowling's own mind. As well as Tory giants such as Churchill, Salisbury and Oakeshott, particular attention is paid to a group of Cambridge dons of the forties now hardly known but perhaps ultimately more influential than many more modish thinkers.

These academics – Kenneth Pickthorn, Charles Smyth, Edward Welbourn and Herbert Butterfield – gave expression to a Toryism both reactionary and religious, based on a notion of Britain as a Christian community. Utley was, like Cowling, a student at Cambridge when all four were dons, and he outlined the core of their vision in his *Daily Telegraph* article.

We were encouraged to believe that the State could not be indifferent to the moral assumptions of its subjects. Society rested on Christian foundations, and it was the positive duty of government to protect these foundations . . . we learned that the nation-state was probably the best means which human ingenuity had discovered of reconciling freedom with public order, that a government's principal task was to maintain the nation against the seldom distant threat of foreign aggression and the never absent danger of social disintegration.

Above all, we were taught to despise and distrust all forms of utopianism: socialist, liberal or any other.

These themes – the importance of supporting the Christian foundations of civilization; the defence of the nation-state from threats, without and within; and the passionate rejection of the claims of utopian projectors – are the themes of some of the most controversial of Portillo's speeches.

Michael Portillo is as much a product of his time as any politician. He came to maturity under Margaret Thatcher, but the cast of his mind had been set before then, and the mould was Maurice Cowling's. His contemporaries and supervision partners attest to Portillo's enthusiastic engagement with Cowling's provocation. Ian Docherty remembers that Portillo's political opinions certainly were firmly Tory by the February 1974 general election: 'he, like most of us, was sorry Heath had lost.' Another who knew him suspects he was more exercised by the victory of the miners in provoking Heath's defeat than any particular regard for the humbled premier.

Influential though Cowling was, he was not the only Tory teacher to make a mark on Portillo's young mind. While Portillo was an undergraduate, writing and other work took Cowling away from teaching. He arranged that, in his place, some teaching should fall to a female academic, Shirley Robin Letwin.

Shirley Letwin died in 1994, shortly after the publication of her most 'political' work, *The Anatomy of Thatcherism*, leaving behind her a generation of Tory writers, MPs and politicians who owe her huge intellectual debts. A more explicitly worldly academic than Cowling, she had a natural grasp of economics, gleaned from postgraduate work at the LSE, hardened by her doctoral study at Chicago University, monetarism's true home, and deployed during her time with the Institute of Economic Affairs. A disciple of sound money and free markets, she was an admirer of Enoch Powell, then more celebrated in intellectual circles for his economic rigour than for his populist patriotism. But she was more than just an economist. An historian of ideas, a literary critic and a philosopher, she imbued study of every aspect of culture with a coherent, deeply Tory, worldview.

Like Cowling, her work seeks to root the energy and power of Thatcherism in an older Conservative analysis. An opponent of the sort of liberal Conservatism that seeks an accommodation with its enemies, she was far from being a barbarian. In *The Gentleman in Trollope: Individuality and Moral Conduct* she provided an elegant guide to the thought of one of present politicians' favourite writers but also brought out delicate moral questions that celebrated a traditional Tory view which was in tune with the moral emphases of Margaret Thatcher.

Those emphases were brilliantly delineated in *The Anatomy of Thatcherism*, which presents Thatcherism not as a simple economic doctrine or a bundle of prejudices but as a coherent project to reverse national decline by the cultivation of the 'Vigorous Virtues'. She lists those virtues early in her work with a description of the 'model' Thatcherite: 'Upright, self-sufficient, energetic, adventurous, independent-minded, loyal to friends, and robust against enemies'. It might almost be a flattering description of Portillo himself.

Letwin then goes on to argue that these virtues were necessary to remove the collectivist encrustations that stifled the real spirit of Britain. Thatcherism was not an aberration from Toryism but Toryism in concentrated form, applied to allow older virtues, in time, to be reasserted.

Her attitude towards Thatcherism, and the stress it placed on economic revival, was developed during the eighties, but even in the seventies Letwin knew what she wanted. The basic analysis of what must be done had been supplied by Powell, and the view she argued for in senior common rooms in the seventies is outlined in the third chapter of *The Anatomy of Thatcherism*, which deals with 'The Historical Setting':

What emerged from Powell's thinking was not an economic lesson, but rather a way of thinking about Britain. At the heart of it was a fierce resentment against the 'enormous and steadily increasing dead weight of organisation and constraint', the great and growing host of organisations advising, exhorting, cajoling, planning, interfering', all endeavouring to promote uniformity, to 'eliminate all scope for choice and initiative', and to evade the Rule of Law.

Cowling himself believes that Letwin's elegant post-Powellism had more of an influence on Portillo the politician than he did. It may be tactical modesty, but it is certainly the case that her intelligence and coherence had an effect on the shaping of the young Portillo's mind. Portillo remembers her and her teaching with enormous affection, commenting, 'She was fantastic.'

Outside supervisions, politics was not much talked of, but one of the seventies Peterhouse generation remembers some early political conversations with Portillo in which the lineaments of the type of Conservatism he was adopting were becoming clear, the influence of Cowling's mind all too apparent: 'I remember he had a particular attachment to institutions – the college, the British constitution, and so on – that was strong without being soppily romantic. Of course his attachment, as with so many children of immigrants, was a form of gratitude, but I believe his feelings went beyond that. There was a hard-headed belief that these institutions embodied values which were not easy to articulate but which preserved the best instincts and prejudices of a genuinely free people.'

Maurice Cowling now divides his time between teaching in America, his rooms in London's Albany and a house in Glamorgan, where he lives happily with Patricia, widow of the journalist George Gale. He is modest about the influence his teaching may have had on Portillo. He accounts him a clever pupil, but not necessarily his best. However, he gives Portillo high marks for having avoided the pit of undergraduate politics. Cowling believes that student politicians feel the need to strike attitudes and lay claim to beliefs and knowledge they do not have. He exonerates

Portillo totally of that sin, and believes the considered nature of most of Portillo's public utterances to be the consequence of quiet intelligence and settled convictions unsullied by immature vote-grubbing.

During his intellectual and social explorations at Cambridge, Michael Portillo also found time and energy for some romantic excursions.

When he went up to Peterhouse Carolyn Eadie was his girl-friend. Despite the strains imposed by her being at Oxford, they stayed very close for most of the time he was an undergraduate. Bill Baker remembers her being 'very much in evidence' during Portillo's second year, and she was popular with his circle, finding little difficulty fitting into the secluded, all-male, society of Peterhouse.

But the subsequent path to the altar was far from uninterrupted. In the summer between his second and third year Portillo took a job as a tour guide, taking parties, mainly of Americans, around Europe. The work was congenial for a cultured young man who spoke fluent Spanish and decent French, and the self-possessed young Englishman enjoyed flirting with some of his clients. His manner charmed them, and more than charmed one fellow guide.

Ann Moses was American, her family was wealthy, and her home, at that point, was in Switzerland. She and Portillo struck up a friendship which soon developed into something more. He was reportedly quite smitten with her, and whatever money he had made as a summer guide was soon dissipated in visits over the winter of 1974–5 to see her in Switzerland. Whether out of a desire to show her off, or just to share the fun, he travelled on at least one occasion with close friends from Peterhouse.

Ann was attractive, vivacious and worldly as well as very keen on Portillo. But, if it was difficult for him to sustain a relationship with Carolyn at a distance of a hundred miles, it was certainly not easy to keep things going with Ann when separated by three nations and the Channel. Perhaps fittingly, Portillo would be the minister who brokered a deal between European governments that liberalised air travel in the late eighties, but in the early seventies one of the consequences of *dirigisme* was the drifting apart of Ms Moses and her English boyfriend.

The break-up of the relationship did, however, allow Portillo to concentrate more on his work.

The history course in Cambridge was divided into two parts. At the end of the second year was the lesser, preliminary, exam known as the first tripos. At the end of the third year, for those who persisted with history, came the main final exam, the second tripos. Possibly as a result of his enjoying himself so much, Portillo, while acknowledged as the cleverest historian in his year, only took an upper second in his first tripos – good, but not outstanding. There were only twenty-one firsts out of almost 200 candidates, but Portillo could have been one of them – especially since Maurice Cowling was one of the examiners who had set and marked the papers.

Spurred on by this check Portillo worked more keenly than ever in his final year. His industry was rewarded: he took an excellent first – the only one awarded to Peterhouse. It was a significant intellectual achievement, and could have led easily into academic life. But by then Michael Portillo had other ideas.

The socialist schoolboy had become an adult Conservative influenced by the allure of entry into a subtly superior set, charmed by an environment defiantly at odds with the temper of the times and challenged by encounters with bracingly sceptical and original intellects. Portillo's maturing was more than political. Socially, he had left Stanmore far behind and become attuned to life lived at a faster pace. The only question was, which path would take him to the inside track quickest?

CHAPTER FIVE

Apprentice Apparatchik

By what method or methods can the able men from every rank
of life be gathered, as diamond-grains from the general mass
of sand – and set to do the work of governing, contriving,
administering and guiding for us?

Thomas Carlyle, *Latter Day Pamphlets*

In the four years after graduating, Michael Portillo was to move
from the defiantly unworldly and unfashionable courts of Peterhouse to play a pivotal role at the centre of British politics – the
man closest to an election-winning party leader at her moments
of greatest vulnerability in the battle for Number Ten.

But there were a few faltering steps before he made that leap.
When Portillo left Peterhouse in the summer of 1975 he had an
impressive degree, a broad and loyal circle of friends, an assured
manner but also, given the way in which he had enjoyed himself,
and the circumstances of his parents, no very secure financial
position.

The need to make some money influenced his initial choice of
career. He chose not to follow some of his contemporaries into the
City but opted for a more transparently wealth-creating post as a
management trainee in industry. He joined a large freight concern,
Ocean Transport & Trading. His eldest brother, Charles, had
an enjoyable and challenging job with British Airways, and the
transport world seemed attractive. Portillo spent his first ten days
in OT & T's offices in Liverpool, a city he has retained an affection
for since then. Unknown to him at the time, his schoolfriend Geoffrey Perkins had also joined the company.

OT & T had concerns across the country and interests across
the globe. It also had a small office at the end of one of Heathrow's
runways – to where the young Portillo was next dispatched. Having
left Stanmore three years previously, he was apparently far from
happy to find himself dumped a few miles south-west of there
on the London Orbital in a Hounslow block. According to one

acquaintance, he had expected to be placed on some form of fast-track career path, groomed for business greatness – 'The last thing he anticipated was to be plonked on a stool in the equivalent of a Victorian counting-house.'

He developed a deep distaste for his clerical and administrative duties: booking freight space on aircraft, trying to juggle the weight and size of goods to maximise commission. He was bored rigid, and his friends knew it. Living in a dingy flat in Maida Vale, having to get up early to make the long journey to his place of work – an office where he had to walk a full ten minutes to buy a newspaper, further for a sandwich – it was a far cry from champagne breakfasts in morning dress.

He stuck it out for several months before, in despair, contacting an old friend from Peterhouse, Nick True. True, a fellow historian, had not been a particularly close friend, but he and Portillo had both been favourite sons of Maurice Cowling. True was at that time working for the Conservative Research Department. Chatting to Portillo, he made the environment seem attractive. Certainly the company of other clever young men with an interest in politics and an air of cultivation was infinitely preferable to sticking around at Heathrow waiting to get into dead men's Clarks' Commandos.

True had been recruited to the Research Department by a friend of his from Fitzwilliam College, Dermot Gleeson, heir to a south London construction firm. At True's suggestion, Portillo contacted Cowling and asked if he would help him get a job at the Research Department. Cowling was genuinely surprised that Portillo wanted to pursue a political career, since 'He had shown absolutely no interest in politics as a profession while an undergraduate.' Nevertheless, he wrote to the department's then director, Chris Patten, asking him to interview Portillo. With a first, True's introduction, and Cowling's blessing, Portillo didn't have much difficulty securing a post as a desk officer at the CRD.

A nursery of Tory talent, the CRD is part of the party machine but subtly superior to the rest of it – in much the same way as the Guards are to the rest of the Army, the Treasury to other government departments, or members of College to other Etonians. It is primarily a secretariat to the party when in government, an alternative civil service when in opposition, a supplier of ammunition at elections, and an intelligence-gatherer and disseminator at all times. But its status and influence extends beyond the sum of its functions.

Its directors have been skilled at winning the premier's ear, adept at using their lines of communication to MPs and constituencies to massage party feeling and respected for their ability to get clever young men and women to work extraordinary hours for a pittance, perhaps tempted by the solid phalanx of former Research Department employees they see in the Commons and the prospect of public service in the future, but certainly not motivated by immediate financial incentives like many of their fellow Tories. Having wanted, primarily, to make money on going down, Portillo was now prepared to postpone earning significant sums in order to work in an area that provided him with a feeling of being at the heart of things.

When Michael Portillo arrived at the Research Department in 1975 the Tories were in opposition after having lost two elections to Labour in the space of eight months. The party had just undergone a bruising leadership campaign, and its new leader, Margaret Thatcher, seemed a shrill suburban throwback compared to experienced statesmen like Harold Wilson, Roy Jenkins and Jim Callaghan. The Thatcher campaign team and the defeated Heathites eyed each other with suspicion and fear. It seemed, superficially, an unpromising time to join the Tory Party, but the power of the Research Department to shape the Tory Party, and future governments, was traditionally greatest in the years after defeat. Michael Portillo might have expected to join an organisation preparing to help Mrs Thatcher in her Risorgimento of the party's feuding bands; however, the Research Department was not playing its traditional role.

Originally the brainchild of John Buchan, the novelist and Scots Tory MP, who proposed a combined research and adult-education institute to counter the growing menace of socialism in the twenties, the Research Department was eventually set up under Baldwin's leadership, when the Tories were in opposition during the 1929–31 Labour government. Its first champion was Neville Chamberlain, and as he grew in power and influence throughout the thirties so did it, doing his personal devilling.

It suspended operations during the war but it came into its own in the period after 1945. The scale of defeat in that year's general election forced a radical overhaul of the party organisation, and part of that was a transfusion of gifted men, many of them with impressive war records, into the CRD. From 1948 to 1951, under Rab Butler's chairmanship, the Research Department boasted the talents of three Tories who were to dominate their party during the next twenty years – Iain Macleod, Reginald Maudling and Enoch Powell – and it played a key role in the regeneration of the party.

Butler and his thirty-something recruits – war veterans, but political greenhorns – used the CRD to shift the Tory party away from its ossified stance as an opponent of the social change that Labour was then introducing. Macleod, Maudling and even, at that time, Powell encouraged the Tories to present themselves not as opponents of welfarism but as enlightened guardians of socialism's gains. The Tories, they said, knew better how to harness the enterprise of the British people than a socialist government stifling business with regulation. But they believed economic growth should be used to pay for an improved Welfare State. The stance was summed up by Macleod in a CRD draft note for speakers at the 1948 party conference when he argued that the Tory position should be 'not that the social services are too expensive but that only a prosperous country can afford schemes of such magnitude'. He went on, 'We do not, of course, want any cheese-paring in the National Health Service or in any of the social measures.'

For Thatcherite revisionists these sentences give off the unmistakable odour of rot setting in. Correlli Barnett and Andrew Roberts have, with pungency and vigorous attention to detail, rehearsed the arguments against the surrender to the socialist tide made by the Tories immediately after the Second World War. The postwar settlement finds fewer and fewer defenders on the Right now, as the rising costs of health and social security place strains on even the most vital economies. But, whatever advantages hindsight lends us, there can be little doubt that, given the scale of Labour's victory in 1945, the Tories had to make an accommodation if they were to recover political popularity and climb back to power.

In their second significant postwar period of opposition the Tories again made good use of the CRD. After defeat in 1964, Edward Heath appointed the CRD's director, Michael Fraser, as party deputy chairman. It was, suggest John Barnes and Richard Cockett in their study of Conservative Party policy formulation in *The Conservative Century*, designed to 'reflect the need felt as the Conservatives went into opposition to integrate their activities in a carefully planned strategy to regain power'.

Few governments were as well supplied with politics as the Heath administration that took office in June 1970, and the Research Department's hand lay behind them. John Campbell, Heath's biographer, points out that the shadow Cabinet from 1964 to 1970 merely rubber-stamped policy worked out by the leader and his cronies or the Research Department. The fruits of the CRD's labours were unpacked at a conference in the Selsdon Park Hotel in January 1970 the themes of Heath's programme had been drawn out, and presented as a sharp shift to the Right. 'Selsdon Man' was Harold Wilson's characterisation of this, intended to portray Heath as 'planning a wanton, calculated and deliberate return to greater inequality'. In fact the term gave an even sharper definition to Heath's appeal. In the end, however, 'Selsdon Man' had less influence on the Heath government than Wilson had feared, and the administration expended most of its energy entering Europe and then lost its remaining momentum in a tangle of incomes policy, industrial interventions and Irish peacemaking.

The Tory Party was picking through the wreckage of the Heath era when Portillo joined the CRD in 1975. If history were any guide then this should have been a moment of maximum leverage for the Research Department. A new leader sought a new direction and was in the market for new ideas. The director, Chris Patten, was more cerebral and stylish than most Tories of his generation, and well placed to influence the party's path back to power. He had money, as well as time, to make his presence felt.

When Labour took power in 1974 they were responsive to the argument that an opposition party needed extra cash to buy in expertise, to match the government's access to civil service wisdom. The lord president, Ted Short, introduced the only, and limited, example Britain has of state funding of political parties by making sums available to the opposition to buy in research help. Every MP has a research allowance, but this 'Short money' was designed to buttress the efforts of the main opposition spokesmen. Short money was introduced early in the life of the Labour government, and Portillo was one of the first beneficiaries. It is perhaps ironic that a man who would become a supremely anti-interventionist employment secretary got his first post in politics as a result of a socialist job-creation scheme.

The CRD staff of 1975 were certainly a talented generation. Patten himself was a fine writer and a skilful secretary to the shadow Cabinet. David Nicholson, the head of the political section, although a haphazard researcher, had a rare ability to ferret out powerful ammunition to throw against the enemy. Bruce Anderson, now a columnist with the *Sunday Express*, was his chief collaborator in the blacker political arts. Anderson was then a strong supporter of Sir Ian Gilmour, the Whig baronet who gave the most elegant expression to the concerns of the Conservative Party's Left, but he more than made up for any centrist tendencies by the vigour with which he set about Labour. Also there at the same time were Adam Ridley, now deputy chairman of Hambro's; Michael Jones, owner of the independent television production company Panoptic; Michael Dobbs, the novelist; John Ranelagh, who went on to help create Channel 4; Robert Shepherd, the biographer of Iain Macleod; and several others who have since scaled greasy poles in commerce, politics and the media.

But, despite this bank of talent, and the fortunate timing, Chris Patten failed to secure the status for the Research Department it had enjoyed in previous periods of opposition. When Portillo joined the CRD it saw itself as the élite cadre of an internal opposition to Margaret Thatcher. The outlines of what Thatcher would do with power were still only dimly discernible in the mid-seventies, but the *apparatchiks* in the Research Department did not like the little they saw.

When she toppled Ted Heath, Margaret Thatcher had not presented herself as a neo-liberal economic purist itching to prune and privatise: she had simply ridden the wave of distaste for Heath's leadership that had swept the party after two successive defeats. Indeed, her campaign manager, Airey Neave, was the archetype of a traditional Tory, with no free-market 'form' to scare off centrists. And there had been a third candidate in the first fight between Heath and Thatcher, Sir Hugh Fraser, designed to appeal to those Tories who thought Thatcher insufficiently right-wing. His claims were pressed by, among others, the young Jonathan Aitken.

However, support for Thatcher from John Biffen, Nicholas Ridley and Jock Bruce-Gardyne, not to mention the brooding presence at her shoulder of Sir Keith Joseph, sent unmistakable signals to the elegant young men at the CRD who had been drawn to the party under Heath – here was a woman at the head of a movement of economic neanderthals determined to unstitch the careful compromises that held Britain's social fabric together, and all in the name of abstract monetary theory.

Opposition to Thatcher was based on more than just suspicion of her ideological agenda: it was deeply rooted in distaste for her 'style' and 'tone'. For many of the fastidious young men of the CRD, she was a dreadful embodiment of the petit-bourgeois prejudices of the 'women in hats' who made Conservatism socially uncomfortable.

For a certain sort of Conservative, acceptance in the eyes of 'opinion-formers' is secured by the assiduous distancing of themselves from the mass of the party. Horror is expressed at the ghastliness of the conference, hands are thrown up at the atavistic prejudices of the activists, greater passion is displayed when arguing against, say, capital punishment than in favour of any root Tory policy. That sort of Conservative predominated in the CRD in 1975, as John Ranelagh, a desk officer at that time, noted in his book *Thatcher's People*:

Within the party bureaucracy it was felt essential to hold on to the respect of the media by indicating privately to journalists that the new leader was an aberration on the part of the MPs who elected her, that she would soon be out and Willie Whitelaw would replace her. In pursuit of these objectives, the Research Department acted as unofficial custodian of the Heath/Whitelaw flame, arguing against such Thatcherite ideas as free collective bargaining in industrial relations or educational vouchers or the replacement of the rating system with a poll tax – all of which were studied and proposed behind the scenes in the 1975–79 period.

Another CRD employee at the time, and one of the few Thatcher fans, was Matthew Parris. Tory MP for Derbyshire West from 1979 to 1986 and now parliamentary sketch-writer with *The Times*, he recalls a certain bitchy hostility to Thatcher: 'People thought, "Oh God! That woman again", and quite enjoyed trying to ask her questions that we thought she wouldn't be able to answer. I don't think she was made to feel that we were particularly on her side.'

Aware that she could not trust the Research Department to fulfil the same function for her as it had for Butler and Heath, Thatcher went private and set up her own rival think-tank in competition to the CRD. The Centre for Policy Studies was Sir Keith Joseph's brainchild, and its thinkers – in particular Hugh Thomas, John Hoskyns, Norman Strauss, Alfred Sherman and Alan Walters – played a far larger part than the Research Department in developing what we now call Thatcherism.

The sense that the Research Department was a rebellious province uneasy at submitting to the Thatcherite yoke was compounded by its geographical position. Even though it was under the nominal control of Central Office, and of Thatcher's appointee as chairman, Peter Thorneycroft, the Research Department was jealous of its independence. It was based in Old Queen Street, a Georgian terrace just the other side of Westminster Abbey from the Commons and marginally nearer Parliament than the rest of the party organisation, based in Smith Square.

The Research Department occupied the best part of two terraced houses. At number 24 there were the director, the political section, which monitored other parties and developed campaigning material, and the economic section, which covered Treasury, employment, trade, industry and energy policy. Number 34 housed the home affairs section, which covered Home Office policy, the social services and local government, as well as the foreign-affairs section, which also dealt with the then European Economic Community and defence. Number 24 was the more important site, accommodating Patten's office and the weekly meeting of the whole department. The surroundings had a certain fading elegance, and the insulation from both the Commons and Central Office reinforced the sense that this was the home of the 'real' Tory party in exile.

Some of Portillo's CRD colleagues were on the Right – among them Robin Harris, later to work for Margaret Thatcher; Alistair Cooke, then the Ulster desk officer and now director of the Conservative Political Centre; and Peter Cropper, head of the economic section – but the prevailing tone was liberal. It may have seemed an odd ideological environment for a devoted pupil of Maurice Cowling to find himself in, but, while Portillo was certainly not 'wet' in manner or beliefs, neither was he an obvious Thatcherite radical according to those who knew him when he joined.

Matthew Parris remembers him as 'Highly intelligent, numerate, cool, unsentimental – not particularly ideological. He didn't strike me then as being naturally on the Right or Left of the party.' To others he seemed discreet, ultra-competent and technocratic. But two desk officers who considered themselves on the traditional Right detected definite signs that he was one of them. Alistair Cooke recalls him expressing no very strong opinions on the details of economic policy, eschewing discussions on privatisation, but firmly Right on 'the fundamentals': in favour of capital punishment, sceptical of Europe (without going so far as to be classed a Powellite), and always possessed of a clear conception of the sort of country Britain should be – traditional, vigorous and independent. Another desk officer believes that, from his conversations about the Heath government, Portillo regarded Heathism as 'socialism with an inhuman face'.

It would be a mistake to assume that Portillo arrived at the CRD with a set of prejudices, kept them hidden from all but a few friends, and then unpacked them for public display after Margaret Thatcher was safely installed in Number Ten. Those who knew him best believe he was not wholly in sympathy with the political direction of those at the top of CRD but far from set in his views on many issues, keen to give a good account of himself, and personally well-disposed to his superiors. They argue that his views developed while he was in the CRD, and afterwards, but judge that the core prejudices of a traditional Tory were there when he joined. The experience of working with a variety of shadow ministers – not least Thatcher herself – helped nudge him further to the Right on a number of issues, but the political course on which he was set was probably clear from Cambridge. His compass bearings had been set to the Right, and any yawing was easily counteracted by the personal magnetism of Margaret Thatcher. Portillo has described himself as 'naïve' about the Tory party's internal politics when he arrived at the Research Department. Whatever the truth, his natural reserve at that time stood him in good stead.

Despite not being wholly in the mould of the men who ran the

CRD, Portillo found it a congenial place to work in other ways. There was something of Peterhouse about it, characterised by one former employee as 'something between an Anglo-Catholic theological college and Oxbridge'. There was a distinctly louche air about the place. Hard work was done, but the seriousness was never allowed to become solemnity and a good deal of effort was put into enjoying oneself. Michael Fallon, Tory MP for Darlington from 1983 to 1992 and an education minister under both Thatcher and Major, describes the CRD team of his and Portillo's time there as 'an unruly mob. There was a lot of falling in and out of taxis, drunkenness, late-night visits to Soho, large bills at L'Epicure, and people losing control.' Though Portillo joined in, he stood just a little apart. The capacity to appreciate a good time without ever putting himself in a position where his enjoyment of the night cast a shadow over his morning had been acquired at Peterhouse, and the temptations of the capital did nothing to make him drop his guard.

Of an evening, Portillo would drop in to the CRD's favourite pub, the Two Chairmen, just round the corner in Queen Anne's Gate. Never a big beer-drinker, on those evenings when he was inclined to push the boat out he would drift up to the West End.

London in the mid-seventies was very far from offering the range and quality of entertainment it now boasts, but Portillo was seldom inclined to settle for second best, even then. He would go a long way in search of a good glass of wine and a decent meal. He had a number of favourite restaurants, in particular one just north of the National Portrait Gallery. In an age before sun-dried tomatoes and buffalo mozzarella were regular fixtures on metropolitan plates, traditional trattorias competed on cost and atmosphere more than culinary excellence, but the young Portillo nevertheless taxed his friends' patience in pursuit of cutting-edge cuisine. Increasing prosperity – both Britain's and his own – have meant a maturing of the Portillo palate, but his favourite restaurant in Southgate nevertheless remains an old-fashioned Italian a few yards north of his constituency-association office.

Food and drink were the most obvious but far from the only vices that were widely popular at the Research Department. As with Peterhouse, the combination of being oh-so-subtly out of step with the tenor of the times and the heavily masculine air made the environment attractive to some homosexuals. The influence of those desk officers who were gay permeated the atmosphere of the place. One contemporary of Portillo's remembers raucous talk about buggery after hours in which even the most vigorously heterosexual would join. There was camp gossip, bitchiness about MPs deemed dull, and vaguely lubricious nicknames – Chris Patten was 'Fluffy', and Portillo 'Portaloo'. Friends remember Portillo happily joining in the banter, albeit with his customary caution.

One colleague who has kept up with him believes that alongside his taste for the traditional and decorous there is a side to Portillo that appreciates raffish, louche and provocative company. At a mixed but decidedly decadent Mayfair dinner party held by a long-standing mutual acquaintance from Cambridge, one of the guests staggered drunkenly out after advising the table, 'Never, my dears, with a rural dean . . .'

One MP colleague who knew Portillo's CRD generation points out that several of Portillo's friends are gay – including the only 'out' Tory MP, Michael Brown, and some from Research Department days who are now no longer in politics. He points also to Portillo's friendship with the former Thatcher adviser and millionaire property developer David Hart. Hart, an emphatically heterosexual figure, is a libertarian with a relaxed attitude towards conventional pieties. He gives some more cautious Tories sweaty palms, but Portillo enjoys his company and sees no need to apologise for having a catholic range of acquaintances.

As with Peterhouse, so with the Research Department: given the flavour of the place suspicious minds assume that Portillo must have been caught up in the camper excesses. As an opera-goer, Peterhouse graduate and party-lover, Portillo was assumed to share other tastes with some in the Research Department, and there has been speculation about his past by political opponents anxious to suggest he could not have passed through Peterhouse and the CRD without being compromised. But, despite the best efforts of enemies, no evidence has emerged. Portillo has, however, never hidden or felt the need to apologise for having friends whose personal lives are not straightforward. He appreciates the company of a wide circle, but has kept himself aloof from their intimate activities.

Some of his gay friends were disappointed that he declined to vote to equalise the age of consent for homosexual and heterosexual acts in 1994, but, while no prude, Portillo is still a conservative. Those who know his thinking say he believes it is wrong for Parliament to travel too far in advance of public opinion on sensitive matters.

While the Research Department did have a definite flavour, it was far from being a totally male institution. Working alongside the universally male desk officers and directors were a corps of all-female, overwhelmingly attractive and usually well-born secretaries. Many were keen on finding a husband who would be a future minister; others just enjoyed the company of self-confident young men. Almost all of them were keen on Portillo.

One Tory secretary of the time who was attracted to Portillo remembers a presence about him she found curiously compelling. Herself a daughter of the gentry, she recalls a figure still finding himself socially but nevertheless assured. She remembers the young Portillo in badly cut shiny suits and towelling socks – in her own words, 'decidedly non-U' – but the sense that he was going places boosted his charm.

While always correct in his dealings, Portillo was sometimes seen as 'libidinous and direct'. Two of the secretaries, in particular, stepped out with him: Maureen Maloney and Sarah Gurney. Portillo's dalliances attracted gossip in the small world of Old Queen Street, and one friend in particular incurred Portillo's displeasure after an indiscreet disclosure about Portillo's friendship with Sarah Gurney. Portillo forgave him, but couldn't resist a final dig – for his birthday he was given a copy of Andrew Boyle's *The Climate of Treason*, inscribed from 'Michael and Sarah'.

Portillo's free time was also spent more seriously – he was devoted to music. When he joined the Research Department he was an opera fan in much the same way as he was a right-winger: never questioning where his heart lay, but acknowledging that the finer points of his enthusiasm needed developing. He already had a large record collection, but did not pretend to be an opera buff. With a small circle of friends, predominantly but not exclusively from the Research Department, Portillo made regular trips to Covent Garden. One of those he regularly went with was an oil-company executive, Richard Ritchie.

Ritchie encouraged Portillo in two respects. As a talented

musician, he broadened the range of Portillo's tastes, and, as an associate of Enoch Powell, he encouraged Portillo to stiffen his views in certain areas. Portillo was at that time still working out his beliefs, Ritchie believed, and was keen to meet Powell, whose certainty and rigour he admired and some of whose instincts he shared.

In the mid-seventies those on the Right most scornful of the Heath government's record were more often than not classed as 'Powellites', even though Powell himself was no longer a Tory MP, having advised the country to vote Labour in 1974 and then being returned to the Commons as Ulster Unionist MP for South Down. Powellism was a powerful cocktail of positions which were united by the man's intellect and their lack of appeal to enlightened opinion of the time. Powell is perhaps most vividly remembered now for his apocalyptic warning of the dangers of mass immigration, but that was only one facet of his programme. He was also a defender, to the point of purism, of Westminster sovereignty, and thus an opponent of both the EEC and reform of the House of Lords, as well as of devolution to any subsidiary parliament. The third leg of his stand was economic: he rejected the claims of Keynesianism and any place for the government in management of the economy other than safeguarding the public finances and the values of the currency. The statutory incomes policies and complex new industrial-disputes courts of the Heath administration were anathema. Overlaying all these was a mystical sense of Englishness which led the Black Country grammar-school boy to ride to hounds, romanticise the Anglican Church's history, and distrust anything which bore the stamp of America.

Powell's apparently adamantine adhesion to principle had a strong appeal for a particular sort of Tory, exhausted by accommodation with the enemy, but many on the Right, such as Nicholas Ridley, while fellow travellers with Powell, declined to go the whole way with him. The two most prominent supporters who remained loyal to him on the Tory benches at this point were John Biffen and Nicholas Budgen, Powell's successor in Wolverhampton South-West.

Powell's anti-immigration stance, in particular, made many uncomfortable. Ever since referring to the Roman who saw 'the River Tiber foaming with much blood' in a speech to the West

Midlands Area Conservative Political Centre on 20 April 1968 he had become a bogeyman, the politician who had broken the most powerful unspoken political rule in Britain and played the race card. Cynics believed it was a deliberate flouting of shadow-Cabinet responsibility and an attempt to undermine Ted Heath. Some thought it was an irresponsible attempt to ride a wave of prejudice into power. Supporters argued that it was a singularly brave attempt by a supremely principled politician to articulate the concerns of his electors lest those fears become the possession of darker forces outside the established polity. Whatever his motives, Powell was summarily sacked by Heath.

There is evidence to suggest that even natural allies of Powell's thought the speech was unnecessarily inflammatory. Certainly, with its references to 'wide-grinning picaninnies' and anti-integrationist groups who sought 'the exercise of actual domination, first over fellow immigrants and then over the rest of the population', as well as descriptions of excreta pushed through the letterbox of an anonymous and never-identified white constituent, it was strong stuff. It did, however, strike a chord with Powell's working-class Wolverhampton voters and with London's dockers, who marched in his support. The biggest swing to the Tories in the election which followed his speech was in his native West Midlands. Ever since then Tories have searched for the issue which would harness support for the Right from the working class.

There was, according to Portillo's CRD colleague Alistair Cooke, perhaps more curiosity than admiration in Portillo's attitude towards Powell. Nevertheless, any wish to meet Powell would have marked him out from the majority of his colleagues in the Research Department, who regarded Powell with distaste. It has been a mark of Portillo's career, though, that he is insouciant almost to the point of being unembarrassable about whom he sees. A taste for spirited debate, an interest in ideology and confidence in his own views have resulted in his dining in a way others might think unwise, but he has broad enough shoulders to shrug off malicious overinterpretation.

He met Powell, with Richard Ritchie, on 1 June 1978, at Covent Garden, for a performance of Wagner's *Tristan and Isolde*. Whatever else they shared, all three were captivated by the performance and, whatever else they may have disagreed on, all three remain admirers of Wagner above all other opera composers. Portillo is, according to his friend Neil Hamilton, MP for Tatton, a particular admirer of Bryan Magee's study, *Aspects of Wagner*. Ritchie considers this a particularly good choice of criticism for a politician in a Western democracy, providing as it does an analysis that stresses the sympathetic elements of Wagner's art at the expense of the unattractive authoritarian and anti-Semitic strains.

After that first meeting, Portillo has returned to the opera with Powell, and the two men share mutual acquaintances, but it would be going too far to assume that Portillo was, or ever has been, a Powellite. There are resonances – parallels even – but other politicians have exercised a closer influence on his thinking and development.

The four to whom he was closest in his first years at the CRD were Tom King, John Nott, John Biffen and Cecil Parkinson – all destined to serve in Margaret Thatcher's Cabinet, none in the least 'wet', but otherwise quite different characters. He met them through the jobs he was given on joining the Research Department. Tory spokesmen who shadowed government departments were assigned a CRD desk officer for each policy area. Partly as a tribute to his talents, partly for economy, Portillo was given two areas to cover, energy and trade/industry and as a result served two masters. When he joined, Biffen was trade and industry spokesman and King was shadow energy secretary. Biffen was a witty, diffident Powellite, King a more mainstream figure, credited with the most attractive features any aspirant minister could ask for – a safe pair of hands.

Portillo's responsibilities were various. He monitored government policy, scrutinised legislation, and prepared briefings for back-benchers on lines to take. He also wrote guidance notes on relevant topics for Tory spokesmen and candidates, and contributed to the pre-election bible, 'The Campaign Guide', as well as occasional pamphlets in the 'Politics Today' series for distribution to activists. In addition, he acted as minutes secretary to the back-bench policy committees and, finally, made himself useful as general dogsbody, bag-carrier and speech-drafter to the shadow ministers. Colleagues remember him making himself useful to both men.

With King, he spent time touring power stations, checking

figures, looking at oil-rigs and so on. They travelled as far as America together, to investigate alternative energy sources among other things. This second trip across the Atlantic certainly made an impression on Portillo. He was shown aerogenerators, solar-power installations and a plant that created electricity from the steam produced by burning rubbish. Recalling the trip in a speech to the Commons in 1985 he remarked, 'The smell of the plant was truly unforgettable.'

Energy was a sensitive area. Following the Yom Kippur War in 1973, OPEC had dramatically increased oil prices, provoking fears of an energy crisis from which the UK was only partly insulated by North Sea oil. Additionally, the miners' role in bringing down Ted Heath in 1974 meant their muscle was feared in Tory folklore and they needed to be handled with care. Energy needed sensitivity, but also imagination. As a minister, Tom King was never conspicuously ideological or imaginative. His shortcomings as defence secretary were ruthlessly anatomised by his deputy, Alan Clark, in his *Diaries*, where King's official MOD position was described as 'On-the-one-hand, on-the-other-hand balls'.

As shadow energy secretary, King was far from radical. Energy policy was a fruitful area for Tory propagandising – the Labour government had set up a complex regulatory framework for developing North Sea oil which it was easy to exploit. Additionally, the Labour energy secretary from 1976 was Tony Benn. 'Wedgie' was not yet quite the bogeyman he was to become, but he was certainly a tempting target for opposition goading. However, instead of ruthlessly exploiting these advantages, King adopted a tone of benign bipartisanship in the Commons. The vigour of private enterprise in exploiting the resources of the North Sea was lauded, but there was no slashing critique of the British National Oil Corporation, the state leviathan established by Labour to ensure government ownership of a slice of production. Rather than making arguments for the liberalisation of the energy market the centrepiece of his assault, he adopted a tone of solidarity in the face of shortage, remarking, in the Commons in June 1977, 'I think that it is common ground between us that the most flexible approach must be adopted towards the uncertain future facing the world.'

King was almost too flexible. His attachment to keeping an open mind meant the Tories came to power in 1979 without a single significant policy proposal. But the problem was never King's: after 1979 he was moved from shadowing energy to become minister of state at the Department of the Environment.

As a desk officer at CRD Portillo would have enjoyed a good deal of access to Tom King. Opposition spokesmen relied heavily on party researchers. Looking back now, with the benefit of hindsight, Portillo has criticised Tory thinking on energy at that point as 'absurdly cautious'. Did he fail to make it more radical because he himself was still working out his own views at that period and, not yet a fully-fledged free-market fundamentalist, would have been disinclined to push King too far in that direction? Or was it simply that the twenty-something Portillo knew his place and would have thought it presumptuous to have sought to shape the shadow minister's policy agenda? Whatever the reason, Portillo enjoyed a smooth and cordial working relationship with King, and the capacity to serve loyally a superior with whom he was not altogether in sympathy was to come in useful later.

Much more ideologically close, though less so personally, was John Biffen. Portillo's responsibilities meant he had less day-to-day contact with Biffen, but the rigour of Biffen's monetarist analyses had a clear attraction. In a Commons speech on 'The Industrial Situation' in February 1979, during the 'Winter of Discontent', Biffen argued a case which Portillo is still arguing today. Biffen alerted his colleagues to 'the profound challenge coming . . . from new economies, frequently . . . from Asia', and insisted, 'It is a cruel deception to suppose politicians can protect jobs.' He attacked the policy of high spending and borrowing, claiming, 'There is absolutely no way in which prudent financing of the national economy could proceed on a public-sector borrowing requirement of £10 billion.' And he advocated 'speedy cuts in the top rates of taxation . . . to restore management morale [and] . . . facilitate the growth of entrepreneurial small business'.

The threat from the Far East and the folly of thinking that government can create jobs were dominant themes of Portillo's tenure as employment secretary. The case for not just low but ultra-low taxation was advanced by Portillo in early 1992, and has been trumpeted often since. The danger of a public-sector borrowing requirement running out of control was the dominant theme of Portillo's period as chief secretary to the Treasury, although he was responsible for a PSBR four times the size of the total that Biffen thought so disastrous.

Biffen was a clear thinker, but had little taste for details, and he often had occasion to be grateful for Portillo's grasp of the recherché fact. At a boardroom lunch in the run-up to the 1979 election, Biffen had kept the company entertained throughout, but at the end he was asked direct about the precise ramifications of some proposed legislation: 'I turned to Michael, who'd been quiet throughout, and said, "I'm very glad you asked that, because it's Mr Portillo's area and I want to give him a chance to talk to you." He coped magnificently.'

Biffen had an influence on the young Portillo's economic views in particular, and Portillo clearly felt a debt to him, demonstrated by his loyalty at a dark moment for the shadow minister.

Biffen was a sensitive man, possessed of strong views but a weak constitution, and he retired from the front bench for a year in 1977. One of those who knew him at the time believes he was suffering from overwork and that personal factors conspired with professional strains to place his nerves under great pressure. Even though he had been an early supporter of Margaret Thatcher, there was no guarantee that she would reappoint him to the front bench. A colleague who knew Biffen then keenly remembers the sensitivity shown by Portillo. At a time when Biffen's future hung in the balance, Portillo took time out to visit and reassure him, travelling up to Biffen's home in his Oswestry constituency with Carolyn, with whom he had remained friendly after their 'separation' in 1975. They spent the weekend with Biffen, walking in the woods and chatting affably. Biffen remembers it fondly: 'They were a charming couple. I hope they enjoyed the trip. I was unmarried at the time, and I don't think the food was terribly good.'

The episode reveals an important part of Portillo's character – the premium he places on loyalty – recognised by a CRD contemporary: 'For Michael, there is no higher virtue. Show him loyalty and he will remain utterly steadfast. He makes a point of sticking by his friends whatever. There's no element of calculation – it's a point of honour.'

Portillo certainly inspired, and inspires, loyalty in those who have worked with him, but there are some friends who have had occasion to feel frozen out as his career has progressed. Some of his CRD cronies remain very close – Stephen Sherborne, a former political secretary to Margaret Thatcher who now works for PR firm Lowe-Bell, and Michael Jones, of the TV company Panoptic, are two – but others see him less often. One or two who always observed a certain reserve in his personal dealings now notice a coolness, almost distance, in his manner. One dates it from his first attempt to get into Parliament, in 1983; another from his entry into government.

One of those with whom relations have cooled is Nick True. True secured Portillo's place at the CRD, but since then Portillo's success has overshadowed his old friend. Viewed as very nearly Portillo's intellectual equivalent, and in the eyes of some contemporaries a more elegant thinker, great things were expected of him. But, while Portillo is a power in the land, True remains a backroom boy – albeit one of a quite exalted kind. He was until recently currently number two in John Major's Number Ten Policy Unit – a drafter of speeches, a source of political wisdom, an ideas man; but not Prince Hamlet, merely an attendant lord.

Mutual acquaintances say the contrast rankles. Both competed for the glittering prizes at the Research Department. Both tried to elbow the other out of the way in the race for a plum posting to Brussels. Perhaps fortunately for Portillo, given his subsequent stance, neither was successful. Portillo's success came as a consequence of greater inner steel and a quicker apprehension of what it took to succeed as a politician, as a CRD contemporary observed: 'When they both joined the CRD they could both be a touch thin-skinned, but Nick True's skin was thinner. Anyway, while at the Research Department Michael was developing himself for a proper political career. He conducted himself in such a way as to make that easier – he acquired a carapace, put on armour and became an astute political character.'

When Portillo had joined the CRD he had been far from fixed on making politics the whole of his career. His Conservatism was not in doubt to those who knew him, but the prospect of working for the party long-term certainly was. Shortly after joining he took Matthew Parris to lunch at The Albert, a cavernous pub on Victoria Street, just off the CRD circuit. Over a steak and kidney pie and a pint of beer, Portillo quizzed Parris about the Foreign Office, where Parris had spent two years, and which Portillo was thinking of joining.

Parris recalls, 'He had either been offered a job in the Foreign Office or he was going through the selection procedure, doing the CRD thing in tandem, and had not made up his mind which, in the end, he wanted to go for. I told him why I hated the FO – I'd felt constrained by the red tape and by the civil service way of doing things – and why, in my view anyway, it was more interesting to be in the Conservative Research Department.'

Portillo abandoned the idea of a diplomatic career. Although his headmaster had predicted a future for him as an ambassador, he clearly felt his destiny lay in politics. But working at the Research Department was a far from automatic passport to a proper political career. Many used it as a stepping-stone to the City or journalism, but the seriousness with which Portillo was thinking about his political future was evident in his decision to get involved at the grass-roots as well as at headquarters.

In 1976 he was living in Islington, in a small flat at 493 Caledonian Road. He lived alone, but he had a spare room in which he used to put up friends from Cambridge, and which he let for a few months to Alistair Cooke, when the latter moved to London to work on Northern Ireland policy at the CRD. Islington then, as now, was not the most fertile ground for aspirant Tory politicians, but Portillo got involved with the local Conservative association.

In May 1978 he stood for election to Islington Borough Council in a Labour-held marginal ward. The Labour government was at the height of its unpopularity, and the Islington Labour Party had a reputation as something of a Catholic Mafia, but even with these advantages Portillo failed to get elected.

Portillo and his Tory running-mates in the three-councillor ward were considered high-flyers, so defeat was all the more galling. However, the faith the Islington Tories had in their young meteors was eventually proved right. All three were to make it into the Commons, Jonathan Sayeed beating Tony Benn to take Bristol East in 1983, only to lose it in 1992, and David Nicholson finally winning a seat in 1987, as MP for Taunton, which he still represents.

Portillo's electoral blooding was good preparation for the

approaching call to arms – the general election expected in the autumn of 1978 but delayed, disastrously for his own fortunes, by the Labour prime minister Jim Callaghan until the following spring. The delay resulted in the Tories being given the greatest propaganda coup they could have wanted – the 'Winter of Discontent'. Years of IMF-imposed austerity had been grudgingly borne by the unions, and pay rises had been held down by means of a 'social contract' – an incomes policy. But in 1978 the painstakingly brokered deal that guaranteed differentials and moderated increases was torn apart by the trade unions, tired of seeing their members tighten belts and never getting even the most distant sniff of jam tomorrow. A rash of strikes paralysed the country – the dead went unburied, rubbish piled up uncollected, and Tory poll ratings climbed with it.

Scenting an appetite in the country for trade-union reform, the CRD looked again at the draft manifesto for the forthcoming election. The shadow employment secretary, Jim Prior, and his CRD desk-officer ally, Stephen Gilbert, had been fighting a rearguard action against the leadership to keep employment proposals vague and the language conciliatory, but the Winter of Discontent was a window of opportunity for those who wanted a harder line, and the manifesto was beefed up. Some in the Research Department, however, were disappointed that the reforms were still milk and water stuff, and said so. Portillo was one of them. He made his doubts explicit: 'He was convinced we could go much further. I realised then how firmly on the Right he was.' Robin Harris also recalls Portillo's deployment of shifting public opinion to bolster his case, displaying a feel for the mood of potential Tory voters that set him apart from others.

Whether as a result of his views, or the growing confidence with which he expressed them, Michael Portillo was shortly after singled out for one of the plum jobs in Chris Patten's gift. He was to have compiled the 'Daily Notes' – a pamphlet of bullet-pointed 'lines to take', and answers to running stories for ministers on election tours and spokesmen at press conferences – but, a few weeks before the election, Portillo was promoted. He was appointed to brief Margaret Thatcher before her daily press conferences. The responsibility for preparing the party leader for her most visible, and

vulnerable, hour every day rested on the shoulders of a twenty-
five-year-old.

During the campaign Portillo had to collect the first editions of
all the papers late at night, scan them for the significant stories
that would dominate the next day's questioning, snatch a few
hours' sleep, rise before six to monitor the later editions and the
Today programme, then prepare a detailed digest and brief before
meeting Thatcher and rehearsing her responses.

Daily access to the party leader could have gone to the young
Portillo's head, and there were obvious temptations, which others
close to her fell into at other times. It would have been tempting
to hide bad news, bowl soft questions, or hesitate to expose the
flaws in the leader's thinking. One of those who worked with him
at the time, and has worked for Thatcher subsequently, states
unequivocally that Portillo never fell into those traps. Indeed, on
one occasion Thatcher objected to the harsh interrogation which
the young Portillo was subjecting her to. Portillo did not apologise,
simply pointing out that the press would not pull their punches:
'I have to be hard on you, Mrs Thatcher, because they will be. I
have to be as tough as Fred Emery.' Thatcher smiled sweetly, 'Oh
Michael, you're not like Fred Emery . . .' Portillo was expecting
a magisterial put-down; instead she continued, 'He's not clever.'
It was high praise, delivered with all the flirtatious charm she
could muster. Portillo was smitten, and his devotion has not
wavered since.

In a tense campaign, none of his colleagues can remember a
gaffe, and friends of Margaret Thatcher confirm that it was during
this period that she formed a very high opinion of the young Portillo, as she confirmed in the second volume of her memoirs, *The
Path to Power*: 'One of my impressions of the campaign was that
Michael was a young man who would, and deserved to, go far.'
But while she admired him, she realised he was just one of many
clever young men around her. Unfortunately, Portillo over-
estimated the esteem in which she then held him.

The day after the election victory Portillo and some friends,
nursing hangovers, moved into Number Ten. Along with Adam
Ridley and some other Research Department colleagues, Portillo
installed himself in a room in Downing Street, believing that their
contribution to victory would be rewarded with posts in the new

prime minister's Number Ten Policy Unit. When they returned to their desks on the following Monday they found Ian Gow, Thatcher's PPS, waiting for them with a simple message: 'Get out.' The premier didn't want any Research Department alumni, no matter how *simpatico*, under her roof. The Policy Unit was to be the preserve of Sir John Hoskyns from the ideologically pure Centre for Policy Studies.

Now that there was a fully fledged policy unit and hundreds of civil servants clustered around the ministers to whom Portillo and others had so recently enjoyed easy access, staying at the CRD lost its lustre.

CHAPTER SIX

A Very Special Adviser

Michael Portillo is exceptional . . . something quite out of the
ordinary.

Nigel Lawson, chancellor of the exchequer, 1983–9

When Margaret Thatcher became prime minister in 1979 she was
still not mistress of her party, let alone the country. For the first
three years of her administration she was under constant threat of
a coup from a Cabinet which contained a majority of men who
had never voted for her, she endured the hostility of sections of
society never reconciled to having a woman as premier, and she
plumbed depths of public unpopularity unknown to previous prime
ministers.

During these years Michael Portillo – the man who had held
her hand in the battle for Number Ten – was to come close to
tears when her leadership was at its most vulnerable, and was to
enter into Parliament after an assault on her life nearly claimed
his own. A young researcher was to become the quiet authority to
whom her revolutionary guard deferred – but not before he had
done a lot of growing up.

Thatcher had owed her victory over Ted Heath to profound
discontent among Tory MPs who had tired of an aloof yet equivo-
cating leadership. In 1979 that feeling had spread to the voters of
the United Kingdom, who rejected the experienced but exhausted
Jim Callaghan without any very clear notion of what was to come.
The Tory campaign had been vigorous in its assault on Labour,
but unspecific in its own prescriptions. Tory ministers who now
damn Labour for their lack of detailed policies might with profit
reread the manifesto that brought the Conservatives to power in
1979. Jack Straw and Tony Blair have, and have drawn appropriate conclusions about the wisdom of advancing on a broad front
and never making exploratory thrusts into detailed policy thickets
that risk yielding hostages to fortune.

Thatcher had talked about lower taxes but had not explained how VAT would rise. Her advertisers, Saatchi & Saatchi, had dramatically illustrated that 'Labour Isn't Working' with a wonderful poster of a dole queue snaking into the distance, but there was no hint in Tory propaganda that the fight against inflation would see unemployment more than double. The frontiers of the state were to be rolled back, but no details were given on which budgets would be cut, and therefore who would be excluded when the frontiers of the slimmed-down state were redrawn.

The provisional nature of the programme underwrote a sense among many Tories that Margaret Thatcher was a provisional prime minister. In her first Cabinet, Ian Gilmour, Peter Carrington, Norman St John Stevas, Christopher Soames, Peter Walker, Francis Pym, Jim Prior and Mark Carlisle were firmly out of sympathy with the direction of her government. Michael Heseltine, Humphrey Atkins and George Younger were not natural allies. The only partisans she could rely on throughout were Geoffrey Howe, John Biffen, John Nott, Keith Joseph and Willie Whitelaw, the last of whose natural instincts were not hers but whose supreme loyalty meant he never wavered in support of her. Those most opposed – the 'wets' – orchestrated a sly mix of background briefing, caballing and coded dissent which provided a discordant descant to her efforts.

Thatcher knew, from the moment she crossed the threshold of Number Ten, that she needed all the allies she could secure – at every level. So, even though the CRD had been far from a loyalist stronghold, she was keen to advance the career of anyone who had been 'one of us'. The Policy Unit was the preserve of Sir John Hoskyns, but there were other jobs in her gift.

The proliferation of aides and the professionalisation of politics, begun in earnest with Harold Wilson's kitchen cabinet, had gathered pace throughout the seventies. Ted Heath had Lord Rothschild and William Waldegrave as his policy wonks in the Central Policy Review Staff to supplement the civil service; the CRD had grown thanks to Ted Short's largesse; and Labour itself had appointed an increasing number of political advisers to bolster ministers' authority. For some, like Jack Straw, apprenticeship to a Cabinet minister led to a life in full-time politics. It was the growth of these posts that allowed Margaret Thatcher to promote Michael Portillo.

Since 1979 it has become commonplace for the brightest stars of the CRD, like John Whittingdale, a former aide to Tebbit and Thatcher, now MP for Colchester South, and David Cameron, a former adviser to Lamont and Howard, now working for Carlton Communications, to move smoothly into a special advisership as a form of political fast-tracking. But when Portillo was appointed the path had not yet been staked out. His CRD specialism meant that Portillo was sent to the Department of Energy, to work for a secretary of state, David Howell, whom he had hardly known before. It was not a smooth period for either of them.

The Department of Energy was a many-tentacled beast, responsible for one of the most regulated areas of the British economy. The team that Margaret Thatcher appointed to run it in 1979 was impeccably free-market. Howell, although one of the first 'Heathmen' and later a prominent supporter of Willie Whitelaw, was an economic liberal of considerable erudition. An Old Etonian with a first from Cambridge, he has none of the condescension such a background might imply and Thatcher thought sufficiently highly of him to put him in charge of her speech-writing team for the 1979 election. Having presided with grace and humour over the speech-writing, he was delighted to be rewarded with a Cabinet seat. His number two was the Ross and Cromarty MP Hamish Gray – an oil and gas expert who was the department's token Scot.

The importance of the North Sea for both energy policy and the Scottish economy meant it had been a matter of political prudence to have a Scot in the department since the early seventies. John Smith had done the job in Harold Wilson's last government. The practice was abandoned only when the Tory collapse in Scotland in 1987 left the government straining to fill the Scottish Office with Scots, never mind any other department of state. Even then, the oil minister, the late Sir Peter Morrison, made much of his Scottish roots – his family own a significant slice of Islay.

The other Energy ministers in 1979 were Norman Lamont and John Moore. Both had City backgrounds, promising careers ahead of them, and were on the Right economically.

They inherited a policy vacuum. Given that Michael Portillo had spent four years covering the area and loyally serving the man who had presided over the energy policy in opposition, Tom King, there was an initial tension between him and the new departmental leadership. But Portillo knew that the secret of being a successful courtier is the mastery of inner feelings in the service of the wielder of patronage. He set to work helping Howell and his ministers turn the department round, and any personal tension was lessened by Howell's attachment to free-market principles which were broadly in line with the young Portillo's thinking.

Howell hoped to lay the framework for the slow withdrawal of the state from the energy market, in line with the general abandonment of intervention, but he faced opposition from two camps. Many in the Cabinet felt that energy was a strategic resource that should stay in state hands for economic and security reasons. In the late seventies and early eighties the grip of OPEC's sheikhs on the oil market, the further instability caused by the fall of the Shah of Iran and fundamentalist control of so much oil production, combined with the broader sense of panic about the future of fossil fuels, and fears about foreign exploitation of 'our oil', to make state control seem sensible to many. Additionally, the abiding Tory fear of being left dependent on NUM-mined coal made Energy a particularly sensitive department. The state owned the national grid, the generators, nuclear reactors, the vast majority of all coal mines and gas, and, through BNOC, it had a significant stake in most North Sea oil production. Dismantling that structure would take time.

However, while most of the Cabinet urged caution, a small, but significant, faction in government was pushing for greater radicalism. In the Treasury, Nigel Lawson was keen to sell everything off as quickly as possible.

Howell tried to steer a middle course. He laid the framework for the privatisation of BNOC, but was reshuffled out of office before he could announce the flotation. The credit was taken by Lawson, who announced the sell-off in his first week in office. Steps were taken to prepare other industries for privatisation further in the future. Sir Denis Rooke at British Gas was forced to remove the bias against business in his pricing policy, to make his company more of an enterprise and less of an amenity. Legislation was also introduced to make the national grid and the power generators behave in a more market-oriented way, and plans were laid for an expansion of nuclear energy to increase diversity of supply and promote competition in the long term.

Howell believes it would have been politically impractical to have moved faster. He argues that 'back then the very idea of privatising utilities was viewed as pretty racy stuff', and the anti-nuclear mood engendered by the disaster at the American reactor on Three Mile Island meant that the department had a limited stock of political capital to draw on for radical adventures.

Whatever the prudent course may have been, there is evidence that Portillo was not wholly in sympathy with the pace of reform. He was impatient with some aspects of his boss's style, and chafed at the tendency for those at the top to be too sensitive to the opinions of others and insufficiently vigorous in working out the correct course and pursuing it, whatever the conventional wisdom decreed. The relationship between Howell and Portillo was not characterised by the warmth the adviser had usually shown his superiors. Portillo was observed to be consistently more 'radical' and 'incisive' than his boss.

The most conspicuous example of caution, or irresolution, during their period together was the coal closure plan, which saw first blood go to the miners.

In late 1980 the chairman of the National Coal Board, Sir Derek Ezra, and David Howell became convinced that several uneconomic pits had to close if the industry as a whole was to survive. Plans to close as many as fifty mines leaked into the press. Uproar ensued. Even though the NUM was not yet in the hands of Arthur Scargill, he and his Scottish Communist ally Mick McGahey were in the ascendant, and the NUM president, Joe Gormley, threatened strike action unless the plans were dropped.

A miners' strike in February 1974 had brought down Ted Heath. In 1980, with limited coal stocks at the power stations, the government trailing well behind Labour in the polls and opposition growing within the Cabinet to the government's economic policy, this was no time for a new confrontation. Within three weeks the government surrendered. A series of meetings with unions, management and government watered down the closure plan at the cost of increasing the external financing limit of the industry from £800 million to well over £1 billion and, perhaps more importantly, loss of face in a big battle with organised labour.

Joe Gormley cherished the victory. As he put it in his memoirs, *Battered Cherub*, 'It was as near to a total climbdown as we could have hoped.'

During this period Portillo was often in the Commons, taking the parliamentary temperature and keeping Howell informed of the broader reaction to his managed retreat. Norman Lamont recalls there was general relief at a crisis averted but regret that retreat had been so total and public. One minister at the time recalls Portillo congratulating Howell in a double-edged fashion by saying, 'MPs think you've extricated yourself well from a difficult problem. They just want to know how you got into it in the first place.' Howell's coal minister, John Moore, had been warning of trouble at the pitheads for months, and, although a convinced free-marketeer, had had doubts about the NCB's plans.

Determination that the next confrontation with the miners should not result in another defeat prompted the secret 'Ridley Plan' for a future coal strike, which saw power stations slowly start to stockpile coal throughout the early eighties.

The lesson of preparing public opinion for radical reform and then advancing, rather than having provisional plans untimely leaked and then retreating, was not lost on Michael Portillo. His cast of mind means he is seldom happy with compromise, and his admiration for Howell's skilful climbdown did not disguise his sense of frustration that the NUM had won.

Portillo's duties as special adviser brought him into contact with MPs and journalists, but most of his time was spent in the department. He struck up a good relationship with the civil servants, in particular those in the press office. Press officers and political advisers can sometimes step on each other's toes in the closed world of the lobby, but the press office at Energy was impressed by the tact with which Portillo handled himself.

Also impressed was the department's most senior civil servant, the permanent under-secretary, Sir Donald Maitland, an ex-diplomat and a former press secretary to Ted Heath. This wily Whitehall insider remembers Portillo with respect: 'I found on joining the department in 1980 that there was no formal arrangement for coordinating advice to David Howell, so I established a Permanent Under-Secretary's Steering Committee consisting of the deputy secretaries and certain of the under-secretaries. Despite

the misgivings of some of my colleagues, I invited Michael Portillo
to join. It seemed to me that the civil servants would benefit from
his perception of ministerial thinking and that he, in turn, would
be able to support our advice. The arrangement worked well. He
showed himself to be well informed on energy issues and fluent in
discussion, and his judgements proved sound. There was no doubt
that he was both shrewd and talented, and his agreeable personality ensured he was soon regarded as "one of the team".'

Whitehall was still resistant to outside appointees. Portillo's success in overcoming that suspicion so quickly to become a valued
adviser not just to ministers but also to mandarins was another
sign of his charm, and ability.

A few months after the coal retreat Howell was moved to become
transport secretary, and Portillo decided to leave the department
– a twenty-eight-year-old who had tasted politics at the top but
still lacked the financial cushion a political career often requires.
He had valuable and potentially lucrative experience of government, but even in those days long before judges would be asked to
take a view on the probity of MPs' extra-parliamentary businesses,
Portillo was punctilious about trading on benefits accrued at the
taxpayers' expense, and he imposed a six-month quarantine period
on himself before accepting an energy-related job as a consultant
with the British subsidiary of an American energy firm, Kerr
McGee Oil (UK) Ltd.

The man responsible for the move was Kerr McGee (UK)'s
chairman, Frank Sharratt, a bloody-red-beef Tory whose reputation as a trencherman almost matched his record as a schmoozer
in Tory circles. Sharratt is a man of robust views who, among
other interests, is a trustee of the Social Affairs Unit, a think-tank
run by the *Spectator*'s food columnist, Dr Digby Anderson. The
SAU has published pamphlets on the health benefits of alcohol
and conducted a guerrilla campaign against the improving agenda
of the Department of Health under Virginia Bottomley. Sharratt
and Portillo had met when the latter was at the Research Department, and they got on very well, very quickly.

On joining Kerr McGee, in December 1981, Portillo was
installed in his own office adjacent to Sharratt's and was encouraged to use his expertise to advance the firm's interests in the
North Sea, and elsewhere. Kerr McGee certainly found it useful

knowing a sure-footed political operator with links to the press, given the unhappy publicity the firm endured as a result of the 1983 film *Silkwood*. This featured Meryl Streep as Karen Silkwood, a worker at one of the parent company's nuclear plants who contracted leukemia and was forced to pursue a reluctant company for compensation. The link between Silkwood and Kerr McGee was brought up during Portillo's 1984 by-election campaign for Enfield Southgate, but was brushed off as a matter that had happened thousands of miles away and years before he joined the firm.

As a consultant, Portillo's tasks were varied. He was involved in negotiating joint operating agreements with partners in the North Sea, he oversaw a project which explored the wisdom of Kerr McGee becoming involved in bidding for UK gas fields, and he subsequently assisted in putting together bids for the government's oil and gas concessions. He also deployed his knowledge of Whitehall to prepare a submission before the 1982 Budget on the case for reforming petroleum revenue tax, a reform finally carried through when he was a Treasury minister himself ten years later. And on several occasions he travelled to Kerr McGee's headquarters in Oklahoma City to liaise with his ultimate employers. It was a stimulating and stretching two years which gave him experience of industry at a level where he was treated seriously by serious players.

Portillo also developed new political contacts while in the oil world: two who have become close friends also worked in the industry. Both social security secretary Peter Lilley and back-bench strategist Alan Duncan made their money in oil – Lilley after a grounding in banking, Duncan as a trader. Peter Lilley recalls meeting Portillo while he was at Kerr McGee and having the odd chat, but not about the oil trade: 'He was always keener to get on to politics.'

Sir Peter Morrison, who knew him while at Kerr McGee, believed Portillo was hired as a long-term 'investment' by Sharratt. They certainly remain close, dining together at the Roux brothers' Waterside Inn at Bray in the Thames Valley, and keeping each other abreast of developments in each other's worlds.

Portillo was not idle in the six months before he accepted his post with Kerr McGee, but the work he did then is the only job he does not advertise in his *Who's Who* entry. A surprising post for a future Cabinet minister, it was one he shared with Richard Ryder, owed to John Moore, and coyly alluded to in his by-election address: he was a researcher on the first Channel 4 series of *A Week in Politics*.

This was then a little more serious than the current knockabout round-up of Westminster presented by Vincent Hanna and Andrew Rawnsley, and it boasted the politics professor Tony King as its anchor. However, the same woman was in charge then as now: Anne Lapping, of Brook Productions.

Lapping recruited Portillo after a conversation with John Moore, a university contemporary of hers who had got to know Portillo well at the Department of Energy. Moore had been the party's deputy chairman in charge of 'youth' in the late seventies, and Lapping approached him to find an intelligent young man with excellent Tory contacts and the self-possession to master television quickly. Portillo took the post, and Lapping was delighted with her find: 'He was a brilliant researcher with a very good mind, an extremely good colleague, with a disarming charm, intellectual and flexible.'

Portillo was involved in preparing interview plans, choreographing studio discussions, ferreting out stories and picking up long-term trends, as well as going out in the field to direct short films. One of these was on proportional representation – a reform for which Portillo has a visceral hatred. He went to the Irish Republic to film the complicated arrangements for an election by single transferable vote. The film led the viewer through the tangle of tallymen, transfers, third preferences and split tickets to render intelligible the complicated voting system. Lapping describes the film as 'most brilliant': scrupulously balanced and luminously clear.

Portillo apparently mixed easily with his colleagues, including Labour activist Diane Hayter, now chief executive of the European Parliamentary Labour Party, and fitted in surprisingly well with the prevailing atmosphere that Channel 4 sought to foster in the independent sector, which one veteran producer describes as 'broadly counter-cultural'.

Several of Portillo's friends at that time were in television. The closest was Michael Jones, but Portillo would also often share a drink with a friend of Jones who was also on the Tory Right, Hugh

Bygott-Webb, who ran Lady Olga Maitland's anti-CND ginger group 'Families for Defence'. A less political acquaintance was Nicholas Fraser, Michael Jones's partner for a while at Panoptic before becoming a Channel 4 commissioning editor, and the three occasionally dined together. Another Channel 4 commissioning editor, John Ranelagh, was a Research Department contemporary but not as close to Portillo as Jones or Bygott-Webb.

During his period out of full-time politics, Portillo maintained his connections with Westminster by a variety of means. In 1982 he moved from Caledonia Road to a larger flat in Battersea, where he played a prominent part in constituency life, rising to become constituency deputy chairman and helping to select Rupert Allason for the 1983 general election. Allason – son of a Tory MP, an espionage writer and right-winger – narrowly failed to topple the sitting Labour MP, Alf Dubs.

Battersea activists in the early eighties remember Portillo as typical in many ways of the young professionals moving into the shabby-genteel terraces just south of the river from fashionable Chelsea and a short taxi-ride from Westminster. Two other aspirant MPs were also involved in the constituency association around that time – Alan Duncan and Charles Hendry, now the members for Rutland and High Peak respectively. All three were ambitious, pink-cheeked and energetic, and well regarded by the old biddies who had been stalwarts of the two Labour-held constituencies of Battersea North and South before merger and middle-class migration created a Labour marginal.

In addition to his grass-roots work, Portillo was keeping his contacts at the highest level in good repair. As well as maintaining his friendship with John Moore, Portillo was developing a close relationship with Cecil Parkinson. Parkinson was opposition trade spokesman when he first met Portillo, and he was struck by the bearing of a twenty-three-year-old who was 'very clever and not remotely deferential'. They remained on good terms while Portillo was Howell's adviser and Parkinson was number two at Trade. In the reshuffle that provided Portillo with an opportunity to leave the Department of Energy, Parkinson was appointed party chairman. Shortly after his appointment, he received a call from Portillo, suggesting a drink and a chat. After a general conversation, Portillo offered his services to Parkinson as an unpaid adviser. At that time

Parkinson had no formal special adviser. Portillo also offered to act as an ad-hoc speech-writer and sounding-board. Parkinson accepted happily.

Portillo dropped in about once a fortnight, and Parkinson found him the perfect speech-writer – 'He had a gift for finding another's voice and giving it a greater clarity.' They would toss ideas around, Portillo noting down Parkinson's thoughts and expressions and polishing them. Parkinson remembers Portillo bringing order to the material he wanted to include in his first big conference speech in 1981.

Parkinson had taken over as party chairman from Peter Thorneycroft, a former chancellor with an impeccable Tory pedigree. Parkinson could not, and would not have wanted to, command deference from the audience in the same way as the elder statesman he had succeeded. What he could do, more effectively than most, was show that he was a true Tory of the eighties – an activist who shared the party workers' concerns and was lucky enough to be in a position to make a difference. Portillo encouraged Parkinson to list his record as a constituency worker, his experience as a self-made businessman and the firmness of his devotion to the leader as three bonds in common between chairman and conference.

Portillo also shaped the anti-Labour passages, painting the opposition into a hard-Left corner. One passage in particular placed Labour firmly on the fringes and also ended with a pithy statement of difference between the opportunity offered by the Tories and denied by Labour:

At the end of their conference they were committed to a series of measures which could turn the United Kingdom into exactly the sort of society which Poland is trying to cease to be. The flow of trade would be decided by the government; the direction of investment decided by the government; the investment of savings controlled by the government; in pensions, education and health there would be one choice: Hobson's choice.

The direct tone, straightforward argument, certainty of tone and vigour of the attack on the opposition confirmed to the audience that Parkinson was one of them, securing him a prolonged standing ovation, the further favour of Margaret Thatcher and the affection of the party. The importance of carrying conference was not lost on Portillo, and making himself invaluable to the party chairman was good politics for a young man angling for a place on the approved list of candidates and a recommendation for the right seats.

Parkinson was not the only powerful ally Portillo made in the early eighties. It was while working with David Howell at the Department of Energy that Portillo first met David Hart. Their acquaintance turned into firm friendship while Portillo worked with Parkinson, and Hart is now one of Portillo's most trusted friends and advisers.

Hart inspires strong reactions. He has admiring friends drawn from very different circles, including the nuclear scientist Edward Teller, foreign secretary Malcolm Rifkind, rock singer Eric Clapton and publisher Anthony Blond. He also has a number of enemies: former allies with whom he has fallen out, ideological opponents whom he has made it his business to frustrate, cautious Tories who baulk at his style, prudent figures who wonder how wise it is to entrust anything to a man so fond of the flamboyant gesture or risky manoeuvre, and those simply jealous of his success and self-possession or suspicious of his easy charm.

Hart left Eton without securing a place at university, set himself up as an entrepreneur, and dabbled in pirate radio and property. He made a small fortune with a series of daring property deals, lost it, and then, with money inherited from his father, who founded the merchant bank Henry Ansbacher, made it back again. His unconventional financial history has invited comparisons with Jeffrey Archer, another Tory adviser who recovered from near-ruin, was close to Thatcher, is possessed of irrepressible self-confidence, and continues to enjoy access to the powerful but is considered not quite twelve annas to the rupee.

Like Archer, Hart is also a published novelist, but his *œuvre* is very different from that of the best-selling peer. His first novel, *The Colonel*, charts a family history similar to Hart's own and weaves in observations about British political life and culture. The second, *Come to the Edge*, has a hero, Dov, whose career mirrors Hart's but whose development diverges in key areas to allow Hart to explore the limits of libertarianism. Dov sleeps with his mother, steals to revenge himself on his enemies, and ends his days in a lunatic asylum. Both books have fine, almost lyrical, passages, but they are far more discursive novels of ideas in the style of Thomas Love

Peacock, or even Disraeli, than accomplished realist recreations of the world around us.

It is, however, as an adviser, not as an author, that Hart is best known. He came to public prominence during the 1984 miners' strike, when he earned notoriety for his part in funding the working-miners network that led to the creation of the UDM. His chutzpah in running the campaign from Claridge's and his commitment in spending time on the ground with the working miners won him Margaret Thatcher's admiration and her ear. However, he left a decidedly mixed impression in the minds of others. The energy secretary at the time, Peter Walker, found his intervention unhelpful, and some senior UDM figures now look back on his involvement with regret.

Although those who worked on Thatcher's staff when she was prime minister believe that Hart is inclined to exaggerate his closeness to her, there is no doubt that he has a great deal of influence with other ministers. Many in the Ministry of Defence – not least Air Chief Marshal Sir Michael Graydon and other service heads – felt distinctly uneasy about Hart's easy access to Malcolm Rifkind when the latter was secretary of state. Several of Norman Lamont's friends thought his acquaintance with Hart unwise; but Lamont remained gloriously unperturbed, saying, 'I like his company and see no need to apologise for it.'

But it is Portillo to whom Hart is closest. Hart claims he knew Portillo would be a success from their first meeting: 'Like Diaspora Jews, we instantly recognised that element in the other which set us both apart from those around us and brought us together. Michael is interested in politics because he has principles. He has deep core beliefs and wants to put them into practice. I only work with people who believe in something. Our politics diverge slightly, but we have the same attitude: he minds deeply what happens to this country.'

Hart believes Portillo is 'operationally brilliant and very cultured' and, even before Portillo was a candidate, was convinced he would make the Cabinet.

Throughout Portillo's career, Hart has provided aid and comfort: helping write speeches, introducing Portillo to potential supporters, entertaining the Portillos in Suffolk, and Scotland, and planning Portillo's ascent. Portillo has reciprocated Hart's kindness, taking him into his confidence and involving him fully in his thinking.

Some of Portillo's friends have advised him to drop Hart: they argue Hart is someone to sup with at a distance. Some of the suspicion arises from jealousy. In the same way that some Blairites resent the influence Peter Mandelson has with the Labour leader, so certain Portillistas want to detach Hart from the defence secretary. They argue that Hart is too impetuous, too much a romantic, for the politics of the present. They fear that behind the respectability of the Suffolk country house and the weeks spent stalking on Lord Dalhousie's estate, Invermark, there is a figure with an erratic approach to personal relations and a fundamental lack of 'bottom'. But, when Portillo first met Hart he found him simply a supporter who shared his convictions and enjoyed his company. Portillo is extremely unlikely now to distance himself from a man who has championed him for more than ten years.

The thoughtfulness and the cultivation of the well-connected was nothing new, but some friends detected a definite maturing in his attitude at this point, as he adopted a more disciplined approach to climbing the political ladder. One colleague from the Research Department who had not seen Portillo for a couple of years remembers an invitation to lunch coming out of the blue in the early eighties. He rang another acquaintance whom he knew had always got on well with Portillo without ever being particularly close, to ask why he had been invited. 'Oh, he's taking us all out – one lunch each,' the acquaintance said. 'Keeping us all on-side.' The one lunch was duly eaten, and the months ahead saw other old colleagues also being processed.

Some were more privileged. Robin Harris saw Portillo fairly regularly in the early eighties. He too recalls the growing professionalisation, but his most vivid memory of Portillo at that period is not of the controlled exterior but of the mask slipping to reveal the emotions of the man within.

During the Falklands War he and Portillo had agreed to meet for breakfast at the Carlton Club. On the day of their morning date Harris was in no mood for food. HMS *Sheffield* had been sunk the night before and Britain's position had never been more perilous. He had wept in the bath. As they toyed with their soggy toast and congealed scrambled eggs, they discussed the progress of the war. Harris was particularly depressed by the grudging support for the fight shown by so many of his former colleagues – but there was nothing half-hearted in Portillo's demeanour. He remembers Portillo colouring and his eyes reddening at the thought of those killed on the *Sheffield* and the prospect of defeat. 'Portillo was very worked up. He thought the war was all that mattered – *all* that mattered. It was a matter of national honour. The sinking of the *Sheffield* was like a bereavement.'

Harris believes that, despite or because of his background, Portillo has an affection for his country deeper than many: 'I know he's a patriot, and I know it's as true of him as any politician, other than Mrs Thatcher, that I know. Even when I disagree with him, I'm sure that he can be relied upon to do the right thing for Britain.' Others attest to an almost paradoxically Latin sense of honour aroused in Portillo by the Falklands War, and remember him excoriating cynics and opponents of the conflict.

Victory in the Falklands War was a decisive turning-point in Margaret Thatcher's fortunes, and in seeing off the Argentine junta, she also saw off the threat from Labour and the newly born Alliance of Liberals and the SDP. The Tories jumped from third to first place in the polls, and the return of public support gave the Thatcher administration the authority to carry through other parts of her programme. Victory seemed to vindicate her determination and single-mindedness, and the sense of purpose with which she had prosecuted the war was seen as of a piece with her broader governing style – a style summed up by the 1982 Tory conference slogan: 'The Resolute Approach'.

Sensing that a Tory election victory was looming but sensitive to the importance of ensuring there were policies in place to absorb the energy of the new administration, the think-tanks of the Tory Right set to work in the second half of 1982. One of the most fecund of them, the Adam Smith Institute, which had seen some of its ideas adopted piecemeal over the previous three years, decided to embark on an altogether more ambitious programme. It drew up detailed policy papers to cover every area of government, under the umbrella title 'The Omega File'. The title, with its sci-fi overtones and faint whiff of swagger, was very much in the style of the ASI's director, the bow-tied libertarian Dr Madsen Pirie.

Pirie assembled teams to shadow each department of government, and each team brought together MPs, businessmen, academics, party *apparatchiks* and journalists. Pirie knew only one or two in each group would do most of the work, but a broad base of involvement would maximise the eventual impact. Portillo was drafted into the energy team, and quickly established himself as the dominant presence according to Peter Young, Pirie's lieutenant charged with coordinating the teams' efforts. Also on the team were Algy Cluff, proprietor of the *Spectator* and owner of Cluff Oil; Ivan Fallon, City editor of the *Sunday Telegraph*; Duncan Burn, an industrial economist; Daniel Lux, the commercial director of Cluff Oil; and Peter Lilley, at that point an energy consultant with Greenwell's and the prospective parliamentary candidate for St Alban's.

The energy report was completed in June 1983 and published on 7 September. Written when Labour were advocating renationalisation of privatised concerns and an extension of public ownership, it reads, even now, as a remarkably radical document.

The report argued for the encouragement of private mining, though stopping short of full privatisation of the NCB. It claimed, 'The National Coal Board has failed in its statutory duty to produce coal cheaply and efficiently, and the coal industry will always be in trouble unless it is completely restructured.' Portillo, the adviser at David Howell's side when he retreated in the face of NUM opposition to the NCB's closure plans, showed his true colours in his analysis of the fundamental weakness of the mining industry, writing, 'The problems in the coal industry stem from the fact that it is politically controlled, and not structured to meet the demands of consumers. The industry has become uncompetitive because politicians, fearful of unemployment, have shored up uneconomic pits to bring political benefits, instead of gains to coal consumers.' He went on to argue that 'The political nature of state mining will always hold back growth and development.' Sceptics might wonder if it is decades of political control or its abandonment that in 1994 left only a tiny clutch of mines thinly scattered across a country once built on coal.

The same free-market principles applied to coal in the report were extended to North Sea oil and to electricity generation. The separation of the functions of suppliers and regulators was urged as a precursor to privatisation. The report also advocated the abolition of all taxation of North Sea oil, to be replaced by a straightforward auction of field franchises. Most radical of all, it urged the development of a private nuclear industry, arguing that competition between rival nuclear generators would provide a stimulus to innovation in safety and an improvement of standards all round.

Portillo has since supported the implementation of all the proposals he argued for, save the last. The young adviser who argued that 'a competitive [nuclear] industry would be less inclined to unite against any criticism, and this would result in more open debates about safety methods and standards', became the Cabinet minister who supported the plan to privatise two already separate state nuclear companies as a single concern. With disappointed voters crying for tax cuts, even the purest principles can prove too expensive.

The report was not noticeably more radical than anything else produced by the ASI at that time, but Portillo's participation identified him as travelling with the furthest-out free-marketeers of the day.

The report was labelled 'the real Tory manifesto', by the Labour party and the *Sunday Telegraph* – the former to frighten, the latter to excite the voters. With his tongue hovering just inside his cheek, Pirie described the proposals as the product of disinterested thought by a few like-minded souls hopeful that a future government, of whatever colour, might feel inclined to implement them. He remarked, with a degree more chutzpah than honesty, that 'Even with a Labour administration I would expect a lot of them to command merit.'

Those words have an added irony over a decade later. That all those and hundreds of other ideas have been implemented and are unlikely to be reversed by any incoming Labour government is widely accepted now but does nevertheless constitute a revolution in public policy. Suggestions that brought a shudder to patrician Tory shoulders twelve years ago are now being implemented by the Communist government of Vietnam.

The political pies in which Portillo had a finger were numerous, but his career was not his sole concern. It was in the early eighties that Portillo's friendship with a key group of friends deepened, and he returned to the first, and most important, woman in his life, his eventual wife, Carolyn.

Although after graduating they had agreed to go their separate ways romantically, they moved in the same London circles and shared friends from school and university. While Portillo was winning his political spurs, Carolyn was serving her apprenticeship in business. After leaving St Anne's with her geography degree she joined the accountancy firm Arthur Anderson. After three years, and one hiccup when she failed a set of qualifying exams, she became an accountant and then quickly established herself in the quintessential eighties profession – as a management consultant. Portillo started to see Carolyn again more regularly in the late seventies, and she soon became more of a fixture in his life, as they went to the opera and on holiday together.

Holidays have always mattered to Portillo. From the long childhood summers in Spain through the adolescent exploration of Paris to the student tours and the varied entertainment they provided, he had always enjoyed relaxing abroad. Although a British patriot and jealous defender of these islands' sovereignty his Euroscepticism is a considered political stance, not a crude outgrowth of xenophobia. Some sceptics, like Labour's Peter Shore, and even Neil Hamilton, prefer to holiday in the UK. Margaret Thatcher shared their suspicion of abroad as anything other than a stage for diplomacy – her most exotic holiday was an occasional week in the Alps. Portillo, however, relishes travel. In the early eighties he and an evolving core group of friends spent their summers in a series of villa holidays in the South of France and, in particular, Italy.

Those with whom he holidayed included Michael Jones and Stephen Sherborne, close friends from the CRD; Richard Ritchie; Charles Mosley, editor of *Burke's Peerage*; Alan Rubin, owner of the Pelham Galleries in Mayfair, and his wife; John Whittingdale, Hugh Bygott-Webb, Leeds MP Keith Hampson and his journalist wife Sue Cameron; Anne Strutt, a lobbyist who went on to marry Colchester MP Bernard Jenkin; and his own future wife, Carolyn Eadie.

One holiday regular remembers Michael and Carolyn as far keener on languid relaxation by the pool than totting up Tiepolos in Tuscan churches. Hard workers keen to switch off totally, both were happy to spend their days doing little more than flicking over the pages of a novel. In the evenings, however, they would become a little more active, and their competitive streak came out as they threw their all into late-night card games – in particular a byzantine variant of whist called Fosdenovo. Initially relaxed, they soon became 'obsessive' about winning.

The conviction that holidays were for doing very little but making sure that what was done was perfect carried over to other evening arrangements. Portillo was remarkably choosy about where they would dine each night. The Michelin guide was his bible, and John Whittingdale recalls a two and a half hour journey to reach the right restaurant. Another acquaintance believes Portillo was too inclined to trust to the stuffy formality of Michelin's recommendations instead of showing greater culinary self-confidence in exploring the area, but no one denies the formidable seriousness with which he planned the party's eating arrangements. In a late-night game one holiday when each member of the party had to think of the sentence least likely to pass the lips of one other, it was agreed the words Michael Portillo was least likely to say were 'I don't care where we eat.'

Throughout his career Portillo has been keen to maintain a strict demarcation between work and leisure. Some ministers are inclined to squander time during the week and pester colleagues over the weekend or during the silly season. Portillo insists on the swift dispatch of business, the better to concentrate on recharging his batteries at other times. He discourages weekend calls, and is sparing in his media appearances on Sundays, preferring low-profile but influential radio interviews on the telephone to the formal paraphernalia of a TV joust with a Humphrys or a Dimbleby.

Friends are surprised by the speed with which he discards the newspapers at the weekend in preference for a Trollope or Armistead Maupin. Portillo is not one of those ministers who take red boxes with them on holiday and recreate the air of a private office in a distant hotel suite. Once abroad he is *hors de combat* and is scrupulous about keeping his life in balance, making time to relax with his wife rather than burdening her and other friends with the cares of office.

Friends now cannot imagine Michael relaxing without Carolyn, and all agree on how well they are attuned. They share a sense of humour, high standards, an impatience with trifles, a formidable and sometimes cutting intelligence, political views, ambition, a taste for good living and a way of viewing the world.

Carolyn is an attractive woman to whose features animation lends considerable charm. A liveliness and directness in her manner are disarming, and she inspires devotion in friends. Several attest to her occasional shortness with those who try her patience, but all agree that she is excellent company with those who have won her trust. They say she is, if anything, a little tougher and wittier than her husband, but never inclined to show him up in the manner of some political wives who seem to think they should be wearing the trousers.

Like Cherie Blair, she is a talented woman with her own career who sees no need to live through her husband, and thus has the self-confidence to give him total loyalty. One friend believes it is a sign of Michael's strength that he chose to marry a woman who had a successful career in her own right and would never be in his shadow.

Her professional success also marks her out from many Tory wives. After her stint as a management consultant, she joined the corporate-recruitment firm Spencer Stuart. As a head-hunter, Carolyn mixes with senior executives in a wide range of blue-chip companies and has developed a knowledge of British business from the boardroom level. There is no doubt she is highly prized by her own employers, but one acquaintance believes too close an association with those at the top has led to a distancing from those lower down, and a friend in a middling capacity at one City concern remembers Carolyn being put out that he did not know more of the directors in the firm he was temporarily assigned to, most of whom were on first-name terms with her.

Carolyn's salary is put at anything up to £250,000 a year, and, while there is a tendency for head-hunters' remuneration to be exaggerated because it makes the company look busy, friends say there is little reason to doubt that she earns well in excess of six figures.

It was Carolyn who first set her cap at Michael when both were still at school. One mutual acquaintance believes Portillo deliberately played hard to get, enjoying the admiration but taking

his time about deciding whether to reciprocate it. The acquaintance detects a manipulative streak in Portillo: he thinks Portillo
has always been aware of his power and charm, and enjoys conducting his relationships in such a way as to make it clear that
he's in control. Carolyn's persistence paid off, and few doubt now
that their relationship is far more equal than most ministerial mar-
riages, but their path to the altar was far from smooth.

Carolyn was a regular visitor to Peterhouse during Portillo's first
two years, but the seventies were a period of changing expectations
and Portillo had no wish to trammel himself too young. Both
allowed themselves full freedom in their early twenties. As well as
student flings and dalliances with CRD secretaries, Portillo also
had one other, slightly deeper, relationship.

He was briefly attached to an American woman, Jamie Ball,
whom he had first met on his schoolboy trip to the States. Years
later they were reintroduced by a mutual acquaintance in the City.
Heiress to an East Coast fortune and with perfect preppy looks,
she was thought a 'good catch' by one friend. Portillo's mentor at
the Department of Energy, John Moore, had an American wife,
and it was thought that Portillo would cement his own transatlantic
alliance, but the relationship foundered. It may have been a simple
mismatch, but one schoolfriend suspects that Portillo realised that
Carolyn had been right for him all along.

Carolyn was living in Muswell Hill in the early eighties with
another mutual friend, the actor Simon Chandler, while her
relationship with Michael was rekindled. She and Michael agreed
to get married late in 1981.

They married on 12 February 1982 at Harrow Register Office.
It was a low-key wedding, reflecting their joint dislike of unnecessary fuss and a prudent regard for how their large families' money
might be spent. The witnesses were Michael's brother Jolyon and
Carolyn's sister Irene. Only a few close friends and family members
were present. Most of their larger circle of friends were invited to
a buffet supper held later that day, instead of a formal reception,
in their new home in Battersea. Most of the guests were friends
from school, university, the Research Department and their
respective jobs. The only MP present was John Moore, who stood
slightly stiffly aside from the general merriment, sipping a soft

drink while the twenty-somethings threw back the Spanish champagne.

The honeymoon was spent, as so many previous holidays had been, in Italy. They enjoyed a fortnight in a villa near Ferrara belonging to Geoffrey Tucker, a PR man who had known Portillo when they both worked for the Tory party before 1979. It was an idyllic start, but the Portillos' marriage was put to the test very soon.

In late 1984 Carolyn developed cancer. The extent of her illness was kept from her friends. Two who were particularly close had no idea how sick she had been until they were telephoned one evening while playing bridge to be told, by Michael, that Carolyn had pulled through a traumatic operation. They immediately rushed to her bed in St Mary's, Paddington, to find Michael keeping vigil. One friend believes it was only prompt surgical action that saved Carolyn.

Most friends are, understandably, defensive about the details of the illness, but even though Carolyn is fully recovered the experience has had lasting effects. The first was a strengthening of her relationship with Michael. His devotion, the testing of his emotions and the tenderness with which he helped nurse her back to full health deepened the bond between them.

The second consequence was the impact of the illness on their plans to have children. One close friend believes the nature of Carolyn's medication made conception difficult. Others suspect that, whatever the medical factors, the fear that the illness might return and leave a young family without a mother made Carolyn reluctant to risk starting a family. One particularly close ally believes, however, that they tried for children in the early nineties, without success, and still feel a sense of regret that they have no family.

The Portillos have had to adjust to life without children. Four of their closest friends, Peter and Gail Lilley and Neil and Christine Hamilton, are childless – in the Hamiltons' case out of deliberate choice, so they could lavish their time on each other – and the Portillos have often joined them in making a virtue out of the extra leisure they can enjoy. One friend detects in the expensive holidays, fine meals and attractive flat a care invested on fine-tuning a lifestyle that could have been directed towards children. He believes the Portillos lead as full a life as any couple – possibly closer than many who do not have the time they enjoy to pursue shared interests – but suspects that buried underneath it all there may be a sense of loss.

Another friend, once quite close but who now sees them less often, suspects that life without children suits them perfectly. He thinks Michael is happier travelling light through life, but believes he is well aware of the political cost of not having children. Families, even in this cynical age, are reassuring for voters, and a childless marriage raises questions in some minds about the warmth of the couple. Despite the inevitable speculation about their childlessness, the Portillos never discuss the reasons with anyone other than their closest friends.

There is no doubt that Portillo enjoys children's company. Lord Harris of High Cross remembers a holiday in Scotland with most of the grown-ups clustered round the whisky talking politics while Portillo played snap and chatted unselfconsciously with the children: 'He seemed to get on better with them than their parents.' There was an unaffected and genuine rapport between them.

The lack of children may mean the Portillos have more time and money at their disposal to enjoy themselves, but after her cancer scare Carolyn's socialising developed a quieter tone, understandably. Before she fell ill she had been a supremely lively party-goer, sharing her husband's fondness for champagne and enjoying a social cigarette. Friends noticed an obvious change after her illness. She gave up smoking altogether and became a much more moderate drinker. She has never lost the relish for the right party, but now takes things at a different pace.

Carolyn's absence from her husband's side at certain public functions has often been remarked on – not least by Peter McKay in a mischievous diary piece in the *Evening Standard*. This was a disingenuous observation. Carolyn has been seen at more political functions with her husband than, say, Norma with John Major before he became prime minister. However, she is a busy woman with her own career and without the experience of conforming to the daily grind of politics that fits so many Commons secretaries for life as an MP's wife.

Carolyn is not a natural suburbanite, and immediately before her husband was selected for Enfield Southgate she confided in the wife of another hopeful that she would never want to live there. However, a pledge to do just that was wrenched from her husband during the 1984 by-election. It was honoured, and they lived in north Enfield briefly in the mid-eighties. But Carolyn was mightily relieved when they made their Victoria flat their base.

Carolyn does have several friends among the constituency party. Two of the closest are David Conway, an Enfield councillor, and his Czech-born wife, Nadia, a former mayor of the borough. Both couples share a love of opera and also go to concerts together, but most of Carolyn's circle tend to be friends from school, university, business and Westminster rather than Southgate.

One friend believes Carolyn finds semi-detached Southgate uncomfortably reminiscent of her Stanmore background. He suspects the last thing she wants, having worked so hard to better herself, is to return to the narrow streets of her youth.

For most of Michael's parliamentary career the Portillos have divided their time between a basement flat in a mansion block by Westminster Cathedral, in the same block as the dowager Duchess of Portland, and a country retreat, a converted rectory in Wingrave, Buckinghamshire.

Most MPs maintain two residences because they need to have a base in London and also in their constituency. For the Portillos, with Michael's London seat only an hour away from Westminster, the second home was more a genteel accessory to their lifestyle, a statement of solidarity with country Conservatism and a comfortable bolt-hole away from the Wen. However, the pace of the Portillos' lives, the metropolitan focus of so much of their socialising, and the number of free weekends spent staying with friends with more handsome houses and broader acres meant the Portillos visited Wingrave less and less. Increasingly, weekends would be spent with friends like Charles Welby, an Old Etonian Lincolnshire landowner whom they met through Michael Brown, or with David Hart.

Hart believes the Portillos have a talent for country-house life: 'They're extremely civilised. Michael is very cultured. He's knowledgeable about music, engaged by ideas, and a wide reader, but he also appreciates what I consider to be the finest flowering of English culture – country-house living. The French may be better painters, the Germans or Italians greater musicians, but the

English created a supremely civilised environment in the country house, and Michael understands it instinctively.'

Hart recalls 'five or six sublime conversations' at weekends with Portillo and other friends. One guest at a dinner in Hart's home, with the Portillos present, recalls Hart, dressed like a Turkish pasha, choreographing the conversation and managing the pace of the evening: 'Portillo was quite quiet, but Hart would occasionally ask him his opinion and encourage him to open up. Portillo was not inclined to hold court, but it's clear Hart hung on his words.'

Increasingly unvisited, Wingrave was eventually sold in 1995, and the Portillos also put their London flat on the market. Consolidating their finances allowed them to move decisively up-market: they bought a handsome terraced townhouse in a Belgravia square, a stone's throw from Buckingham Palace.

The Portillos moved into their new house in autumn 1995, the character of their home life already apparent, in miniature, from their approach to their mansion flat.

The Portillos' Victoria flat had the formal charm of a well-cared-for apartment block unsullied by ill-disciplined children or untutored tastes. The table in the main hallway normally bore the ubiquitous ministerial red box and a batch of new novels and the latest biographies. The main drawing-room was tastefully, if unflamboyantly, decorated in the style of what one friend describes as 'the better class of hotel'. Deep sofas in Colefax & Fowler-style fabrics fringed a large room whose walls were hung with wildlife and architectural prints as well as some striking engravings of scenes from the Napoleonic Wars. There was little evidence of vanity. On the mantel-shelf there were two vases bearing the Portillo family crest, and the lavatory had its fair share of mocking cartoons of Michael, but otherwise the stamp of Michael Portillo's personality was unobtrusive.

Both are keen entertainers, but neither is a particularly good cook. They usually hire caterers, and take great care over the quality of their table. Portillo also appreciates good wine, especially champagne, but tends to serve Spanish wine – Rioja or Cordon Negro. Whatever some might think about the quality, another friend attests to the generous quantity of entertainment always on offer, saying simply, 'They are very good hosts.'

The marriage of two strong-willed and ambitious people will obviously be buttressed by their shared successes, but there is nevertheless potential for friction. Neither is used to having to play second fiddle or to back down. Despite that, friends attest to the rarity of open rows, and indeed to almost kittenish displays of affection.

One friend, herself an MP's wife, remembers the couple embracing tenderly when they thought themselves out of sight at someone's wedding. And they are remarkable for the range of nursery nicknames and pet terms of endearment they use: 'It's always "Splodge" and "Squirrel", "Bear" and "Snookums".' The adolescent billing and cooing even extends to puppy-love-style gift-giving, with teddy bears and toy parrots exchanged, jokily but sincerely, as tokens of affection. Ministers who faced him while he was chief secretary may find it hard to imagine the austere steward of the public finances as a soppy sentimentalist, but close friends recognise a pronounced romantic streak. One thinks it far from insignificant that his two favourite films are *Jules et Jim* and *About Last Night*.

But, close though Michael and Carolyn's alliance is, and successful as each partner is in their sphere, there is still a sense in which Michael is the more senior partner, his career the more powerful influence on the shape of their lives. The pace of ministerial life means they have occasionally to live staggered existences. One acquaintance who lived near Wingrave thought it odd that the Portillos would often arrive separately for weekends together.

Sacrificing spare hours together is not the only accommodation that Carolyn has made to making life easier for her husband. Another friend, a former Tory candidate, considers it significant that the Portillos' holiday companions are drawn overwhelmingly from Michael's circle of friends rather than Carolyn's. Several summers have been spent with Michael and Carolyn and one or two other couples in the company of some of his more louche friends from Research Department days and Commons allies like Michael Brown. The friend thinks Portillo's loyalty to old friends commendable, and Carolyn's readiness to accommodate his bachelor pals indicative of her attachment to him, but wonders if it is wise for Portillo to have spent so much of his free time with acquaintances whose company may be enjoyable but whose lifestyles attract gossipy attention.

Portillo's fidelity to close friends, whatever the reservations of more cautious colleagues, did not prevent him behaving more prudently overall as he moved towards his thirties and his thoughts turned increasingly to a parliamentary career. Marriage marked another stage in the maturing of Portillo. From the age of eleven he had always maintained a certain reserve with all but the most intimate of friends, but around the time of his marriage he became still more careful.

During this period Portillo attended the wedding of a female friend who had worked as a special adviser. The reception was held in a handsome country house. While speeches were being made paying tribute to the bride's virtues, Portillo hatched a plot to pay his own tribute. He rounded up all her old flames behind a marquee and photographed them as a statement to her charm and generosity. It was a mischievous gesture, but there were loud guffaws from all concerned.

Shortly after Portillo's own wedding, one of those present when the snap was taken asked, light-heartedly, if he could have a copy. Portillo claimed he could not remember taking the picture. The acquaintance is convinced Portillo was anxious to ensure there were no embarrassing impediments to his acquiring a parliamentary seat. Photos of the former lovers of an influential party *apparatchik* taken in an irreverent vein could be misconstrued. It was only a minor matter, but symbolic of the care Portillo was taking to safeguard his political career.

Whether that care was necessary or not, Portillo did not have to wait long to enter Parliament. But, for reasons he could not have expected and certainly not prevented, it was a far from easy passage.

He first tried to enter the Commons at the 1983 general election – fighting the Perry Barr division of Birmingham, held by Jeff Rooker, an articulate Labour member with a record as a free-thinker on educational and electoral reform. The seat seemed highly marginal. Rooker had held it in 1979 by only 491 votes, and the Tories entered the 1983 election confident of victory. Few first-time candidates are selected for seats with such an apparently good prospect of victory, especially at the age of only twenty-nine, even if they have written speeches for the party chairman.

Portillo fought a campaign aimed more at the prejudices than the pockets of his West Midlands electorate. On polling day he toured the constituency soliciting votes by pointing out that he supported hanging and Rooker didn't. Even though his support for the restoration of capital punishment probably placed him closer to constituency opinion than Rooker, it was still a crude campaigning gambit for someone who had been a political professional for seven years.

Portillo took the campaign seriously and entertained serious hopes of success. His wife even approached city contacts to drum up extra cash to support the campaign. She would not have expended her capital, or tried to secure theirs, unless she thought there was a realistic chance of winning. Rooker, however, believes Portillo never stood a chance: 'The boundary revision in 1983 increased the size of the seat by 50 per cent – most of them Labour voters from Handsworth.' He also believes the Tory high command did not expect Portillo to win, but were simply blooding him in preparation for better things: 'A senior Tory whip told me they were trying him out. I got the impression I was there to rub him down with an oily rag and send him back soiled.'

There were no public meetings during the campaign and only one occasion when the three candidates met. A service at Holy Trinity Church in the constituency was curtailed to allow the candidates a chance to talk to the mainly black congregation. Rooker recalls, 'The Liberal and I stood at the front, but Portillo walked up and down the aisles. It didn't work – half of them couldn't see his face.'

In the end, the result was bitterly disappointing for Portillo. Rooker increased his majority fifteen-fold, to 7,402. The full result was:

Jeff Rooker (Labour)	27,061
Michael Portillo (Conservative)	19,659
Gus Williams (Liberal/Alliance)	4,773

What added to the hurt was the success of near-contemporaries in securing favourable swings in nearby seats. Twenty-seven-year-old former Oxford Union president Daniel Moylan, a friend of Alan Duncan, came within 231 votes of wresting Birmingham Erdington from Labour, and former Research Department crony David Nicholson was only 702 votes off toppling Labour's Bruce George in Walsall South. Nicholson's success did nothing to bring the old friends closer.

It was a dispiriting time. Entry into the Commons seemed at least another four years off. The Thatcher government had a three-figure majority, a radical agenda, momentum and scores of ambitious young back-benchers. Portillo wanted to be part of it. Eighteen months outside the party machine had done nothing to wean him off his addiction. If he could not get into government by the front door as an elected MP, he would sidle in the back way – by appointment.

CHAPTER SEVEN

Joining the Praetorian Guard

The spirit has stirred and the nation has begun to assert itself.
Things are not going to be the same again.

Margaret Thatcher

Margaret Thatcher's majority in 1983 was 144 – the biggest since
Labour's 1945 landslide. It was a personal triumph for the leader
and signalled a decisive shift to the Right, in the party and in the
country. The pleasure for Portillo was, however, all vicarious. He
was not one of the winners.

Thatcher instantly set about reconstructing her Cabinet and
reinvigorating her government. The promotion of her allies on
the Right gave Portillo friends in high places; the entry of a new
generation of back-bench radicals gave him a network of supporters
and allies in a changing parliamentary party. The momentum of
Thatcher's victory was to carry the Right, and Portillo, forward,
with only a few judders, to the next decade. But, at the time, even
as he saw his friends advance, he was excluded from the real inside
track – a seat in the Commons. He itched to be a part of the
revolution.

Even as Hemsworth, Bradford and Renfrew turned Tory there
were those who argued that the Conservatives had no mandate for
their radicalism. Sceptical pollsters put the scale of Thatcher's
victory down to the disastrous divisions in the opposition – the
creation of the SDP in 1981 and lingering dissension in Labour.
Progressive commentators, such as John Rentoul in *Me and Mine*,
argued that the collectivist assumptions of most British people had
not altered despite four years of the enterprise culture, but most
barometers of national feeling suggested that conditions were favourable for the form of leadership, evangelical and ideological, that
Thatcher had made her own.

Her new Cabinet was much more in her own image. Francis
Pym, the man who had tried to reach an accommodation with the

Argentinians during the Falklands conflict and who had warned of the dangers of too big a majority during the election, had seemed more eager to please the enemy than his own leader. He was replaced as foreign secretary by Geoffrey Howe, the loyally monetarist chancellor of the first four years. Howe's place was taken by the free-market radical Nigel Lawson. Another right-winger, Leon Brittan, was installed at the Home Office, and Cecil Parkinson was placed in charge of the new joint Department of Trade and Industry.

Parkinson had originally been earmarked for the Foreign Office. As a junior trade minister he had travelled widely, and during the Falklands War his knowledge of Latin America and distaste for Foreign Office temporising had made him a valuable ally of Thatcher in the War Cabinet. Thatcher thought a commercially minded politician with the right principles would be the best person to reform FO thinking, but an act of folly meant Parkinson could not accept. He had been conducting an affair with an aide, Sara Keays. When Parkinson told Thatcher this on the night of her victory, she thought he could still go to the Foreign Office. She changed her mind the next day, when Sara Keays's father wrote to inform her that his daughter was pregnant.

Her loyalty to the man she thought had done so much as party chairman to mastermind her victory was still undiminished. She gambled that he could survive exposure in a less sensitive Cabinet post.

The merger of the Departments of Trade and Industry gave Parkinson considerable clout, even in a free-trading and anti-interventionist government. His position also meant he was entitled to a special adviser, and he knew who he wanted: 'There was no doubt Michael Portillo was the most able person I could have picked.'

He had a battle getting him. Portillo was anxious to get back into politics, but Parkinson was not alone in wanting to tempt him back. Nigel Lawson had heard of his abilities, and tried to persuade him to go to the Treasury. This would have meant a more prestigious post, but Portillo declined. Parkinson was an old friend and had been his sponsor in the past, and Portillo, not for the last time, put loyalty before a narrow calculation of self-interest.

Parkinson was in office for only four months, but he laid the groundwork for the liberalisation of the Stock Exchange which led to the 'Big Bang' in 1986 and consolidated the City's reputation as the world's pre-eminent financial centre. He persuaded the Stock Exchange to dismantle some of their traditional restrictions on trade voluntarily, without having to use the blunt weapon of the director general of fair trading. The changes wrought made the City better able to exploit the growth of global financial markets in the eighties. It was a technical finesse, but a hugely important one.

Portillo was in sympathy with the approach Parkinson took to his task, but his main work in the department was preparing for the political speeches his boss had to make. The most important of these was the speech at the October 1983 conference, made a week after it was publicly revealed that Sara Keays was pregnant. Parkinson's fate hung in the balance.

Parkinson's conference speech was well received and did much to firm the ground under his feet, and the loyalty of his wife further strengthened his position. But on the Friday of the conference his position gave way when *The Times* published an interview with Sara Keays. She was in no mood to let the matter lie, and her continual visibility in the media could only undermine Parkinson's ability to carry on. He tendered his resignation in the early hours of the conference's last day.

That morning Parkinson was due to open a new heliport in Blackpool. His place was taken by Denis Thatcher. Parkinson and his wife were driven back to London by Portillo, and as they moved off-stage politically their driver had his first taste of public exposure.

The three-hour drive was far from easy, but Parkinson remembers Portillo as 'supportive and discreet'. When they arrived at the Parkinsons' home they were met by a pack of photographers and reporters. The press were uncertain who the mystery man with the Parkinsons was. The next morning he was on the front of *The Times*, described as the minister's detective. The Parkinsons rang the Portillos to joke about the mistake that morning. It was a rare moment of light relief at a difficult time.

One of Parkinson's last ministerial acts was to safeguard his protégé's future. Knowing of Lawson's admiration for Portillo, he persuaded the chancellor to take him on as special adviser. Lawson did not hesitate.

Lawson, a formidable intellect whose ghost still stalks the Treasury, thinks very highly of Portillo. He believes he is 'of quite exceptional calibre and something quite out of the ordinary'. It's a generous compliment, and doubly so when one bears in mind the company Lawson kept. For Portillo to shine in Lawson's Treasury required something special.

Lawson was sufficiently sure of himself as a minister to seek out the best minds in his field and fence with them for the sheer fun of it. It was more than just intellectual braggadocio: he sharpened his own views by testing them against others. Outside economists like Alan Budd of the London Business School and Treasury insiders like Terry Burns, the government's chief economic adviser, were taken on in regular discussions. One Treasury civil servant recalls Portillo more than holding his own in discussion, impressing Burns and Budd, who were to be the Treasury permanent secretary and chief economic adviser respectively when Portillo returned after 1992 as chief secretary.

Portillo joined too late to have much to do with the 1983 Autumn Statement, the annual negotiations on what government departments can spend, but he was involved in the run-up to Lawson's first, triumphant, Budget in 1984. A tax-cutting and tax-reforming Budget, it abolished two taxes, set in train a progressive reduction in corporation tax, and marked a subtle shift in Treasury tactics from the all-out fight against inflation to a broader strategy of reforming the supply side and making Britain more competitive.

Portillo was involved in the shaping of the Budget, closeted with ministers and weekending at Chevening, the government's grace-and-favour home in Kent, with the chancellor's closest advisers. As a special adviser his policy input was limited, and Lawson was not the sort of minister who needed reassurance that he was doing the right thing, but Portillo was more than a bag-carrier. The chancellor commanded respect and affection in the Treasury and carried the department with him in support of his policy, but he needed allies with political nous to square party opinion and detect potential hazards ahead.

As well as acting as a political fire-fighter, Portillo also wrote speeches for Lawson. Much of the process of speech-writing for ministers is hack-work: a standard recitation of achievements, ritual knocking of the opposition with a few weak jokes, and a dash of visionary rhetoric at the end. Apart from at party conferences, little care is lavished on such speeches. The chancellor, however, is different. His every word is scrutinised by the markets, MPs and journalists sensitive to the impact of even the slightest nuance on the economy and political fortunes. Indeed, when Lawson and Thatcher were at odds over exchange-rate policy in the late eighties, the Commons press gallery subjected the chancellor's utterances to the sort of close textual analysis more appropriate to authenticating biblical fragments than political speeches.

As well as the general sensitivity of the chancellor's position, Lawson was also particularly jealous of his reputation as an economic thinker and a former financial journalist, making the process of speech-writing particularly testing for his advisers. Portillo was a skilled drafter of Lawson's thoughts who rarely disappointed.

The one exception was the chancellor's speech to the 1984 party conference. An over-intellectual exposition of policy, it failed to win a standing ovation – almost unheard of for a senior minister, and particularly damaging for the chancellor. However, Lawson's poor performance was soon overshadowed by a tragedy which changed everything that week – not least Michael Portillo's future.

The Brighton bombing was a calculated attempt on the lives of the entire Cabinet by the IRA. At 2.55 on the morning of 12 October a bomb planted by republican terrorists ripped through the Grand, the conference hotel. It had been positioned to kill as many ministers as possible and to inflict the maximum possible damage on the prime ministerial suite. Fortunately it failed. Unfortunately two people were killed, many more were injured, and some were left permanently paralysed.

Republicans justified the attack as revenge for the deaths of terrorist hunger-strikers. In her conference speech the next day Margaret Thatcher described it as 'not only an attempt to disrupt and terminate our conference. It was an attempt to cripple Her Majesty's democratically elected government.'

Portillo was in the Grand in the early hours of the morning of the 12th, deep in discussion with a journalist. Exasperated by, as he saw it, the obtuseness of his drinking companion, David Rose of the *Liverpool Daily Post*, he eventually lost his temper and stormed out. It may have saved his life. He told the story of the events of that night in his maiden speech to the House of Commons, a few months later:

The discussion became heated. To emphasise his point, the journalist beat the pillar beside us with his fist and said, 'This is a pillar; that is a fact. Your policies are to create unemployment, that is a fact too.' The discussion became even more acrimonious and the journalist rather abusive, so I left the Grand Hotel and went safely to bed in my hotel down the road.

In the morning I reflected on two things. First, I was grateful to the journalist for having been abusive towards me; otherwise I might have stayed in the Grand Hotel and been there when the bomb went off. Secondly, I reflected on the fact that the pillar which he had thumped with his hand and which represented for him absolute certainty was probably a pile of rubble. I thought that, in the light of day, the journalist, too, was a little less certain about the motives of government policy.

One who was not so fortunate was Sir Anthony Berry, a former deputy chief whip who was member for Enfield Southgate. He was standing when the bomb went off and was crushed by the collapsing roof. An Old Etonian with a distinguished military record and a gentle manner, he was much missed by his colleagues.

After the death of any member, colleagues inevitably reflect on the achievements, impact and memories provoked by the loss. But, politics being politics, thoughts soon turn to the future. The tragic nature of Tony Berry's death delayed it perhaps longer than on most occasions, but speculation soon began on who would fill his vacancy in the ranks of the House.

Tony Berry had held Southgate in 1983 with a majority of 15,819. A London seat within half an hour of the Commons, it was a tempting prospect – particularly given the rumour that the other parties might stand aside as a mark of respect. It was too tempting for some, who sent their CVs to the agent within days of Sir Tony's death. Their letters were not answered.

By-elections were not then the automatic bloody noses for the government they have since become, and a large number of applications were expected, even when it became clear that the election would be contested by the other parties. The government expected to win, but it was still a significant test of public opinion and important for party morale. The interest in the contest, from applicants and from party headquarters, was correspondingly intense.

The constituency party, under its then chairman David Solomons and agent Tony Dey, were determined to conduct the by-election in their own way. They did not want to rely on the lottery of random applications from hopefuls, nor did they want the heavy hand of Central Office intervening in their campaign. Donald Stringer, the agent for the London area and an experienced party professional, tried to exert his influence, and pressure was exerted from Number Ten. The party establishment wanted a late election – preferably after Christmas – and had strong views about certain candidates. Their views were listened to, but rejected.

Both Dey and Solomons were convinced that an early election was imperative. They thought delay would give the main challengers, the Alliance, the chance to build up a proper campaign. They were aware that a hurried election might lay them open to the charge of insensitivity, and the *Times* Diary did draw malicious attention to the proximity of Tony Berry's memorial service and the election day, but they thought, as friends of Sir Anthony, that the best tribute to him would be the election of a Conservative successor.

Rather than invite candidates to write to them, they scoured Central Office's approved list, looking for those who knew London and had already fought one previous seat. They also decided to interview any local party member who applied, purely in the interests of keeping egos unruffled.

After wading through over 100 CVs, the association executive whittled down the list of hopefuls to twenty-five, among them Michael Portillo. They were all invited for a half-hour interview over a weekend in November. Donald Stringer tried, unsuccessfully, to shoehorn several Central Office favourites on to the list, including Emma Nicholson, now member for Devon West and Torridge, but the association had its own, very clear, preferences. One of those who was interviewed was David Lidington, now MP for Aylesbury, who was then a precocious Young Conservative. As a local constituency activist and a bright lad who was to go on to work for Douglas Hurd as a special adviser, he was offered an interview as encouragement. He acquitted himself better than many more experienced hands, but was not among the final four selected.

After the initial selection panel, the next hurdle was the executive council – some thirty-plus local officers and branch workers. At this stage the front-runner was the recently elected MEP for North London, John Marshall. Enfield Southgate lay within his Euro-constituency, and he and his wife were well-liked by the local activists. Stiff on a public platform, he can charm in person and he was on the same wavelength as many of the Southgate Tories.

The other three candidates were Alan Amos (the borough's chairman of education), James Arbuthnott (an Old Etonian) and Portillo. Amos had his supporters among some of the more radical and younger party members, who appreciated the imaginative way he was reforming the running of schools. Arbuthnott attracted those nostalgic for the patrician self-confidence and plummy tones of Sir Anthony. Portillo had no local connections and no grand manner. He did work for the chancellor, but Lawson's reputation had suffered a precipitate slide in the second half of 1984, after his first Budget, culminating in his poor reception at the party conference. Portillo had nothing to recommend him other than his talent.

All four were invited to speak and answer questions. Unemployment, law and order and the miners' strike featured. Portillo's self-assurance and knowledge put him head and shoulders above the rest.

After the speeches the executive began a series of votes to select the candidate. After one round Arbuthnott was eliminated, then Amos. In the final round, between Marshall and Portillo, the executive was divided equally: it was a draw. Marshall was shocked that the thirty-one-year-old with the too-tight suit might pip him to the nomination for a seat he had known for years and represented in Strasburg.

His fate lay in the hands of the constituency chairman, David Solomons, whom he knew and had worked happily with in the past. According to the agent, Solomons had the casting vote. With his executive council divided, Solomons felt he could not choose, and recommended that both, rather than just one candidate, should be placed before a selection meeting of the entire association. And so a few days later, on Friday 16 November, at Arnos

School, a comprehensive in the southern part of the constituency, nearly 300 party members gathered to choose the man they hoped would be their next MP. Portillo knew that Marshall's appeal to a few old friends would be diluted by the size of the audience and, in the view of one observer, he performed with a fluency and confidence even more impressive than anything he had previously shown. One question in particular impressed itself on the memory of the agent. Portillo was asked if, in the event of losing to Marshall, he would contest the then vacant Euro-seat. He said, simply, 'No', and gave an elegant argument for the supremacy of the sovereign Parliament at Westminster.

That response was not the only respect in which he shone. The agent, Tony Dey, had his own informal method of marking the candidates, for presentation, content, star quality and so on – much in the manner of the judges of the acts on the then popular ITV talent show *New Faces*. According to Dey, Portillo was clearly ahead in every department. The ballot was secret, but those present all expected Portillo to win.

When he did, he embraced his wife, acknowledged the congratulations, and enjoyed his first victory in any election. But he knew a sterner test was still to come. Sixteen months before, in a by-election in Penrith, a Tory majority over the Liberals of the same size as in Southgate had been cut to 552. If defeat could come so close only weeks after an electoral landslide, how much riskier might an election be as mid-term unpopularity took hold? Two other by-elections, held in May in Surrey South West and Stafford, in the wake of a successful Budget, had seen swings against the Tories which could deny them Southgate on a low poll. In June a 12,000 Tory majority in Portsmouth South had been swept away by the SDP. Victory was far from assured.

But since the summer a shadow had fallen over British politics. Arthur Scargill had led the NUM out on strike. His refusal to ballot his members had split the union and led to angry clashes on the picket line. A miners' strike had finished off Heath, and some Tory supporters were discomfited by the confrontational stance taken by Margaret Thatcher. Southgate was hundreds of miles from the pitheads, but, with unemployment still rising, the stridency of Thatcher's stance and the suggestion that Scargill was fighting on the side of a devastated manufacturing sector did not reassure fractious Tory supporters.

Tony Berry's main challengers in 1983 had been the Liberals. They won 10,652 votes to Labour's 8,132. The Liberals' 1984 campaign received an early boost when Labour selected their candidate, Peter Hamid, the councillor for the Ponders End ward of Enfield Borough. Unemployed, a poor speaker, with a history of erratic campaigning and no great charisma, he was not a figure designed to tempt wavering Tories. The Liberal, however, was. Tim Slack, a fifty-four-year-old Wykehamist, had been headmaster of Bedales, the public school which educated Princess Margaret's children, and also director of the Foreign Office's conference centre, Wiston House, until he resigned in protest at government cuts. A well-spoken older man with a background in education, he was well-placed to exploit the issue that caused the greatest damage to the Tory campaign – the threatened abolition of student grants.

The education secretary, Sir Keith Joseph, was a gifted theorist and an impassioned advocate for the free market, but, while he was a man of far greater intellectual calibre than most Tory ministers, his inability to grasp low political tactics meant he occasionally shot himself in the foot, or inadvertently strafed his colleagues. In 1974 he had destroyed his own hopes of succeeding Heath as Tory leader with a speech in Edgbaston where he declared, 'The balance of our population, our human stock, is threatened' by children being born to mothers 'least fitted to bring children into the world', having been 'pregnant in adolescence in social classes 4 and 5'. It had him labelled as a mad eugenicist, and his reputation took a long time to recover.

As Margaret Thatcher's first industry secretary he had provided his civil servants with impressive reading lists but little leadership. As education secretary he diagnosed many of the faults in British education which had taken hold since the sixties, but he grievously underestimated the power of the progressive lobby in the universities, the schools and, most fatally, his own department. He did not have the skill to smuggle in the policies he wanted, and when he tried to be daring he succeeded only in squandering a diminishing stock of political capital.

Student finance was a case in point. In the run-up to the 1984

Autumn Statement Sir Keith realised he would have to reform the funding of higher education. His twin aims were to expand spending on the universities and bear down generally on his department's expenditure. In order to find extra finance for the universities – and in particular for the science research budget – Sir Keith and the chief secretary, Peter Rees, agreed to abolish the maintenance grant for all students and make better-off parents contribute to the cost of tuition fees.

The chancellor, Nigel Lawson, and his adviser, Michael Portillo – at that point on the verge of selection as candidate for Southgate – did not know of the deal reached by the chief secretary and the education secretary. They found out, along with everyone else, when the departmental press releases accompanying the Autumn Statement were published on 12 November. In Nigel Lawson's words, 'All hell broke loose. Keith was asked to appear before the back-bench Education Committee, where he robustly defended the changes, and was given a roasting.'

Student maintenance grants were an expensive anomaly, unknown in the rest of the advanced West. No other comparable country forced the taxpayer to subsidise the parents of the wealthiest element in society, but that was of no concern to MPs in marginal seats. They saw a middle-class benefit disappearing at a stroke, and believed it was political folly to victimise their supporters. Lawson astutely summed up their concerns in his memoirs:

The real problem was the people who would be hurt by the proposed changes. These were not the poor, who were fully protected, nor the rich, who could take the increased parental contributions in their stride, but the people in between. They were the people who comprised the bulk of the Party activists in the constituencies and, in particular, the local Party officers.

And, the bulk of the electorate in Southgate.

In one of their 'Focus' leaflets the Liberals exploited the government's discomfiture. With a selective, but successful, attempt to cost the proposals they created an effective scare. The leaflet skated over the amount of maintenance already paid in order to exaggerate the cost of abolition, and suggested that every parent, and not just the wealthiest, would have to pay tuition fees, claiming, 'Some families will have to find nearly £10,000 to pay for a three-year course at university. The introduction of £520 a year tuition fees will also hit parents hard.'

Tory canvassers in Southgate, and Tory MPs in the Commons, pleaded with the government to abandon a deeply unpopular policy, and, with the same speed with which she had retreated from confrontation with the miners in 1981, the prime minister U-turned. Lawson brokered a deal on 6 December, just a week before the Southgate by-election. The Treasury bumped up the education budget, Sir Keith Joseph reduced the research allocation, proposals to introduce tuition fees were withdrawn, and maintenance grants were reduced but not abolished.

In his first two election addresses Portillo had steered clear of education, concentrating on crime, transport, the Tory record on inflation, and employment. In his final address, published after the Lawson–Joseph-managed climbdown, he felt he could tackle the subject, admitting that student grants had been one of the two biggest issues on the doorstep, but taking a share of the credit for the policy reversal. He was quoted as claiming, 'Many people told me of their concern about student grants. I understood those concerns and conveyed them strongly to the government. As a result of all the representations made to the government, it has withdrawn its proposal to charge tuition fees for students.'

It cannot have been easy for the young radical to take pride in defending a state subsidy to the well-off. Ten years later, with that by-election a distant memory, Portillo told the North-East Fife Conservative Association that it was the duty of the government to oppose the 'acquired privileges' of the middle class and argued that lobby groups should be resisted, because 'What they want for themselves may often seem eminently reasonable – but to grant it to them may not be in the interests of the nation as a whole.' But granting it to them might well be in the interests of a vulnerable candidate in a difficult by-election.

Central Office gave Portillo heavyweight support during his campaign. As well as Nigel Lawson, the home secretary Leon Brittan and the defence secretary Michael Heseltine addressed public meetings on his behalf. A battery of other ministers attended the morning press conferences which provided entertainment for journalists but did little to bring the issues to the people.

In many by-elections the ministers are there to soak up the questions and shield the candidates from scrutiny in their weak areas. That was not the case in Southgate according to Tony Dey: 'Michael handled all the encounters with the press quite brilliantly. I sat in on nearly all the press conferences, and Michael consistently outshone the ministers who came during the campaign.'

Impressing the stubby-pencil brigade might help him when he got to Westminster, but Portillo had to impress the voters first. In order to introduce him to the electors in a short campaign, Dey organised a cavalcade with a sticker-plastered car to tour the main streets of the constituency and a team of helpers leafleting the homes they passed. If any voter was at home and wanted to meet the candidate he was introduced for a short chat, but Dey was careful not to allow Portillo to become bogged down in detailed discussion or distracted by in-depth canvassing. It is a method of campaigning Portillo has stuck to, and at the last election he blitzed the constituency in a Range Rover to the accompaniment of an Andrew Lloyd Webber arrangement of a Purcell theme, glad-handing supporters rather than involving himself in doorstep debates with opponents.

The reception from the voters in the first week of the campaign was broadly favourable. Portillo's first election leaflet played on the anger of voters at the murder of Sir Anthony Berry – an anger detected by visiting journalists like Alan Franks of *The Times*, who reported an elderly voter remarking, 'I think it's a shame there should be an election. It used to be that when an MP got killed in action the other parties ceded the seat.'

The backdrop of Sir Anthony's murder gave Portillo's initial campaign emphasis on law and order an additional resonance. This is a Tory theme that has been played so often that even variations on it now have a tired quality, but it was congenial to Portillo. Capital punishment had been central to his campaign in Perry Bar. In Southgate he was subtler: as well as evoking middle-class anxieties about mugging, he also played on the picket-line violence that was such a feature of the miners' strike. In his first election leaflet the first policy issue he alluded to in his personal message was crime. In his second leaflet he headlined the presence of the home secretary at the campaign launch and interweaved commitments to create more neighbourhood-watch schemes with 'concern at the amount of violence on TV, particularly in the coalfields'. What started as a Mary Whitehouse-ish whinge turned into an association of the Left with disorder – good, hard campaigning, but directed at the wrong target.

The Labour candidate may have had the odd heavyweight, like Roy Hattersley, supporting him, but more noticeable on his platforms was the presence of GLC leader Ken Livingstone, inveighing against Thatcher and Reagan and predicting the final crisis of capitalism. The *Enfield Gazette* reported his telling a public meeting at Bowes Road Infants' School, New Southgate, that there would be 'a sensational collapse in the economies of the Western world because of the policies pursued by Mrs Thatcher and President Reagan'. Such apocalyptic rhetoric might have gone down well in County Hall, but in suburban Southgate the only historical inevitability was that Marxist theorising would alienate middle-class voters even more effectively than abolishing student grants.

The Liberals exploited the imploding Labour campaign by presenting themselves as the only credible challengers. Most early polls showed the Tories well ahead, but the Liberals gave widespread publicity to a 'what-if' poll in the *Observer* on the Sunday before polling day which suggested that as many voters would go for the Liberals as the Tories if they thought the Liberals could win. They argued that the twenty-fifth safest seat in Britain could fall if the opposition coalesced around Tim Slack. In the final week they tried to give the impression of a gap being closed by quoting journalists who suggested the race might be close. The *Guardian*'s invocation of a previous Liberal by-election triumph was gleefully seized on, and its suggestion that 'Southgate might turn into another Orpington' was splashed across the Liberals' 'Focus' leaflet.

In their determination to squeeze the Labour vote, the Liberals also indulged in hard campaigning, releasing a leaflet designed to look like Labour literature urging Labour voters to switch to the Liberals. The leaflet was printed in red, tagged 'Labour News', and its Liberal origins were disguised by a tiny and uninformative 'Printed by ESLP' tucked away at the bottom. The Liberals probably would not have objected if voters thought that that meant Enfield Southgate Labour Party, rather than the Liberal Party. Local Labour activists were incensed. It is a trick the Liberals and their successors, the Lib-Dems, have pulled since, most notably in Tower Hamlets in 1990, and have ended up expelling party members as a result. All Labour could do in Southgate was to fume and watch their support drift away to Tim Slack in an attempt to deny the Tories victory.

The Liberals also targeted wavering Tories. A 'Focus' leaflet released in the final week featured a retired couple straight out of a private-pension-plan ad, all floral frocks and woolly cardigans, who were alleged to be switching to the Liberals. Skilful quotation presented their move as a natural way to protest. 'We've always been Conservative,' the anonymous couple were quoted as saying, before they gave their reasons for deserting Maggie:

We'd never dream of voting for anyone else in a General Election. It might let in a Socialist Government, and that would be a disaster for Britain. But, in a by-election, things are different. We're a bit unhappy with the Government at the moment and, for the first time in our lives, we're thinking of voting for someone else. We're not alone. Many of our friends and neighbours feel the same. A by-election here gives us a unique chance to influence Government thinking and improve Government policies. It's a chance too good to miss.

The policies the couple objected to, and sought to moderate with their protest votes, were not mentioned. It was an invitation to kick the Tories, cost-free. And it seemed to be working.

Another artfully cloaked leaflet was released in the same week. Styled the 'Enfield and Southgate Courier', it contained nothing to suggest it was a Liberal leaflet apart from the agent's name. Looking like a standard local free-sheet, it also deployed another anonymous quote, this time from a 'senior local Conservative' who was alleged to have said that the party 'might live to regret its choice' of candidate.

The Tories were increasingly nervous in the last week. Both the agent and the chairman feared the worst, and found their only solace in the quality of their candidate and the wisdom of going early. The Liberals' canvass returns showed a large swing in their favour. Their candidate, Tim Slack, recalls, 'My agent told me at the beginning of the final week that we were on course to win, and I believe he was right then.'

The Tories drafted in extra support from neighbouring seats, and ambitious outsiders. Most help was warmly welcomed; some less so. One MP, Staffordshire South's Patrick Cormack, whose high opinion of his own abilities he felt should be more widely shared, turned up to do his bit on one day when the cameras were expected. It was late in the campaign, with the Liberals closing fast. He was given a sheaf of canvass cards with the names and addresses of wavering Tories highlighted, and was asked to see if their support had firmed. 'I only canvass off virgin cards,' he told the harassed party worker. It was too much for the helper, who exploded, 'If you'd been here a little fucking earlier you'd have virgin cards. Now get going or get out.'

In an effort to shore up fraying morale, a message of support was sent to Portillo from Norman Tebbit. Tebbit, the most cruelly injured of all the ministers who survived the Brighton bomb, had been recuperating since the blast and was still in hospital. The images of his body being extricated from the rubble, in considerable pain, lingered long in the minds of all those who saw the TV coverage of the bomb's aftermath. Coming from such a high-profile victim, Tebbit's message, quoted in the Tories' final leaflet, was a sharp reminder of the reason for the by-election: 'The murder of Tony Berry robbed me of a good friend as well as robbing Southgate of a devoted member . . . [Michael Portillo] is well qualified to succeed Tony and I look forward to seeing [him] sitting in Tony's place.'

The use of Berry's name by another victim of the Brighton bomb was a calculated attempt to exploit the sympathy vote, and was denounced as such by both the Liberals and Labour. Coming in the same week as Tony Berry's memorial service, it may have helped the Tories firm up their support. Tim Slack certainly thought so: 'We really noticed our vote falling off in the last two days. I'm convinced it was the Tories reminding the electorate how Tony Berry died.' Nevertheless, the momentum seemed to be with the Liberals.

Polling day, 13 December, was a depressing one for the Tories. The weather was foul, some of their older voters were unwilling to make the journey to the polling booths, and there was an apparent jauntiness about the Liberal campaign that grated. That night the tension got to the Tories, and sharp words were exchanged between party workers and the BBC *Newsnight* reporter Vincent Hanna, whom they thought was slavering a little too obviously at the prospect of a Tory defeat and a juicy story. In the end the methodical counting of Enfield's town clerk denied Hanna an on-air declaration, and it wasn't until 1.45 a.m. that the returning officer announced that Michael Denzil Xavier Portillo had been returned as the member for Enfield Southgate.

The Liberals had secured a 10.4 per cent swing away from the Tories, but Labour had lost their deposit. The full result was:

Michael Portillo (Conservative)	16,684
Tim Slack (Liberal)	11,973
Peter Hamid (Labour)	4,000
A. Polydorou (Troops out of Cyprus)	687
J. W. Kershaw (National Party)	80
R. E. Shenton (English Nationalist)	78
I. I. Burgess (Restore Middlesex)	50
G. Weiss (Captain Rainbow)	48
H. M. Anscomb (Death off the Roads)	45

It was a Tory majority of 4,711.

Portillo put the reduced majority down to the low number of voters who bothered to turn out on a wet winter Thursday: 'I believe most of the decrease in our majority can be explained by the low turnout, and lack of urgency among some Conservatives who knew the Government's large majority in the Commons was not at stake.' The agent, Tony Dey, claims he has no head for numbers but says he will never forget the figures 4.7.1.1. He believes that if the campaign had gone on for longer, as Margaret Thatcher wanted, even for another week, the Tories would have lost.

The Tory party has not been kind to candidates who are careless with safe seats, as the losers in Newbury, Christchurch, Eastleigh and Eastbourne know only too well. Having transformed a Labour majority in the low hundreds to one in the high thousands in his only previous electoral outing, Portillo could have seen his hopes of a seat disappear if he had lost in Southgate.

Michael Portillo owed his place in Parliament to the U-turn on student loans and to his constituency association's rejection of the prime minister's express wishes on the timing of the poll. He was in Parliament despite Thatcherism and Mrs Thatcher, but, now that he was in, both platform and premier had their loyalest supporter.

Portillo took his oath and his seat in the House of Commons on the Tuesday after the by-election, 18 December, just a couple of days before Parliament broke up for Christmas. He did not speak in the House until well into the new year, choosing a debate on public expenditure on 4 March 1985.

Maiden speeches are, by tradition, uncontroversial and mainly a tribute to the previous member and the constituency. Portillo's was, as one might expect, cast in the most traditional mould. He praised Sir Anthony's dedication to his constituents, remarking on his habit of visiting those in trouble in their homes like a latter-day Dr Finlay. He caught the shock of the House at Sir Anthony's murder by the IRA, calling it a 'stunning paradox that such a kind, courteous and gentle man should lose his life at the hands of the men of violence'. He quoted from Sir Anthony's own maiden speech, which asked for the widening of the North Circular Road in the constituency. Portillo ruefully pointed out that, twenty years later, his constituents were still waiting.

A brief historical *tour d'horizon* of the Middlesex suburbs he now represented was then quickly followed by a short feint in the direction of policy. His comments were suitably non-controversial and only gently pointed. There was a plea that the opposition understand the government's good intentions. In addition, he tentatively suggested the merger of the Autumn Statement of expenditure plans and the spring revenue-raising Budget. It was a prescient plea: he was the chief secretary at the Treasury in 1993 when the then chancellor, Norman Lamont, brought the two together.

The nine-minute speech was well-received. The next speaker, the Liberals' Treasury spokesman, Richard Wainwright, called it 'admirable'.

Having broken his silence, Portillo was free to play a more active role on the floor of the House, and he did his best to make himself useful to the government. He got himself elected as secretary to the Tories' back-bench Energy Committee, and used most of his questions to enable ministers to make statements or launch attacks on Labour.

It is a convention of Parliament that all announcements of

importance have to be made to the Commons first. Given the huge growth in the government's responsibilities since the convention arose, another convention has grown up to get round it and allow departments to make statements and unveil policies without clogging up time on the floor of the Commons. Tame back-benchers are roped into asking questions framed for them by the whips, for written reply. These, ironically named 'inspired questions', are used as occasions for issuing any news a department has. Portillo facilitated the work of his old colleagues in the Department of Energy by asking detailed questions about onshore licensing arrangements and the fate of BNOC, and on one occasion he assisted the Environment Department by asking about the future of dolphinaria. In so doing, the future enemy of red tape was midwife to a barrage of new regulations, but he was doing nothing more than working his passage as a scrupulously loyal new boy, anxious to impress.

As well as getting in with the government whips by his diligence, Portillo also recommended himself to two other, equally shadowy, sets of colleagues.

The 92 Group is, like MI5, a much-misunderstood organisation. The parallels are various. The group's hand is seen behind imaginary plots, its appetite for intrigue is assumed to be insatiable, its power is variously overstated and undervalued. Both organisations keep their membership lists hidden and say that they act only rarely, and then in the best interests of honest patriots. But there the parallels end. The 92 is not so much a secret society as a private one. It is the largest grouping within the parliamentary Tory Party, and exists to provide support for those who consider themselves broadly on the Right.

It was founded in 1965 by a group of MPs who had supported Reggie Maudling in his unsuccessful bid for the Tory leadership that year. Maudling had not been markedly to the Right of Heath at that point, but he was distinctly more Euro-sceptic. The only defiantly right-wing candidate had been Enoch Powell, who had stood on a purist free-market platform with the support of Nicholas Ridley. However, Maudling was the more traditional of the two front-runners. Heath was the moderniser, and had the support of the party's most progressive figures, including Iain Macleod.

Maudling's traditionalist supporters, fearing that Heath would drag the party away from its historic roots, set up a group with the aim of, in the words of one of its founders, 'keeping the Conservative Party conservative'. It took its name from its first meeting-place, 92 Cheyne Walk, the Chelsea home of one of its founders, Patrick Wall, the member for Haltemprice (now part of the Beverley constituency).

Marginal during Heath's years in opposition, with fewer than twenty members, the group grew in numbers and influence during Heath's period in government as more Tories became dismayed by the drift to the Left. When Margaret Thatcher launched her leadership bid, her campaign manager, Airey Neave, although not a member, asked the 92 for help, and its members brought on board other friends to lend her challenge momentum.

Thatcher herself never joined the group, partly because one member would always veto any woman, irrespective of ideology, because he believed women had no place in Parliament. However, she always looked to the group to sustain her, and thought its leading lights were all 'one of us'.

The 92 would arrange a slate of candidates for the annual elections to the party's back-bench committees. These committees have no power, but their chairmen have access to ministers and, perhaps more importantly, the airwaves, as representatives of back-bench opinion. Control of these posts can influence the reporting of the party's mood, and shots can be fired across the bows of departments which seem to be steering too far to port.

The Left of the party has its own organising caucus, known as 'The Lollards', named after the Lollard Tower in Lambeth Palace where its first organiser, Sir William van Straubenzee, had rooms. Throughout the eighties and since, the Lollards have usually been beaten by the 92 in any straight fight, unless the 92 itself has been split.

The Lollards' lack of success was partly due to their skill in advancing clever young men on the Left quickly into the government, giving them power but denying them a vote in any back-bench tussle. It was also due, according to the Lollards' current leader, Leominster's Peter Temple-Morris, to the civilised nature of much of their support. He believes the greater ideological zeal of right-wingers makes them more amenable to being dragooned into voting the line in committee rooms at six in the evening, while the Tory Left are in the Smoking Room wondering if whisky or gin is a better base for the night ahead.

Portillo joined the 92 on arrival. There were no black balls. Those who knew him thought of him as incontrovertibly on the Right, and membership was a natural move. Some ambitious MPs – John Major was a case in point – calculate it is better never to identify themselves too obviously with any faction, to avoid making unnecessary enemies. This was not an option for Portillo. His association with Parkinson, Lawson and Thatcher, his support for the death penalty, his work with the Adam Smith Institute and even his Peterhouse origins all marked him out.

Membership of the 92 did not require any subscription to a set of policies, simply a broad identification with the Right in the party. That meant that within its ranks there were economic liberals, social authoritarians, the occasional pro-European or imperialist nostalgic, High Tories, monetarist technicians and simple reactionaries. What united most of them was an attachment to the traditional Tory principles that they believed predated what they saw as the guilt-ridden, patrician, liberal Toryism of Macmillan and Gilmour.

They were at one in their distaste for progressive Toryism – the wetness that, if they could not always describe, they knew when they saw. Whether as libertarian purists or reactionary romantics, they would tend to oppose equal-opportunity legislation; whether as defenders of private property or in the interests of economic efficiency, they would demand lower taxation and a smaller state. Closer to the grass-roots' prejudices than the gubernatorial class of Chris Patten, Francis Pym and Jim Prior, they made a virtue out of staying in touch with saloon-bar opinion in preference to *bien-pensant* salon thinking.

The 92's current chairman – holder of that office since 1983 – is the Reigate MP Sir George Gardiner. A member of Margaret Thatcher's first campaign team and one of her earliest biographers, his loyalty has never wavered even though he has remained on the back benches throughout his career. A typical member of the 92, he is a confirmed Euro-sceptic without any tinge of fanaticism, a free-marketeer who is not bound to any narrow doctrine, a supporter of strong defences and the shortest way with offenders. A gaunt, almost etiolated figure with the looks of a particularly melancholic bloodhound, he has a reputation for caballing and plot-hatching which he does nothing to play down.

Other back-benchers occasionally disparage his attachment to faction, but all acknowledge his organisational skill. Even those few members of the 92 who disagree with his Euro-sceptical line, such as Ray Whitney, accept that he has been effective in keeping the group together and maximising its influence. But, while he is a clear thinker, he is not considered a profound one. In that respect he is at one with many members of the 92.

The Lollards take some pleasure in their own back-bench impotence, because it implies that the Left has most of the MPs with the talent to become ministers. That is part of the story, but only part. There has certainly been a reluctance among all recent prime ministers – even Margaret Thatcher – to advance the claims of many right-wingers. This is partly a cultural backwash from the days before the Tories elected their leaders. A persistent form of snobbery has dictated that although the Tories may be led by someone from a humble background, the leader should be surrounded by a patrician caste of 'moderate' ministers to palliate the harshness of lower-middle-class Toryism.

Heath had Hume and Carrington to lend his government tone. Thatcher relied on Carrington and Whitelaw, Prior and Hailsham to convey an impression of moderate Conservative continuity. John Major has had Douglas Hurd and Michael Heseltine as his chief lieutenants – their expansive suiting and polished vowels complementing the appeal of the boy from Brixton.

But, as well as this persistent social and cultural bar to the Right making its presence felt at the top, there has been a more difficult barrier – simple lack of talent. One senior left-winger who spent a long stint in the Whips' Office claims he was in despair that there were not more right-wingers worthy of promotion. He wanted to stop the government becoming too unbalanced in relation to the back benches, but, he claims, 'We had difficulty in the early eighties finding any who could do joined-up handwriting.'

While the Tory Left found its recruits from Oxbridge and Edinburgh, in the seventies and early eighties the Right's foot-soldiers were in the redbrick universities or making money. Their professional approach might have added ballast to the administration, but it could not supply the elegant thinking or stylish writing of a Patten or a Waldegrave.

All that changed in 1983, however. The landslide, as landslides do, swept in a lot of rubbish, but there was evidence of a subtler shift in the party's make-up behind the sheer increase in size. A generation of intelligent young politicians who had come to political maturity despairing at the Heath government's abandonment of principle and who had been enthused by Margaret Thatcher's leadership entered the House. A smattering were Oxbridge-educated, smooth and assured, but a surprising number came from another university – defiantly provincial but certainly not redbrick, ancient, but in the political avant-garde – St Andrew's. Among the 1983 new boys were Michael Forsyth, Michael Fallon, Robert Jones and Christopher Chope, all graduates of the small Scottish university, and all former pupils of Ralph Harris.

Harris had been one of the driving forces behind the Institute of Economic Affairs, the think-tank which had fought for the free market during the decades-long rule of Keynesian orthodoxy and which had supplied the Thatcher government with an armoury of economic arguments. He had been ennobled for his efforts, and, as Lord Harris of High Cross, had set up a club of peers, known as the Repeal Group, dedicated to advancing individual liberty by repealing unnecessary legislation.

He suggested to his disciples that they set up a similar group in the Commons, to argue for liberal economic policies and provide some intellectual support for Margaret Thatcher. The St Andrew's circle decided to invite a few like-minded colleagues from the 1983 intake, but thought better of setting up a simple Commons branch of Harris's Lords' club. Instead, they decided on their own name, lighting on the prime minister's most famous repudiation of accommodation, her rejection of a U-turn in her economic policies at the 1981 party conference, when she had taunted her critics, 'You turn if you want to. The lady's not for turning.' Making no secret of their inspiration, the No Turning Back Group was formed.

As well as the St Andrew's core, the first members included Alan Howarth, David Heathcoat-Amory, John Butcher, Eric Forth, Neil Hamilton, Gerald Howarth, Francis Maude, Angela Rumbold, Peter Lilley, Ian Twinn and Edward Leigh. All were bright, right-wing and new to the House. They extended an early invitation to

Leigh's Lincolnshire neighbour, Michael Brown, who, although of the 1979 vintage, was considered sufficiently sound to fit in and was thought to be a source of amusement when the theorising became too technical. They met once a month in the IEA's offices in Lord North Street, for dinner. They dined simply – a buffet of cold meats and salad, a little white wine, followed by cheese and fruit. After a general gossip, a formal topic for discussion was chosen and kicked around the table. Neil Hamilton might light a cigar, Lord Harris his pipe, but, that apart, the atmosphere was far more cerebral than sensual.

Since its inception the NTB has grown. Right-thinking ministers who returned to the back benches, such as Allan Stewart and Bob Dunn, were invited to join, as were later entrants such as John Redwood of the 1987 intake and Alan Duncan, David Willetts, Liam Fox, Bernard Jenkin, John Whittingdale and Iain Duncan-Smith from the 1992. Its most notable new attender has been its president, Lady Thatcher, who attends annually, when smoked salmon is served.

In its infancy the NTB was assumed to be no more significant than the many other dining societies that Tory MPs form to fill the long hours between the time for the first drink and the last vote. Kenneth Clarke had his own, the Amesbury, named after the street in Birmingham where he lived and aimed at 'One Nation' colleagues who entered the House in the seventies. Another was simply called 'The One Nation'; founded by Iain Macleod, it staggers on still. Others on the left have joined 'Nick's Diner', a wettish group of *bon viveurs* under Nicholas Scott's wing. On the right, the 'Snakes and Ladders' provides a forum for Sir Rhodes Boyson and Jim Pawsey to entertain a gallery of sympathetic colleagues, journalists and businessmen. Among new members 'The Standard Bearers' caters for ambitious public schoolboys, and the 'Dresden Group' for privately educated members with an eye to office.

Some of the societies are collections of friends with a similar outlook or who have known each other since student years or early days in the House. Others have an ideological edge. Most have a varying mixture of both those elements.

One of the most famous, and influential, has been the 'Blue Chip' group. Formed, like the NTB, from a nucleus of new boys, but from 1979 rather than 1983, its ideology is less capable of easy classification than the purely Thatcherite NTB. It is leftish, but includes the High Tory and arch-Unionist Robert Cranborne as well as the early Thatcher fan Matthew Parris. It is toffish, but includes John Major and Robert Atkins. And it is Oxbridge, but includes a fair smattering of Scots – notably Ian Lang, Peter Fraser and Michael Ancram.

John Patten, another member, characterises its philosophy as 'the continuation of the Queen's government'. He may be seeking to suggest its members are nothing other than loyal Tories with an affection for established institutions and no taste for radicalism of any stripe, but cynics might detect in the avoidance of commitment a reluctance to proclaim any principle other than holding on to power. Its main members, apart from those listed above, are William Waldegrave, Tristan Garel-Jones, Chris Patten, Douglas Hogg and Richard Needham. They have been immortalised in a group portrait by Cranborne's wife which hangs in reproduction on all their walls and adorns the table mats in the Garel-Joneses' house in Catherine Place, where they usually meet.

Its influence rests on the extraordinary ability of its members to win, and hold office. They succeeded under Thatcher, and under Major every member of the Blue Chip group in Parliament has been in the government. Its presiding genius, Tristan Garel-Jones, is now on the back benches, but some on the Right think his influence on the others is such that he is an ex-officio member of the government anyway.

The founding members were all clever and civilised, and they also, as all young MPs should, showed an early independent streak which brought them to others' attention without creating too many waves. In 1981 they published a pamphlet, entitled *Changing Gear*, which called for not so much a U-turn as a period of consolidation to allow reforms to 'bed down'. Whatever the merits of their case, the Blue Chip group had laid down a marker. The lesson was not lost on the NTB.

Fearing that the radical energies of the second Thatcher administration could be squandered, in 1985 the NTB published its own pamphlet, *No Turning Back*, arguing for further privatisation, greater choice in the provision of health and education, and yet lower taxation. The authors' names were listed on the back – the first public roll-call for Parliament's young radical Right. The pamphlet was not, however, the work of any MP. All the NTB members had contributed sheafs of ideas to Michael Forsyth, who was asked to select and edit. He handed the contributions over to Madsen Pirie at the Adam Smith Institute, who wove the mass of radical ideas into a simple and easily recognisable standard for the group to raise.

One MP who contributed more than most was the recently elected member for Southgate. Although not a 1983 entrant, Michael Portillo was an instant recruit to the NTB, and an obvious one.

Even though he was among the youngest, he quickly established himself as the group's de-facto leader. Until Margaret Thatcher's return to the back benches they had no president. Administration was shared between the 'senior man', Michael Brown, and Lord Harris. Different figures led in different discussions. Peter Lilley was the group's first member in the Cabinet, John Redwood had run Thatcher's Number Ten Policy Unit, but no one had the combination of political authority and sinewy intelligence which Portillo enjoys. He does not assert himself, but other members recognise him as the biggest beast around the table.

One member says, 'There are some very clever people in the NTB, but he's the sharpest. He doesn't say all that much and he seldom leads off, but we all acknowledge he weighs his words more carefully and argues more effectively than anyone.' Other members attest to his unwillingness to dominate any discussion and his tendency to draw the skeins together at the end, rejecting weak arguments and appraising strong ones. The obvious comparison they draw is that of a good prime minister summing up at the end of a lively Cabinet, and imprinting his personality on all the deliberations.

Portillo's position has been strengthened by his long period as a minister and his status in the Cabinet, but members of the group are keen to stress that they meet as equals, with back-benchers encouraged to lay into ministers and argue against their policies. Indeed, one of the favourite sports of the junior members is goading the ministers with evidence of their 'selling-out' or 'going native', trading their principles for promotion. As a clearly ambitious young man who achieved office early, there was always the chance that Portillo might be accused of going native, and one or two early decisions were seized on as possible policy wobbles. However, his behaviour in 'The Emergency', when Thatcher fell, vanquished any doubt about his soundness for even the flintiest NTBer.

His credentials and ability were to make life as the NTB's unofficial leader difficult later, when he had to talk to Major about Maastricht on the group's behalf, but in his first years in Parliament membership provided a ready-made support network.

Membership of the 92 indicated to any interested observer that Portillo was on the Right. But that could have been deduced from his well-advertised support for the rope, or the ministers he'd worked for before becoming an MP. Membership of the NTB was the clearest demonstration possible that Portillo was on the free-market right, but that would have been a precondition anyway for a junior special adviser to Nigel Lawson. What would have eluded instant detection was the High Tory strain in Portillo's political make-up. His public free-market radicalism obscured the Peterhouse influences and the deeper attachment to the British state and its institutions which had drawn him to the Right in the first place.

In an attempt to suggest that the new generation of Thatcherites were not really Tories, wet writers such as Julian Critchley tried to suggest they were simply 'Manchester Liberals' – nineteenth-century utilitarian free-marketeers with no feel for the fabric of the nation, who knew how much a hospital founded in the twelfth century cost to run but had no idea of its real value. This was understandable but inaccurate propaganda by a faction determined to wrest back control of 'their' party. Portillo's own Toryism is evident from the speech he made to an almost empty chamber on the afternoon of Friday 5 July 1985.

Fridays are Parliament's fag end. They are normally taken up with debates of minority interest or private member's bills. Most MPs are in their constituency. On this Friday, with only half an hour to debate it, and no chance of it passing into law, the Labour back-bencher John Marek introduced a bill to abolish the House of Lords. A pure free-marketeer would not have wasted his breath defending a House built on the hereditary principle. A Manchester Liberal on the economic right – an Andrew Neil or Stephen Haseler – would probably have put his name down as the bill's co-sponsor.

But Portillo was the only Tory who opposed it on the floor of the House.

His speech was a spirited defence of the Upper House. He began with an assault on the Opposition's restless need to remake British democracy: 'I am sometimes perplexed how it is that the Labour Party's first instinct when faced with a problem is turn to constitutional reform.'

That point, which could be made with even greater force now, as New Labour abandons economic radicalism for constitutional experimentation, was followed up by the suggestion that it was self-interest not principle that drove Labour to devolution: 'they acted without regard to whether those actions would be good for the long-term constitutional health of the United Kingdom. They found a way of getting themselves out of a tight corner politically and they were willing to throw constitutional tradition and history to the winds in the interest of self-preservation.'

Portillo praised the expertise of the Lords, and argued that televisation had meant that his constituents had seen it at work and now agreed with him that it was a 'splendid place'. He acknowledged that it had not always been Thatcher's poodle – voting against the abolition of the GLC for example – but praised it for all that, arguing, 'the House of Lords is willing to consider carefully and independently the legislation that comes from this House'.

He summed up by characterising the assault on the Lords as a cry of frustration from a party rejected at the polls that wanted to change the rules so that it could at last win. If the British people would not vote for a Labour government, they had to be given a system that would allow Labour to govern:

In effect it is a call by the Labour Party for a recount. If it loses a general election, it wants a second bash at it when it has a second House.

Constitutional reform by the abolition of the House of Lords would merely be the prelude to a much more devastating constitutional reform. With the House of Lords out of the way, our ability to stop that devastating change would be that much more restricted.

Portillo has used every available opportunity to defend the Upper House. In 1991 the Lords were attacked for their impertinence in twice rejecting the War Crimes Bill. The bill was framed to allow prosecution of Nazi war criminals still living in Britain and had the overwhelming support of the Commons. After a short delay, the Commons allowed the bill to pass into law, but there was frothy talk about constitutional crises as the Lords had twice defied the electorate's representatives.

Portillo used the platform of his local newspaper, the *Enfield Independent*, where he had a weekly column, 'The Commons Touch', to defend Their Lordships' right to defy the elected chamber:

I think the episode shows that our constitution is working well and no reform is necessary. The Lords point to formidable legal questions about the difficulty of gathering witnesses and evidence for either prosecution or defence after so many years.

These problems are serious enough to ask the Commons to think again. We have done so but have not changed our mind. I think we get the best of both worlds. Our upper chamber, full of experienced people, checks our lower chamber when it sees that important issues are at stake. But our elected House of Commons finally has its way. No crisis here and no need for reform.

As he grew more confident in the Commons, Portillo was prepared to place himself out on a right-wing limb. His High Tory stance on the constitution was complemented by a staunchly socially conservative and economically liberal position.

As a traditional right-winger, he twice voted in favour of capital punishment: once in support of a bill introduced by Geoffrey Dickens to bring back hanging for child-murderers in January 1987 and once on a free vote in April of the same year. He was anti-abortion, supporting the Lancashire Catholic Tory Ken Hind's Unborn Children (Protection) Bill in October 1986.

As a defender of individual liberty, he defied the government only one month after his election, by rebelling on the vote to introduce compulsory fluoridisation of water.

As an economic liberal, he devoted most of his time to nudging the government more firmly towards the free market in energy.

In a debate on the Oil and Pipelines Bill, on 14 May 1985, Portillo argued that the replacement of the state leviathan BNOC with a privatised Britoil and a new agency was welcome, but still suggested a willingness to intervene *in extremis*. He counselled the minister of state at the Department of Energy, Alick Buchanan-

Smith, to stop taking tiny steps to full liberalisation of oil production, comparing his progress, loosely, to that of a timorous flea
trapped on a table. 'My right honourable friend the minister of
state is not in the least like a flea, but I should like to see him steel
himself and, with one great bound, get himself free of the table.'

In 1985 the energy secretary, Peter Walker, introduced a bill to
privatise British Gas. It was to be one of the most successful sell-offs
of the Thatcher years, the attractions of popular capitalism captured by the 'If you see Sid, tell him' advertising campaign that
saw manual labourers learning the language of stags, bears, offer
prices and flotations. Portillo, however, had reservations about the
bill. He thought it did not go far enough. In the debate on the
second reading, on 10 December, he made his doubts explicit:

Privatisation of a monopoly has three important benefits – commercial
freedom for the company, regulation to protect the customer and competition. I believe the greatest benefit to be competition. I am not sure
whether the bill recognises competition as the most important aspect.

One thing missing from the bill is the duty, present in the British
Telecom Act, on the director-general to promote effective competition.
I was surprised by that. There used to be a cartoon character who stuck
his head over a brick wall and said, 'Wot, no Watney's?' When I stuck
my nose into the bill I said, 'Wot, no duties to promote effective competition in the industry?'

What he lacked in wit, he made up for in ideological rigour. As
a back-bencher on the standing committee that scrutinised the bill,
Portillo proposed an amendment to compel any future regulator
to promote effective competition. After some discreet lobbying
behind the scenes, Walker was persuaded of the merits of Portillo's
case and amended the legislation accordingly.

Portillo was still not pleased, however. In the debate on the
third reading of the bill, on 25 March 1986, he thanked the government for accepting his amendment to promote competition among
suppliers but signalled his disquiet at its reluctance to maximise
the competition British Gas would face in obtaining supplies from
the North Sea and elsewhere. His comments betray a suspicion
that British Gas had ensured that some of its old monopoly advantages would remain: 'The government statement was not exactly

the statement for which I had been hoping, because I had been hoped for an entirely free regime of imports and exports.'

Portillo wanted the government to follow the logic of privatisation right through: 'My thesis is that it is better to rely on competition to ensure the good of the customer than to rely on any kind of regulation, because competition would always do the job better for the customer.'

Even in its imperfect state, however, the bill got Portillo's vote.

His efforts to toughen up the Gas Bill were not the only back-bench campaign he waged in an effort to encourage the government to be true to its Tory conscience. In March 1986 he used a rare slice of Commons time allocated to back-benchers to press the case for greater parental choice in education. He had won a place in the ballot for a slot on the debate on the Consolidated Fund, a Commons device which allows members to raise matters of personal concern. Flanked by allies from the No Turning Back group, including Robert Jones, Michael Forsyth and Edward Leigh, Portillo outlined an agenda for reform, radical at the time, but accepted even by the Labour Party now.

Developing some of the ideas in the NTB's first pamphlet, Portillo argued for the publication of all examination results (a practice dear to the heart of the first headmaster of his own grammar school), the ability of parents to make an unfettered choice on the school for their children, a system of cash following pupils to reward and expand good schools, the involvement of parents in running schools, and the devolution of control from education authorities to schools themselves. In 1988 the suggestions were to form the core of Kenneth Baker's Great Education Reform Bill; the first significant reform of schooling since the 1980 Education Act introduced assisted places and a measure of open enrolment.

Portillo summed up his vision by putting his faith in market principles, given a populist expression: 'Trust parents; give them responsibility and they will prove to be responsible. I would rather rely on the collective wisdom of parents than on the accumulated experience of civil servants, educationists and, dare I say, ministers.'

These radical forays marked Portillo out as impeccably Thatcherite. If not 100 per cent loyal, he was running a little ahead of the government rather than holding it back or trying to knock it off course.

After his first rebellion on fluoridation he gave the whips no cause for concern. Indeed his willingness to ask the right questions, snipe at the Opposition and put in hours on dull Friday afternoons recommended him to the party's Stasi. In an administration hardly overendowed with talented right-wingers he very quickly became an obvious candidate for promotion.

During the 1984 by-election campaign *The Times* had tipped him as a certainty for the Cabinet. The week after he was elected, the *Enfield Gazette*, under the headline 'Tomorrow's Tory', drew parallels with the last Enfield member to dominate his party, speculating, 'We could have another Iain Macleod in our midst.' On the Sunday after his election the *Sunday Mirror* became the first paper to tip him for the top, suggesting he could become the first Tory prime minister in the twenty-first century.

Margaret Thatcher wanted to promote Portillo early, but her initial plans were frustrated. Even though she was near the zenith of her powers, the cracks that would bring her down were beginning to appear. The second half of the eighties were a time when the Thatcherites thought the big battles had been won, but for Portillo the biggest of all were still to come.

CHAPTER EIGHT

Climbing the Greasy Pole

Power without principle is barren, but principle without power
is futile.

Tony Blair

One afternoon in the autumn of 1985 Margaret Thatcher spent a
difficult hour with one of her most junior ministers. It was quite
a long time with a lowly member of the government, but then this
minister was explaining why, unless she acted quickly, everything
for which she had worked would be set at naught.

The minister was Bob Dunn, parliamentary under-secretary at
the Department of Education and Science, and his message was
simple: the majority of members of Mrs Thatcher's government
were loyal neither to her nor to her ideas, and, unless that was
remedied, both she and her programme would inevitably suffer.
In the room where her Cabinet would gather every Thursday,
Dunn told her her government was not her own. When she pro-
tested that the Gilmours and Pyms were now fuming impotently
on the back benches, he produced a chart with the name of every
member of her administration, down to the lowliest junior whip.
Beside each name was a mark: Left, Right or mainstream loyalist.

Thatcher began by pointing to the number of allies she had in
the Cabinet, from Dunn's boss, Sir Keith Joseph, through Lord
Young to Geoffrey Howe. That these allies were on the way out,
isolated in the Lords or growing disaffected did not deflect Dunn
from his main point. He took her through the ministers of state,
parliamentary under-secretaries and the Whips' Office, pointing
out how firm the grip of the wets and their protégés was on the
levers in the engine room of government. Dunn warned that even
if she won another election Margaret Thatcher's future Cabinets
would be drawn from figures, like the Blue Chips, who might be
talented but were never in sympathy with her.

He went on to draw her attention to the new talent that had

entered in 1983, loyal to her and thirsty for office – not for status, but simply to carry forward her policies. He stressed the reservoir of support for her on the back benches, which felt increasingly distanced from her and feared she was being deliberately kept away from her supporters by ministers anxious to dim her radicalism. He pointed to the many ardent supporters whose careers she had not advanced and whose loyalty had not been rewarded.

Thatcher resisted Dunn's arguments initially, but as he took her through the ministers in every department she slowly buckled and recognised the strength of his case. Instinctively she had been both prime minister and, at the same time, the most effective leader of the opposition the government had, as the most trenchant critic of her administration's own backsliding. Dunn was trying to point out that she should rely on loyal supporters to act as her eyes and ears, implementing her will, rather than having to rely on her own energies to chivvy every department.

When Dunn left, Thatcher resolved to act. She decided to accelerate the careers of the true believers. Cecil Parkinson recalls, 'It had quite an effect on her. She realised she had to do more to bring her supporters on.' But, before she could, her hand was forced and her leadership was threatened by precisely the sort of headstrong, wet-driven sabotage from within of which Dunn had warned.

The Westland affair is proof, if proof were needed, of Pope's belief that great occasions rise from trivial things. The future of a Yeovil helicopter firm was a pretext for Michael Heseltine's challenge to Margaret Thatcher as the Tory Left provoked the war of Hezza's chopper.

In January 1986 Heseltine walked out of the Cabinet in protest at being unable, he claimed, to put the case for the Westland helicopter firm merging with a European consortium in preference to the American Sikorsky firm. He was to develop his protectionism while on the back benches, arguing in words that appealed to members in West Midlands marginals that the British car industry should stay out of foreign clutches. The depth of Heseltine's attachment to British ownership of British firms did not stop him welcoming BMW's take-over of Rover in 1994, but in 1986, when Thatcher prevented him making his case to the Cabinet on foreign control of our helicopters, it was a resigning matter.

In an effort to undermine Heseltine, a war of leaks and unattributable accusations was unleashed. Blame for the unauthorised disclosure of a law officer's letter designed to embarrass Heseltine lay, pretty clearly, with Number Ten, but the sacrifice of DTI secretary Leon Brittan and a forensically incompetent performance by Neil Kinnock in a censure debate saved the prime minister.

Michael Portillo saw Heseltine's resignation as more than a principled stand about the future of a West Country factory, but he was generous towards the man who had, just a year before, spoken on his hustings. At the time he said, 'I am sorry for Heseltine because I thought he was a very able Cabinet minister, but it is difficult to believe this is all about Westland. I suppose it is about a long-running personality clash between Mrs Thatcher and Heseltine. I just wonder why it has taken seven years.'

Many on the Tory Left sought to portray Heseltine as the champion of a muzzled Cabinet and hoped to paint Thatcher as a distant, wounded autocrat. Unsurprisingly, Portillo tried to reverse the image: 'There is only a small group of Heseltine supporters, and a very large number of those concerned about the damage done.'

Part of that damage was a reconstruction of the Cabinet which saw one interventionist enemy and one talented ally, Heseltine and Brittan, leave, to be replaced by another instinctive anti-Thatcherite, Malcolm Rifkind, and an ineffectual and un-ideological loyalist, Paul Channon. But the damage also went deeper in tarnishing Thatcher's image of invulnerability and providing a vigorous focus for opposition behind her. If she were to keep the insurgents at bay, her allies thought, she needed fighters around her. One of the schemes they hatched involved the advancement of Michael Portillo from back-bencher to bodyguard.

Throughout 1986, figures on the radical Right argued that Margaret Thatcher should have two PPSs. The PPS – parliamentary private secretary – is a minister's link to the back benches. The first rung on the ladder of promotion, the post carries no extra salary but PPSs are included on the government payroll and are considered, de facto, members of the administration.

For the first years of her premiership Mrs Thatcher had been supremely well-served as PPS by Ian Gow, who was utterly committed, ubiquitous and shrewd. His successor, Michael Alison, although also on the Right, was thought less sensitive to the nuances of parliamentary opinion, less active on his mistress's behalf and less in touch with her natural supporters. Rather than moving him and losing the asset of a trusted and experienced old hand, right-wing radicals wanted a younger Thatcherite appointed to provide a more energetic and committed link. Their man was Michael Portillo. It was, in the words of NTB member Michael Fallon, 'A straightforward right-wing plot to strengthen her position.'

Even though Portillo had only been in the house for just over a year, he was already in demand. He had acted as 'minder' for Matthew Carrington, the defeated Tory candidate in the April 1986 Fulham by-election, a sign that he was trusted not to trip up on a sensitive and very public platform. The new, and suitably Thatcherite, transport secretary John Moore wanted Portillo as his PPS and appointed him in July 1986. Moore had known Portillo from their time at the Department of Energy. They were good friends, and Moore was also positioning himself as a long-time successor to Thatcher. Portillo was his link to the new boys, the core of a future leadership electorate.

One back-bencher recalls Portillo adapting easily to the role of a minister's eyes and ears. Seldom an assertive figure over the muffins in the Pugin Room, he remained more a listener than a talker, but he was broadening his circle: 'When he first came in he'd spend all his time with extremists like Hamilton, Howarth and Forsyth. I think he realised he had to talk to more members.'

Portillo's sojourn with Moore was always meant to be brief. Over the summer, speculation about an autumn reshuffle grew and the prospect of Portillo becoming a second PPS for Margaret Thatcher was floated by his friends.

When Michael Alison read the rumours he exploded. With a display of passion in defence of his dignity greater than he was accustomed to deploy on behalf of his mistress, he threatened to resign if she appointed Portillo to 'assist' him. Sensitive to the damage such a move would inflict, Thatcher backed down.

Portillo took the rebuff on the chin. He told the *Daily Express*, with, given the origins of the rumour, delicate disingenuousness, 'I was flattered to see myself tipped for such a splendid job, but I never knew more than I read in the newspapers.'

But, blocked though she had been on this matter, Thatcher was not to be deflected from her main aim: the reconstruction of her government to favour the Right. Well-sourced stories in the early autumn had made it clear she wanted 'a major reallocation of middle-tier and junior ministerial posts'. Bob Dunn had had an effect.

The main reshuffle came in September and, despite heavy tipping, Portillo's name did not feature. That was because Thatcher had a better job in store. On 16 October 1986, just after the Tory conference but before Parliament resumed, Portillo entered the government as a junior whip. In the words of Sir Archie Hamilton, he had joined 'the Broederbond'.

The Tory Whips' Office has been compared, variously, to a superior school for future ministers, the secret service and the sewers. The mystery that surrounds the whips' work – fuelled by Michael Dobbs's fictional chief whip, Francis Urquhart, in *House of Cards*, and fanned by a BBC documentary that gave a tantalising glimpse of a system of blackmail, threats and informers – obscures the prosaic nature of much of the job. Whips are responsible, simply, for dispatching government business. They make sure legislation passes through Parliament on time and, as far as possible, intact. They additionally act as an information-gathering network, spotting talent, detecting trouble and developing a feel for the mood of the parliamentary party.

Each whip is given a group of MPs to monitor. According to Sir John Cope, deputy chief whip at the time, Portillo was responsible for London members. The whip's responsibility is to get to know his flock, communicate their worries to the top, develop an understanding of their passions, weaknesses and principles, and know how to pressure them into supporting the government when other factors might incline them to rebel.

Even at school Portillo had relished exercising a hold over others by winning their friendship, expending time and charm to make them feel special, and occasionally expressing his displeasure in such a way as to make the recipient yearn for the return of his favour and do anything to avoid losing it again. The late Sir Peter Morrison, Thatcher's PPS at the time of her fall, attested to the power of the full-force Portillo charm: 'He has the incredible ability to make the person he's talking to feel they're the only one he wants to talk to that decade. Others are quite jealous of him.'

That one-on-one ability made Portillo an effective, albeit junior, whip. He had responsibility for the progress of some legislation, but in the hierarchical world of the Whips' Office, with the chief whip in one room, the senior whips in another and the juniors at the bottom, he remained a lowly creature.

The chief whip at the time, John Wakeham, was, according to those who served under him, addicted to intrigue. One right-winger believes he sometimes deliberately let some situations become more complex and threatening because he took such pleasure in defusing them and thus consolidating his reputation as a 'Mr Fixit'. Sir Peter Lloyd, a whip at the time, suspects Wakeham's style was not entirely to Portillo's taste, believing that Portillo was fascinated by his feel for manipulating events but suspicious of his fondness for politics as a game. Portillo, he believes, saw politics less as an opportunity to relive life in a byzantine court and more as a matter of doing the right thing.

Whether or not Portillo appreciated Wakeham's approach, he gave the chief no cause for complaint. Lloyd recalls Portillo as 'Quiet, courteous and contained – a bright boy doing his time.'

The sense that Portillo was good at the job but not a whip to his fingertips is supported by Sir John Cope's memory: 'He was a useful member of the team. We always used the Whips' Office to bring in people who were likely to be promoted. He was brought into the office as one of those who wasn't likely to be a long-term whip but nevertheless would do a year or two as a whip and would be a better minister for it.' And not just any old minister: only weeks after Portillo's appointment, in an article that had the chief whip's fingerprints all over it, it was revealed that Portillo and his colleague Richard Ryder, appointed at the same time, were 'being deliberately groomed as future Cabinet ministers'.

Old hands argue that the best whips are not too attached to either wing of the party and should be interested more in the process of politics rather than the product – happier with gossip, intrigue, faction-play and expediting business than with discussing policy and exploring ideas. They cite Richard Ryder, who became chief whip in due course, as a model process member. Portillo was considered pre-eminently a product man, driven by the need to get the policy right. His stint in the Whips' Office was designed to help him get ahead by giving him an insight into the means required to pursue his ends.

One or two close to Portillo believe his interest in human motivation and his talent for bending people to his will would have made him a more natural whip than some allow. Tristan Garel-Jones, himself a former deputy chief whip, believes Portillo may be less of the purist ideologue, interested only in pushing through yet more radical legislation, than some think. 'Michael would have been, if his career had panned out a different way, a very good chief whip.' Other contemporaries remember Portillo's assessments of his members as shrewd and brief, and all of them thought him a team player. There was an expectation that he would stay for two years, but it was not to be.

The 1987 general election saw the Tories win another term and another 100-plus majority. In retrospect, with the economy booming, taxes tumbling and the opposition divided, victory was always obvious, but the professionalisation of the Labour campaign and tensions between Margaret Thatcher and her party chairman, Norman Tebbit, meant it was far from a smooth election.

For Michael Portillo, however, 1987 was a breeze compared to the by-election campaign. He had a house in the north of Enfield, had spent his first summer as an MP going walkabout throughout the constituency, and had a large and enthusiastic association.

Although his public bearing can sometimes seem a touch stiff – even haughty – Portillo's constituency profile was very different. As a new MP he happily posed for the cameras of his local papers in any pose they suggested. The undergraduate who was seldom seen without a tie was pictured break-dancing, sliding down a fireman's pole, decked out in party crowns, and modelling handmade Easter bonnets, smile fixed firmly in place.

Martin Summers, a researcher who has helped him with his constituency mail, claims Portillo genuinely enjoys these staged events. But, beyond that, he thinks Portillo is ideologically attached to the idea of constituency members and is strongly opposed to any weakening of the link between MPs and voters through proportional representation. But the attachment is more than abstract, according to Summers. Portillo has been active in pursuit of constituency casework, but never in a high-profile way. Blessed by never having had to champion his constituents' interests in defiance of government policy by arguing for factories threatened with closure or ancient hospitals facing merger, he has been a low-key advocate for his electorate.

Apart from lobbying long-term to improve the North Circular Road, which bisects the constituency, his most notable constituency campaign has been on behalf of a voter who suffered a miscarriage of justice. Enghin Raghip was one of three men found guilty of the murder of PC Keith Blakelock during a night of violence on the Broadwater Farm estate in nearby Tottenham in 1985. The most famous of those accused was Winston Silcott, a Tottenham greengrocer who already had a violent criminal record. In the aftermath of PC Blakelock's murder there was enormous pressure on the police to arrest the killers of their colleague. Silcott and Raghip were arrested and imprisoned against a background of widespread public outrage. It was only after the anger abated that the case against the men was seen to be so flimsy. Portillo was approached by Raghip's family, and, after assessing the evidence on its merits, agreed to fight for an appeal. After years of discreet lobbying, an appeal was allowed and Raghip was acquitted.

Many Tory MPs would have baulked at taking on the case, but, actuated by respect for the law, sympathy for victims of obvious injustice and a sense of duty towards his constituents, Portillo worked energetically for Raghip.

Portillo's attentiveness to Raghip's case is part of a broader sympathy he feels for Southgate. Portillo feels a sense of pride at representing a slice of middle England, and enjoys identifying with an area both naturally Conservative and entrepreneurial. There is also, Summers believes, something in Portillo, the former boy actor and student drama hack, that relishes the performance element in campaigning.

Portillo's election address was, like the man, glossy and assured. A four-page A4 colour sheet, it was designed to appeal to a variety of constituency interests, with snaps of the candidate in local hospitals and schools. The large Jewish vote was not neglected, with mention being made of Carolyn having visited Jewish refuseniks in Moscow and a prominent picture of the candidate meeting the most famous refusenik, Anatoly Shcharansky.

The message to the electors was simple: Vote Tory and you'll get strong defences, support for the police, low inflation and tax cuts. The temptation to vote for the Alliance, his main challengers, was presented as risking a dangerous step back to the days of the Lib–Lab pact and 'that awful winter of discontent'.

On a personal note Portillo paid tribute to the support of his wife, who had also 'managed to run a home and a career'. He also drew attention to their home in Enfield – the last time he was to do so. His message was superimposed on a montage of letters from grateful constituents and press clippings which chronicled his unhappiness with the level of the television licence fee and, in a nod to a large local population, his concern with the troubled affairs of Cyprus.

Portillo and his team eschewed detailed canvassing with the candidate, preferring the cavalcade method of whipping up interest pioneered by Tony Dey during the by-election. It worked handsomely. Portillo turned his slim majority of 4,711 into a thumping 18,345. It was an increase of nearly 16 per cent on the 15,819 Sir Anthony had won in 1983. The full result was:

Portillo, M.D.X. (Conservative)	28,445
Harvey, Nicholas (Liberal/Alliance)	10,100
Course, Richard (Labour)	9,114
Rooney, S. (Green)	696

The Southgate association had been confident and large enough to devote much of its time and energy to helping Portillo's neighbour, Ian Twinn, hang on to his ultra-marginal Edmonton seat, and their generosity paid off, helping secure an increase in Twinn's majority from 1,193 to 7,826.

Victory gave Margaret Thatcher an opportunity to reshuffle her administration again and to introduce a radical edge to departments hitherto insulated from change. During her first two terms the institutions of the Welfare State, in particular the NHS and social security, had not been fundamentally reformed. The temperamentally unshowy and deeply conservative Norman Fowler had resisted doing anything too dramatic as secretary of state at the DHSS for the previous six years. When Fowler published his memoirs, *Ministers Decide*, one who knew him commented, 'Yes – in his case to do fuck all.'

It was a somewhat harsh judgement. Fowler had done much to

simplify certain aspects of social security, not least in the 1986 act, and he was at least astute enough not to bite more off than he could chew. But Thatcher wanted to give the DHSS a more politicised feel, and so she appointed a new secretary of state, John Moore, and a new under-secretary with responsibility for social security, Michael Portillo. It was a post just vacated by another rising star, John Major, and once occupied by Thatcher herself.

It may have been a sign of favour to be made a minister, but the post was one of the worst jobs in the government – known as 'the letter-writing job' or 'minister for moaning minnies'. One of the main responsibilities was signing the replies to the thousands of highly specific queries which MPs addressed to the department on behalf of constituents. Hitherto these had been regarded as an unwelcome burden. Portillo, however, saw them as a golden opportunity to extend his power-base. Whereas before MPs were used to a curt civil-service draft with an inky scrawl at the bottom, they now got a personal, sometimes lengthy, always polite, Portillo postscript.

Whether it was a simple expression of hope that the foregoing helped, an enquiry after the member's own welfare, or a personal comment based on information gleaned as a whip, Portillo always wrote something himself. And members noticed. It was not only Tories who were so favoured, even Labour MPs got a simple little sign-off, but the series of very different notes to colleagues sent out one message: a man many thought a cold ideologue was both more human and a better politician than they might have allowed.

Those who have known Portillo since school believe his good manners are inborn. They remark on the correctness of his bearing even then, and on the old-world graciousness of his father which he inherited. Others compare his politeness with that of John Major, another talented boy from the suburbs keen to get on the inside track rather than rattle the bars from outside. Whether it was upbringing, class-consciousness, natural grace or cold calculation, it had its effect, and even those who had not liked the clever young Thatcherite when he first arrived confessed themselves disarmed by the time and care he took over their cases even as he was burdened by other administrative work.

While his boss was obsessed with larger matters, Portillo introduced all manner of detailed regulations to a complex system, replacing family income supplement with family credit and defending the accompanying harsh treatment of child benefit from the criticism of a concerned back-bencher, Virginia Bottomley. He also steered the 1988 Social Security Bill through committee. His experience as a whip was invaluable in this, and his principal Labour opponents, Margaret Beckett and Robin Cook, expressed respect for his political and technical ability even as they maintained a distaste for his policies.

One of the most controversial provisions of the bill was clause 4, the withdrawal of supplementary benefit from sixteen- and seventeen-year-olds. The move was defended by the government as an inducement for the young to take up places on a training scheme or stay in education if they could not get a job. It was slammed by Robin Cook, who argued, 'Competition among the clauses of the bill to see which may be regarded as the most objectionable is intense. However, when history makes its judgement on the bill it will be by clause 4 that it will be best remembered. The proposal is as lonely and friendless as any adolescent whom it will affect.'

Portillo was unmoved by the opposition's rhetoric, retorting, 'Labour believes an eighteen-year-old should collect as much benefit, never having worked, as a fifty-five-year-old with forty years' work behind him. We do not.' The clause was included unamended.

Portillo did not, however, go out of his way to cultivate an impression of flinty hard-heartedness. In debates on the disabled and pensioners Portillo has defended generous treatment for the unfortunate and, writing his first article for the *Sun*, in April 1988, he took pride in the increase in his budget, writing, 'If you believed everything you heard in the last few days you might think we were actually spending less on social security than before. This year, taxpayers will spend £48 billion on social security – that is £2 billion more than last year.'

Whatever might be thought of his policies, Portillo tried not to alienate any section of the House with an unfortunate manner at the despatch box. From his first speech on the front bench on 22 July 1987 onwards he has usually succeeded in showing courtesy to his opposite numbers, eschewing personal abuse and contenting himself with attacks on their arguments.

The delicacy of much of his work meant there was huge potential for embarrassment, but one civil servant at the DHSS at the time believes Portillo's attention to detail helped the department avoid several pitfalls. Useful though that was, she thinks it was not the biggest reason for his safe passage. She believes that, paradoxically, Portillo's best protection was the growing political weakness of his boss. Sensing John Moore was wounded, the opposition directed most of their fire on him, hoping for a kill.

Moore's rise and, more importantly, his fall have had a profound effect on Portillo. Like Portillo, Moore was a clever, charming, handsome and numerate Thatcherite from a humble direct-grant school. He had taken a shine to the younger man when they worked together under David Howell, and had given him his first post as PPS. Portillo repaid the loyalty, taking time as a junior minister to tour the lobbies and tea-rooms talking up his boss and gently rubbishing any speculation that Moore was on the slide.

Moore was an unlucky minister, but he was also an over-ambitious one. At one of his first Cabinets as secretary of state he outlined the massive extra expenditure his civil servants had told him was required on the NHS. Margaret Thatcher, disappointed that the man she had chosen to adopt a radical approach was brandishing the begging bowl, challenged him. His response was not impressive. He argued that he was not, er, ahem, actually asking for more money, just laying out the options as part of a technical exercise. Thatcher gave a fair impression of a basilisk before moving on.

Not abashed, Moore pressed on with his personal campaign. A series of adulatory profiles was discreetly arranged in the *Telegraph* and *Today*. Cooing over his looks, they charted his rise from working-class roots, and speculated on how much more attractively Thatcherism might be presented by this laughter-lined professional.

The most egregious of all the profiles was the work of Angela Levin in the *Mail on Sunday*. It was not an effective pitch for the vote of the average Tory MP, resentful at his lack of preferment and overfond of the solace provided by a palace with seventeen bars and a smoking-room. The cloying tone, the uxorious double-act by Moore and his wife, the holier-than-thou healthiness of the breakfast and exercise regimes described, the sheer shameless self-advertisement got up colleagues' noses, even among those on the Right who might have been well-disposed. When the article was published, there was an unseemly delight among many Tories that Mr Moore, the decaffeinated health minister, had been struck down with pneumonia.

When ill, the man who had delivered a speech entitled 'The NHS: Problems of Success' booked himself into a plush private hospital. A few weeks later, while Moore was recovering – physically if not politically – Willie Whitelaw fell ill. He used the NHS.

Aware that his career was coming to resemble his exercise bike – for all his hard work, he was getting nowhere – Moore nevertheless struggled back to his office early. But, with no faction and few roots, he was a political lone wolf, easily picked off.

His attempt to hype his talents and fitness for office had not been accompanied by any effort to cultivate a caucus of support on the back benches, and he had been careless of the few allies he might have had. His colleague at Energy, Norman Lamont, was one of many offended by Moore's habit of telling others how to do their jobs rather than just getting on with his own. His sponsor at Energy, who took him to the Treasury, Nigel Lawson, was far from delighted that Moore associated himself with many of his initiatives, dubbing himself 'Mr Privatisation'. Others in the Treasury had a shorter, and crueller, nickname.

Robin Cook had been making hay in his absence, raising fears about the horrors that the allegedly radical Moore might be plotting to inflict on the NHS he could not be bothered to use. Moore returned to face an opposition-day debate early in 1988, but his voice had not yet fully returned and he croaked through an unconvincing defence of his position. In the *Daily Telegraph*, Nicholas Comfort summed up the state of opinion on the back benches: 'Some Tories are pleading, "Say something, even if it's only goodbye."'

Portillo was one of those who, loyal to the last, believed Moore could recover, but a few months later Thatcher humiliated Moore by splitting his department in two, handing over responsibility for Health to Kenneth Clarke, and leaving Moore in the ghetto of Social Security.

A journalist who was lunching with Portillo at the time remembers the junior minister asking what had gone wrong. The lessons were obvious, and have lingered. Moore had seemed to want to take the credit for others' efforts, had sought to curry favour at the top, and had spent little time building up a faction of supporters in the Commons, let alone the country. He had taken over a department and promised much without any very clear idea of what to do or any strategy for reform. And, above all, he had sought, like an American presidential candidate, to use the press and details about his personal life to present himself as the Coming Man.

Portillo has been determined not to repeat those mistakes. As a deputy he was wise enough not to step on others' shoes, even when he had to bite his lip. He has been assiduous in building up a circle of like-minded members on the back benches and sufficient appeal to activists in the country to insulate him from temporary squalls. He has been careful to make no extravagant promises and has, most of the time, made careful tracking of departmental work his top priority.

Perhaps most importantly, he has kept the press at a distance. There have been any number of Portillo profiles written, but none has been solicited. A willingness to make himself available to broadcasters to defend the party line has been balanced by an absolute unwillingness to be interviewed about anything other than his job and his vision. Having seen what happened to John Moore, Portillo has no wish to reveal what he has at breakfast. It may result in an impression of a dry, cool, detached politician afraid to show a more human side, but one close ally thinks it is more than just prudence. David Hart believes Portillo has a profound distaste for the appeal of the superficial as well as a keen awareness of how image manipulation can backfire. Portillo understands that his appearance will inevitably affect how he's judged, and he takes care with it, but he sees no need to tailor, or advertise, any other part of his life.

Portillo was sorry to see Moore brought low, but as his star faded so Portillo's was more firmly in the ascendant.

He had charmed the civil servants with whom he worked. Every birthday of even the lowliest clerk was always remembered and marked. He was particularly close to his private secretary, Caroline Rookes, a woman unlike the standard civil-service blue-stocking. Considered attractive and strong-willed, with none of the public-school polish of other private-office high-fliers, she was not a natu-

ral ally, but another civil servant at the time remembers her and
Portillo getting on so well that baseless office gossip started to
spread. They travelled to America together to investigate com-
puterisation of social-security administration – a reform Portillo
subsequently initiated.

The effective working relationship he struck up with Rookes is
typical of a number of the alliances Portillo has formed during his
career. Carolyn and Margaret Thatcher are not the only strong
women in his life. He is still close to a former researcher, Angela
Casey, who is now MD of Government Policy Consultants, a
public-affairs firm, and two of the most important women in his
working life are his constituency secretary, Clemency Ames, and
his special adviser, Alison Broom. Ames worked for Sir Anthony
Berry but has transferred her loyalty completely; Broom has a
background in local government and lobbying and first worked as
Portillo's adviser at the Department of the Environment. Like
Casey, they are strong, self-disciplined women whom Portillo trusts
and whose advice he respects. Broom and Casey often join Portillo
for a glass of champagne to celebrate small successes and review
progress. Casey, Broom and Ames often go out together for a drink,
and have dubbed themselves 'The Portillo Bureau'.

Rookes was very much in the mould of the strong and self-
confident women whose company Portillo appreciates, but she was
not the only one in his private office who grew to appreciate their
minister. Portillo worked efficiently but not overearnestly, once
joking with his private office about having to face the new Bristol
South Labour MP Dawn Primarolo, claiming he found her so
attractive he would be unable to deal toughly with the baby
Bennite. The mix of hard work and humour charmed his civil
servants so comprehensively that on his own birthday Portillo
arrived to find his office decked out in bunting.

Portillo left when the DHSS was broken up in July 1988. His
private office was not the only place where his work had won
female admirers: Margaret Thatcher wanted to do just what she
had done with John Major and pitchfork Portillo straight from the
DHSS into the Cabinet. The whips were against it. Some thought
it would only harm him to accelerate his promotion; others thought
he simply did not deserve it. Portillo himself did not expect any

dramatic rise, but he did harbour hopes of a leg-up from under-secretary to minister of state.

On the night that Thatcher put the finishing touches to her reshuffle her political secretary, John Whittingdale, was a guest of the Portillos at their Victoria flat. Carolyn Portillo badgered him to spill the beans, but all he could do was hint that her fears that her husband might be on his way to Northern Ireland might be misplaced. While the Portillos might have found his discretion and loyalty frustrating that night, the impression that he could be trusted with a confidence lingered.

Portillo was told about his promotion the next day. Knowing it would, perhaps, have been a step too far, Thatcher did not put him into the Cabinet, but she did give him a department to run: in July 1988 he was appointed minister of state at the Department of Transport – the youngest minister of state in the government. He was officially number two to the secretary of state, Paul Channon, but in reality, as Thatcher knew, he was the man meant to turn around a department adrift.

Since Nicholas Ridley had left in 1986 the department had had two secretaries of state, Moore and Channon, but no leader. Morale among the civil servants was low, and scarcely helped by a spate of accidents, such as the fire at King's Cross, which contributed to Channon's misery. The bad luck was exploited by Labour's transport spokesman, John Prescott, who made much of Channon's fondness for holidaying with Princess Margaret on Mustique while the infrastructure cracked and frayed at the edges. The accidents were certainly unfortunate, he said, but not simple Acts of God. Rather, Tory penny-pinching had made safety a low priority and put passengers at risk.

One civil servant who was unhappy with Channon's style remembers an instant difference with Portillo. On their first meeting Portillo was modest enough to introduce himself – imagining the official would not know who he was – and was switched on enough to know just who his subordinate was, what his job entailed and the length of time he had been doing it. The official was also aware that Portillo had definite ideas about what he wanted to do. He suspects that Portillo might have preferred a job at a more prestigious department, rather than going to the concrete stump at the bottom of Marsham Street staffed by the civil servants the neighbouring Department of the Environment did not want. But if Portillo had such fears they were mitigated by the chance to make a difference and then banished as he got to grips with transport policy.

Portillo's principal private secretary on arrival was an official called Steve Bramall. He expected a capable minister, but he was not prepared for the reaction from Portillo's former private office at the DHSS, who were 'in a state of high emotion' at having lost him. He also recalls Portillo arriving with a clear agenda, dedicated to privatising and deregulating in every area of the department. Bramall was impressed with the access Portillo enjoyed to the Number Ten Policy Unit and the prime minister's political secretary, and by the care he took in formulating a coherent policy package in common with Number Ten. It was a degree of direction the department had been missing, and civil servants from other parts of the department soon came to Portillo for policy steers, bypassing the secretary of state.

As Portillo grew to recognise the scale of the task so he also became more determined not to be distracted by the petty problems of junior office. One civil servant recalls Portillo's first public engagement being the opening of the hundred and fiftieth refurbished railway arch sold to a small business. After hours spent travelling there and back for a photo-call, he informed the official who had arranged it, 'I hope I don't have to pose next to any other brick walls while I'm here.' He didn't.

Instead he set to work on several massive policy problems. Economic growth was tearing ahead, and, although inflation was poised to return, most voters were enjoying greater prosperity than ever before. Political attention was focusing on 'quality-of-life' issues, the Greens were scooping protest votes by channelling concern about the environment, and no environmental issue was more important, especially for the Tory-voting commuters of the South-East, than transport.

Portillo's main tasks were to lay the ground for British Rail privatisation, press ahead with deregulation at home and in the air over Europe, prepare for the Channel Tunnel, solve the transport problems of London in general and Docklands in particular, and cope with a number of niggling worries – not least the future of

England's most picturesque but least profitable railway line, from Settle to Carlisle.

Solving London's transport problems would have posed problems at any time. Having to cope with the needs of what was meant to be a new city growing out of the dereliction beyond the East End made it all the worse. Margaret Thatcher had, famously, made saving 'the inner cities' the crusade of her third term on the night she won the 1987 election, and Docklands was the most high-profile redevelopment the government faced.

The transport needs of Docklands had been ill thought-out. The roads east were inadequate, and the one new public-transport development, the Docklands Light Railway, was seen as a clockwork carrier, more suitable for a Swiss resort than for the fastest-growing commercial zone in Europe.

The centrepiece of the *Drang nach Osten* was to be Canary Wharf, the skyscraper being built by the Canadian property tycoons the Reichmann brothers, rising from the mudflats at the mouth of the Isle of Dogs. Portillo was attracted by plans outlined by the Reichmanns' company, Olympia & York, to extend the Bakerloo tube line eastwards to Canary Wharf, but he ran into departmental opposition. He believed the Reichmanns' investment had to be protected and the quicker progress was made the better. Civil servants felt that transport policy could not be dictated by a single company, no matter how big or influential, and demanded an inquiry to ensure the best route was chosen and accountability to the public was preserved.

Portillo fought, but he could not overcome the internal inertia. In the end he had to relent, and he set up what became known as the East London Rail Study. After long deliberation it recommended the extension of the Jubilee Line.

Portillo was not instinctively in sympathy with massive public works – in every other area he was deeply sceptical about spending taxpayers' money on 'prestige projects' – but he had a job to do, ensuring the prime minister and her Canadian favourites got the links they needed. His loyalty to her meant that even though he was frustrated in his preferred plan he supported the eventual solution. Years later, when he was at the Treasury and Margaret Thatcher in the Lords, he took a different view.

The Treasury was always sceptical about the cost of the extension of the Jubilee Line, even though the Reichmanns were putting up hundreds of millions of their own money to bankroll the project, and in 1989 the then chief secretary Norman Lamont tried hard to block it. Halfway through the whole process Channon had been replaced by Portillo's old friend and former boss, Cecil Parkinson. Parkinson prided himself on his hands-on business experience and invited Paul Reichmann over from Canada to sway Lamont.

On the morning of 15 November, the day the Treasury's Autumn Statement was due to be made, Reichmann and Parkinson met at dawn. After hard bargaining, Reichmann made clear he could offer no more than £400 million to support the project. This was a figure the Treasury had already rejected, and when Lamont met Parkinson at noon he still refused to give the scheme the go-ahead, agreeing only to talk things over again that night at Number Ten. Knowing this was his last chance, Parkinson ordered Portillo, the man who knew the arguments best, to cut short a ministerial visit to Bristol and be ready to do battle with Lamont.

When they met that night in Downing Street, Thatcher listened to all the arguments before turning to Lamont, a career politician who had spent a few years in the City between acting as a Cabinet aide and entering the House at a by-election. With her first question to Lamont she made it clear whose side she was on: 'Norman, you have never made any money, have you?' Parkinson made the announcement the next day. Portillo had helped win the argument, but the attack that deflated Lamont could so easily have been flung at him.

The insensitivity of officials had delayed a decision on Canary Wharf, and their inability to understand the broader political context in which they were operating took some overcoming. Bramall also remembers Portillo being driven to distraction by the dithering of British Rail over the route for the Channel Tunnel and their inability to appreciate the political cost of the delay in choosing a route through Kent.

He even ran into trouble with his boss. Cecil Parkinson was an old friend, but that did not prevent them falling out over policy. Portillo wanted the Channel Tunnel's north-London terminal to exploit derelict land behind King's Cross. One of the lessons of Docklands, according to Portillo, was that rail routes were always inadequate unless the road links were in place first. If the rest of the country was to benefit from a new Channel Tunnel terminal at King's Cross/St Pancras then a redevelopment of the roads to the north of the terminal was required. Plans for this had already been drawn up by a group previously set up in the DoT by Nicholas Ridley to 'think the unthinkable'. They would have meant some disruption to the 'quality of life' in marginal seats but a clear long-term benefit.

When Portillo outlined his plans to Parkinson, his boss spelt out the potential unpopularity of what he proposed. Parkinson still remembers his junior's response: 'We weren't elected to do what is popular. We were elected to do what's right.'

The same principle guided Portillo's approach to another problem he had inherited – the future of London's taxis. A study had been commissioned, just as Portillo arrived, into the future of the capital's black cabs. The black-cab drivers were furious, and the DoT received over 600 letters of protest about the study.

As a free-marketeer, Portillo was against the restrictions the black-cab drivers had erected to limit competition. Under laws dating back to 1847, the only drivers allowed to tout for custom on London's streets were those licensed by the Hackney Carriage Office after passing a test of their familiarity with the capital's routes – 'The Knowledge'. Portillo wanted to free the roads and allow minicabs to compete, subject to appropriate licensing, hoping to bring down prices and bring under the umbrella of light regulation the burgeoning trade in unlicensed minicabs.

Portillo planned to reform not only London's cabs but what he saw as the overregulated provincial taxi trade. He told the *Sunday Times*, 'I strongly disapprove of local authorities who distort competition and the free market by rationing the number of licences that they issue.'

The radical back-bencher who had taken on the lobbying machine of a powerful monopoly like British Gas in order to promote competition was not afraid of taking on another vested interest. But, while the principles were consistent, the politics were not. Taking on nationalised industries is one thing; attacking the privileges of a caste of C2s who have daily contact with MPs and journalists is quite another.

When Portillo's plans reached the ears of the rest of the government there was a near riot. He was called in to see the whips.

One of them recalls, 'We asked him, "Do you really want to be responsible for the headline 'Portillo abolishes Knowledge'?"'

Even more horrified than the whips was the prime minister. Margaret Thatcher's Finchley constituency was home to many of London's cabbies, and she was sensitive to the worries of working-class entrepreneurs whose instincts in so many areas chimed with her own. After a short interview with the prime minister, Portillo shelved his plans. Proposals leaked to the *Sunday Times* were binned and, not for the first or the last time, he was forced, against his own instincts, to execute a U-turn. The screeching of brakes was heard all over Whitehall and his reputation for political nous suffered a set-back.

To have outflanked Mrs Thatcher on the ideological Right took either rare radicalism or questionable political judgement. A more experienced minister would have been unlikely to go so far in trying to reform a popular service in the name of purism. Every MP knew what Portillo had planned, and his climbdown was seen by some as proof that he had been overpromoted. However, while the reverse might have harmed his reputation for low-profile efficiency, it did confirm him in the eyes of the flintier right-wingers as a man of near-adamantine principle.

Although frustrated in these areas, Portillo did get his way in others. As the activist minister in the department – and one with a mission to bring the market to a sheltered area – there was still much to do, and he was prepared to intervene vigorously in the interests of promoting a more commercial approach, justifying the sullied means by the purist end.

He influenced fare structures to nudge them towards market-sensitivity, and, according to one civil servant, impressed his colleagues by doing so in a way that would limit the pain in politically sensitive areas. The same civil servant also remembers Portillo acting on one occasion in a less ideological and much more political fashion, taking minute care in calculating London Underground's tariffs. The member for Southgate was apparently happy to adopt a quite interventionist approach in deciding what his constituents would have to pay on the Piccadilly Line.

But in every other area of policy his attachment to free-market principles was as marked as the energy he deployed in getting his way. Civil servants satisfied that deregulation had gone far enough were at first politely and then firmly told to go much further. One civil servant recalls Portillo's junior minister, Peter Bottomley, who was an enthusiast for regulation in the interests of road safety, having several schemes gently decommissioned.

On British Rail, Portillo encouraged a more competitive structure as preparation for privatisation, presiding over the sell-off of the company's engineering arm, BREL, and also improving the quality of the food by opening up on-board catering to tender.

He resisted demands for state subsidy of the Channel Tunnel fast link. An effective lobbying campaign drew unfavourable comparisons between the carriages trundling along Kent's ageing track and the speed with which French trains sped through the Pas de Calais. The case for state spending to upgrade the link was pressed by a coalition of transport 'experts', south-eastern Tory MPs and the opposition, but Portillo stood firm. He believed BR should be weaned off subsidy and be prepared to compete with other transport providers. He told a Kent County Council conference on the regional consequences of the Channel Tunnel that 'The argument that the tax-payer should subsidise rail services through the tunnel, regardless of the level of demand for such services, is groundless. We believe that BR are taking the right way forward, planning to meet the demonstrated, commercially viable needs of those wishing to travel.'

Portillo's hostility to subsidising the rail network led some critics to believe he was a prisoner of the department's powerful road lobby, but, according to Steve Bramall, Portillo was keen to submit road transport to the most rigorous commercial pressure possible. He pressed for the shadow tolling of roads to see if road use could be rationed by price, and tried to make road-building more a matter of market demand than government diktat, encouraging private finance with the publication of the consultation document *New Roads by New Means*.

It was a common complaint that the *laissez-faire* approach of the department during Portillo's period was no substitute for a properly 'coordinated' transport policy, with the government designing, and investing in, the most appropriate ways of getting from A to B, avoiding messy duplication of services and 'getting Britain moving'. On a pragmatic level, Portillo defused the attack by pointing to activity in solving the problems of the state's main transport responsibility, British Rail, and the level of money spent on investment. In an opposition-initiated debate on 7 February 1989 he ran through a series of investments from the £720 million modernisation of the London Underground's Central Line to the purchase of 158 new Sprinter expresses for the provinces.

But trading statistics was only one tactic. Portillo preferred to fight a battle of ideas instead of a numerical war of attrition. The mind-set of advocates of a 'coordinated' transport policy was totally alien to him. When he worked at the Department of Energy he had believed the best energy policy was to liberalise the market and allow a proper price structure to govern decisions about energy use. It would be futile to imagine that the decisions of a government department, however wise, would be more sensitive to fluctuations in supply than the myriad decisions taken in market-places every day. The best conservation policy was the ingenuity of entrepreneurs forced to look elsewhere as economic laws forced up the price of scarce resources. According to Steve Bramall the same approach governed his analysis of transport policy – any attempt to favour rail over road would distort the rational decisions of travellers. The cleanest, quickest, most efficient way of moving people and goods would emerge from the market.

Cecil Parkinson tells the story of Enoch Powell asking to see him shortly after his appointment as transport secretary and arguing that 'One should never underestimate the ability of the public to make sensible choices provided that they are given a sensible range of options.' This was also, unsurprisingly, Portillo's view.

Portillo accepted that there were problems as a result of pursuing a *laissez-faire* policy, but they were often the problems of success. He argued that congestion – a growing problem in the late eighties – was a consequence of economic growth. It was evidence of the success of Tory policies in revitalising the economies of large cities and would, in itself, encourage the exploration of alternative routes and locations. It was a point Portillo made in the House: 'Congestion in Central London . . . came about because of an unprecedented reversal in the long-term declining trend of commuting to London. The economy in our capital has prospered, and London has proved to be still one of the most magnetic cities for international business.'

The free-market case was, according to its advocates, not just bolstered by economic principles but historically rooted. Britain acquired more miles of waterway and railway per square mile of its territory in the eighteenth and nineteenth centuries than any of its competitors, through the vigour of capital rather than the efforts of the state. For the radical Right, the answer to transport problems was the withdrawal of government rather than the extension of its powers.

Portillo successfully applied that analysis to one area of the transport market where Britain's deregulatory principles were having an effect beyond its shores. The European aviation network was one of the most constricted markets in the world, as countries, attached to their own airlines as a matter of national pride, sought to protect them by rigging prices. The privatisation of British Airways, where Portillo's eldest brother worked, had rippled through the airline industry and increased pressure for deregulation, and in autumn 1989 Portillo conducted a series of negotiations to liberalise Europe's air routes as part of the preparations for the 1992 single European market. Although he had to accept a three-year delay before full implementation of his policy, he got his way.

It was his first experience of negotiating in Europe, and he found success oddly easy – confessing, 'Countries with more restrictive air-transport regimes mounted surprisingly little resistance to the new measures.' It was not always going to be that way.

Portillo's efforts across the board, however, were frustrated, as so many transport ministers' have been, by a series of disasters. The horrific loss of life in the sinking of the *Herald of Free Enterprise* and the King's Cross fire had overshadowed the efforts of Paul Channon. While Portillo was at Transport there were rail crashes in Glasgow and at Clapham, where thirty-five were killed. Forty-seven died in the Kegworth air crash, and 270 at Lockerbie.

One official remembers Portillo staring straight ahead, the morning after one disaster, drained of his usual energy. Portillo turned to him, almost beseechingly, and said, 'I feel quite helpless.' The official was struck then by 'a sense of commitment different to most ministers'.

One thing Portillo could do was tighten airport security, and colleagues were bawled out by an irate Portillo when breaches in Heathrow's security were exposed by investigative reporting.

There was one disaster, in particular, that put Portillo in the public eye. The *Marchioness* was a Thames pleasure-boat which revellers could hire for a party with a difference, drinking and dancing while water-borne. On the night of 19 August 1989 the *Marchioness* collided with another boat, the *Bowbelle*. In the confusion, many of the party-goers – photographers, agents and models, with haunting, young and beautiful faces – were drowned. Both Cecil Parkinson and Margaret Thatcher were abroad, so it fell to Portillo to represent the government in a climate where a succession of disasters had given the opposition sticks with which to beat the government.

His calm and grave demeanour, on the scene and in the House, impressed. Portillo had had television outings before – including an early *Question Time* appearance with an up-and-coming Labour MP called Tony Blair – but the grace with which he handled a difficult situation, on main news bulletins, *Breakfast Time* and *Newsnight*, marked him out as a communicator who could be trusted in a government, then as now, with its full complement of gaffe-prone ministers.

But if he was developing a reputation as a smooth broadcaster, Portillo was also determined to get known as a hard one. One official recalls Portillo's behaviour during a pre-recorded interview with a BBC reporter, designed to secure a short clip for inclusion in a longer report. The reporter asked a series of questions on the Channel Tunnel high-speed rail link, all of which were essentially the same question in a different guise, in an effort to provoke a slip. Portillo responded in exactly the same way each time, with an even temper and a wry smile.

After twenty minutes the tape ran out and as a new one was installed Portillo expressed his irritation that time was being wasted. The reporter apologised and promised they would move on. When the cameras started rolling again the same line of questioning was resumed. The official foresaw the worst and closed his eyes, imagining that Portillo would stalk off. Then he heard Portillo repeating his answer with the same modulated tones he had employed when first asked half an hour before.

This is not a technique peculiar to Portillo – any reporter who has interviewed Tony Blair or Gordon Brown with a view to securing a short clip will know how difficult it is to get them to express themselves in a different way throughout the interview, especially if they have just been talking to Peter Mandelson. It is an approach only the tough-minded can use effectively, and it prevents wilful misinterpretation, but it is not calculated to endear the interviewee to the press.

Endearing himself to the press was, however, not among Portillo's priorities while at the DoT. He was civil to the lobby, and had his friends on certain papers, but did not seek the limelight with the energy of other junior ministers. It was perhaps just as well, given the dangers of early over-exposure, because he was shortly to be thrust from a post vital in policy terms, but still relatively low-profile, into the toughest job in government.

During his time at the Department of Transport, Portillo had sought to revitalise an area of government that had been unglamorous, unlucky and under indifferent direction. He set in train a host of policy initiatives, trying to liberalise transport and lend policy coherence.

His record was not unblemished. Support for the Jubilee Line extension could be seen as an expensive departure from free-market orthodoxy. His attachment to the same orthodoxy when it came to London's cabs betrayed a lack of political feel. But, in the eyes of his civil servants, Portillo had, at a difficult time, restored the morale of a neglected corner of Whitehall. Steve Bramall comments, 'I regard the whole experience of working for him as a period of fascination – watching a politician operate with immense charm and vision. He was completely in control, unbelievably bright, very demanding and conscientious. Even the Labour members of his private office would have voted for him.'

That high opinion was shared across Whitehall, as the spring reshuffle of 1990 was to prove.

The issue of the moment was local-government finance. Future historians may look at the last days of Margaret Thatcher and wonder that the manner in which citizens pay for rubbish collection and libraries should have brought down the woman who saw off Gilmour and Galtieri, Scargill and the Soviets. But it was the reform of local taxation that provoked Tory councillors in Cabinet ministers' constituencies to resign the whip, forced the solid citizenry of Tunbridge Wells on to the streets in protest, and led to a riot in the heart of London which culminated in scenes of lawless anarchy unlike any witnessed in recent history.

The community charge – the poll tax – was, Thatcher proclaimed, the 'flagship' of her third term. An attempt to fundamentally reform the old rating system, which was thought to discriminate against Tory voters, it became a focus of opposition, internal and external, to her government.

In early 1990 the situation seemed critical. A complex web of exemptions, reliefs and reviews had done nothing to mitigate the unpopularity of the flat-rate tax. Local authorities had smuggled in spending rises with the new tax, making a nonsense of government estimates of what levels would be. The minister responsible, David Hunt, had taken heavy flak, and it was thought he deserved a respite. The retirement of the Welsh secretary, Peter Walker, gave the Welsh-born Hunt a chance to enter the Cabinet.

Just before the reshuffle, the whips met, as was their custom, to review the talent available to replace Hunt. The then chief whip, David Waddington, asked his colleagues who was the best-equipped minister at that level in the government – minister of state. Most agreed there was one obvious candidate: Portillo. However, one right-winger dissented, for his own reasons. According to Michael Fallon, himself on the Right, another whip on the Right who was a friend of Portillo's tentatively suggested that putting Portillo so young into such a sensitive post might not be good for his career. Waddington exploded, saying, 'I don't care what it will do for his career. If he's the best he'll do the job.'

Portillo's appointment was floated in the final week of April and confirmed in the first week of May. He took over on 4 May, the day after the local-government elections.

The previous few weeks had been a momentous time for the tax, and for Margaret Thatcher.

On Saturday 31 March agitators had turned an anti-poll-tax demonstration in Trafalgar Square, one of the largest displays of public feeling these islands have seen, into a violent riot. There had been disturbances before during Thatcher's premiership – in Brixton, Bristol and Liverpool in the early eighties, and at Orgreave during the miners' strike – but this was something different. The sight of Trafalgar Square disfigured by violent pitched battles, shops in Soho looted, and bricks, bottles, fire-extinguishers and oil drums flung at police officers less than a mile from Parliament was supremely shocking.

A month later the Tories suffered heavy losses in the local elections. From an already low base after poor results in 1986, hundreds of Conservative seats were swept away. But that was not the
message that Margaret Thatcher heard, for, on the same day that
Tories in shires and cities across the nation were losing their seats,
there was also a rout in London – but this time of Labour councillors.

In Wandsworth and Westminster, the two authorities with the
lowest level of poll tax in England, there was a Tory landslide.
Knife-edge majorities were turned into safe ones, and in Wandsworth, where it once controlled all the parliamentary seats, Labour
was driven into a tiny Tooting redoubt. The ripples also reached
other boroughs, and a cost-cutting low-poll-tax Tory group took
over Ealing, the London suburb that was home to Labour leader
Neil Kinnock.

The Tory chairman, Kenneth Baker, had spent election night
on the phone to tabloid editors talking up the significance of the
London results. The Wandsworth and Westminster Tory leaders
were trenchant communicators who argued that the poll tax was
a vote-winner because it brought home to every elector the cost of
socialism. The next day's headlines and news bulletins were therefore dominated by a significant, but highly unrepresentative, set
of results. When Baker, notorious for his ever-present grin, was
tackled by a reporter who asked him why he was so pleased with
himself when it was Neil Kinnock who had woken up with more
good news to smile at, he shot back, 'Of course Mr Kinnock's
smiling – he woke up in Tory-controlled Ealing, so he'll face a
sharp cut in his poll tax.'

The results were capable of giving comfort to both the supporters
and the opponents of the tax. In high-spending Labour areas and
low-spending Tory authorities there had been a swing to the
Tories. But in areas where the message was muddied by high-
spending Tory councils or efficient Labour ones the national swing
to Labour had been stronger. The effect was clearer in areas where
there was only one council tier, like London, than in much of the
rest of the country, where the impact of a split between Labour
counties and Tory districts led to confusion.

In May 1990, before the poll tax had really begun to bring home
the electoral costs of inefficiency, *The Economist* concluded, 'Judged

by its first outing in England and Wales the poll tax could yet achieve the principal aim for which it was designed . . . It does look likely that the poll tax was taken by a sizeable number of voters as a reliable guide to the efficiency and competence of the local council.' But the massive losses in many areas worried fractious back-benchers. Labour was well ahead in the polls, and headline poll-tax figures still seemed far too high in too many areas. A review was promised following the local results, and Portillo was now put in charge.

The hope that the review might presage radical reform, or even abandonment, of the tax was seized on by Michael Heseltine, his nostrils flaring on the back benches as he scented blood. A week after Portillo took office Heseltine published an article in *The Times* calling for a battery of changes to soften the tax's blow. The most crucial of these was banding according to income – a policy advanced earlier in the eighties by Heseltine's lieutenant, Michael Mates. According to Tony Travers, Andrew Adonis and David Butler in their study of the poll tax, *Failure in British Government*, it was a well-aimed shot across the bow of the Thatcher flagship: 'The abolition of the poll tax in its existing guise was all but declared, despite his protestations to the contrary.'

The Cabinet spent much of late spring reviewing the options. There was press speculation about possible change, and on 22 May Portillo told the House of Commons that he was 'listening' to critics. But anyone who expected radical change was to be disappointed. Margaret Thatcher was very anxious to improve the tax, but she did not believe it was fatally flawed. She thought the problem lay with the councils.

Her answer was to centralise control of council spending. According to her memoirs, she was keen to cap all excessive local-authority spending. This might drive a Chieftain tank through the accountability argument, but it was the only way to prevent the merits of the tax being obscured by high-spending authorities. In her memoirs she argues an earlier and more vigorous control of council expenditure should have been tried:

The conclusion I draw is that whatever reform was chosen, we should have accompanied it with draconian restraints on local government spending from the centre in order to prevent local authorities – alas

Conservative as well as Labour – from using the transition to jack up spending and blame it on the Government.

While wrangling went on behind the scenes on how wide the government's capping powers were, Portillo moved to dispel doubt about the future of the tax. At a meeting of the Association of District Councils in Harrogate on 29 June he made it clear he had come not to bury the poll tax but to praise it. In a speech *The Times* called 'uncompromising', he spelt out that the Cabinet review was aimed at ironing out 'anomalies'. Sweeping reform, Heseltine-style, was not on the agenda. 'What we are not doing is looking at root and branch changes to the community-charge system. The basic principle of the charge is that almost every adult should make a contribution to the cost of local services. There is no intention to change that.'

One former civil servant who saw a lot of him at the time believes the speed with which Portillo became acquainted with the complexity of the legislation did not blind him to its many faults, and, according to one friend, Portillo had his worries about the chances of the tax's survival. But, as with Canary Wharf, he allowed his loyalty to the leader who had brought him to the verge of the Cabinet to obscure any doubts he may have had.

Portillo's skill in grasping detail was in contrast to the more broad-brush approach taken by his boss, the environment secretary, Chris Patten. Patten had moved Right since he was Portillo's superior at the Conservative Research Department, but he was still not on Portillo's ideological wavelength. Nevertheless their personal relationship was cordial and the division of responsibilities was clear. It was to become clear to many on the Right that Patten was keen to ditch the tax, but at the time he worked hard to make it more palatable, fighting for more money at Cabinet level and negotiating capping criteria with the prime minister. Portillo dealt with the detail and sold the tax in public.

Over the summer, agitation died down, even though Labour's lead in the polls stayed stubbornly high. The Right suspected the tax was bedding down. Scots Tories – even moderates like Ian Lang – thought the tax could work, and reported a decline in non-payment. Their case had been bolstered by Scottish chairman Michael Forsyth's savage assault on Labour's 'roof-tax' proposals.

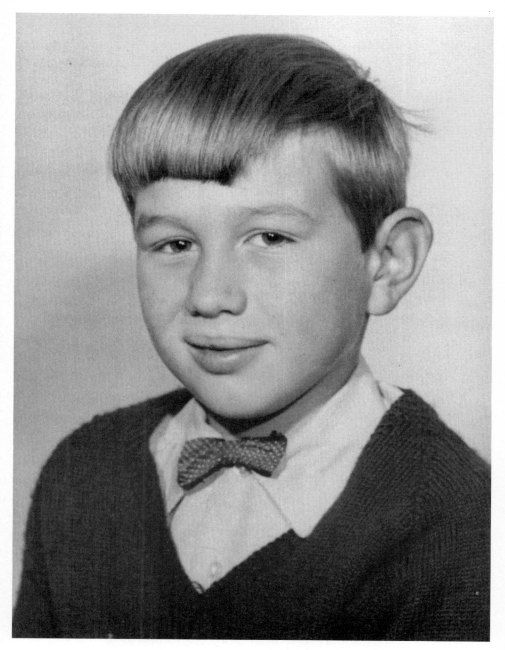

Michael Portillo, about eight years old (© Cora Portillo).

The Portillo family in 1959 at home in Stanmore. Top, left to right: Jolyon Cora, Justin, Luis, Michael and Charles, lying on the ground. Bottom, left to right: Michael, Jolyon, Justin, Charles and Cora (both © Cora Portillo)

Michael with a cart-load of Spanish holiday
playmates in Cantalapiedra (© Cora Portillo).

On holiday in 1963 on the beach at Ventnor,
Isle of Wight (© Cora Portillo).

A talented young generation at Harrow County School for Boys. Michael
Portillo is in the middle row, fourth from the right; on his right is Clive
Anderson. Nigel Scheinwald is in the back row, fourth from the left; Francis
Matthews is on his right; Matthew de Lange is in the middle row, sixth from
the right.

Portillo plays hookey in Paris, 1971 (© Matthew de Lange).

In the sixth form dressed with senior prefect's bands at Harrow County Grammar School, Michael is seated third from the right. Matthew Francis is standing second from the right and the master in charge is Bernard Marchant (© Bernard Marchant).

As a student visiting then-girlfriend Ann Moses in Zermatt during the Christmas vacation with Simon Marquis, in his final year at Cambridge, 1974 (© Bill Baker).

Summery student days, June 1975 – en route from Cambridge to Audley End are, back row from left, Michael Portillo, Simon Marquis, J. M. T. Ambrose, front row from left, M. N. P. Ramsay, ?, Trevor Woolley (© Bill Baker).

The graduation photograph in Peterhouse Old Court. With Michael Portillo is
Simon Marquis (© Bill Baker).

December 1984: Michael and Carolyn Portillo acknowledge their supporters after winning the Enfield Southgate by-election (Press Association).

Outside the Houses of Parliament in 1984 with his father Luis on his arm.

A call was made on you today — sorry you were out. If you have a problem, please do not hesitate to contact me on 360 2210.

Michael Portillo

MICHAEL PORTILLO

Published by A. Dey, 814 Green Lanes, N21 2RT
Printed by Pika Print Ltd. Genotin Road, Enfield.

IN TOUCH

ISSUED BY YOUR LOCAL CONSERVATIVES
—— Spring 1992 ——

View over Westminster
by Michael Portillo, M.P.

As the election approaches, the policies of both parties are being tested. Labour has promised more spending by Government based on higher taxes and National Insurance. We have heard such promises before. Last time Labour gave us higher taxes, but cut back investment in hospitals and cut out the pensioners' Christmas bonus. This time it is not just the rich who would pay more: Labour's proposals would hit teachers, police officers and others on similar pay. Many people doing overtime would face a steep rise in National Insurance.

The Conservatives want lower taxes for everyone – including pensioners. Lower taxes will stimulate our economy by giving people more money to spend, and more incentive to work and to invest. Lower rates of tax have led to higher revenues to the Government as the economy improves. It really would be mad in a recession to penalise those who invest in the businesses of tomorrow: the creators of jobs and of wealth.

As well as wishing to create more prosperity, we are making better use of the money that we spend today.

We are tackling standards in schools. The National Curriculum helps teachers to cover the necessary subjects. Testing children reveals to parents the progress that each child is making. Local management of schools gives the parents, governors and head teachers more choice about where money is spent and how teaching is done.

In our health service, family doctors are encouraged to monitor patients' health, not just to treat illness. Some of them have chosen to exercise more choice about how to organise hospital treatment to the advantage of their patients. And in the hospitals, managers, consultants and ward sisters have more responsibility to choose the best care for the people in their charge.

We cannot make the poor richer just by making the rich poorer so Conservative policies are designed to create wealth, and to spend it well.

The election literature has become more sophisticated as the contrast between the homely 1984 postcard and the January 1992 leaflet shows. (Opposite, top to bottom) The endless round of profile-raising photo-opportunities from local schools to a newly opened Docklands creche in 1990; from supporting the police as environment minister with responsibilities for inner cities to the 1991 opening of a Westminster exhibition where Michael Portillo is accompanied by the then leader of Westminster Council, David Weeks and Archbishop Gregorios (all pictures © Enfield Conservative Association).

Pressing the flesh: complete with newly buoyant quiff these are posed campaign photographs from before the 1992 General Election – all are Enfield Southgate Tory loyalists. Most of the campaigning was done by leaflet and Portillo's majority was never threatened. He worked tirelessly coordinating the Conservative effort in London generally and his team of canvassers moved to neighbouring Edmonton to secure, just, fellow Conservative Ian Twinn's re-election (© Enfield Conservative Association).

Enfield Southgate Conservative Party constituency officers with their MP and his wife at a campaign dinner in 1992.
(© Kenneth Prater)

Clive Anderson, Matthew de Lange,
Robert Ironton, Barry Jones,
Francis Matthews, Geoffrey Perkins,
Michael Portillo, Graeme Rocker,
Nigel Sheinwald and Philip Smith
invite

MR. B. MARCHANT

to a dinner
twenty years on
Friday 29th November 1991
in Dining Room B, House of Commons
London SW1
at 7.15 for 8 p.m.

R.S.V.P.
Michael Portillo MP
House of Commons
London SW1A 0AA

Dress:
Lounge Suits

Harrow County Grammar School alumni hosted a dinner for their teachers twenty years after they had cooked a farewell supper for those same members of staff. In the group photograph Michael Portillo is seated fourth from the right, Matthew Francis sixth from the right, and standing second from left is Clive Anderson and sixth from the right is Bernard Marchant (both © Paul Thompson).

Two conference favourites with many shared characteristics in style – the young tiger versus the old lion – the two Michaels, Portillo and Heseltine, face each other in Downing Street in 1994 (© Kipper Matthews/*Guardian*).

Carolyn and Michael Portillo in St James's Park.

This had drawn blood, and rallied Tory support in middle-class Scots areas. There were hopes that time, capping and a counter-attack could see the tax survive.

The counter-attack was launched at Bournemouth that autumn. The venue for the final offensive was the Tory party conference. The leader of the charge was to be Michael Portillo, in his first platform address.

The audience were restive. Many had lost their council seats that spring, or had tired of seeing their voters punished by a tax designed to benefit them. But there were vigorous speeches in the tax's defence – not least from the candidate for Aberdeen South, Raymond Robertson, who argued that the tax was now working in Scotland. The only lingering problem, he told the conference, was non-payment, and he urged the government to withdraw services from those who would not pay for them. It won him a lusty roar from the Thatcher loyalists.

When Portillo rose to speak there was a dryness in his throat that made him seem to swallow his words and almost took the edge off his first joke. 'When the prime minister offers you a hot potato, there is only one thing to say: "Take responsibility for the community charge, Prime Minister? There is nothing I would rather do." The funny thing is, I meant it.'

Whether he supported the policy with all his heart or not mattered little. He was fighting on her behalf where the heat of the battle was greatest, and he went at it with gusto, claiming, 'The community charge is the most potent weapon ever put in the hands of ordinary voters to defeat incompetent and malign Labour councils. Labour's hatred of the charge has nothing to do with fairness and everything to do with fear – their fear of being chucked out in local elections.'

Warming to his theme, Portillo advanced an ambitious thesis, linking his defence of the poll tax with a long-held belief, which was to resurface again, that the British system of government had not been defended vigorously enough by the élites charged with its stewardship:

Before the community charge, local government often aroused contempt amongst the well-informed and apathy among the rest. When democracy is held in such low esteem, it is only a matter of time before you lose it altogether. The apathy has been ended by the community charge. In the pubs today they speak of little else. Just about everyone in the land knows exactly what they are paying in community charge – in many cases all too well . . . The community charge is a courageous, fair and sensible solution. Far from being a vote loser . . . it will be a vote winner.

Portillo was greeted with a standing ovation. One observer remembers a conference which still had its doubts about the tax but few about its advocate. Outside the hall, however, the speech came across as hubristic hype. The tax showed no sign of winning widespread support outside a Tory redoubt no matter how vigorously it was sold.

With hindsight, Portillo's speech in defence of the charge was as likely to turn the tide as the charge of Polish lancers against German Panzers in 1939. It was the last flamboyant hurrah of a doomed regime. At the time, though, few suspected the tax would soon be buried – one of the casualties in a struggle that nearly tore the Tory party apart and which saw Portillo at the centre of a battle to save the leadership he had served so loyally. It was a battle he was to lose.

CHAPTER NINE

Never Glad Confident Morning Again

I was sick at heart. I could have resisted the opposition of
opponents and potential rivals and even respected them for it;
but what grieved me was the desertion of those I had always
considered friends and allies and the weasel words whereby
they had transmuted their betrayal into frank advice and concern for my fate.

Margaret Thatcher, *The Downing Street Years*

Shortly after Chris Patten's appointment to the Cabinet in July
1989 his friends noticed a new concern stealing across his already
well-lined features. Questioned by friends, the new secretary of
state for the environment was initially reluctant to share his
worries. Only after a while did he begin to unbutton – and the
reason why he had been so reticent was understandable: Patten
was becoming convinced that Margaret Thatcher had 'lost it' and
was becoming an impediment to re-election. He was not alone.
Even as Thatcher's hegemony over her party seemed total, so
the accumulated grievances of slighted ministers began to reach a
critical mass and the persistent plotting of the dispossessed and
never-possessed grew.

That autumn her 'brilliant' and 'unassailable'' chancellor, Nigel
Lawson, resigned. Ostensibly he was annoyed at her refusal to
disown criticism of his exchange-rate policy by her economic
adviser Sir Alan Walters. But behind the resignation lay years of
growing disaffection as the two architects of victory in 1987
squabbled over the way ahead.

In October one of the most fateful reshuffles of Thatcher's time
as prime minister saw John Major become chancellor, Douglas
Hurd foreign secretary and Tim Renton chief whip. The consequences of the moves, for the prime minister and her party, were
to be two devastating internal explosions, but at the time it seemed
that she would ride out her unpopularity. She had seen off

Heseltine, so why not Lawson, whose base on the backbenches was, if anything, smaller?

In November of that year an obscure Welsh baronet notable mainly for his opposition to the Falklands War and his passionate European federalism challenged Thatcher in the annual leadership contest allowed under party rules but not previously called for during her reign. It was a 'stalking-horse' challenge, designed to allow a pot-shot at Thatcher to weaken her before another challenge was launched, led by Michael Heseltine, lean and hungry after four years in the wilderness.

The 1989 stalking-horse, Sir Anthony Meyer, was less Rosinante and more of a dissidents' Don Quixote, his natural nobility making up for the inadequacy of his qualifications as a rival to Thatcher. Nevertheless, his candidature secured 33 votes and saw another 27 decline to support the prime minister. Nearly one-sixth of the parliamentary party wanted her to go.

Her campaign manager, 'Gentleman' George Younger, calculated that a similar number had been bought off only by his promise that she would change her ways. Tristan Garel-Jones, the former deputy chief whip she had appointed minister for Europe, warned her of a hundred assassins lurking on the back benches.

To avert further trouble, she agreed to spend more time listening to opinions in the Commons tea-rooms and instituted a series of meetings with back-benchers. In her memoirs she claims, 'There was frank speaking on both sides – on one occasion a back-bencher told me it was time for me to go. I may not have complied but I did listen.' Not according to one who remembers the sessions: 'They were a dialogue of the deaf.'

In addition to back-bench unease, there was trouble enough at the top. Just before the 1990 party conference Thatcher was persuaded, against her better judgement, to put the pound in the Exchange Rate Mechanism of the European Monetary System.

It had previously been the long-term aim of Lawson and Howe as chancellor and foreign secretary to tie the pound into the system of fixed exchange rates. Lawson believed this would provide the necessary anti-inflationary credibility sterling needed; Howe wanted Britain on Europe's inside track. Whatever their mixed motives, they worked together to secure their goal. But, despite their considerable combined weight, they did not succeed. In 1989

Lawson resigned, and Howe was reshuffled out of the Foreign Office to become leader of the House and deputy prime minister. It was only when Major moved to the Treasury and Douglas Hurd took over the globe-trotting that Thatcher eventually relented.

Major had been a disciple of Lawson's orthodoxy, and Hurd was as committed a European as Howe. Both were keen on ERM entry and agreed, one breakfast, to force the prime minister's hand. They knew – and she knew, after Lawson's departure – that she could not afford any more resignations.

Unfortunately, her reluctant agreement to lock the pound into the currency corset did not prevent the resignations. On 1 November, less than four weeks after the pound entered the ERM, Sir Geoffrey Howe left the Cabinet. He had apparently been driven to distraction by Thatcher's vigorous extemporising during her reporting back to the House from an EC summit in Rome. She had closed the door on a single currency, nudged open the week before, on *Walden*, by Howe, and had swept aside a three-pronged proposal of European Commission president Jacques Delors to turn the European Parliament into the EC's House of Representatives, the Commission into its Executive and the Council of Ministers into its Senate – rejecting them together: 'No, no, no.' It was meant to be a point-by-point put-down, but it sounded like a tantrum.

In his resignation letter, Howe justified his decision with reference to 'The mood you had struck . . . in the House of Commons last Tuesday.' Thatcher's allies tried to use the reference to 'mood' to imply that there was no substantial policy difference between Howe and her. It infuriated him. His anger simmered for two weeks, given the occasional stir by his wife, Elspeth, until it boiled over in a devastating speech in the House of Commons on Tuesday 13 November.

The night before, Thatcher had tried to defend herself, saying, 'I am still at the crease, though the bowling has been pretty hostile of late. And, in case anyone doubted it, I can assure you there will be no ducking bouncers, no stone-walling, no playing for time. The bowling's going to get hit all around the ground.' The *Independent on Sunday* political columnist Alan Watkins has often warned politicians about the inadvisability of using sporting metaphors. Margaret Thatcher would have done well to follow his advice.

The next day Howe rose from the unfamiliar obscurity of the back benches, a brooding Lawson by his side. It was one of his best, and most destructive, speeches. He touched on the way in which Thatcher's words on the single currency had hindered the freedom of manœuvre of her chancellor and the governor of the Bank of England, commenting, 'It is rather like sending your opening batsman to the crease only for them to find, the moment the first ball is bowled, that their bats have been broken before the game –' He paused, and then slipped the knife he had been fondling for months right between the shoulder-blades: '– by the team captain.'

If anyone had any doubt about what Howe now hoped for, he put them to rest with his final line: 'The time has now come for others to consider their own response to the tragic conflict of loyalties with which I have myself wrestled for perhaps too long.'

The way was clear for Heseltine to launch his assault. The next morning he contacted Cranley Onslow, chairman of the 1922 Committee, and thus the back-benchers' shop steward, to notify him of his intention to challenge Thatcher for the party leadership. The contest was fixed for the following Tuesday, 20 November.

The only period during which a formal challenge may be mounted to the leader of the Conservative Party is in the fortnight after the Queen's Speech, which normally falls in November. Was it coincidence that Sir Geoffrey Howe could stand no more in November, when ERM entry had been safely secured, rather than in, say, June, when a stubborn premier was still holding out against any entry into the system and just after she had rejected reform of the poll tax – the greatest worry to the back-benchers? Was it coincidence that he had delayed his speech until after the Loyal Address, until two days before the close of the period allowed for nominations, with Michael Heseltine ready to spring? Almost certainly it was – politics usually owes more to chaos than to intrigue – but during the next week some Thatcher loyalists were inclined to see intrigue where it was alleged all was chaos and chaos where they hoped to see intrigue. It is an impression that time has done nothing to efface.

Margaret Thatcher's hold on the party had never been as strong as it appeared, and even as figures on the Left – like the Pattens, Clarke and Hurd – found the magnetism of her leadership pushing the country, and them, to the Right, so they found themselves increasingly repelled by her style of governing. Her old feel for the parliamentary party had slackened following the departure of Willie Whitelaw from the government in 1987. It was dealt a devastating blow in the summer of 1990, when her old PPS and back-bench conscience and contact, Ian Gow, was murdered by the IRA.

Increasingly she had come to rely for advice not on elected politicians but on a coterie of appointees. Her private secretary, Charles Powell, and press secretary, Bernard Ingham, were brilliant men and utterly loyal, but they were not MPs. By cutting herself off from day-to-day contact with her immediate electorate, Thatcher was running huge risks. Her instincts may still have been those of the vast mass of Tory supporters, but her time was rarely spent with their elected representatives, so she was in a poor position to head off the rumblings in the undergrowth.

The concerns of the old Left and other grandees' grumbles had been expressed to her face at a private dinner in Peter Carrington's house one Sunday in April 1990. Her former foreign secretary advised her that she should go with dignity. Thatcher herself has made it clear that he meant sooner rather than later. She was not about to take his advice. The view of many in the parliamentary party was that if she did not go quietly, other methods would be required.

During much of this period Michael Portillo was absorbed with the minutiae of local-government finance. Some NTB members had been keen to provoke Heseltine to, in Bernard Ingham's words, 'put up or shut up'. They thought a challenge would see Heseltine humiliated, and an end put to back-bench sniping. Portillo was not among them. Temperamentally opposed to picking unnecessary fights, his priority was to solve the biggest domestic policy problem the Tories faced by teaching voters to learn to love the poll tax.

When Heseltine did launch his challenge, there was an efficiency and *élan* about his attack that bespoke careful preparation. He had had nearly five years to plan his strike, but, even so, the manner of his assault suggested a battle-readiness that did his political instincts great credit.

Operating from his offices in Victoria Street and the House

of Commons, a team of twenty 'Heselteenies' drew up charts of colleagues' potential preferences. From the start Heseltine's support was broadly from the Left. His campaign manager, Michael Mates, and his main lieutenants, Keith Hampson, Anthony Nelson and Peter Temple-Morris, were all ideologically anti-Thatcherite, as well as opportunistically tied to the coat-tails of the coming man.

Other members of the campaign team, such as William Powell, the member for Corby, and Heseltine's two proposers, Sir Neil McFarlane and Sir Peter Tapsell, were less easily placeable. Powell, with a majority of 1,085 in Corby, was typical of Tories with tight marginals – anxious to ditch the bitch and axe the tax. McFarlane and Tapsell were men who felt slighted – the former by being sacked, the latter by never having been appointed – and whose careers might have a chance of an Indian summer under Heseltine. McFarlane was an old golfing partner of Sir Dennis Thatcher, and Tapsell, although an avowed anti-monetarist, was easily as sceptical of Europe as Mrs Thatcher, but both calculated their lot would improve under a new dispensation.

Inevitably, after eleven years, those who had never been reconciled to Margaret Thatcher's leadership were joined in an enemy alliance by those ejected from office early and those whose chance of office seemed to have receded entirely. Swelling their ranks were those weaker brethren fearful of a ten-point lag in the polls and restless for a change. Driven by hunger, ambition and, in some cases, desperation, the Heseltine team were, in the words of one whom they canvassed, 'assiduous'.

The Thatcher team were anything but. The prime minister chose a bizarre combination of out-of-touch grandees, ministerial failures and ineffectual loyalists. She appointed George Younger to head her campaign. He had helped see off Anthony Meyer, but his heart was not in the fight this time. He wriggled, claiming responsibilities as the new chairman of the Royal Bank of Scotland would take up much of his time, but in the end he accepted. He was to be supported by former chief whip Michael Jopling, former number three in the Whips' Office Michael Neubert, the overlooked Gerry Neale, the hapless John Moore and the once-estranged Norman Tebbit. Their efforts would be aided, it was hoped, by the PM's PPS, Peter Morrison.

Norman Fowler, who had been in her Cabinet scarcely a year before, initially agreed and then almost instantly declined to help, claiming he was too close to Geoffrey Howe to support her. Jopling faded from the scene. Moore was out of the country for much of the period. And, as will become apparent, the rest of the team hardly exerted themselves.

Fowler's lack of loyalty might not have been surprising, but it should have been proof – if proof were needed – of the danger Thatcher was in. But, instead of being provoked by this into getting into the gutter to scrap, her team elected to mount an aloof, presidential campaign. The media – vital to past Tory election victories – had access to the candidate rationed. There were interviews, in the *Sunday Times*, the *Sunday Telegraph* and *The Times*, and that was it.

In contrast to Heseltine's team, canvassing for Thatcher was desultory. One MP rung three times by the Heseltine team – including once in the bath by the man himself – found out only after the vote that an oblique conversation with an old friend which included a general enquiry into his welfare was a canvass from the Thatcher team.

A summit dinner was held to talk tactics at Chequers on the Saturday before the vote. George Younger could not attend, owing to a prior arrangement in Norfolk. He could not spare one evening to help the woman who had brought him into the Cabinet and whose re-election he had pledged to secure. And, if he was absent that night, he was scarcely more visible over the next few days.

Most of the dinner guests were family or friends from outside the Commons – there was no feel for the mood of the Parliamentary electorate. At that dinner Peter Morrison confidently predicted 220 votes for Thatcher and 110 for Heseltine. Thatcher was sceptical of the size of the margin, aware that she had benefited from double-dealing in the secret ballot when she had challenged Heath, but she was told not to worry.

The next day, Sunday 18 November, she flew to Paris for the Conference for Security and Cooperation in Europe summit designed to mark the end of the Cold War. It was thought that it would be more dignified, and effective, to be seen taking credit for defeating Communism and bringing peace to the Continent rather than grubbing for votes in the tea-rooms. That might have been the case if there was someone else grubbing for her, but all the flesh-pressing and ego-massaging was the work of the Heseltine team.

Thatcher's natural supporters were worried. Sir George Gardiner called ad-hoc meetings of the 92 Group to discuss the situation and see what could be done. Michael Neubert and Gerry Neale attended the meetings but said nothing, and gave no indications of how help could be given. Many of the members of the 92 had no idea that Neubert and Neale were even on the Thatcher team.

In Thatcher's assault on Heath the 92 had been used as a cadre with connections to marshall support on the Right and beyond. In the past decade its leaders had shown their mastery in winning the Tory party's internal elections. At the moment of greatest risk for the prime minister it had fought so hard for, no attempt was made to make use of its muscle.

Members of the No Turning Back Group were, if anything, even more alarmed. One, Michael Brown, had launched his own 'private-enterprise' bid to rally support for Thatcher. Like the 92, the NTB decided to meet daily during the crisis to discuss what could be done, but offers of assistance to the Thatcher campaign team were genially dismissed as unnecessary.

On the eve of the vote even the Commons' cleaners must have been aware of the effort expended by the Heseltine team. This was no gentlemanly tilt at the top. Heseltine was not a reluctant grandee allowing himself to become the focus for the discontented to register their unhappiness. It was a determined attempt to channel even the slightest discontent with the Thatcher leadership into a strike designed to kill.

In retrospect, the complacency of the Thatcher team seems remarkable. A few votes might make all the difference. The Tory party has a fair number of preening egos and self-important dullards on its back-benches, and half an hour with a handful of them might have secured their support. In the end she was denied the majority necessary for victory by just two votes. Of course, if she had won, she would have had a tough job reuniting her party, but it would have been her tough job, not a junior's.

When the result was announced – Thatcher 204, Heseltine 152 – it was Kenneth Clarke who exclaimed to a friend, 'That's it, she's finished.' Even though she had a majority of 52, it was not enough to prevent a second contest. For that, she would have needed a clear majority of 15 per cent of the parliamentary party: 56. If two MPs had switched she would have been safe. Now she had been so grievously wounded, the game was up. Another ballot in a week's time would be decided by a simple majority. Several ministers might feel they had discharged their duty to Thatcher by voting for her in the first round and could now switch. Heseltine looked set to seize the leadership.

Thatcher herself – still in Paris – did not think so. She knew she was in trouble, but it had been agreed that in the event of an inconclusive victory she should indicate a willingness to go on while planning to return to London to review the options. A bold front would stop speculation and allow a more considered view to be taken. When she came down the steps of the British embassy to confess her 'willingness' to let her name go forward, the diffidence intended in the careful phrasing was completely effaced by her delivery. The words' nuances were overshadowed by the impression of the old, imperious Maggie sweeping past the BBC's unfortunate chief political correspondent and apparently determined to go on regardless. What was designed to be an exercise in buying time seemed a stubborn refusal to recognise the scale of her rebuff.

Meanwhile, at Westminster, a number of MPs found themselves talking to colleagues who announced to anyone who wanted to hear that they were no longer prepared to support Thatcher but would switch to Heseltine for the second ballot. The impression was created of a swing to the challenger decisive enough to secure victory. One back-bench psephologist, the Bristol MP Rob Hayward, calculated there would be at least thirty straight defections.

But all was not as it seemed. The Heseltine team had instructed some of their silent supporters, in the event of a close result, to declare themselves as former Thatcher supporters only now planning to desert. Many of these 'defectors' had gone over long before. It was an artful attempt to create a sense of momentum in Heseltine's favour, and it worked.

While the Heseltine team manipulated the electorate, Thatcher was at Versailles, celebrating the collapse of Communism. As she tried to face a bleak future with dignity, her supporters were distraught. When the 92 and the NTB met, there was still a sense among the majority that not all was lost. It was thought that a new campaign team – or, as one wag put it, any campaign team – could turn matters round. Portillo was convinced that victory could still be hers.

On the night of the vote the NTB met in a free room on the lower ministerial corridor just before the ten o'clock division. Discussion was acrimonious. Anger at the campaign team for 'a monumental cock-up' was channelled into harsh words for those who thought that the writing was on the wall for the prime minister. Neil Hamilton, Gerald Howarth, Michael Brown, Michael Forsyth and Michael Portillo were the most adamant that she could still win. MPs in the room that night remember raised voices from the die-hards berating their friends for faintness of heart. Portillo had no time for the arguments of colleagues counselling 'realism'; he was determined, almost to the point of imprudence, that no one should be in any doubt where his loyalty lay.

After the result of the first ballot had been announced, Portillo had declined an invitation to another cabal. His old friend from the Whips' Office Tristan Garel-Jones wanted a few friends to come round for a drink at his house in Catherine Place to discuss matters.

Much has been written about the meeting, to suggest it was part of a plot to ease the prime minister out, but it is a caricature of the evening to see it as that. If it were, then Alan Clark would not have been invited to join Garel-Jones, John Patten, Chris Patten, Tim Yeo, Norman Lamont, Malcolm Rifkind, Tony Newton, Richard Ryder and Douglas Hogg. While most were on the Left, Clark was a Thatcherite Ultra and Lamont and Ryder were on the Right. What united them – as rapidly became clear – was not a desire to plot against Thatcher but a feeling that fatal damage had been done and the pressing need now was to stop Heseltine.

Moreover, if it had been an anti-Thatcher occasion, then Garel-Jones would not have invited Portillo to join him. But, even though it was not a plot, Portillo had no stomach for a meeting that would involve discussing alternatives to defending the prime minister. While she remained in office he would not contemplate surrender.

Garel-Jones recalls, 'His reply was: "The prime minister has said she's going on. There is nothing to discuss." Now that shows, I think, on the one hand, admirable loyalty to Mrs Thatcher – not a quality to be flicked away. But it also shows, in my view, a total lack of judgement. I would say he – and I think he is an emotional man – had said to himself, "This woman is not only leader of my party but represents everything I believe in, has given me my chance in politics, and if I have to die with her in the bunker I will die." The interpretation I put on it is, if you like, almost a Castilian nobility – but, in the real world, foolhardy.'

The Catherine Place consensus had been that a 'wider choice' should be offered, and opinion had divided on the merits of Douglas Hurd or John Major as a 'unity' candidate. But all were firmly of the view that Thatcher was finished. It was a view that rapidly became the orthodoxy even among those who had no strong views on the merits of the alternative candidates. Once the advocates of a Hurd or Major premiership realised the party could coalesce around either in preference to Heseltine then the need to persuade Thatcher to resign in time to let them stand became paramount. Nominations would close at noon on Thursday, 22 November. The Major/Hurd partisans had to persuade her to go before then, otherwise, they thought, she would hand Heseltine the prize on a plate – or, if by some supreme effort she survived, it would be as mistress of a broken party. A number of half-hearted attempts were made to press the message home.

One of those on whom the case for an early resignation was forcibly impressed was her new campaign manager, John Wakeham. He asked the new leader of the House, John MacGregor, to survey Cabinet members' opinions and communicate their fears. Cranley Onslow did the same with the executive of the 1922 Committee, but came back with a confusion of opinions. The chief whip, Tim Renton, trawled the parliamentary party for opinion to buttress the other surveys.

At a lunch of cheese and ham sandwiches with mineral water on the day after the vote they delivered their judgements, but in such a diffident fashion as to decide nothing. Renton, who thought her finished and had never sympathised with her Euro-stance, muttered darkly that matters were 'too close to call'. Sir George Gardiner believes Renton 'only talked to those he wanted to talk to'. But, if his intention was to persuade Thatcher to resign then, he failed. Onslow's delphic utterances gave comfort to both the fighters and the withdrawers. MacGregor, who knew she was no longer mistress of her own Cabinet, said nothing.

That afternoon Margaret Thatcher left for the Commons. Her press secretary, Bernard Ingham, released a brief statement: 'I fight on. I fight to win.'

John Wakeham, with the unerring ability all Thatcher's campaign managers had of being off-stage for much of the action, had spent the morning at a London hotel, presiding over the next stage of electricity privatisation. That afternoon he was surprised to see her still in the field after the advice he knew she should have been given. He believed she had to be forcibly shown that she was a liability. He determined on death by twenty-two cuts. The Cabinet should tell her, one by one, that she would lose – before it was too late to allow other candidates to enter. He convinced a reluctant Peter Morrison that Thatcher should talk to the Cabinet individually late that afternoon and early that evening to gauge how strong she really was.

The interviews were to be no random sampling of the Cabinet's opinions. Before the majority entered, they had agreed a formula: they would declare their willingness to fight for her if she wanted to stand, but also that they thought she would lose, and should resign. Just before the first Cabinet member entered, around six o'clock, a plum fell into the laps of those who wanted her to go. Francis Maude, an impeccably Thatcherite junior minister who nevertheless thought her a goner, passed by her room. It was a heaven-sent opportunity to convince her that her bodyguard had no stomach for the struggle. He was ushered in to deliver his own gloomy message about her prospects.

The first two Cabinet ministers to see her – Kenneth Clarke and Peter Lilley – could not have been more carefully chosen to destroy her resolve. Clarke was brutal; Lilley was the driest member of her Cabinet. Clarke's candour and the pessimism of Lilley coming after Maude's fears – above all the insistence that defeat was almost inevitable – sapped her remaining strength.

While these melancholy interviews took place, the members of 92 were gathering in some confusion above, in a room off the Commons main committee corridor. When they assembled at seven o'clock they were unaware that the *coup de grâce* had already been administered below. Most still assumed that Thatcher would go forward to the second round, and a general chat to see what could be done to help began.

Before the discussion got properly under way, it was interrupted noisily by the arrival of David Maclean, the aggressively right-wing Scot who sits for Penrith. Never a man to underplay his hand, his face was a deeper shade of red and his voice more ragged than his colleagues had seen before. 'We're wasting our time,' he exclaimed – 'the Cabinet are already being lined up to force her out.'

Deciding that the Cabinet should not force a coup against their wishes, the 92's leaders set off to see the prime minister to assure her that, whatever the Cabinet thought, the back benches were hers. George Gardiner led the delegation of Bob Dunn, John Townend and Michael Portillo. When they arrived, they found her door locked and were told to go. A message was sent in, and then eventually Peter Morrison came out. He politely declined their request to see Thatcher, calculating that his mistress had suffered enough and did not need another emotional meeting.

The 92 were not convinced. Portillo advanced and squared up to Morrison's formidable bulk. Hands were raised, fists were clenched and oaths were exchanged, but Morrison remained obstinate. Then Norman Tebbit, who had been inside the prime minister's room, came out to see what the commotion was. When he saw the culprits he sighed, 'Thank God, the 92 has arrived.' They were ushered in, with Portillo at their head.

One witness remembers Thatcher, moist-eyed, turning to Portillo and saying, 'They tell me my support is evaporating.' Portillo shot back, 'They are wrong,' and told her she was being badly advised and there were troops ready to fight for her, if only she would lead them.

Thatcher recalled the exchange ruefully in her memoirs: 'He tried to convince me that the Cabinet were misreading the situation, that I was being misled and that with a vigorous campaign it would still be possible to turn things round. With even a drop of this spirit in higher places it might, indeed, have been possible. But that was just not there.' Thanking him for his support, she asked Portillo to lead the delegation out and said she had to return to Number Ten to write her speech for the no-confidence debate Labour had called for the following day.

Portillo left in a state of high emotion. His next meeting did little to calm him. That night, quite by coincidence, was the monthly dinner of the NTB and there, at least, he might have expected to find allies with an appetite for counter-attack. But when he arrived at Lord North Street he found the group split, with a minority faction led by Francis Maude and Peter Lilley pronouncing Thatcher finished. One member remembers Lilley declaring simply, 'She's going' and a furious Edward Leigh storming out, determined not to listen to any more defeatism.

Portillo's reaction was more measured. He was visibly angry with those friends who had lost stomach for the fight, but he marshalled his thoughts and words carefully, to try to convince fainthearts. His conviction that victory could still be wrested from Heseltine was buttressed by the passion of some others of those there – in particular Michael Forsyth and Michael Fallon. Fallon thought other candidates should be encouraged to enter the lists, in order to split the anti-Thatcher protest vote. He believed that if she could survive until a third round then she could still win. There was a desperate edge to the scheming, but it was underpinned by a determination to try anything to save her.

Their discussions were cut short by the arrival of John Butcher, the Coventry South West MP, who had heard in the Commons that Thatcher had definitely decided to resign. The die-hards resolved to do everything in their power to change her mind. Portillo, Forsyth and Fallon drove immediately to Downing Street, where Thatcher was closeted with John Gummer, Peter Morrison, Norman Tebbit and her political secretary John Whittingdale, writing her speech for the next day's debate.

Once again, Portillo found his way barred. He was ushered into an ante-room with Fallon and Forsyth, and kept waiting. One of those there remembers Portillo sipping a glass of white wine proffered to pacify them and commenting, 'I was here on her first night as prime minister and I shall be here on her last.'

Eventually they were met by Whittingdale, who explained that an emotional Mrs Thatcher had only recently calmed down and set to work and, sadly, he could not risk upsetting her again. All the three Michaels could do was persuade him to take her a note scribbled by Forsyth.

They left unhappy, and Portillo returned to the House. After a strained drink in the Commons, he then set off for his flat, hoping there might still be a chance for the inevitable to be averted. As he walked past his office in the Commons he heard the phone ring.

In no mood for late-night gossip or business, he was minded to ignore it but something prompted him to answer. It was Whitting-dale. The prime minister had been informed that he had called earlier and wanted him to come round. It was his last chance.

He gathered together Forsyth, Fallon and Neil Hamilton and set off again. He hoped to convince her that all was not lost, but when they were shown in it was a deflated and 'clearly distressed' woman they found. Portillo tried to rally her spirits, but it was apparent that her mind had pretty much been made up. A conversation with Dennis, who was determined to protect her from the humiliation of defeat, had decided matters.

While the others waited, she and Portillo exchanged a few private words. No one had been more loyal to her and her policies. He had striven to do her will in every job he had been given, even when her wishes strayed from the path of purist orthodoxy which he would have preferred to follow. She had promoted him and given his political career a purpose. Now, at the last, he was still willing to fight. While every politician with an eye to the future was manœuvring to position themselves favourably in the eyes of her successor, he was demonstrating that he thought none of them could come anywhere near her.

Cecil Parkinson believes there is something almost Latin in Portillo's romantic attachment to Margaret Thatcher when so many had deserted her. Others see something of his mother's Scots background in his stance – his dogged attachment to Thatcher's cause when no advantage lay in it echoing the Highlanders who remained loyal to Charles Edward Stuart after Culloden.

When Portillo left Thatcher that night she promised to sleep on matters, but everyone in the room knew it was over.

The next four days were frenziedly active for most members of the parliamentary party as John Major and Douglas Hurd launched their campaigns for the leadership. Official business, on hold since Heseltine's fatal wounding of the prime minister, was ignored while the three candidates and their supporters threw themselves into furious campaigning. Ministers who had taken a relaxed approach in defence of Thatcher displayed an energy and skill in advancing the claims of her potential successors that took some aback.

Ian Twinn contrasts the enthusiasm of some members of the

Cabinet in support of Messrs Hurd and Major with their efforts on behalf of Mrs Thatcher. He is disinclined to think that it was shock at the failure of the Thatcher campaign that galvanized them into action, commenting, 'I could say more, but I've no wish to add to the current leadership's troubles.' There was a widespread sense of betrayal among many Thatcherites at the time, and the more some have learned about the manner of her going, the less happy they have felt about some colleagues. It was, however, shock rather than resentment that meant that some, like Forsyth and Portillo, had no desire to join any of the candidates' campaign teams.

All three candidates made a bid for the votes of the Right. Tristan Garel-Jones tried to sell Hurd as the most authentic Tory of the three, but he managed to convince only Nicholas Budgen and Michael Fallon. Garel-Jones might have been more successful had he not with typically sinuous, yet honourable, logic refused to press the point too vigorously because it would have meant revealing just how left-wing his friend John Major really was.

Heseltine sold himself as the most genuinely radical of the three, and sought to convince Tory cavaliers that in style, energy, imagination and *élan* he was closest to Thatcher. On those grounds he attracted right-wing Midlands populists like Jim Pawsey and Dame Jill Knight. He also secured the support of two Ultras, Edward Leigh and Michael Brown, not so much out of admiration for his policy platform but because, in the words of one, he had had the courage to 'stab her in the front'.

But it was Major who enjoyed the support of most of the Right. Although a Blue Chip, he had been careful never to alienate any faction. His PPS, until entry to the ERM prompted his resignation, had been the tinder-dry Stockport MP Tony Favell, and he had won the admiration of some economic right-wingers. However, the decisive factor in his favour was the support of Margaret Thatcher. Portillo was one of a number on the Right inclined to support Major but by no means certain.

On the Monday after her resignation, the day before the second ballot, Margaret Thatcher threw a lunch party for those who had been loyal to the last. Most of the guests were members of the NTB, but neither Peter Lilley nor Francis Maude was present.

It was not an easy occasion, but most of the guests were determined to buoy her up. She was in better spirits than many expected, confident that John Major would win and carry on the torch. She spent some time lobbying Leigh and Brown to transfer their support from Heseltine, and lost no opportunity of convincing doubters to back Major. According to Michael Fallon, 'She wanted her troops to stay as a solid phalanx, and she wanted them to go to John.'

There were words for every guest but she spent a particularly long time with Portillo. Another MP remembers a note of disagreement entering Portillo's tone at one point, prompting Thatcher to raise her own voice a little to settle things, saying, 'Michael, it's the ideas that must go on.'

Portillo openly declared for Major, but, apart from voting for him, played no other part in his campaign. Advancing his own cause was the last thing on Portillo's mind after Thatcher fell. As a talented middle-ranking minister he was unlikely to be dropped, but he did not exert himself to impress the new leader in the hope of promotion.

On the Tuesday night, 27 November, when Major's team celebrated their victory at Number Eleven, Portillo was not among the revellers, although he did congratulate the victor later. Curiously, the candidate whom he spoke most to that night was one of the defeated. After the excitement of the election the business of government had been resumed, and Portillo found himself trooping through the division lobby for a vote at ten that night. As he walked through, he found himself face to face with Michael Heseltine.

The man who had brought down the leader Michael Portillo loved was alone. His own dreams of the leadership seemed to have disappeared for ever, and there was something diminished about him. Portillo, prompted by a sense of honour, and sympathy, went over and commiserated with Heseltine. Without for a moment indicating that he would have wanted to see Heseltine succeed, at the moment of the man's defeat he found a few magnanimous words. It was politeness more than anything, but, if he had not realised before it was soon brought home how, in politics, politeness pays. The next morning Portillo discovered that Heseltine was to become his boss.

The centrepiece of Heseltine's challenge had been his pledge to fundamentally reform the poll tax. Neither Major nor Hurd could have afforded to be outflanked on that issue, so both also pledged to reform it if elected.

When Major won it was natural and tactically necessary that he should invite Heseltine to join his new Cabinet of Unity, and what could be more appropriate than allowing the man who was so keen on a review to preside over it? If he failed, the damage for Major would be contained. If he succeeded, then it might help the Tories – and Major – win another term.

Heseltine could hardly refuse, but he did make one request: he wanted as his deputy the man who knew the tax better than any other politician – Michael Portillo.

Portillo had been expecting to move, and had said as much to an NTB colleague at the Thatcher lunch on the Monday before Major's victory. He realised the tax would go, but he thought it unlikely that its most vigorous partisan would be asked to get rid of it. But he was the expert, and a clever party manager like Major may just have been aware that it would hardly help the career of the darling of the Right, and a potential long-term threat, to be seen scuttling Margaret Thatcher's flagship.

In the reshuffle following Major's election some old Thatcherites like Parkinson and Waddington bowed out, one young Thatcherite, Michael Spicer, was sacked, and a number of new faces – many from the Left – were brought in. One of those was the Salisbury MP Robert Key, who had been PPS to Chris Patten and Ted Heath. Key was appointed Portillo's deputy in a restructuring of the Department of the Environment that saw Portillo encircled by wets. But, having worked well with Chris Patten in the past, Portillo was unfazed. His grasp of the detail of local-government finance placed him in a strong position, and he soon found himself developing a good working relationship with both Heseltine and Key.

Heseltine has always been a broad-brush politician, disinclined to get bogged down by details. The review, or, more accurately, replacement, of the poll tax was perhaps the biggest and certainly the most complicated policy problem he had ever faced, but that did not worry him. As far as he was concerned he had not been given this job to immerse himself in the technical nitty-gritty of revenue support grants. That was what junior ministers were for.

Key says, 'I remember the day Michael Heseltine came back

from a Cabinet meeting and he called Michael and myself into his room and said, "Right, boys, Cabinet has decided you've got to go away and get rid of the poll tax and introduce something else. You've got three months – and make sure it works."'

To defuse the political dangers of reversing the centrepiece of the Conservative's third term and disarm the opposition, Heseltine proclaimed that nothing would be ruled in or out and invited the other parties to talks to help him thrash out a new tax. How then could they damn a process that they had had a part in? Labour saw the dangers and declined to cooperate, but all the other parties agreed. The meetings were largely charades designed to string the Liberals and Nationalists along, and none of the opposition suggestions made the slightest difference to the shape of the poll tax's successor, but the tactic did spike some of the guns pointed at the government.

One of those present at these meetings remembers Portillo being not entirely at ease. Portillo, he suspects, found the ruse gimmicky and had some difficulty in disguising his natural distaste for coalitions and consensus, but he remained civil throughout.

Although all three candidates for the leadership had pledged in effect to scrap the poll tax, and Heseltine had airily told Portillo and Key that the Cabinet had decided to 'get rid' of it, there was no agreement within the government, let alone the party, on what shape the successor should take. Some ministers were still attached to the poll tax, and they were not all residents of right-wing ghettoes.

The then health secretary, William Waldegrave, a politician who sometimes cannot see the dangers lurking in the political wood because he is so attracted by the beauty of the policy trees, was very attached to the tax. As a junior environment minister he had had a hand in its design, and he still felt the intellectual appeal of a flat-rate charge for services even though a welter of exemptions and exceptions had come to obscure the essential simplicity of the initial concept.

Ian Lang, the new Scottish secretary, was, like Waldegrave, a Blue Chip with no Thatcherite 'form', but he was the Cabinet's most determined defender of the tax. Having ridden out one more year of agitation than his colleagues, as the tax was introduced a year earlier in Scotland, he could see how the tax benefited Tory voters. His deputy, Michael Forsyth, had increased the Tory vote in that spring's Scottish local elections by appealing to the interests of the middle classes and eviscerating Labour's proposals for a property tax. Lang foresaw only trouble if the poll tax, only now beginning to bear fruit, was uprooted altogether. The adoption of a property tax would allow the opposition to throw back in the government's face everything the Tories had ever said against Labour's plans. As a new member of the Cabinet, Lang was in no position to make demands. He had seen his predecessor, Malcolm Rifkind, squander goodwill in the past with resignation threats and leaks. But, despite his weakness, he fought ferociously to keep the principle of a personal charge.

Portillo himself had invested a lot of political capital in defence of the original tax. His stance had been governed, to some extent, by the need to seem strenuous in defence of his mistress's policy, but he had been a believer. And the tax's strongest supporters, such as Michael Forsyth, were his closest political friends. However, he was a middle-ranking minister who had been given a clear task by the Cabinet. If he caused a fuss now, his capacity to make a stand later would be diminished.

It was not easy to swallow his words, and his ability to do so, while retaining the loyalty of his friends on the Right is, perhaps, a reflection of the political capital he had built up with them. Perhaps a wiser politician would not have been so vigorous in the tax's defence – neither former heavyweights such as Nigel Lawson, nor up-and-coming right-wingers like John Redwood had been enamoured of it. But, having stuck his neck out and survived, it was time to duck back below the parapet and toe the line.

Portillo did not always see eye to eye with Heseltine during the review. Heseltine was keen to move as much as possible to a property-based tax, whereas Portillo was temperamentally more cautious about such a move. However, Heseltine did acknowledge that Portillo was the master of the minutiae, dubbing him the "AA man', after the TV ad. Heseltine might not have all the answers, but he knew a man who did – Portillo.

As an adroit operator, Portillo moved quickly to put water between himself and the sinking flagship. A profile in the *Sunday Telegraph*, penned by a Portillo-friendly staffer, explained away his apostasy: 'He has shed few tears over the poll tax because, for him, it was not really a matter of ideological principle – as, say, privatisation, the extension of ownership or other moves to mini-mise the state are.'

The difficulty of designing a workable replacement meant Portillo took longer than the three months first allotted by Heseltine to come up with a solution. And while he was working on a new tax, the old one was still causing problems. April 1991 would see the second round of bills in England and Wales – many of them driven up much higher by non-payment of the first year's tax.

The time taken to come to a conclusion about the shape of a replacement allowed the opposition to paint John Major as a ditherer, unable to choose between advocates of a property tax and defenders of a personal charge like Lang, Waldegrave and, it was thought, Portillo. But some close to Major considered delay a wise course, anxious to put off as long as possible any backlash from the Right when abolition was announced.

Whatever the internal considerations, external factors – in par-ticular the voters – concentrated minds. On 7 March the Tories lost a by-election in their thirteenth safest seat, Ribble Valley, a Lancashire constituency whose voters had been hard-hit by the poll tax. Labour sought to harness electoral impatience by using a scheduled opposition day debate on 13 March 1991 to call on the government to scrap the poll tax immediately and return to a reformed rating system.

Six days later the government acted to avert any further damage. In his first Budget, the new chancellor, Norman Lamont, cut £140 off every poll-tax bill by increasing VAT to 17½%. Some on the Right were unhappy with the flashiness of the announcement and the implied acceptance of an ineluctible increase in state spending, but it bought the government time.

Two days later Michael Heseltine unveiled the fruit of his underlings' labours. The council tax looked like a property tax, smelt like a property tax and sounded like a property tax, but there was one fig-leaf for the poll-tax nostalgics. The council tax placed properties in one of seven – later to be eight – bands based on a rough estimation of market value and charged accordingly. Like the rates beforehand, it was only crudely related to ability to pay, but it was a tax, and not a charge.

It was billed as a hybrid property tax/personal charge. Half of the amount levied was supposed to be personal, and based on a two-adult household, so if only one adult lived in a property then the charge would be reduced by one quarter. The distinction from a pure property tax was entirely sophistical. The level of the total charge was decided solely by a rough valuation of the voters' property. It was not calculated by merging a property element with a separate personal levy, nor could it have been – the survival of a poll-tax element in practice would have been offensive to its opponents. The single-persons' discount was a sop to the Scottish secretary, designed to allow Lang some dignity in defeat. The poll-tax purists were not taken in.

Douglas Mason, one of the inventors of the original charge, thought the council tax a retrograde step. Some MPs, like Sir Richard Luce and Sir Rhodes Boyson, with a large number of elderly and single constituents, were also sorry to see the poll tax go. But, while there were grumbles, there was no rebellion.

As far as Portillo was concerned, if colleagues had wanted the poll tax to stay then they should not have removed Margaret Thatcher. His shortness with some critics who were quick to find fault with the new policy was hinted at in an interview in the *Financial Times* at the time of the new tax's passage through the Commons: 'A lot of water has flowed under this bridge. We did have a system where everybody paid, and in the end it was found not to be acceptable, not least to the majority of Conservative MPs.'

The same day that the interview appeared, Portillo wound up the debate on the second reading of the bill to introduce the tax. He took the House through the detail of the new tax and predicted a net reduction for most payers. It was a straightforward and careful defence of the new measure, but the speech was spiced with passion. It came alive towards the end, but in an unapologetic defence of the past, not a ringing defence of the new:

Certainly I defended the community charge, which gave Labour councils in many areas the fright of their lives. I am asked whether I am sorry. I am sorry that we did not manage to pin the overspending of Labour authorities on those authorities and that we did not have a chance to repeat across the country the electoral triumphs that we enjoyed in

Trafford, Southend, Brent, Hillingdon, Ealing, Wandsworth and West-minster.

Then, in an audacious policy pirouette, after having hymned the poll tax in tones that echoed his conference speech of a year before, he moved straight to commending the new tax, but with a rueful twist. 'So I am happy to say that the government have changed their mind on local-authority finance, but the world still goes round and the Conservative Party is still a Conservative party.'

Portillo had done the job he was asked to, but there was in his tone more than a hint of regret for the good old days. It was an echo picked up during the committee stage of the bill by Portillo's opposite number, David Blunkett, the blind Labour member for Sheffield Brightside. Blunkett describes Portillo as 'my friend Michael', and confesses to an admiration for his intellect as well as a liking for him as an individual. Both are interested in ideology and capable of riding out unpopularity because of the strength of their convictions.

Blunkett believed that Portillo would not be at ease disposing of the poll tax, and tried to tease him for his abandonment of past principle. Portillo was never tricked into an unwise word, but Blunkett detected in Portillo's caution, and the occasional aside, a sense that he was far from committed to the new tax. 'He did exactly what he had to do to satisfy the brief – but he did it with a mischievous glint.'

Portillo and Blunkett had a number of informal conversations during the passage of the bill, and the two enjoyed each other's company. Even though their paths have now diverged, they still talk, and meet occasionally for lunch. Blunkett is convinced that Portillo believes the poll tax was right – and certainly superior to its replacement – but he was prepared to see it go because he did not see reforming local government as central to the Thatcherite project.

Blunkett believes the ideology that lay behind the poll tax appealed to Portillo. It was one of the purest ripostes to collectivist assumptions that the Tories advanced in the eighties. Paying for local-government services through progressive taxation, and in particular a property tax, meant there was no incentive for the feckless, rootless and irresponsible to vote for efficient local government. Levying a charge brought home to every elector the consequences of their actions.

Both economic liberals and High Tories are wary of the universal franchise, although for subtly different reasons. Both, however, recognise the danger of extending the franchise to people who will not bear the costs of the programmes they vote for. Blunkett believes Portillo was a committed supporter of the poll tax because it addressed both his liberal economic preoccupations and his High Tory instincts. Blunkett also thinks Portillo was particularly uneasy about a return to a property tax because he thought it was a Tory's duty to defend property rights and property-owners.

Blunkett's antennae picked up Portillo's unhappiness not only with his new policy but also with his new boss. Behind the façade of loyalty and the relative smoothness of their working relationship, there was a lack of warmth in Portillo's attitude to Heseltine. Other MPs recall that Portillo would refer to his boss simply by his surname in private conversation. Blunkett recalls that Portillo made no effort to defend Heseltine's absence from the committee stage of the Council Tax Bill.

Whatever his attitude towards his superior, Portillo's stance to his opponent was one of unbending ideological hostility garnished with civility and dry humour. Blunkett recalls one joke designed for Portillo's opposition colleagues. 'I'd been ridiculing the new system of valuing houses before placing them in council-tax bands. I asked how can you value if you don't assess each property, looking at gardens, extensions, conservatories and so on. I suggested the government would have to hire balloons to survey every property in the land. Michael dismissed the point, but I must have hit home. The next day there was laughter from my colleagues – Michael had come into the committee with a tie covered in little balloons.'

The bill, introduced in November 1991, had to be in place before the expected election in early 1992, and so the committee stage was taken at a rattling pace. The committee sat three days a week, rather than the usual maximum of two, and on some occasions carried on debating until the early hours of the morning, finishing off one clause at 4.50 a.m.

Portillo's long immersion in detail insulated him from attack, Blunkett recalls: 'He could do double somersaults in the middle of the night without wincing. He didn't make mistakes, and seemed remarkably strong right through the long nights.'

Blunkett was not the only member of the committee impressed by Portillo's relaxed but sure grasp. Robert Key helped Portillo while away the long committee sessions by competing with his superior to see who could note the greatest number of clichés deployed by their colleagues, winking at each other when they both noted an 'I must say . . .' But, more than the jokes, he remembers Portillo's industry and application. 'I learned a very great deal from him about how to be a minister. I had already come across a brand of ministers who weren't particularly assiduous, and I found that very tiring . . . but Michael was a man for great detail, and I realise that in his working method mastery of a brief was simply a prerequisite.'

This view is echoed by another member of the committee, the former Scottish local-government minister, Allan Stewart. 'He was immensely impressive, I must say. On a committee you really have to know what you're doing – especially in a complicated area like local-government finance and a new tax – and you have to try to take the committee with you as far as possible. Atmosphere in committee is important. He was extremely pleasant, and technically he really knew what he was doing and he was a minister in charge of his bill.'

The council tax, barely amended, made its way on to the statute-book, and since then local-government finance has faded from the political foreground. In so far as it was his job to defuse the issue that had done more than anything else to undermine Margaret Thatcher, Portillo had succeeded.

But there have been costs. In his 1990 conference speech, and subsequently, Portillo identified the accountability gains secured by a personal charge. Local elections, briefly, and patchily, became local referenda on the costs of councils. As the recent elections conducted on the basis of the council tax suggest, the relationship between the council tax and the quality of the council has become blurred, and the only issue on which electors focus is the unpopularity of national government.

Some nostalgics argue that if the amount of money subsequently showered on reducing the poll tax, and then amending it, had been invested in making it work from the start it could have survived.

Thatcher herself argues, 'Its benefits had just started to become apparent when it was abandoned.'

This is a seductive thesis, but it ignores certain uncomfortable realities. If the government had realised how much it would have to spend to save, then bury, the poll tax, would they ever have embarked on such an expensive adventure just to tame a few local authorities? Even if more government money had been available earlier, would that have prevented councils simply spending more? Even if the levels of the tax had been lower, wouldn't the number of new people brought into the paying net have created a well of resentment that could have been drawn on anyway by rioters and agitators? And, with the economy overheating and interest rates rising, would any radical change in taxation ever have had a chance to bed down?

Whether or not the tax could have survived, the hope that greater local accountability could be rescued from its wreckage seems an increasingly forlorn one. And the drive to bring local government nearer to the people has also been frustrated by the problems created by another Heseltine-driven, Portillo-designed reform.

In his *Times* article of 10 May 1990 which had suggested reform of the poll tax, Heseltine also had argued for single-tier local authorities and elected mayors. The latter was a piece of American gimmickry, but the former point had validity. The biggest swings to the Tories in that spring's local elections had been in London, where there was only one layer of local government and therefore less chance of obscuring who was responsible for the level of the poll tax. So, when the council tax was unveiled, a year later, it was accompanied by an announcement from Heseltine that legislation would also be introduced to create a commission to look at the structure of local government. The commission would be encouraged to create a system of unitary authorities.

At the time, the structure of local government seemed far less contentious an issue than its finance. In Scotland and Wales there was considerable opposition to reform plans, because the respective secretaries of state decided to dispense with the advice of any commission in redrawing the local-authority maps. Opposition MPs suspected the dwindling Celtic corrals of Tory voters would be ring-fenced by politically motivated ministers. Given that there are now no Tory-controlled councils in either of these parts of the kingdom, they need not have worried.

In England, however, while there were worries, the insistence placed on the independence of the commission did something to assuage opposition concerns. The choice of the former CBI director Sir John Banham was applauded by some as proof that the commission would not be Whitehall's poodle. Whitehall should perhaps have started to worry then, but instead it took the chorus of *bien-pensant* approval as a reassuring sign. Some of the strongest expressions of concern came from Tory county councillors, worried that their power-bases would disappear in any reorganisation.

Portillo piloted the necessary bill through committee. He made much of the flexibility the commission would enjoy, although he also made the government's preferences clear in the second-reading debate in the Commons on 20 January 1992:

We are predisposed towards unitary authorities. When there are two tiers of local authority people tend to become confused about who is doing what. Accountability suffers. People do not know which authority they are paying for particular services. It leads people to believe that there is excessive bureaucracy and overlap and the potential for waste.

As well as having an institutional bias in favour of a single-tier solution, Portillo also felt the commission should respond to loyalties that predated the last reorganisation, under Peter Walker and Ted Heath in 1974. He was motivated by sentiment and tradition, not just administrative convenience:

To the people of England, it is more than a question of who administers local government: the lines on the map, the cricket teams, the lords lieutenant and signposts are important . . . It matters very much to the people of the Wirral whether they live in Cheshire or Merseyside. It matters very much to the people of Coventry whether they live in Warwickshire or the West Midlands.

As with his initial attachment to the poll tax, so with his defence of the reform of local government's structure, Portillo was motivated by two instincts. Both the poll tax and unitary authorities made government more transparent and placed a premium on efficiency, but both also attempted to focus the voters' attention on their locality and to encourage an engagement with institutions rather than a casual indifference. In advancing both policies, economic efficiency was the handmaiden of traditional Tory virtues like loyalty and responsibility. By harking back to the collectivist accretions that encrusted local government, older virtues would be allowed to develop and assert themselves.

That, at least, was the theory. But both policies foundered in practice. While the poll tax was snuffed out some time ago, the consequences of local-government reorganisation still haunt the Tories. John Banham's commission succeeded in alienating councillors, MPs, ministers and many voters. Banham's interpretation of the injunctions to think of traditional ties and single tiers was an eccentric one, and prompted some ministers to consider resignation if his proposals were accepted. He was unceremoniously sacked, and his efforts were hastily amended by ministers. The high hopes with which the venture was launched were realised in certain areas, like Lincolnshire, which says goodbye to Humberside, but seem to have been replaced with resigned cynicism elsewhere.

But by the time Banham had begun his rural rides Portillo had left the Department of the Environment. He had taken his second complicated council bill through committee and emerged unscathed. The executive problems would be somebody else's.

Portillo had had his own fair share of executive responsibilities during his time at Environment. He was minister for the inner cities in general, and Merseyside in particular. He got to know the area well, and one departmental colleague confesses himself surprised at the affection Portillo developed for the city that had symbolised militant resistance to Margaret Thatcher.

In the summer of 1990 Portillo led a campaign to highlight Merseyside's role as a television-making centre, during which he revealed his own first brush with the cameras as the Ribena Kid. He made regular visits to help promote the city's regeneration, and developed close links with Liverpool's businessmen and clergy, returning to give an important lecture there in January 1995.

He also encouraged the ex-Beatle Paul McCartney's attempts to create a school for the performing arts in Liverpool, supporting McCartney's efforts to turn his old school, the Liverpool Institute, into a Mersey version of the Manhattan school featured in the film *Fame*, and recorded his impressions of touring the site with McCartney in his column in the *Enfield Independent*:

For McCartney every room was full of memories, all of which I found rather reassuring. First of all, it seems that whatever you do in later life it is still memories of the school which are the strongest. And second, it was good to see a man who has made millions return to his roots and want to help young people in his native city to climb the ladder.

Portillo certainly wanted to see Liverpool, and other cities, enjoy a renaissance, but he did not display the same warmth to every scheme that he showed to McCartney's. One departmental contemporary remembers Portillo's scepticism when Heseltine unveiled his 'City Challenge' proposals. The scheme, which invited local authorities to compete for funds by outlining their own ideas for new prestige projects, did not appeal to the more austere side of Portillo's character.

Robert Key also recalls the fiscally prudent and anti-interventionist instincts of his boss coming to the fore on several occasions. 'I remember one particular submission which had come up from ministers about how you would focus government resources on inner-city regeneration. Officials had come up with a partnership which suggested that ministers should "pick winners" in urban regeneration, and I recall that I had written on the submission, which had subsequently gone to him, that I thought that this was something we could consider. I remember a withering Thatcherite look at the concept of ministers picking winners.' That idea didn't get any further, but the relationship between the two men did. 'We had a good laugh about it, and I think that was actually something that broke the ice when I realised exactly where he stood.'

A similar flinty friendliness is recalled by Margaret Hodge, now Labour MP for Barking but then leader of Islington Council. Hodge recalls being rung on holiday by an anxious DoE civil servant worried that Portillo was planning to pare an urban-development budget even further. She was asked by the official to show Portillo what had been achieved with money from the budget in the past, in the hope that he might relent. She took him to an indoor sports centre, funded by the development cash now under threat, where children who might otherwise have been on street corners were playing tennis and keeping out of mischief: 'He was very polite and friendly but completely unconvinced. He clearly thought this was not an appropriate use of public money. I couldn't get through to him.'

Another councillor, Sir Jeremy Beecham, leader of Newcastle City Council and chairman of the Association of Metropolitan Authorities, was also struck by Portillo's politeness, contrasting it with the gauche and difficult manner of his successor, John Redwood. But more than the politeness he remembers Portillo's grip on his work, which was much firmer than Chris Patten's, and how invulnerable he was to appeals for extra money: 'It was very much the iron fist in a very decorative velvet glove.'

Hodge did penetrate the defences on one occasion. She was arguing that London, as the entry point and often the terminus for most immigrants and refugees, needed extra funds to cope with the extra strains this placed on local authorities. 'He showed some sympathy. I think I actually got to him. We got a little bit of what we were asking for. I like to think his family's experience had an effect.'

It was a rare instance of a lobbyist making an impact on Portillo. And his apparent inflexibility in the face of supplicants is not restricted to pleas from those on the Left: he is as difficult to persuade when it is an industrialist or a potential ally who is asking him to change his mind on a matter of policy.

One old friend from the Research Department, Tony Hutt, who now works full-time for the political lobbyists GJW, believes Portillo is one of the toughest ministers to deal with. His initial friendliness is disarming but deceptive. He usually knows his mind before a pitch is made, and he is more critical of cases put to him than are other colleagues.

Although his special adviser, Alison Broom, has worked in government relations with a Saatchi subsidiary, and a former researcher, Angela Casey, is now managing director of a lobbyist's, GPC, Portillo has been sceptical about the worth of lobbying. He counselled one other researcher very strongly against a career in the trade, and has not disguised his lack of enthusiasm for it. However, those lobbyists who have dealt with him all attest to his polish in handling them: coming out of his office to meet them, rather than waiting for them to be ushered in while he hides behind a desk, introducing himself and never assuming knowledge, generous with his time, and always, always briefed before any meeting.

His manner has always been scrupulously polite, and he has always been aware of his power to charm, but, according to his friends, Portillo assumed an even more 'professional' edge following Margaret Thatcher's fall. Part of that was prudence. Without his protectress he would have to be a little more careful. Part of it was also learning from his new boss. Heseltine's measured yet supremely effective deployment of charm and charisma meant he carried a weight in government that his intellect alone might not have justified.

Even though their relationship was marked by reserve at first, as personal and ideological factors inevitably intervened, Heseltine and Portillo did develop a fruitful partnership. They were never very close, but Heseltine admired Portillo's intelligence and political skills as well as valuing the efforts he made. One departmental colleague at the time believes Portillo admired aspects of the Heseltine style and learned a lot from him.

One of the most obvious influences was Portillo's abandonment of the pudding-bowl crop of his schooldays for a hairstyle that echoed the flamboyant mane of the young Heseltine. Portillo, who had been interested in the cultivation of 'style' since he was a schoolboy, had already been influenced by Heseltine in small ways: there was a thicker weave in his silk ties and a better cut to his suits after 1990. But the hair was something altogether different.

Portillo was entertaining Alison Broom, his new constituency agent Malcolm Tyndall and one or two others to lunch during the Tory party conference in October 1991 when the conversation turned to his appearance. Although not a platform speaker that year, no one around the table doubted it would be long before Portillo was in the Cabinet. It was Tyndall who suggested that before he became any more publicly prominent he should do something about his hair, commenting, 'You can't carry on looking like a Rugby player who's just come out of the shower.' The rest of the party agreed, but Portillo, self-conscious about his hair ever since he had been mocked for its childish kinks, just let the subject pass.

Three weeks later Tyndall was waiting at Arnos Grove tube station in the constituency on a Friday, expecting to take Portillo on a tour of a police station. While he was staring into the middle distance he saw what he still considers an 'extraordinary' sight as Portillo's new quiff crested the escalator, followed by the man himself. In its first incarnation it was cut very closely, almost shaved, at the back and then rose up in two dark waves. Tyndall mentioned that he had not foreseen anything quite so radical, but Portillo had already prepared a defensive quip: 'I got it changed before Brussels told me to.'

The self-conscious remodelling, and the foppish edge to the new style were the mark of a man aware that appearances count – especially when going for the biggest prizes. But the pre-emptive self-deprecation also showed a man alive to the dangers of being seen to be too attached to the superficial. And Portillo's echo of Heseltine's halo-building was studied: he went to Heseltine's London barber for his new style.

Heseltine's own standing in the party grew during his time as environment secretary. In the months immediately after his return to the Cabinet he still bore the stigma of Thatcher's assassin and received a cool reception at the hands of party activists at their spring central council meeting in 1991. However, by the autumn of that year, with the announcement of the council tax behind him, he returned to the barn-storming, conference-waving form of old. His skill as a campaigner had never deserted him, and the talents that had seen off CND as defence secretary in the early eighties were deployed to scorch off the shine of Neil Kinnock's New Model Labour Party.

In the run-up to the 1992 election Heseltine assumed a more prominent role, and he scored a direct hit on the opposition during a debate on the economy. Norman Lamont had introduced a tax-cutting budget on the eve of the election to emphasise the divide between the parties, and Heseltine was determined to follow through by exposing Labour's pretensions to being the party of business. It was a curious role for an environment secretary to take, but Heseltine used his position to advantage.

In writing his speech, Heseltine hoped to use a survey of City opinion to show that Labour's long march through the boardrooms – the so-called 'Prawn Cocktail Offensive' – had failed to convince finance that Labour was no longer a threat. Closeted with Portillo, his PPS, William Powell, and David Cameron, the young head of the CRD's political section, Heseltine tried a number of lines.

Eventually it was Portillo – himself no mean mimic – who, realising how effectively Heseltine had deployed a sub-Churchillian tone in the past, suggested an ironic twist on his boss's orotund style. He thought Heseltine, when invoking the Prawn Cocktail Offensive, should reveal, gravely, how badly it had gone, and then intone, 'Never have so many crustaceans died in vain.' Heseltine, seeing the comic potential of his position, shot back, 'And, with all the power vested in me as environment secretary, I say, "Save the Prawn!"'

It was hardly Ciceronian, but the careful histrionics and double punchline, when delivered with Heseltine's customary brio, had the Tory back benches barking like seals with laughter. As the last successful parliamentary performance before the election campaign began in earnest, it placed Heseltine in a strong position for what was to be a difficult fight. But, more than that, it established an ease and rapport in Heseltine's dealings with Portillo which, while falling far short of intimacy, was to prove useful for both.

While the 1992 general election approached, Portillo was still adjusting to the loss of Thatcher. He had been in the same post for the eighteen months that followed her fall, and had played a part in burying her inheritance. The sense of united purpose and ideological certainty the NTB enjoyed while she led the party had, to some extent, dissipated as some members moved to the Left to make life easier. Restiveness on the Right at seeing Major move so quickly from Thatcherite positions, on everything from Europe to aid to haemophiliacs, had yet to find an appropriate focus. Fears about the consequences of defeat were tempered by the first stirrings of a desire to recover in opposition and come back to govern refreshed after a Labour collapse.

CHAPTER TEN

The Most Unpopular Man
in the Cabinet

We believe that unless the state is controlled by the constant
and rigorous effort of the people it will grow inexorably and
eventually like a parasite destroy its host.

Michael Portillo, May 1991

Very few people apart from John Major were certain he would
win the 1992 general election. Michael Portillo was not one of
them.

At lunchtime on election day, 9 April, David Blunkett received
a call wishing him well from an old friend. It was Michael Portillo,
passing on sporting good wishes and enquiring after the health of
Blunkett's guide dog. He was calling from his favourite constituency haunt, an Italian restaurant just up from the party offices in
Green Lanes. Judging from the laughter in the background, the
Portillo party were in festive mood.

Blunkett asked Portillo, 'Do you think you've won?' Given Portillo's 18,000 majority, he was clearly referring not to Portillo's
own prospects but the Tories' overall chances. Portillo ducked the
challenge. 'Oh yes, I've won,' he remarked, before laughing and
then signing off.

Journalists who talked to Portillo during the campaign detected
a sense that he was preparing for defeat. Party workers who were
with him during the campaign agree that for much of it he was
disinclined to believe that the Tories could survive.

He had been placed in charge of the London campaign as well
as charged with coordinating the assault on Labour's record in
local government. He was asked to use evidence of Labour's incompetence locally to highlight the party's unfitness to govern
nationally. As a prominent campaign figure with a higher profile
than several Cabinet ministers, he did not shirk the fight. He even
forecast Tory gains in the capital owing to the 'London effect' –

the perception that the party in London was well to the Left of the mainstream. Portillo claimed the Tories would win seats in Newham, Tottenham, Lambeth, Brent and Ealing. They didn't.

Behind Portillo's bravado there were doubts. One Cabinet minister on the Right who talked to him during the campaign was deeply sceptical about the chance of victory at the outset, and the conduct of the election did nothing to reassure him, or Portillo. As a former Central Office employee during the 1979 victory and Parkinson's aide in the run-up to the 1983 landslide Portillo had experience of efficiently run campaigns. The 1992 campaign was anything but efficient.

The party chairman, Chris Patten, was an excellent performer – skilled at hitting Labour hard and low – but he had never been a natural administrator and his tenuous grip on Central Office was not helped by his need to nurse his marginal seat in Bath. 'Master-fixer' John Wakeham was assigned to help run Central Office, but his management style, appropriate for running a parliamentary party with a 100-plus majority, was not suited to walking a twenty-four-hour election tightrope. One party worker described Wakeham's style as the creation of minor problems, the avoidance of bigger ones, and the dropping of the really large ones into the laps of others. One MP who retired in 1992 believes Wakeham's style as a whip was to create tension and then take the credit for resolving it. As acting chairman of the party he could only manage half of that.

As well as the administrative chaos that affected all those who had to deal with Central Office, there was also, especially in the earlier part of the campaign, a lack of political focus. In the later stages of the campaign John Major's stress on low taxation and constitutional stability put the opposition on the defensive, but at the beginning there was an inchoate feel.

The manifesto launch was, for many, the nadir. Primarily the work of the Number Ten Policy Unit, under Sarah Hogg, it drove many on the Right into despair. As far as they were concerned, there was the irrelevant – such as policy statements on hedgerows – and the offensive – such as the suggestion that shortlists for public appointments automatically include a quota of women. There were precious few exciting titbits, and even the two big changes in the shape of government – the creation of the Department of National

Heritage and the promotion of the Citizens' Charter minister to the Cabinet – found little favour on the Right. The first smacked to them of a Continental-style 'minister of culture', and for at least one young Thatcherite the second had uncomfortable echoes of the Department of Administrative Affairs, parodied as the *ne plus ultra* of bureaucratic pointlessness in the TV sitcom *Yes, Minister*.

Portillo was less worried than some. He had seen manifestos written before, and seldom seen them read afterwards, but even he was put out by one policy. One of the first sections he turned to, as an environment minister, was on urban regeneration and housing, where there was a pledge to introduce a bill to reform the law on leasehold – a type of time-limited property ownership prevalent in parts of London. The legislation would force land-owners to sell their freeholds to leaseholders. It was to drive the Duke of Westminster out of the Tory Party in protest at 'legalised expropriation'. To Portillo it was 'stealing private property'.

The exasperation at that policy did not, however, affect the professionalism with which Portillo conducted himself throughout the election campaign. He never betrayed any public unhappiness with the direction it was taking, and friends say he became more confident of a good result in the last few days, recognising the Tory vote solidifying as the prospect of Prime Minister Kinnock concentrated their minds.

However, even though he fought for victory as strenuously as any minister, there were signs that he was already preparing for any eventuality. The drift from Thatcherism that had begun with Major's first days in power and which had led to the 1992 manifesto had been a source of some concern to him in the months leading up to the election. He had outlined his thinking in two speeches – the first broad-ranging or 'philosophical' speeches he had made as a minister. The first was addressed to a meeting of Conservative Way Forward at the 1991 Tory party conference in Blackpool, the second to a meeting of the Conservative Political Centre in Limpley Stoke, near Bath, in January 1992.

CWF was a pressure group within the party, set up following Margaret Thatcher's fall to keep her ideas alive. It was intended to match the influence once exerted by the leftish Tory Reform Group, which had provided safe havens for coded wet dissent during the Thatcher premiership. The Tory Party in the country does not take to internal pressure groups with the same enthusiasm as MPs at Westminster, and neither the TRG or CWF has ever recruited anything like a mass membership. Both, however, attract a disproportionate number of the more committed activists who tend to become, or choose, parliamentary candidates.

The CPC is the political-education wing of the party, run from Central Office by Portillo's old Research Department colleague Alistair Cooke. It provides members with an opportunity to discuss policy, feed their suggestions upwards, and see the reaction filter back down.

Although the occasions were subtly different, Portillo's aims were similar at both. He wished to check any incipient leftward drift and plot a course ahead for the Tory party, in the event of victory or defeat, that would bring long-term success.

That he felt the need to make the speeches was a reflection of several factors. There was the fading from the scene of figures like Parkinson, Tebbit and, above all, Margaret Thatcher herself. There was a sense that a man on the verge of Cabinet should show he was more than just another able administrator. And there was a feeling that the Right's ideas had to be vigorously promoted if they were not to be written off as an aberration. The speeches were subsequently edited down to form a CPC pamphlet entitled *A Vision for the 1990s*.

Both speeches were attacks on Labour, but the ground from which Portillo chose to launch his attack also provided him with a standpoint from which to make an oblique commentary on what was happening within the Tory Party. He launched an attack on socialism's infatuation with greater government expenditure, but Major himself had been presiding over a pre-election state spending spree. Since Major had become prime minister public expenditure had increased by £18 billion in his first year, and £24 billion in his second in office. It was prodigal, even for a recession. Portillo was turning his fire on Labour's demands for still more expenditure as part of their pre-election campaign, but there also was a warning to his own party in his words: 'We have arrived at the essential difference between the Conservatives and Labour. We believe that unless the state is controlled by the constant and rigorous effort of the people it will grow inexorably and eventually, like a parasite, destroy its host.'

The other main thrust of his attack was the corollary of a smaller state – lower taxes. Tax cuts helped the Tories win the election, but for Portillo it was not enough just to have them lower: 'Now we need a new goal: the ultra-low-tax economy.' Arguing on grounds of economic efficiency and morality, Portillo believed a constant downwards drive on taxation would expose Labour's economic illiteracy and demonstrate 'their continuing and deep antipathy to the cause of the market and the individual'.

Portillo's determination to push taxes ever lower again had two targets: the Labour Party of shadow chancellor John Smith, dedicated to tax-raising and redistribution, and the consolidators in his own party whose support for tax cuts was only ever tactical and provisional and who were always happier arguing for new areas in which to expand, rather than cut, public spending.

When the speeches were delivered it was far from certain that the Tories would win. In terms of timing they served a triple purpose. They softened up Labour before the main assault, they set out a path to follow when in power, and they sought to forestall backsliding in opposition if the Tory Left tried to push the party closer to Labour.

Portillo believed that the election of a high-taxing, high-spending, federalist Labour government would give the Tories a chance to delineate the difference between Left and Right more clearly. In conversation with journalists during the campaign, he outlined the shape of any Tory counter-attack in opposition – a ruthless assault on tax increases and European accommodations that would create a new appetite for future Tory tax cuts and a vigorous defence of sovereignty.

Portillo campaigned vigorously. Unlike some ministers, of both Left and Right, he stuck his head above every available parapet. For much of the campaign he was accompanied by Martyn Fisher, a researcher on leave from an accountancy firm, and he had his efforts aided by the Research Department's local-government desk officer, Andrew Caesar Gordon. They were friends of each, educated in the North-West and typical of many of the twenty-something Tories attracted by Portillo's mix of certainty and *élan*.

Fisher acted as Portillo's driver and as a linkman with headquarters when they were out in the field. Their main sphere of

operations was the Thatcher heartlands – London and Essex –
although they made helicopter forays to the West Country. Fisher
recalls Portillo as indomitable for most of the campaign, occasionally openly disconsolate when Labour's lead in the polls opened
up further, but really depressed only when the daily grind meant
he had to hurry lunch. Portillo is a hater of the snatched sandwich.
Rising early and working late have yet to take their toll on his
physique, and part of his routine is a commitment to a hot lunch
every day. Even during the thick of constituency campaigning in
the tightest of marginals time was made for a plate of tagliatelle
or, in Basildon, a pie, chips and beans. Irritation, however, did
break through when Portillo was away from the campaign trail.

In his capacity as coordinator of the London and local-
government campaigns, Portillo spent time in Central Office over-
seeing strategy and commissioning ads. Early in the election
Saatchi & Saatchi pitched to him with their strategy for exploiting
Labour's local-government record. Steve Hilton, the brightest
researcher of his generation at Central Office, had been attached
to Saatchi's for the duration of the campaign and he took Portillo
through their thinking, eventually unveiling the centrepiece – a
poster of an overflowing rubbish bin, supposedly symbolic of socialist waste. Portillo was unimpressed, and politely asked Hilton, and
Saatchi's, to think again.

A week later they had another meeting and Hilton revealed the
same poster, albeit with new justifications. Portillo exploded. One
of those there claims he had never seen a politician so angry.
Portillo was obviously infuriated at being defied on a matter for
which he was ultimately responsible. He took the proposed campaign apart, point by point, and explained exactly what he wanted.
It was a wounding moment.

Portillo's customary politeness went out of the window for two
reasons: anger at not having his orders carried out, however clever
the underling, and concern that no blame should attach to anything he was responsible for throughout the election.

Portillo and Hilton have subsequently got on well. Portillo recognises the importance of skilled salesmen in modern politics, but
his admiration for others' expertise is tempered by a belief that
decisions must rest with those who will be held publicly responsible.

Because of his other responsibilities, Portillo's time in his own constituency was limited, but he had a solid association and Malcolm Tyndall was an energetic agent. Confident of the security of his own position, he again encouraged activists to help in other seats, in particular Ian Twinn's marginal Edmonton, next door.

There was one wobble. A stray comment from the Foreign Office minister and old friend Tristan Garel-Jones on London Greek Radio incensed some of the significant Greek population of Portillo's north-London seat. A hurried clarification might not be reported with the same prominence as the original remark, so Portillo insisted that every Greek voter in Southgate receive a personal letter from him setting their minds at rest. When party workers queried the practicality of such a minutely targeted mailshot he brushed away their worries. Tyndall worked flat-out for forty-eight hours, and eventually managed to reach them all. Portillo was deeply grateful.

Although it had been hard work, Tyndall didn't think Portillo's actions eccentric: 'He's a perfectionist. He doesn't accept mediocrity at any level. He pays attention to every detail – from the table plans at constituency functions down to the shadows on photographs.'

On election day itself Portillo was in the constituency. A leisurely lunch and a call to his Labour opposite number interrupted but did not disrupt his marshalling of the vote.

After a Chinese meal in the evening, he made his way to Enfield Town Hall for the result. His spirits had already been cheered by the victory of his PPS, David Amess, in Basildon – evidence that the late swing he had sensed but was not certain of had come good. He was delighted to find not only that his own vote had held up – reduced by only 18 from 1987 – but that his friend Ian Twinn had scraped home, one of a number of Tories with majorities under 1,000 who ensured that John Major got the majority he wanted, and the Tories their historic fourth term.

For Portillo, another term meant one thing above all: a chance to enter the Cabinet. Four years after the idea had first formed in Margaret Thatcher's mind, eight after it had been confidently predicted by the pressmen covering his by-election and just one before his own fortieth birthday, Portillo was a natural for promotion. Although still young, he had spent four years in two of the most difficult minister-of-state posts in the government. Both the previous poll-tax ministers, Michael Howard and David Hunt, had been promoted to the Cabinet at the end of their stints. After so long in the departure lounge, it was time for an upgrade.

John Major has been criticised for his handling of both policy and personnel, but his long immersion in the parliamentary party and his skilful manipulation of its factions in his rise to the top have given him a shrewder feel for his colleagues' talents than most outsiders are prepared to allow. Although his support for mauled ministers like David Mellor and Michael Mates may cast doubt on his judgement, and his appointment of Jeremy Hanley may perplex, he has also sought to marry man and industry with a care often missing under Margaret Thatcher. From his initial appointment of Michael Heseltine to Environment, when the poll tax needed to be defused, to his talent-spotting of more junior figures like social-security minister Roger Evans and party deputy chairman Michael Trend, to his choice of Michael Brown for the Whips' Office, he has shown an eye for the interesting fit.

His choice of Cabinet post for Michael Portillo was made with care. The man who before the election had stood out for ultra-low taxation and the hacking back of state spending while the deficit went wild was appointed as chief secretary to the Treasury – the man in charge of the nation's purse-strings. Much in the same way as Major had said to Heseltine, 'If you think the poll tax can be reformed, do it yourself,' so he had tossed Portillo the task of controlling expenditure.

Portillo was appointed on the Saturday after the election result – while the Tories were still basking in the warm afterglow of victory. The incompetence of others and his own doggedness had meant the victory was, uniquely, Major's own. The arrogance of the opposition had played a part, their campaign collapsing in the last week with overblown razzmatazz and incoherent constitutional kite-flying. The centrality of tax, at the insistence of Norman Lamont, had given the Tory campaign a focus it initially lacked. The social changes wrought in the eighties by Margaret Thatcher, with a broad coalition committed to the aspirations Toryism embodied, had also contributed. But, in the eyes of his party, the main achievement had been Major's. When so many had doubted, he had stood firm.

He then enjoyed a power over his party he had not had before, and would soon forfeit; that spring he seemed supreme. After four successive Tory victories there was heady talk of one-party rule and the Nipponisation of the British political system, but the unexploded incendiaries of the previous years' errors were still smouldering behind the Tory Party's confident façade. Membership of the ERM, the poor state of the public finances, unresolved dilemmas about Britain's place in Europe, ambiguities about economic policy, all would return to haunt John Major.

Indeed, in a curious way, the manner of Major's victory, even as it entrenched his temporary ascendancy, undermined his capacity to lead long-term. There was a warning in the experience of another Tory premier who had defied the odds to come from behind and snatch victory from the jaws of defeat – Ted Heath. The manner of Heath's victory set an unhappy precedent for his term in power, as his biographer John Campbell has argued:

He had won by his own efforts in his own way, despite them all, and was now inclined to think that he could do no wrong. The years of nagging criticism had made him more than ever solitary, defensive, distrustful of advice and stubbornly self-sufficient, a curious mixture of self-confidence and insecurity. Now victory in such heady circumstances restored his self-belief, freed him to follow his own instincts without obligation to the party faint-hearts who had never believed he could win and released in him a powerful streak of arrogance. This too would bring its nemesis in the years ahead.

Like Heath, Major was to push through European legislation in the face of dogged opposition from his own back benches. Like Heath, he would have to alter key economic policies in defiance of purist critics. Like Heath, he would pursue an Irish policy that alienated traditional allies. Like Heath, he would be attacked for straying from the true path but insulate himself with loyal allies. Like Heath with Alec Douglas-Home, he would follow the instincts of his Old Etonian foreign secretary, Douglas Hurd, in defiance of backwoods grumbling. Like Heath, he would prove himself more progressive in office than many of his supporters had hoped. And, like Heath, Major hoped he would tackle problems his predecessors had avoided, their displays of rhetorical brilliance masking the reality of fudge and failure.

One of the areas Major proclaimed he was determined to see tackled, and which remained a worry for all Margaret Thatcher's loudly-trumpeted good intentions, was public spending. He had presided over a pre-election spending boom, but he knew spending would have to be reined in if he were to deliver further tax cuts. When Michael Portillo became chief secretary the state took more than 40 per cent of the nation's income – and it still was not enough. There was a public-sector borrowing requirement of £28 billion and rising.

As chief secretary, Portillo was a full member of the Cabinet, but still only number two in his department. His boss was Norman Lamont, chancellor since 1990 and architect of the tax cuts before the 1992 election which had prepared the ground for a low-tax campaign.

Within the treasury, the chancellor was responsible for broad economic strategy and the chief secretary was supposed to scrutinise spending. Some chancellors, including Lawson and Clarke, have encouraged their chief secretaries to play a bigger role, but Lamont was a more cautious figure and kept Portillo to his brief. Stephen Dorrell served as financial secretary to the Treasury under both Lamont and Clarke and believes the two men's characters dictated very different approaches: 'Norman is somebody who is a private man who holds his cards close to his chest, and Ken's a much more open, buccaneering fellow, and he encouraged people to pitch in to an extent that Norman was sometimes uncomfortable with.'

Portillo had a big enough job, anyway: John Major was determined Portillo should bring order back to the public finances. Number Ten briefed the press that the government would face 'the toughest spending round in decades' and individual departments would see 'savage cuts'.

It was easier said than done. Margaret Thatcher had tried to bear down on public spending and, in the eighties, her administration had reduced it as a percentage of national income, albeit on the back of an incipient boom. It had even been possible to pay back some of the National Debt. But the success was temporary. The recession of the late eighties and early nineties had driven state spending up to new levels, a situation which pre-election generosity to everyone from the Manchester Olympic-bid team to every adult tax-payer only exacerbated. Given the limited success previous governments had had in cutting spending, even during periods of runaway growth, it was considered almost impossible to make real inroads when recovery was still some way off and the pain of the recession was still being felt.

Despite the scale of the increases in spending, most commentators believed Portillo would not have the muscle to claw back from existing programmes, let alone limit the growth of new ones. Cynical veterans of past spending rounds thought it would be politically impossible to do more than reduce expenditure at the margins. Many potential targets for cuts, such as the NHS and child benefit, had been specifically protected by manifesto pledges. Writing in the *Guardian* in the immediate aftermath of the Queen's Speech, the paper's economics editor, Will Hutton, doubted Portillo could make much of a difference: 'After 13 years' war against the public sector there is little or no fat left: budgets as disparate as housing and trade and industry have already been pared to the bone. To go further means reaching into the marrow.'

A more cautious, or less principled, minister might have scuttled for shelter, using the commentators' predictions as covering fire, deliberately down-playing expectations so he could not be criticised if he failed to force his colleagues to cut. But that was not Portillo's style. Even though he was the most junior member of the Cabinet, he was determined to raise the stakes.

Portillo was not going to try to set small targets and hope he would be praised for reaching them: he wanted to dramatise the battle he faced, and put his struggle at the centre of the government's strategy. It was more than a matter of good management, it was an ideological necessity. He outlined his approach to the House of Commons in the debate on the Queen's Speech only a few weeks after taking up his new post:

Our determination to control public spending and conduct the business of government prudently does not simply arise from our desire for efficient government and sound economic policy. Vital though those both are, there is, for us, a profound question of principle. Unlike the opposition, we do not believe in the inexorable growth of the reach and size of the state. Nor do we believe that the state can and should try to solve all our problems. Unlike the opposition, we believe in rolling back the state and returning to the individual as much automony over his or her life as possible.

And Portillo promised more than just sound public finances: he also dangled the prospect of further tax cuts.

The speech was heavily laced with taunts at the expense of Labour's shadow chancellor and chief secretary, John Smith and Margaret Beckett, who were the 'dream ticket' for the leadership vacated by the resignation of the defeated Neil Kinnock and Roy Hattersley. Using the surprise increase in the Tory vote in Scotland as a jumping-off point to savage Smith, Portillo tried to rub salt in the Scot's wounds with the satirical use of some execrable verse.

Labour members representing Scotland – those who survived the Tory onslaught there – will recall the Tay Bridge disaster. William McGonagall – a fine poet, with whom you, Madam Speaker, will be familiar – tells us that

> The beautiful railway Bridge of the Silv'ry Tay
> Collapsed with the loss of ninety lives
> On the last Sabbath day of 1879,
> Which will be remember'd for a very long time.

The architects of the Tay Bridge never worked again – yet the designers of Labour's disaster are apparently to be commissioned to prepare the next set of drawings, with dispatch and without much of a competition. How can the Labour Party contemplate forgiving the master craftsmen of its defeats? How can it entrust the future to such proven incompetents?

The braggadocio of the approach reflected the confidence of the newly elected government and the newly elected Portillo, but it did not appeal to everyone. The *Mail on Sunday*'s political diarist Black Dog, hitherto a discreet champion of Portillo's cause, thought it smacked of 'sneering triumphalism'.

Black Dog's was one of the first of a series of personal attacks on Portillo which were to grow in volume and ferocity in his time as chief secretary. Portillo knew his job as axeman would make him unpopular. He even joked about it in that speech, claiming, 'I no longer have any friends.' But the attacks were prompted by more than his zeal for economy: they were the first shots in a long campaign by the Left, in the country and in his party, to undermine the man who might reignite the Right.

The confidence which marked Portillo's début as a Cabinet minister in the Commons was carried over to his first hours inside the Treasury. Greeted by the permanent secretary, Sir Terry Burns, whom he had known when Burns was the government's chief economic adviser and Portillo was Nigel Lawson's political adviser, he had a civil, but direct, message: he would not be starting work in earnest until his private office was sorted out and the private secretary, Nick Holgate, he had inherited from the outgoing chief secretary, David Mellor, was removed.

A private secretary screens access to a minister, takes his calls, writes his letters, and acts as occasional understudy in Whitehall dramas. It is a post normally allocated to able young high-flyers starred for the top, or to experienced hands with a feel for intra-governmental relations. Portillo had encountered Holgate before the election and had not enjoyed the experience. He knew his task would be difficult and that the chief secretary's relations with his colleagues are uniquely sensitive. He was adamant that he did not want his principal aide and linkman to be a figure he felt could only exacerbate, rather than resolve, tensions.

Burns got the message, and set about finding Portillo a replacement. The man he chose was superficially a typical Treasury candidate: an articulate and self-confident twenty-something called Peter Wanless.

Portillo was initially suspicious – according to one official, because he feared Wanless was the 'establishment' choice and would be more the Treasury's man than his. But Wanless was far from an 'establishment' candidate. A graduate of Leeds University, he combines intelligence with informality and an undoctrinaire approach to problem-solving.

Throughout his career Portillo has shown a preference for 'outsiders' as aides. His first private secretary at the DHSS, Caroline Rookes, was far from the model of the deferential official. His special adviser, Alison Broom, had a background in the North-East and local government rather than the Westminster inside track. David Hart may be an impeccably connected old Etonian but he is no establishment dry stick, and none of Portillo's other assistants have been Oxbridge men on the make. The reason for this may be sensitivity to his own insulated career path, and a deliberate desire to draw expertise from as wide a field as possible. It may be an echo of Margaret Thatcher's thirst for alternative perspectives to those offered by the party machine and Whitehall. It may be his broader taste for as catholic a range of company as possible. It may even be his own sense of being subtly outside the establishment, as a grammar-school boy with a Spanish name and a Scottish mother.

Whatever the reason, Portillo liked Wanless's style, but it was to take some time for their relationship to move from friendly formality to a firm alliance. Wanless recalls, 'I had to wait seven months for the first word of praise. When I mentioned that a while later he seemed a bit taken aback and replied, half-jokingly, that he'd had to wait even longer before he got any positive feedback from me. But, throughout, he's been a tremendously good person to work for. He sets clear goals, has high standards, and appreciates pains taken.'

Wanless's favourable impression of his boss was shared by other Treasury officials, some of whom had spotted Portillo's promise during his stint as a special adviser. Officials from that period contrast him favourably with other Treasury ministers: 'Portillo always did his boxes – unlike Norman, who didn't master the detail and never gave a clear steer.'

Mastery of one's boxes – the red dispatch bags stuffed full of official papers that constitute ministerial homework – is normally a precondition of a minister being taken seriously by his civil servants. The few exceptions, such as Douglas Hurd, are those whose elegance of mind is best deployed when left uncluttered by the insignificant detail. Wanless recalls Portillo's treatment of the material in his first box: 'He'd list with an A, B and C the points he wanted to make on every document – he always wanted to know where the space was for his comments. He always gave a clear lead on every issue, always knew his own mind – or at least what additional information he needed to make up his mind. There's a tendency with some ministers if a subject is difficult, or boring, to put off the decision. He never did.'

Peter Wanless believes the high standards Portillo seemed to set himself were extended to what he expected of others. Wanless soon learned, in his role as gatekeeper to the chief secretary, not to waste his time with incoherent or slack work from others: 'I often had to ask people to do things again, and they'd ask if it was me or the minister who wanted it redrafted. It was me, but I was simply saving everyone wasted effort.'

One other aspect of Portillo's working method struck Wanless: alongside his determination to do things his way was a respect for the Treasury as an institution, and for its methods, which may have been inculcated during his year as a special adviser. 'He respected hierarchies and knew what the civil service was for. He appreciated how the machinery operated – and fitted in.'

Like Peterhouse, and Parliament, the Treasury was an institution which inspired affection in Portillo. Despite its historic attachment to Keynesian heresies and the keenness of recent regimes on managed exchange rates, Portillo appreciated it. His approach to the place was very much in line with Enoch Powell's definition of a Tory: 'someone who respects institutions more than the people who are running them'.

Respect the Treasury way of doing things though he might, Portillo soon set in train one very significant change. If he was to reduce public spending he would have to win political arguments, but Portillo and his boss, the chancellor, Norman Lamont, made their life a little easier by redrafting the rules of the expenditure game after years when they had become slanted in favour of spending ministers.

Before 1992 the budgets for the various government departments had been decided in a series of exhausting one-to-one negotiations between the chief secretary and his Cabinet colleagues. Starting with an exchange of letters in the spring and culminating in Commons corridor muggings throughout the autumn and bedroom broking at the Tory party conference, it was a messy and, for the Treasury, unrewarding process. Departmental ministers were encouraged to get as big a slice as possible for themselves, and devil take the hindmost. They entered extravagant bids and tried to wear the Treasury down. The sheer volume of submissions helped them, and, even though their initial bids were always high, the process of seeing so many off meant that, on average, departments got two-thirds of what they were after. Given the inflated nature of their initial demands, this was not a significant shortfall.

Lamont and Portillo designed a new method of fixing spending which, as in judo, used their opponents' weight against them. They secured the Cabinet's agreement for the adoption of a 'control total' beyond which spending that was not governed by cyclical factors, like unemployment benefit, could not rise. This was no phantom figure: it was the public target they collectively pledged to hit.

Instead of the chief secretary negotiating with each minister alone, he would now ask ministers for a menu of options, based on suggested spending limits, bring them back to a Cabinet committee, and allow the committee to decide who would lose and who would win, to ensure that spending could be squeezed into the corset. The committee, ED(X), would contain ministers who would have a vested interest in helping the chief secretary cut colleagues' budgets in order to safeguard their own. The persistent attitude that cuts were fine in general, but not in my department – an attitude Portillo called nimdyism – could not be sustained.

Theoretically this meant a diminution in Portillo's role. Rather than being the final arbiter of budgets, he would simply present ED(X) with the figures and calmly point out that an increase in health would have to mean cuts elsewhere, indicate where they might be made, recommend, and allow responsibility to rest with the committee. Portillo was fond of saying he was merely the servant of the committee, but he was its servant in the way that the prime minister is the Queen's servant – he used the name of a greater authority than himself to push his own programme.

Deploying the authority of the rest of the Cabinet, and the prime minister, Portillo got to work early. He arranged bilateral meetings with all spending ministers before they had submitted their initial bids for discussion, and before the Cabinet's scheduled public-spending discussion in July.

Colleagues were not the only ones anxious to protect their budgets who got an early indication of Portillo's determination to safeguard every penny. The day after he took up his new post Portillo took a call from Paul Reichmann, of Olympia & York, whose preferred tube link to Canary Wharf Portillo had championed as transport minister. Reichmann congratulated Portillo on his new appointment, and then touched on the matter of the Jubilee Line extension, hoping he could secure his old friend's support for the scheme at a time when even the most ambitious capital projects were being reviewed. He reminded Portillo that O & Y were in for £8 billion. There was a long pause, and then Portillo remarked, 'Yes, well we're in for £28 billion.'

Other plans still covered with Portillo fingerprints were not spared harsh scrutiny. He asked his old colleagues at Environment to save money by scrapping the City Challenge scheme, even though he had been the minister who had introduced Heseltine's pet project.

Far from offering cuts, most colleagues submitted bids for significant increases. Having agreed, collectively, to fix a control total, and set it at £244.5 billion, they then asked for at least £14 billion more. The biggest culprits included Environment and Transport, where a number of Portillo initiatives were soaking up more spending than initially envisaged; Health, which was protected by manifesto commitments; Defence and Social Security, where Portillo had close connections with the respective ministers; and the territorial departments, Scotland and Wales, where an established formula limited room for manœuvre.

Having set a precedent for breaking rules by revising the whole spending round, Portillo did not feel constrained by sentimentality in other areas. With the reluctant agreement of the Scottish and Welsh secretaries, Portillo abandoned a hundred-year-old safeguard for Scottish spending. The Goschen–Barnett formula, devised by a Victorian chancellor and revised by a Labour chief secretary in the seventies, guaranteed Scotland two-seventeenths and Wales one-seventeenth of public expenditure. Portillo saw no reason why, as these nations' populations declined as a proportion of the UK, and their prosperity rose relative to the rest, they should continue to be so protected. Ian Lang, the Scottish secretary, fought a rearguard action to protect his budget, but, as with his defence of the poll tax, he was again in a minority. Allan Stewart, who was a minister at the Scottish Office at the time, considers Portillo handled the move with 'sensitivity but certainty – he was aware he could bring the weight of the rest of the government to bear'.

The idea that he was the Cabinet's servant helped Portillo fly a number of kites, including a suggestion that entitlement to unemployment benefit be withdrawn after six months rather than a year. But the political wind was not yet gusting strongly enough in his favour to allow him to fly too many. Instead, he had to concentrate on using the discipline of the new system rather than imaginative innovation to pare budgets down. There were scare stories about the fate of the European Fighter Aircraft, British Rail's refurbishment programme and the enormously expensive eastwards expansion of the Jubilee Line, but throughout the Treasury made it clear that expenditure was a matter for the Cabinet to decide as a whole.

Portillo sought to create a greater sense of urgency in his task by allowing estimates of the size of the deficit to mushroom. The Treasury might be forecasting £28 billion, but outside bodies like the strictly non-partisan Institute for Fiscal Studies were predicting a potential deficit of £50 billion. Portillo did little to demur from their view in private, and allowed pressure to build up on advocates of greater spending. Andrew Dilnot, the hyper-numerate director of the IFS, believes Portillo played a skilful political game: 'Our estimates, given the slackness of the pre-election spending round, outran the Treasury's. Our honesty and accuracy were apparently used to great effect to bring errant ministers into line.'

But the bleakness of the broader picture did not stop one or two fierce bilateral battles breaking out – and coming to wider notice. One of the fiercest was a tussle between Portillo and his old boss, Michael Heseltine, then in charge of the Department of Trade and Industry.

The DTI was planning to close a number of pits as a prelude to making British Coal profitable enough to sell, and needed a large tranche of cash to soften the blow at the pit-heads. The politically damaging closure of the Ravenscraig steel mill in Lanarkshire earlier in the year had been cushioned by millions pledged in development aid, but that was before the election.

Portillo stood out against presents for the miners to make redundancy easier, but was lobbied persistently by the DTI. A letter from Heseltine's deputy, Tim Sainsbury, was leaked to the *Guardian*, protesting that the Treasury were offering 'nothing either major or new which can be presented as an appropriate response to the very serious problems coal areas will face'. Heseltine, true to form, intervened personally – before breakfast, lunch and dinner – to get more money. But all the preprandial lobbying came to nothing – Portillo was not prepared to give him what he wanted.

Heseltine was not the only big-hitter to come away empty-handed after haggling with Portillo. Kenneth Clarke, as home secretary, was also disappointed when, before the Tory conference, he tried to prise more money out of the Treasury for police and prisons. He had wanted to throw some red meat to the activists, in despair at rising crime and uneasy at Tony Blair's ability, as shadow secretary, to capitalise on that unease.

But, pressing as Clarke thought his political problems were, they were as nothing compared to the storm about to break over Heseltine's head. His obsession with winning the Whitehall compensation battle had blinded him to the broader need to prepare the ground for the pit closures in the first place. When the scale of the proposed closures was revealed on 13 October, just days after a bruising Tory party conference, it provoked public outrage and a political backlash that nearly ended Heseltine's career.

Sir Marcus Fox, chairman of the 1922 committee, said the closures were 'unacceptable'. Andrew Mitchell, the Tory party's vice-chairman in charge of candidate selection, called the plan 'catastrophic'. The former was a Yorkshire member, the latter had a Nottinghamshire seat, but the outrage they articulated was felt much more widely, as was shown when Arthur Scargill, back from the dead, led a march of thousands in protest through Kensington, cheered by the Royal Borough's lumpenbourgeoisie.

Would greater Treasury generosity have assuaged the hurt? Almost certainly not – the anger was too raw for balm, however expensive. Could, or should, the closures have been averted? Again, almost certainly not. Industrial militancy and changing technology had made British coal the fuel of last resort for too many. Without demand, there was no future for much of the industry. It would have turned the economic logic of the previous decade on its head to intervene to save a few thousand jobs, however high-profile, when the long-term consequences of subsidy seemed so debilitatingly clear.

Heseltine knew the closures had to go ahead. So did Portillo. The only difference was that Heseltine believed that spending more money on cosmetics would make things easier, rather than telling the truth earlier and more often. He was reaping the harvest of expectations sown by his previous protectionist and interventionalist rhetoric. Faced with the harsh realities of office, that rhetoric came to haunt him.

The government's crisis manager, Lord Wakeham, leader of the House of Lords, announced there would be a 'review' on 21 October, feeding the hope among some for a reprieve. Portillo knew the hope was misplaced. In a letter to a constituent on the same day, he commented, 'It is very difficult to see what will change.' He went on, 'The fact is likely to remain that the electricity industry is not taking the coal that is being produced. Despite all this talk about the economies of this or that source of energy, those who have the duty to generate electricity are not buying coal in the quantities they used to.' He was right. After the review, the inevitable came and the closures went ahead after public anger had burnt itself out.

Portillo had simply done his job. Every spending minister threatens crisis unless he gets his cash. It is the chief secretary's job to judge how much is exaggeration, and, even if there is a looming crisis, to what extent more taxpayers' money could avert it. The exchange did little to improve relations between him and Heseltine, however. The good professional relationship they established at Environment had not been characterised by an effusive personal warmth. The coal débâcle cooled things a little further.

It was a month after Heseltine's mauling at the hands of the miners that the Autumn Statement for 1992 was delivered. It was the last of its kind. Portillo had argued for the merger of the Statement, the government's spending plans, with the Budget, its revenue-raising arrangements, in his maiden speech in 1984. Now Norman Lamont had pledged to bring them together, and so, on 13 November, he delivered the final Autumn Statement, the fruit of his deputy's labours. Portillo had spent the days before preparing back-benchers for the wholesale slaughter of some of their pets. In the end, the yelping came from a constituency with few supporters on the back benches – public-sector workers.

Portillo hit the control total exactly. Identifiable government expenditure, excluding cyclical spending, came in at £244.5 billion. Capital spending had been protected: projects from hospital building through the modernisation of Kent commuter routes to the extension of the Jubilee Line to Canary Wharf survived intact. The victims were civil servants. A de-facto pay policy had been introduced. Their pay rises were limited to 1.5 per cent. The only exceptions were senior civil servants, judges and serving officers whose 2.8 per cent increase had already been agreed.

The package was well-received by Tory MPs and most ministerial colleagues. A Treasury civil servant let it be known that Portillo was 'the sharpest minister he had worked with since Lawson'. Even those colleagues who faced cuts agreed he was better briefed and better mannered than his predecessors in the post.

The in-house Treasury view was just as favourable. In an internal post-mortem drawn up by senior civil servants, Portillo was praised for both his firmness in the spending round and his skill in introducing a new method, 'despite the toughness of the remit of a new system designed on the wing'.

But, whatever the Treasury view, spending cuts had political costs, as Portillo knew. While a clampdown on public-sector pay might not seem as dramatic as, say, cancelling the Jubilee Line extension, it nevertheless hit 1.5 million voters and their families.

Portillo defended the policy in the pages of the *Evening Standard*, arguing:

By asking public-sector employees, whose jobs are generally secure, to accept less pay, we have freed £1.5 billion which will immediately and directly create jobs and provide better services.

It is a sacrifice, without doubt. But the government believes in getting our priorities right. At a time when so many are out of work, it seems reasonable to ask that, for one year, those in work should do with less. That helps us to invest now in Britain's long-term future.

The message was reinforced in a round of interviews, and extended in one with ITN, where he argued that the gains of a one-year reduction 'should not be followed by a series of catching-up settlements which would dissipate the benefits achieved'. He went on to add that some industrialists were calling for the private sector to accept a ceiling of 1.5 per cent for their pay increases, commenting, 'I think that is in many ways very desirable.'

That theme was developed in his speech in the debate on the Autumn Statement a week later, on 19 November, when he argued, 'It is up to individual employers to decide what they can afford to pay. But what everyone knows is that the lower the growth in wage costs in general, the better will be the UK's competitive position.'

The desirability of a pay ceiling was not a view shared by everyone on the Right. Lord King, the then chairman of British Airways, a friend of Lady Thatcher and Portillo, spoke for many purist free-marketeers when he commented, 'I think we should be very careful about going back to the awful mistakes of the Heath days, because if you have a pay freeze, then comes a pay thaw.'

Lord King, recently in receipt of a pay rise of 64 per cent which took his salary to £670,000, spoke for more than just the chairmen of privatised industries. His disquiet was reflected in an otherwise warm review of the chief secretary's performance in the *Financial Times*. The *FT*'s political editor, Philip Stephens, described Portillo as 'among that rare group of politicians who manage effortlessly to set themselves apart from their peers', but he took a sideswipe at Portillo's adoption of a 'U-turn' which saw 'The reintroduction of a 1970s-style pay policy'.

The praise meted out to Portillo rankled with Lamont. He had helped design the new system, and yet Portillo got the plaudits. 'He was a highly effective chief secretary, but ED(X) was a collective effort.'

One Treasury official, now in the private sector, believes Lamont's contribution has been unfairly eclipsed by Portillo's publicity, but Tristan Garel-Jones begs to differ. 'To compare Lamont to Portillo is absurd. I can't imagine on what basis people would say that Lamont was underrated. Lamont was overpromoted, and I would guess that his chancellorship, to a great degree, was underpinned by Portillo, frankly. Only one incident that I know of specifically about that chancellorship comes to mind, and there the person who behaved as if he were the senior one was Portillo and not Lamont.'

History may judge Lamont more leniently, but while Portillo's reputation certainly seemed to be enhanced at the Treasury, Lamont suddenly and spectacularly lost his on one bad day in September 1992.

CHAPTER ELEVEN

A Devalued Government

In office, but not in power.
Norman Lamont, chancellor of the exchequer 1990–93

On Wednesday 16 September 1992 the pound was slung out of the Exchange Rate Mechanism, unable to match up to the mighty mark, like a bantamweight boxer after too many rounds with the heavyweight champion. In the preceding days, £11 billion of reserves had been spent trying to prop it up. Two interest-rate increases in one day had done nothing to convince the markets that sterling should continue to be locked into the currency corset.

Membership of the ERM had been the centrepiece of the government's economic strategy and the main plank of its foreign policy, simultaneously the most powerful weapon in the fight against inflation and proof of the UK's Euro-virility. The honeymoon the Major government had enjoyed following its election victory had been short-lived. The humiliating exit from the ERM was more devastating for the Tory party's fortunes than the last major devaluation, in 1967, had been for the then Labour government.

Although Margaret Thatcher had presided over a precipitous fall in the value of the pound when it floated in the eighties, the losses were not associated with the stigma of formal devaluation. When that happened it was doubly traumatic. It was seen as proof that Britain's economic strength was far less than the Tories sought to portray and also, for an electorate unwilling to grapple with the complexities of managed exchange rates, as a simple humiliation. The UK couldn't hack it in an environment where the mark had muscle, the franc had friends and the pound was a puny also-ran.

Even economic revival – ironically, noticeable only once Britain had left the ERM – did little to revive poll ratings. The public saw the recovery as occurring despite rather than because of Conservative policies, so credit for growth was not laid at the door of Number Ten, or even Number Eleven.

The most vigorous public defender of Britain's membership of the ERM, the chancellor, Norman Lamont, had been one of the ministers most suspicious of its benefits. Although Lamont's first sponsor in politics was the impeccably pro-European Duncan Sandys, he had become suspicious of the EEC's claims by the time he was adopted as the candidate for the Kingston by-election in 1972. His experiences as a minister under Margaret Thatcher hardened him in his views.

Chief secretary in Thatcher's government, in the summer of 1990 Lamont was one of a group of academics, businessmen and politicians gathered in a Holland Park house to celebrate Edmund Burke's birthday. Discussion turned to the merits and demerits of entry into the ERM, then a favoured panacea for Britain's economic ills, championed by both the CBI and the opposition parties. Lamont then made no secret of his views. He believed there was nothing Britain could do to fight inflation in the ERM that it could not do outside, and the loss of control inherent in ERM membership was not a price worth paying for benefits that were nugatory if not non-existent.

One of the other guests recalls, 'Norman arrived late, didn't have anything to eat, and contented himself with laying into the drink. But that didn't affect his fluency. He was perfectly clear, and perfectly sceptical.' Given that his boss, John Major, was urging entry to the ERM on Thatcher at that point, given that entry came months later, and Lamont's own elevation to the chancellorship very shortly after that, it is illuminating to know what the man really thought. Like sterling, once Lamont was locked in he had to make the best of it. But he was a happier man outside.

Since leaving the government, Norman Lamont has become the most outspoken, articulate and coherent critic of its European policy – or, as he would have it, lack of one. His support for John Redwood's leadership challenge in 1995, his series of articles in *The Times*, his speeches raising the possibility of withdrawal have all been attempts to force the Tories to rethink their European policy from first, Powellite, principles. Anger at what he perceived as his ill-treatment when the chancellorship was removed from him may lend an additional edge of relish to his attacks, but he is a sceptic to his sinews. His scepticism is not camouflage adopted to make it easier to attack the administration he so lately left.

However, notwithstanding his private doubts, his public defence of the ERM meant that Lamont was intimately associated with the failure of membership.

In 1967 the Labour chancellor responsible for devaluation, Jim Callaghan, had resigned and swapped jobs with the home secretary, Roy Jenkins. Although his career seemed becalmed, he had then gone on to become prime minister, proving once more the fatuity of writing politicians' obituaries prematurely. As a politician with a keen sense of history, and an even keener desire to save his own skin, on 14 September, the day after the ERM débâcle, Lamont told the prime minister that he wished to resign. Implicit in his offer was the hope that room could be found for him in a senior office of state, but more important than the status of his new berth was the need to be seen to act honourably.

Major refused to countenance Lamont's resignation. He considered that the chancellor had been carrying out Cabinet policy and should no more resign than should the whole Cabinet. At a subsequent Cabinet meeting Major specifically instructed other ministers to shoulder some of the blame and warned them against using Lamont as an 'air-raid shelter'.

That, of course, was just what John Major was doing in the eyes of Lamont. If Lamont had gone then Major would have become the focus of criticism for the failed policy, rather than the damaged chancellor. By keeping him in office, Major allowed Lamont to soak up more punishment.

An old friend of Lamont's claims that Major promised Lamont he would stay in office to deliver the first combined Budget and Expenditure Statement – that is, until autumn 1993. When Major removed Lamont from the Treasury in spring 1993, offering him the Environment Department as compensation, Lamont believed he was simultaneously being betrayed and insulted. To his friend, Lamont's bitterness is understandable: 'By not allowing Norman to resign when he wanted, making it seem as though he was clinging to office, and then offering him a humiliating demotion when he had absorbed as much criticism as possible, Major really shafted him.'

Such admirable loyalty skates over the precipitous decline in public and City confidence in Lamont in the wake of Black Wednesday. A spate of stories in the press contrived to turn him from a damaged figure into a ridiculous one. The *Sun* revealed that he had been tardy in paying his hotel bill at the 1992 party conference. The *News of the World* revealed he had unwittingly let the basement of his London home to a sex-therapist. A malicious invention by an off-licence manager about the purchase of cheap champagne and 'tart's' cigarettes in a seedy area of London was given huge coverage. The stories were either trivial, irrelevant or false, but the accumulation of unfavourable publicity hurt Lamont.

A former adviser's judgement is that 'Norman's a proud man who was unfairly attacked for abandoning a policy he never believed in. He didn't deserve the vilification.' Perhaps not. But the public appetite for believing the worst of the chancellor may have reflected a deeper public desire to see someone pay for the national humiliation. In the end Major bowed to the pressure, and evicted a chancellor he thought no longer commanded confidence.

The consequences of Lamont's departure from the government were to linger, but Lamont's criticisms were merely one of the most visible expressions of a deeper discontent simmering within the party brought to the surface by Black Wednesday. Disquiet with John Major's constructive approach to Europe had emerged in 1991, barely months after his becoming prime minister, when his attempts to build an entente with Chancellor Kohl attracted criticism from Norman Tebbit and other Ultras on the back benches.

Many had their worries about the Maastricht Treaty, signed in December 1991, which marked another staging-post in the evolution of 'Europe' from common market to political union. However, Major's skill in focusing attention on the opt-outs from the social chapter and the single currency, rather than the many other provisions for which Britain had signed up, deflected early criticism.

Rumbles in the first half of 1992 were muted in the run-up to the election and quietened by Major's victory. However, they returned with the Danish rejection of Maastricht in a referendum in June 1992. The Danish 'No' gave the sceptics in the Tory party, bolstered by an intake markedly to the Right of previous tranches of new boys, the opportunity to raise their banner.

Using the Commons ruse of an early day motion – a parliamentary means to collect signatures on a matter of general concern –

the sceptics, under Worcestershire South's Michael Spicer, gathered over 100 signatures calling for a 'fresh start' on Europe in the wake of the Danish rejection. Since members of the government – 100 of the 335 Tory MPs – could not sign, it was an impressive show of strength. Nearly half of the party on the back benches had signalled their unhappiness with the Maastricht Treaty, and the strength of feeling persuaded the government to delay introducing the legislation necessary to ratify the treaty until the autumn.

The government hoped that Europe would be a less incendiary issue once passions had subsided during the summer. But, if the Danish referendum had inflamed sceptic feeling, the exit from the ERM set off a forest fire of opposition to further progress towards integration. The party conference in October 1992 was marked by the two faces of Toryism slugging it out for mastery, with Maastricht as the battlefield. Norman Tebbit gave tongue to the pit-bull populism of the representatives opposed to the treaty; Douglas Hurd issued a patrician appeal to the party that had broken itself over the corn laws and tariff reform not to split again but 'give that madness a miss'.

The passions unleashed by the devaluation gave Michael Portillo an opportunity to prove something of his stature as a politician. The collapse of so many policy assumptions allowed him the chance to try to fill the vacuum with a series of speeches that set compass bearings for the Conservatism of the nineties. He was staking a claim to be taken seriously, and the platform he was building was meant, primarily, to remind the party of what it should stand for. But the speeches were inevitably seen as a critique of John Major's government from the inside.

Those who had a hand in writing them are adamant that that was not Portillo's intention. In charting a course based on basic Tory principles while the administration was entangled in the necessary compromises of power, Portillo inevitably became a dauphin for the discontented. But the way in which he handled the discharge of his daily duties showed him to be a politician with an understanding of the realities of power and the limitations of office. Portillo, like Tony Blair, has always believed that, however sophisticated your philosophy, what matters is winning, using and keeping power.

Perhaps appropriately, on Black Wednesday, the day that in the near future was to force Portillo and others to look towards the blue horizon, he had his head down at his desk. While the Treasury and the rest of Whitehall were paralysed by the currency convulsions that eventually ejected sterling from the ERM, Portillo was getting on with the job of cutting public expenditure.

Although number two at the Treasury, the chief secretary has no formal input to monetary policy. Lamont, unlike Lawson, did not canvass the opinions of colleagues on areas outside their responsibilities. Everyone knew that Portillo had his doubts about the ERM, but he did not consider it his place to air them publicly, and Lamont never gave him an opportunity so to do. David Cameron, Lamont's special adviser, cannot recall Portillo stepping out of line once on the issue of monetary policy: 'I can never remember Michael venturing an opinion on our membership, pre or post our exit from the ERM. It simply isn't the chief secretary's job to get involved in that sort of thing.' And Lamont himself claims that he and Portillo discussed the ERM privately only perfunctorily, and without passion.

On Black Wednesday itself, Peter Wanless, Portillo's principal private secretary at the time, noticed in the chief secretary's office an insulation from the atmosphere of crisis in the rest of the building that amounted almost to insouciance: 'That day he was involved in a bilateral discussion with Ken Clarke about Home Office spending. When Clarke came in he said he only had an hour because he had to go off to the Admiralty to see the PM. Rather than waste any time fishing for facts, the chief secretary just got straight down to negotiations and then let Clarke go.' Clarke, who was on the crisis management team, was much better informed about what was happening, but Portillo's priority was to do his job properly, whatever else was going on.

The capacity to concentrate on the matter in hand at a time when any politician might be forgiven for allowing his mind to wander might suggest a certain wintry detachment, but those who have worked most closely with Portillo prefer to see it as a mark of his professionalism. He regards politics as a serious task, and, however attractive the dilettantish and gossipy sides may be, the ability to enjoy them depends on the effective discharge of public duties.

Moreover, Portillo had learned, under Heseltine, the hard lesson of working as number two to a minister pursuing a policy with which he was not enthusiastically in agreement. The luxury of agonising over policy which he could not change was one he could not afford. He did not criticise, or seek to influence, exchange-rate policy, knowing his own stock of political capital could only be diminished by an ill-timed intervention.

Loyalty to the Treasury line may not have endeared Portillo to some of the freer spirits on the Right who exulted in the collapse of the ERM, but it impressed those with whom he worked. David Cameron remembers Portillo as a solid lieutenant in trying times: 'He was always supportive of Norman and, even as Norman came under attack, never attempted to exploit any instability to push himself forward.' Lamont himself, asked if he thought Portillo regretted the exit from the ERM or welcomed it, is clear: 'He saw it as a definite downside.'

Portillo's solidarity with his boss extended beyond the temporary turbulence of the ERM exit to the difficult decisions the chancellor faced in 1993. The 1992 Autumn Statement had made inroads into state spending and had helped control the deficit. The reductions in expenditure had gone beyond what most commentators had expected, but they were still not enough, by themselves, to move the budget into balance. The Budget that had to be delivered in March 1993 – the last of its kind – would be an uncomfortable one. Spending cuts would have to be augmented by tax increases.

Lamont had known the previous autumn that it would be an afternoon unloved by Tory activists, hence his insistence on staying in office until autumn 1993 if he was to be expected to endure the odium of introducing the March increases.

The first 1993 Budget was designed to make a significant dent in the deficit without dangerous increases in direct taxation. The room for manœuvre was limited, and, reluctantly, Lamont concluded that VAT would have to be extended to cover domestic fuel and power. Other EU countries levied a similar tax on these commodities, but throughout the 1992 election campaign Lamont had insisted the government had 'no plans and no need' to raise VAT.

When Lamont unveiled the increases, they proved every bit as unpalatable as he had feared. His attempt to soften the blow, by introducing the increase at 8 per cent and raising it to the full

VAT rate of 17½ per cent after a year, succeeded only in giving a desperate air to an unattractive impost. Teddy Taylor, the Scot who sits for Southend East, called the decision 'one of the most unpopular ever taken by a chancellor'.

Opposition to the increase came from Left and Right. The Tory Left feared VAT on fuel would hit pensioners and the poorest hardest as they struggled to heat their homes. Many on the Right were unhappy that the government's tax-cutting edge had been so clumsily blunted, fearing the effect of any future income-tax cuts would be obscured by this single high-profile indirect increase.

Both fears found a home in the schizophrenic breast of Nicholas Winterton, a politician whose populism embraces everything from doughty defence of the unreformed NHS to vigorous championing of rope, birch and stocks for the criminal classes. His opposition to the increase, on both electoral and sentimental grounds, found an echo among a surprisingly wide range of the party, and he was joined in opposition by several normally loyal back-benchers, including Phil Gallie, the member for Ayr (majority 85), and William Powell, the member for Corby (majority 342).

Their public opposition was matched by the private sniping of many more members, particularly from those on the Right. Several anti-federalists argued that the tax increases were being imposed only because ERM membership had exacerbated the recession and wrecked the public finances. The Stafford sceptic Bill Cash, for one, took the view that the public should not be forced to pay for ministerial folly.

These arguments did not impress Michael Portillo. His views on the pressing need to halt the growth of the public sector were on the record, but nevertheless he was a vigorous supporter of the March 1993 tax increases. Portillo had absorbed the sound-money lessons of the eighties thoroughly from mentors like Lawson and Biffen. However important it was to reduce taxation, it was all the more important to balance the budget. A small deficit could be tolerated, but it was short-sighted to allow borrowing to stay high just in order to keep taxes low – that would only delay an even more painful day of reckoning.

It was an analysis he outlined to the Commons in the debate on the Budget on 17 March:

Next year, the public sector would be borrowing around £1,000 a year for every man, woman and child in the country. The interest on that borrowing is going to have to be paid over many years to come.

The Chancellor could have chosen to postpone action to another day. Many apparently expected just that. But those who create jobs in Britain need to know that the government will reduce its borrowings.

A mischievous disavowal of Spanish practices followed: 'The mañana approach would have done nothing for confidence in the economy.'

Portillo was at some pains to remind MPs that tax increases were not the only difficult deficit-reduction measure the government was trying. He reiterated the commitment to cut spending – spelling out the severity of the new control totals which held increases to less than 1 per cent in real terms, and pointing out that 'At a time when we are also committed to increasing the money for the health service and increasing the number of students and facing pressures on social security, these are very tough ceilings indeed.'

During this period Portillo was held to account for his stance on tax increases by a variety of critics on the Right. At one private dinner in a London club several Euro-sceptic industrialists chided him. They were unhappy with what they saw as an abandonment of Thatcherite instincts. Portillo listened courteously, but, even though he was at a private dinner among the ideologically sympathetic, he did not yield an inch in his loyalty to the Treasury line. One who was there recalled, 'He pointed out the policy he was supporting was true to the one Mrs Thatcher had pursued in the recession of the early eighties. He argued that monetarist orthodoxy demanded the budget be balanced, even at the cost of tax increases. He didn't convince them all, but he was clearly convinced himself.'

Disquiet on the Right of the Tory party with the March tax increases simmered through the summer and, with the prospect of another tranche of tax rises in the joint Budget and Expenditure Statement scheduled for November, it boiled over in August.

Conservative Way Forward, the party's main right-wing caucus, led by a natural Portillo ally, Sir George Gardiner, expressed the anger felt by many on the Right when it argued, in the pre-conference edition of its journal, *Forward*, that increases should be resisted in November. Sir George did not restrict himself to an anonymous editorial deprecating tax increases: he told the BBC, 'I think every department could find further economies.' Defence, foreign and welfare budgets were particularly favoured for the axe.

Sir George's close collaborator John Townend, the Bridlington wine merchant who chairs the Tories' back-bench Finance Committee, also fired a shot across Treasury bows: 'If we do not tackle public expenditure, and we go into the next election as the party that has increased taxation, we don't stand a hope in hell of winning.'

Such critics were expressing Portillo's own instincts, but he knew better than they could just how difficult it was to muster a majority for painful cuts, and how necessary temporary tax increases could be. When their arguments were put to him by ITN, he did his best to politely educate them in fiscal realism. Pressed to attack his natural supporters, he sought instead to enlist their comments as aid in the battles he would have to fight against other, internal, critics coalescing in opposition to cuts:

What they are doing is lobbying in very colourful language to make sure that the government retains its toughness. We are about to face a very difficult spending round. When we come out with some of the decisions we have made, doubtless many people will say, 'We cannot stomach that, you ought to put up taxes.' What the Way Forward is saying is that it is just as difficult to get tax increases through Parliament as spending cuts. That is absolutely true.

In the following week Portillo went on the counter-attack – the champion of the ultra-low-tax economy making the case for tax increases. In an interview with the *FT*, he argued, 'It is essential for the Conservative government to go into the next election with a reputation for sound public finance and in a position where it can explain that it has the public finances in a state where it can plausibly show the path to a low-tax economy.'

He developed the case in an article in *The Times*: 'Failure to reduce borrowing could lead to a permanent increase in national indebtedness which could be addressed only by permanently higher taxes, thus increasing the reach of the state.' He took a sideswipe at the right-wing nostalgics – and by implication his heroine, Margaret Thatcher, among them – who felt he was too soft on the spenders: 'The government's spending plans aim for no real increase in the control total, its measure of public spending, between this year and next year and next year and the year after. "Not tough enough," say the critics. Well, tougher than Mrs Thatcher's record during the 1980s, and tougher than it seems.'

Portillo's task in holding the Treasury line against attack from the Right had become more difficult that summer, following the departure of Norman Lamont from the Treasury and his replacement by Kenneth Clarke. Lamont's departure had been followed by a withering attack on the administration he had just left, in a resignation statement delivered from the back benches attacking Major for being 'in office, but not in power'.

Lamont had been a buddy of Kenneth Clarke at Cambridge, but they were very different men, in character and in views. Clarke had been a Heathite in his youth, a patron of the Tory Reform Group. His willingness to tell Margaret Thatcher to her face that her time was up in 1990 marked him down as a member of the Left of the party. A pugilistic attitude to the public sector and an air of studied East Midlands ordinariness masked instincts as thorough-goingly wet as those of any Gilmouresque grandee.

The Conservative Way Forward snipers had really been aiming at Clarke when they launched their late-summer offensive, fearing a more left-wing chancellor would be softer on spending cuts than the politically weaker but at least more Right-inclined Lamont. Gardiner and Townend may have calculated that their intervention would strengthen Portillo's hand in any intra-Treasury battle on the balance between cuts and tax rises. But, if that was their intention, their sighting-shots were just a little off-mark.

Their comments, coming from back-benchers unencumbered by ministerial experience, would have irked some in the government who realised just how difficult it is to cut. The airy suggestion that there was fat in every department to be sliced away underestimated the difficulty of scaling down the spending of departments like Social Security and Defence, where the withdrawal of benefit and the disappearance of historic regiments could harm social cohesion and inflame back-bench revolts. But, more than that, the comments misjudged Clarke and misunderstood the changes that had been taking place on the Tory Left.

Apart from a few beached relics, like Sir Peter Tapsell and Sir

Ian Gilmour, the Tory Left had quietly abandoned Keynesianism in the mid-eighties. Tory left-wingers were no longer instinctive big-spenders. The perceived success of Mrs Thatcher's monetary policies meant that the battle-ground between Left and Right in the party had changed. Most of the wets accepted that the terms of the economic debate had shifted decisively away from them, in favour of lower taxation and spending, freer markets, lighter regulation and tolerance of higher unemployment. But the mind-set of the Tory Left – conciliatory, inclined to manage decline rather than take risks to reverse it, anxious to avoid confrontation – found its outlet elsewhere. The issue that divided Left from Right became Europe, not the economy.

Whereas Walter Monckton once constructed rationales for retreat in the face of organised labour, and Jim Prior argued for a 'softly softly' approach to trade-union reform, the Tory Reform Group now talked of the inevitability of political integration and monetary union, and Foreign Office ministers deprecated the 'unhelpfulness' of the confrontational stances taken by ministers from Margaret Thatcher to Edward Leigh.

As a result of their attachment to Europe, the Tory Left came to adopt a curious position on the economy of the late eighties, when opposition to Thatcher was given a cause in the shape of pro-Europeanism. They became convinced of the wisdom of the pound joining a single currency; they argued for membership of the 'narrow bands' of the ERM and acceptance of the strict convergence criteria for a single currency outlined in the Maastricht Treaty. But the high interest rates needed to stay in the ERM and the tight budgetary controls needed to observe the convergence criteria meant a Treasury regime as deflationary as any Margaret Thatcher had supported. So, in the early nineties, the positions of a decade before were, for many, piquantly reversed. Old Thatcherites like John Townend were taking risks with the budget by calling for tax cuts, giving succour to those making Keynesian calls for deficit-driven reflation, while the traditional anti-Thatcherites of the TRG called for strict control of the public purse in pursuit of a single currency.

Clarke, whose Left credentials were stronger on Europe than on any other issue, was far from being a let-it-rip big-spending wet of the early eighties who was about to go soft on spending cuts.

His record at Education and Health showed he was unsentimental about making efficiency savings in the public services and about upsetting anyone who resisted his attempts to save money and introduce market pressures.

But Clarke's immunity to big spending was more than just a reaction to running public services – it was part of his impeccably pro-European strategy as chancellor. He realised that his freedom of manœuvre, particularly on potential re-entry to the ERM and eventual entry into a single currency, depended on getting the budget back into balance, as he remarked to his biographer, Malcolm Balen:

I began to talk about the £50 billion spending deficit, myself, right away. Madness, you might have thought – why's the Chancellor going round telling everybody how much we're borrowing? Well, it was to prepare people for tough decisions because I was convinced in my first Budget that I couldn't do anything as Chancellor unless I began to get the public finances sorted out.

Clarke's determination to deal with the deficit may have had different origins from Portillo's, but their aim was the same. If Portillo felt there was an irony in the old wet now enthusiastically embracing the monetarist orthodoxy from which he himself had not deviated, he did not allow it to colour their relationship.

Knowing he had Clarke's full support, and that Clarke was judged the weightiest figure in the Cabinet, helped. Portillo needed all the help he could get. The control total aimed for in the November 1993 Budget was tight. Spending ministers were growing wise to the tricks pulled the previous year. And the coincidence of Budget and Expenditure Statement might tempt some ministers to press for further tax increases, in preference to cuts in their own budgets.

Portillo had set to work on the autumn 1993 spending round at the very beginning of the year, by launching an initiative that did a great deal to raise the profile of his job and expectations about the radicalism of the government. The Fundamental Expenditure Review had been launched in February 1993, after some massaging of opinion over Christmas. It was presented as a no-holds-barred, nothing-is-ruled-out examination of every area of government activity, designed to see if the state should be shorn of any of its functions, and if what remained could be delivered more efficiently. Designed as a rolling review of every area of government, it began with a look at four of the biggest-spending departments: Health, Education, Social Security and the Home Office.

Portillo stressed that the exercise would be run in tandem by the Treasury and the departments concerned, and told the House that the aim would be 'to distinguish between the essential costs of high-priority spending, which we will continue to fund, and avoidable spending, which we cannot afford. We will be seeking to identify areas where better targeting can be achieved or from which the public sector can withdraw altogether.'

His Labour shadow, Harriet Harman, raised the fear – far from restricted to the opposition benches – that the review would result in public services suffering, claiming it would be 'wholly wrong if British people, already suffering in this recession, ended up paying the price in worse policing, worse schools, worse health care and less benefits'.

Portillo defended himself by citing Labour's Commission on Social Justice, set up by John Smith to review the party's commitment to the Welfare State with a brief which 'ruled nothing in, and nothing out'. Portillo tried, as he often did with Harman, a riposte pitched uncomfortably between condescension and blokishness: 'A party which pledges itself to examine everything, but then attacks the government for doing so, is a party which frankly does not know its bottom from its elbow.'

Behind the Commons bravado lay a deeper political dilemma. As soon as a review was launched it was a licence for the press and opposition to raise fears that cherished benefits and services were under threat. New scares could be generated every day. Denial would crab freedom of movement, and make the government look reactive. Refusal to comment would be construed as proof that suspicions were justified.

But, more than giving Labour and dissident back-benchers a chance to raise fears, the review also raised expectations among the City and right-wingers that public expenditure could be cut back dramatically. Veterans of the last Fundamental Expenditure Review, in the early eighties, were cynical about what could be achieved. Peter Spencer, the chief economist at Kleinwort Benson, described it as 'just another case of promises, promises. Previous reviews of public spending have come to nothing.'

The last attempt had taken place in 1982–3. The then chancellor, Sir Geoffrey Howe, alarmed at a Treasury study which foresaw public spending marooned unbudgeably at 47 per cent of GDP in the future, and taxes increasing to cope with that, had commissioned the Central Policy Review Staff, the government's think-tank, to come up with possible long-term economies.

The CPRS team, under Alan Bailey, an official on secondment from the Treasury, produced a plan that raised various proposals, such as education vouchers, an increase in the pupil–teacher ratio, the supplanting of NHS care with compulsory private medical insurance, and the cancellation of the Trident nuclear-missile programme. It was driven by Treasury cost-cutting logic rather than ideological imperatives, but it provoked a violent reaction. 'The result was the nearest thing to a Cabinet riot in the history of Mrs Thatcher's administration,' according to Nigel Lawson, who was energy secretary at the time. The proposals were thrown out, and, if anything, put Thatcher off any further fundamental reviews. As it was, the rapid growth of the eighties boom put off the day of reckoning.

When Portillo came to pick up the knife again, there was deep suspicion at his ability to succeed where Howe had failed. *New Statesman* columnist Edward Pearce was one of the doubters. Pearce was a once fierce supporter of Thatcher who flirted with libertarianism before travelling to the Left and becoming a pacific opponent of the Gulf War, stopping off on the way to write a favourable study of John Major. Skirting the boundaries of good taste, he branded Portillo as the Thatcherite movement's equivalent to the Nazi butcher Reinhard Heydrich, before forecasting that one of the phrases from the review should be picked up by Labour and 'hung round his neck like a dead albatross'. He forecast disaster: 'What we are watching is the construction of a minefield by a high-IQ politician without much sense.'

As the months progressed some of Pearce's prophecy seemed to be uncomfortably close to coming true.

The first significant storm broke in May 1993, following a speech Portillo gave to the Association of Investment Trust Companies. Delivered in the wake of the first of what were to become customary by-election humiliations for the Tories, it was a deliberate raising of the stakes. Portillo wanted to emphasise the scale of his task, flirting with the language of crisis:

Containing public spending means courting unpopularity. It requires political sensitivity in judging which should be the priority areas. It requires endless vigilance, seeking out those elements of spending that no longer relate to today's priorities.

The prospect does not frighten me. The threats posed by excessive spending and borrowing are serious. It is our duty to hide nothing and tell it as it is . . . Something will have to give.

Just before the speech was delivered, an off-the-record Treasury briefing designed to test the water for unpopular cuts to come floated the possibility of extending prescription charges to better-off pensioners and children. Asked to confirm the rumour on ITN, after he had delivered his speech, Portillo refused to rule it out, commenting, 'My job is to look at all sorts of options.'

The prime minister, however, was less than enthusiastic about endorsing any such reform. That same night, on *Channel 4 News*, he dismissed the speculation as 'premature', saying 'those stories always' abounded when spending was under review. The following day, in the Commons, he moved further to dampen down speculation, commenting on suggestions that Portillo was contemplating extending prescription charges that 'He has not yet considered those options . . . No decisions have been made. They will not be made until the public-expenditure round in the autumn. Many will then be discarded.'

Had Portillo put his foot in it? Was he clod-hopping through the minefield Edward Pearce believed he had laid? And why, given the size of the deficit, and the range of the FER's ambitions, was the prime minister sounding so cautious?

One Treasury civil servant, now in the private sector, sees the incident as a rare public glimpse of the frustrating behind-the-scenes battle between a premier fearful of offending interest groups and a Treasury, then still under Norman Lamont, committed to cuts: 'The relationship between Norman and the PM got very strained in those months. Norman and Michael were arguing for deeper cuts, but the PM was always arguing against them.'

Peter Wanless, Portillo's private secretary at the time, saw the speech as an attempt by his boss to emphasise the scale of the task the Treasury faced. Portillo's success in 1992 had given some the idea that controlling expenditure seemed easier than it was. 'The control total increased by 2.3 per cent in 1992 – that's 0.75 per cent in real terms. He [Portillo] was worried that wouldn't hold. If he was to get his colleagues to cooperate, he had to engender the right atmosphere.'

The tension between Portillo's tactics and Major's reactions was the tension between a chief secretary who was keen to talk up problems and fly kites to motivate other Cabinet ministers into making their own cuts and a prime minister who was weakened by events, buffeted by a by-election humiliation and anxious not to further destabilise his position within a bruised party.

Portillo was aware of the disquiet his tactics provoked in Number Ten, but he was nothing abashed. On BBC Radio's *The World This Weekend* on 23 May, just four days after this speech, and three after the PM's 'damage-limitation' exercise, he raised the threat of more cuts in middle-class benefits. It would not just be better-off pensioners paying for their prescriptions – the wealthy might see child benefit affected, or access to hospital accommodation altered. He refused to rule out taxing child benefit, and raised the issue of welfare obligations to the wealthy, questioning the desirability that 'a millionaire's wife can get child benefit, and the fact that a company director gets free food as well as free medical care when he's in hospital'.

For more cautious conservatives – in particular Major and his party chairman, Sir Norman Fowler – Portillo was playing a dangerous game. Electoral success for the Tories depended on reassuring the middle classes most of all. Job security and property price rises looked like relics of the past, the Welfare State was one of the few shelters left from the New Insecurity, and here was Portillo drawing up plans to knock huge holes in it.

Portillo was certainly playing at taking risks, but he thought he had to if the Tories were to have any chance of winning the next election. Without scaring his colleagues into making economies now, the tax cuts on which victory would depend would never come. Ministers had to be confronted with the consequences for the Welfare State if they refused to institute cuts in their own backyards. One Treasury aide at the time is blunt about Portillo's tactics: 'He was deliberately putting the wind up the wets.'

The week may have begun with Portillo taking risks with his position, but it ended with his boss removed from his. Speculation about the wisdom of Portillo's cock-snooking was overshadowed by the reshuffle on 27 May which saw Lamont leave the government.

Following the May furore, Portillo spent less of his time as chief secretary scaring horses but assured his allies on the Right of the wisdom of the balanced course Kenneth Clarke was following. One of his most significant suggestions, however, in an LWT interview with Brian Walden, was that under-forties might have to make private provision for the majority of their pensions, instead of relying on the state. A less immediately alarmist tone was struck than in the spring interviews. The intra-Whitehall politics was less pressing as the spending round moved to its close, but the thinking behind the policy was something Portillo wanted to develop. He was attracted by the idea that there are certain foreseeable events for which individuals can insure themselves.

Andrew Dilnot, who met Portillo at several points during that period, explains: 'The number of pensioners is growing. Portillo argued that, in order to cope, the state pension might have to become "nugatory". Ken Clarke said that was unacceptable, but we're going to have to move in that direction. Portillo opened up the debate, but the inertia against which he was working is enormous.'

The suggestion, raised just as the chancellor and Portillo were putting the finishing touches to the joint Budget/Expenditure Statement, was part of the broader strategy of provoking thought as part of the FER. Its impact on the spending round was limited, but at the time it was marked down as a minor gaffe on Portillo's part. Just two years later the Labour MP Frank Field published a paper calling for universal private pension provision. Today's gaffe can sometimes be tomorrow's commonplace.

In 1993 the spending round was conducted with more drama, but also greater secrecy, than in 1992. Portillo and Clarke used the £50 billion figure to cajole ministers into delivering deep cuts, reminded colleagues of the consequences of the control total being breached. They pointed to the opposition on the back benches to the large tax increases, that failure to cut would require. However, when the Budget was announced, it was a smug Clarke and a smugger Portillo who unveiled a £3.5 billion undershoot. Far from failing to keep increases within limits, Portillo had imposed real cuts.

Andrew Dilnot believes it was 'the best-run – i.e. tightest – spending round since 1979. It was amazing.' Clarke had doubted Portillo's ability to bring in an underspend but when, just ten days before the Budget announcement, Portillo confirmed that he had done better than expected, Clarke's former adviser Tessa Keswick remembers the astonishment: 'We all nearly fell off our chairs with excitement.'

The undershoot had depended on significant cuts in defence spending, the Home Office budget, the housing budget of the Department of the Environment, and the Department of Employment. Significantly, Health spending, guaranteed to rise ahead of inflation in the 1992 manifesto, stabilised, and was projected to decrease in 1997.

At the time, Portillo's performance was acclaimed as 'skilful' by the *Independent* and a 'masterstroke' by the *Daily Telegraph*. A significant part of his success depended on the maintenance of the public-sector pay policy introduced the year before, but there was a general perception of Portillo's effectiveness.

Portillo's performance in the run up to the 1993 Budget had impressed his new boss. A senior aide to Clarke commented, 'Michael and Ken come from different wings of the party, but they developed a relationship that was harmonious and very effective, although they never became what you might call "close". Ken thought he was a first-rate chief secretary: he got to the point with the minimum of fuss, and Ken was particularly impressed by Michael's handling of his civil servants – he really got the best out of them. Ken appreciated Michael's aversion to leaking, and thought he was a guy who said what he meant and meant what he said. He was resigned to losing him after the '93 Budget, but on the day of the 1994 reshuffle I remember him commenting, "Michael Portillo is a class political act."'

The 1993 spending round was the last which Portillo was in place to complete. By the time of the next Expenditure Statement he was himself a spending minister, with his own budget to fight for. But, even though the main business was completed by the end of November, Portillo did not let up.

In the next month he tried to push forward the limits of the Fundamental Expenditure Review. He had already outlined his determination to put Agriculture, Environment, Treasury and legal-aid spending under the microscope, but he accompanied that with specific suggestions, positing the merger of the Inland Revenue with Customs and Excise and the introduction of tuition fees for higher education, and exploring the feasibility of linking unemployment benefit to some sort of 'Workfare' scheme.

Few of these ideas have since been adopted, and the ratio of public spending to national income remains much the same. There have been reforms, but the need for legislation to effect significant change and the political difficulty of winning consent for cuts have all blunted the edge of the FER knife. In Portillo's remaining six months at the Treasury, favourably inclined observers could find little evidence of movement towards a fundamental reduction in the size of the state.

Dilnot believes the FER was a worthwhile, but limited, exercise: 'Some of the analytical work has been good, but it didn't do anything dramatic.' The FER was a useful, two-way, education process – encouraging spending departments to be more imaginative and responsible, but also teaching right-wing radicals like Lilley and Portillo the difficulties of down-sizing the state. Dilnot has had several private conversations with Portillo, and believes 'He, I am sure, became aware that the chances of a truly minimal state are tiny.'

David Cameron, at the Treasury at the start of the FER, cites the pressure applied by the FER as a decisive factor in securing the defence cuts made possible by the 'Front Line First' review and points to future reforms of legal aid and unemployment benefit as real gains.

Peter Wanless, intimately involved with Portillo's search for long-term economies, has a longer list of benefits on his balance sheet. 'The FER played a part in getting the Department of Social Security to equalise the pension age, reform invalidity benefit and statutory sick pay, and introduce the job-seekers' allowance. At Employment it inspired the Training For Work initiative and saw us move to spend up to a third less than before. At the Home Office it influenced the adoption of the Sheehy Report on police pay and conditions. At Education it provoked thinking on options for higher education. And across the government it helped the financial secretary to the Treasury in his campaign to extend market-testing.'

Peter Lilley, doubtful initially, found practical benefits from the review: 'I was equivocal at first, but I decided to grab the bull by the horns and we examined everything. It takes a long time, because to achieve anything you have to legislate, but the existence of the review provided a useful psychological framework.'

Elsewhere there were certainly critics on the Right, disappointed by the failure of Portillo to make more swingeing cuts. When John Redwood challenged John Major's leadership in 1995, he made much of the Major government's failure to cut public spending and provide the money for further tax cuts, focusing on the need to mount a war on waste.

One of Redwood's supporters, Rupert Darwall, a former Treasury special adviser, had argued in the past for the abandonment of capital projects, such as the Jubilee Line extension to Docklands. Money could certainly be saved by cutting back on government investment, but what would have been the political, and economic, cost of abandoning another piece of infrastructural development in order to find money to feed consumption? The Treasury, and Michael Portillo in particular, had agonised long and hard about the wisdom of pursuing the Jubilee Line extension, and reluctantly backed it. It was a one-off cost – the real pressure on the size of the state is not money spent on investment but the growth in recurring annual costs in two areas: wages and welfare.

The cost of keeping so many people in the government's employ was being held down by the process of putting tasks out to tender as well as by the pay freeze, made justifiable by the apparently successful pursuit of low inflation. Ultimately, however, further progress in reducing the public-sector wage bill may depend on reducing the range of services the state provides. Coming up with suggestions on areas from which the state might withdraw was supposed to be the function of the FER, but any really radical conclusions are likely to be implemented only by a future government – with a larger majority. Portillo, from his first call for an 'ultra-low-tax economy' in 1992, has been the highest-profile advocate in British politics of radical action to reduce the size of the state, but the political climate will have to change if progress in that direction is to be made.

Portillo's fight to reduce the size of the state was a technical problem that absorbed two years of his energies as Treasury minister. But, absorbing, and compelling, as his official task was, it became increasingly overshadowed by speculation about a greater game: the struggle for the future direction of the Tory Party, and the search for a lead over Labour. It was a contest to define the essence of Conservatism, and a search for clear blue water.

CHAPTER TWELVE

Bastards

I need not say that I hate the name of Diehard which has done
us no good. But I do not regret the movement for it is a genuine
movement of honest men who have risked their political reputation in order if possible to rescue the Country.

Lord Salisbury to Bonar Law, 1922

On the morning of Michael Portillo's first presentation to the Cabinet he had received a call from a well-wisher. A warm five minutes
passed between Portillo and his older admirer, who shared a few
tips about how to cope.

The caller was John Major. The time taken to reassure a colleague was typical of the prime minister's careful management of
personal relations, but within weeks the cordial warmth was to be
replaced by a frosty distance. The Treasury's first lord became
suspicious of his chief secretary's thoughts, wary of his actions, and
concerned that he was becoming a potential focus for opposition.

The frostiness was more than the suspicion the old stag feels
towards the younger: it grew from an acute understanding on
Major's part of the sense of betrayal felt by many on the Tory
Right, who felt he owed his position to their votes but had done
everything to distance himself from them since his election. Portillo's position, as the developing and deepening voice of the Right,
from 1992 onwards, meant he became the de-facto leader of the
disaffected. Portillo was never inclined to place himself at the head
of any peasants' revolt, as the events of 1995 were to show, but on
a number of occasions his position as Tory tribune gave Major
cause to worry.

Major's nostrils first flared at the scent of danger within weeks
of his 1992 election victory.

The No Turning Back Group had met for its first post-victory
supper in June 1992, when talk had turned quickly to Maastricht.
The Danes had just voted to reject the treaty in a referendum, and
Michael Spicer's 'Fresh Start' early day motion was on the table.

The evening began with an unfocused discussion as various members ran through their objections to the treaty. It was Portillo, who brought order to the debate, according to one who was there: 'There were about twenty-five of us, and Portillo went round the table asking us if we felt we should go ahead with the treaty. No one spoke up in its defence. It was then suggested that if we all felt like that we should tell the PM. It was agreed we'd ask him to lunch and Portillo would let him know what we thought.'

The prime minister was soon acquainted with the sentiments expressed that night, but not in the way the group wanted. Following the NTB meeting another, more open, discussion was arranged, in the House of Commons, to see if the disquiet felt by the NTB was shared by other sceptically inclined ministers. As well as the nominal organisers, Edward Leigh and Neil Hamilton, there were NTB stalwarts including Portillo, Lilley, Michael Forsyth and John Redwood, and other ministers including Steve Norris and a whip, David Davis.

The meeting was presented by the press as a rebel cabal. The presence of a government whip, invited as evidence of the group's bona fides, hardly suggested an insurrection in the making, but all the ministers there were thoroughly sceptical of Maastricht and far from in tune with the prime minister's view, expressed in the Commons that day, that ratification was in Britain's 'national interest'. Edward Leigh expressed the organisers' position: 'I said, straight out, we should abandon the treaty. Michael was far more cautious. David Davis arrived in a fury – he clearly thought the whole thing unhelpful. The prime minister knew that the meeting had been arranged by Neil and me – we were working very closely together – and I don't think the PM ever forgave us.'

Leigh, perhaps naïvely, thought the meeting, intended as an exercise in private lobbying, should be seen as a threat not to Major's leadership, only to the Maastricht Treaty. He believed that a previous initiative, before the election, had been legitimate and helpful. In November 1991, Leigh had met Major as 'spokesman' for a group of sceptical junior ministers, including David Maclean and Archie Hamilton, to press for the drawing of a line in the sand at Maastricht: 'We said there should be no extension of qualified majority voting, no new powers for the court, and so on.' Leigh may have felt that that shot across the bows had stiffened

Major's sceptical resolve, but there was a clear difference between advice on what to do when the treaty had yet to be signed and pressure, after it had been signed, to abandon the whole thing.

The day after the Commons meeting of ministers, the Cabinet met and discussed the treaty. Both Portillo and Lilley voiced their objections to the path of rapid ratification Major was then set on pursuing. However, the Cabinet as a whole backed Major and Hurd, and Portillo and Lilley were bound by collective responsibility to fall into line. Major, sensitive to the damage to his position the apparent public opposition caused, wrung loyalty pledges out of Lilley and Portillo, which drew an overtly supportive statement from Peter Lilley: 'The prime minister negotiated a good deal at Maastricht which gives us a good opportunity to shape Europe in the way we want. The prime minister has set out how the government intends to carry forward this approach in the light of the Danish referendum, and I fully support this approach.'

Portillo was careful to say nothing on the record, but let it be known that he 'associated' himself with Lilley's remarks. In a stronger position politically, he saw less need to bind himself so closely to a course whose wisdom he still doubted. Moreover, he was shortly to act as shop steward for those who were counselling a different course. The NTB was expecting to entertain John Major to lunch on 1 July, and it was intended that that should be an opportunity for the prime minister to see something of the scale and depth of principled opposition to further integration.

On the morning of the lunch, one of the guests was bleeped with a message that it had been cancelled: 'It was only an hour or so before lunch, and we were told the PM had another pressing appointment, but it was clear he'd pulled out because he thought he was about to be ambushed. I realised that one of our number was a Judas, and had tipped him off.'

The NTB had lunch anyway, without the chance for a fruitful dialogue with the prime minister, but Major's failure to attend sent its own eloquent signal: he was in no mood to bend, or treat with potential traitors. The leaker within the NTB may have secured preferment in due course, but he had also damned the group further in Major's eyes, and had damned in particular the man who had emerged at their private meeting as the natural voice of their disquiet – Michael Portillo.

The uneasy tension between Portillo's position as a loyal member of the Major Cabinet and as a Thatcherite heir became all the more pronounced as progress was made towards ratifying the Maastricht Treaty. The bitter rows surrounding ratification helped entrench divisions within the Tory party and posed a series of dilemmas for Portillo and others who were in the government and on the Right.

Following the Danish 'No', Major decided to postpone the parliamentary process of ratification until the autumn, when Britain would enjoy its six months in the EU presidency. It seemed a smart tactical manœuvre, designed to allow tempers to cool and to permit the Danes to work out their difficulties with a sympathetic power at the EU's helm. However, in this instance as in others, a problem deferred was a problem doubled.

Sterling's exit from the Exchange Rate Mechanism in September 1992 blew apart any chance of a consensus re-emerging and turned a debate designed to clear the air into a dangerous test of confidence. The government, at the request of the Labour Party, and following Foreign Office advice, had agreed to allow a 'paving' motion to be debated before proceeding with the bill. It was an occasion for the House to reaffirm its faith in the bill to ratify the treaty. The last Commons vote on Maastricht – the bill's second reading – had been overwhelmingly in favour, but circumstances had changed and so the House was given a chance to vote again.

To offer a mutinous Commons such an opportunity might have been honourable, but it was also close to suicidal. Labour, scenting weakness, said they would vote against the government using the Tory opt-out from the social chapter as a fig-leaf for their tactically seductive but arguably unprincipled about-face. With a majority of just 21, the bill, treaty and government were vulnerable to a sceptical rebellion.

The NTB was riven by divisions on how to vote. Iain Duncan-Smith, the only member of the 1992 intake to abstain during the second reading, was one of those who argued for a big vote against – including, if necessary, ministerial resignations to make the treaty's demise certain. Duncan-Smith refuses to condemn those who did not resign, but thinks it could all have been very different: 'Resignations that autumn, and a vote against the treaty in the paving debate, would have killed it. The Right's failure to act together and flex its muscles meant it was weakened and sidelined after as a result. Our bluff had been called.'

One of those who wanted to resign, and felt he should vote against, was Edward Leigh. After a long period of agonising, and open rubbishing of the treaty in conversation with colleagues and journalists, he reluctantly stayed in the government and voted with the government for the treaty. It did him little good, and he was sacked the next spring. Leigh, a devout Catholic, responded with a tortured article in the *Spectator*, comparing his soul-searching over Maastricht to St Thomas More's over Henry VIII's divorce, and making it clear he should have followed the promptings of his principles rather than clinging to office.

With the benefit of hindsight, and distance, Leigh agreed with Duncan-Smith that the Right suffered from a collective failure of will: 'We discussed a joint resignation. The PPSs wanted to resign but wouldn't go without the junior ministers. The junior ministers wouldn't go without the Cabinet ministers. And the Cabinet ministers weren't convinced resignation was right – they came out with all the usual arguments about having more influence fighting from within. I doubted it then, and I doubt it even more now.'

At least one minister on the Right saw the point of Leigh's case but believes he was naïve: 'Resignations would not have wrecked the treaty. The first casualty would have been Major, not Maastricht. Labour might have played silly buggers procedurally, but they would have supported the treaty in the end. If we'd destabilised Major at that stage we would have risked a Labour government, or the succession going either to Heseltine or Clarke, and it's difficult to know which would have been worse.'

It was a view widely shared by observers plugged into centre-Right Tory thinking, and the same analysis was borne out by events three years later, when many Tory Euro-sceptics baulked at ditching John Major, for fear of propelling Michael Heseltine to the top. Several of the arguments then were echoes of the debates on the Right that had characterised the uneasy progress of Maastricht through the Commons.

The resentment among Ultras at the unwillingness of anti-Maastricht ministers to resign is tempered by the memories of personal kindness and support from those same ministers for those facing the full force of the whips' anger.

One of the rebels was John Whittingdale, Margaret Thatcher's former political secretary. He had been returned as the member for Colchester South and Maldon in 1992, and within months was at the heart of a tug-of-love battle between Major and Maggie. The prime minister who had won the election demanded loyalty to his government. The former prime minister who had got Whittingdale his seat in the first place demanded loyalty to her principles. Whittingdale eventually decided that he could only abstain. It did not endear him to the whips, but allegedly prompted Lady Thatcher unfairly to remark that his spine did not reach to his brain.

He was joined in his abstention by his fellow new boy, and Colchester neighbour, Bernard Jenkin. It is still fresh in Whittingdale's mind: 'When the division bell rang Bernard and I were in the Smoking Room. We stayed there, alone with our drinks, while the minutes ticked by, not knowing if the government would win or lose, and whether or not it would depend on us. They were the longest minutes of my life.'

Whittingdale was criticised by former friends and bawled out by Thatcher. There were rumbles from Colchester Tory worthies about the wisdom of his selection in the first place. Throughout it all, he was grateful for Portillo's personal loyalty: 'Michael was never himself disloyal to the government but he was sympathetic to those of us who rebelled. He knew and we knew what the score was.'

Bernard Jenkin, and his wife Ann, an old friend of Portillo who now acts as her husband's secretary, also had reason to be grateful for Portillo's support. On the day of the paving motion Ann was telephoned by Andrew Mitchell, then party vice-chairman with responsibility for candidates. He tried to pressurise her into changing her husband's mind, exploiting her loyalty to the party as an activist involved in Tory circles long before her marriage. When Bernard found out about the call he was furious. He knew his own position would be difficult, but saw no reason why his wife should face a tough time. Even as the weight of the party machine was being brought to bear on their joint resolve, they were reassured by the support they received from Portillo: 'We won't forget how he helped us.'

Portillo was discreet, almost careful, in his dealings with the rebels, but Major was aware of his attitude from 'whips' narks' at the NTB. Iain Duncan-Smith recognised the risk Portillo was taking: 'During this period the NTB was very much a mutual support group for those of us who were rebels – we were assured of a friendly welcome at a difficult time. There were very few who condemned us, and Portillo wasn't one of them. I'm sure the tenor of those meetings would have been faithfully reported back to the whips.'

NTB supporters were not the only Portillo diary dates to give Maastricht-supporting Major loyalists a twinge of unease. On Thursday 25 February 1993 Portillo and his Cabinet colleague Peter Lilley joined three other Tories for lunch, but an apparently unremarkable breaking of bread with like-minded friends made front-page news the next week. The magnitude of their mistake was summed up by Chris Buckland in the *Daily Express*:

If Michael Portillo and Peter Lilley had lunched with Carlos the Jackal last Thursday to plot Mr Major's assassination, the reaction could hardly have been more hysterical.

But these two bright young Cabinet ministers, their futures, some would have us believe, now stretching brilliantly behind them, were supping with someone far more dangerous – Margaret Hilda Thatcher, Baroness of Darkness, with the demonic Lord Tebbit at her right hand, and at her left hand the fallen angel and economic guru Sir Alan Walters.

The climate of the times was particularly fevered, with Maastricht, and John Major's future, under threat, and Lady Thatcher publicly opposed to the former and privately bitter about the latter. Over fish terrine, beef daube and *crème brûlée*, the conversation centred on prospects for the world economy.

Although the agenda may have seemed innocent, the company was deeply suspect. Hoping to tarnish Portillo by associating him with a nest of rebels, one Cabinet minister leaked details of the date to the press, placing an unfavourable spin on the event, suggesting John Major had been carved up alongside the beef. Michael Portillo was accused of slurping with the enemy.

Portillo had not imagined there was anything very remarkable about a Tory MP lunching with a former Tory premier. He had the engagement marked in his official diary, which would have circulated widely throughout Whitehall. During Margaret

Thatcher's own time in office several of her ministers had travelled to Salisbury's Cathedral Close to eat with Edward Heath. Impeccably loyal members of her Cabinet like William Waldegrave and John MacGregor had not thought it disloyal to dine with their old boss even as he railed at her abandonment of 'traditional Toryism'. But then Heath had never summoned his former acolytes, as Thatcher had with John Whittingdale and others, and ordered them to vote against a central piece of government legislation.

Knowing she had done nothing to make John Major's life easy during the previous months, was Portillo unwise to accept the invitation? Could he really have declined it? John Whittingdale thinks it would have been all the more remarkable if Portillo had not accepted the request to meet from a woman who had done so much for him: 'An invitation to lunch from Lady Thatcher is not the sort of thing you can easily refuse.' Nevertheless the impression had been created that Portillo enjoyed flirting with danger, in the shape of Baroness Thatcher, the Tory temptress. And, within days, another lunch date was leaked in an effort to embarrass Portillo further.

A week after the press revealed Portillo's lunch with Thatcher, they disclosed he had, that same month, invited Labour's leading Euro-sceptic, Bryan Gould, out to lunch. With party chairman Sir Norman Fowler getting aerated at that point at an 'unholy alliance' of Labour, Liberals and Tory rebels undermining the progress of Maastricht, it seemed to pro-European Tories that the Portillo–Gould tête-à-tête was more than a social arrangement.

Portillo was bemused by the attention the meal attracted. As with the Thatcher lunch, he had not hidden anything. The date had been arranged by his private office and was in his ministerial diary. The location for the lunch was the Harcourt Room in the House of Commons, where they would be surrounded by colleagues from all parties.

Michael Portillo had got to know Bryan Gould when they both served on the committees scrutinising the bills to reform local government's finance and structure. They had become friends, as Portillo had with Gould's number two, David Blunkett, because they enjoyed exploring each others' minds. Blunkett's comment on the meeting is succinct: 'Michael is an ideologue – he likes exploring ideas. It's natural he would have got on well with Bryan. The idea that they got together to plot is ridiculous.' Nevertheless the meeting was considered to 'cast doubt on the judgement' of Mr Portillo. It was considered unwise for a minister suspected of sympathising with the anti-Maastricht rebels to be seen consorting so openly with opponents of the treaty.

It probably says more about the fear Portillo inspired in sections of the Tory Left than about any lack of judgement on his part that so much effort was expended by party colleagues to present two unconnected social events as evidence of a plot to undermine the premier.

With speculation about Norman Lamont's future growing daily at that time, several tipsters had been talking up the chances of Portillo becoming the next chancellor. The Left had their own candidate for the top job – the Europhile home secretary, Kenneth Clarke.

Clarke was ahead in the race, but Portillo was gaining fast. A *Sunday Telegraph* poll of City economists made him favourite. It was thought that, if he sacked Lamont, Major might be tempted to pacify the Right by replacing him with another sceptic, and Portillo knew the numbers. For Clarke's backers the answer was obvious – Portillo's standing had to be undermined. The lunches, innocent at any other time, were used, in the difficult months during the ratification of Maastricht, as evidence of fundamental unsoundness. One member of the 1992 intake sympathetic to Portillo is in no doubt who was responsible for the lunch leaks and the accompanying gloss: 'It was a deliberate attempt by the Left to undermine Michael. I don't think it worked, because I don't think Major would have made Michael chancellor, but it showed they were prepared to fight dirty to stop him.'

Major was reportedly 'irritated' by the reports of Portillo's lunches. He would have known how unimportant the events were in themselves, but they had a symbolic significance. They were gossamer-thin, but still tangible, evidence of Portillo's privately held reservations about both Maastricht and the direction of the Major government. Outright treachery would have been intolerable, but it was far more difficult to punish a minister merely for fraternising with the other side. However, Portillo's card was becoming ever more comprehensively marked. And the prime minister's real feelings became cruelly clear only hours after Maastricht finished its turbulent journey through the Commons.

Major had just finished recording an interview with ITN's political editor, Michael Brunson. As was customary, after the formal fencing of the interview, the prime minister was chatting informally with a journalist he had come to like and trust. What Major didn't realise, even as he unclipped his own personal microphone, was that every word he said was still being recorded. His candour about the Cabinet would return to haunt him, and them:

What I don't understand, Michael, is why such a complete wimp like me keeps winning everything. The way people who oppose our European policy go about it is to attack me personally. Think of it through my perspective. You have three right-wing members of the Cabinet. What happens if they resign? Where do you think most of this poison has come from? It's coming from the dispossessed and never-possessed on the back benches. Would you like three more of the bastards out there? What's the Lyndon Johnson maxim?

' "If you've got them by the balls, their hearts and minds will follow"?' offered Brunson. 'No, that's not what I had in mind,' replied Major – 'though it's pretty good.'

The maxim the prime minister was, of course, reaching for was Johnson's famous explanation for not dismissing a troublesome colleague: 'Better to have him inside the tent pissing out rather than outside the tent pissing in.' The point Major was making to Brunson was a simple one: ministers like Lilley, Redwood and Portillo were too dangerous to sack.

The knowledge that he was safely inside the tent, despite unfortunate leaks, allowed Portillo to spend the night of 26 May celebrating his birthday in a style that could have been hubristic, but turned into an investiture. While John Major and his chief whip, Richard Ryder, were in 12 Downing Street plotting the eviction of their neighbour, Norman Lamont, his chief secretary was celebrating his fortieth birthday in the Alfonso XIII Room of the Spanish Club, in Cavendish Square, just off London's Oxford Street.

Lamont was among around 200 guests gathered from every area of Portillo's life. Schoolfriends, university chums, Commons colleagues, mentors and aides turned up for two hours of Spanish sparkling wine and tapas. Martyn Fisher, Portillo's assistant during the 1992 election, described it as being 'like a moving Madam

Tussaud's. Everywhere you turned there was a famous face, from Clive Anderson to Margaret Thatcher.'

As well as friends from every part of Portillo's life, there were friends from every section of the party, from Michael Heseltine to Michael Brown. Lamont – no mean party-goer, a talented jitter-bugger also at home in the eighties in Earl Spencer's Althorp and not averse to raffish company himself – was, according to one guest, a little surprised by the catholic range of Portillo's acquaintance, remarking, 'How brave to invite all these people.'

Just how brave was revealed a little later. Another of the guests was the comedy producer Jon Plowman, a school chum of Portillo. Plowman sought to exploit the comic potential of Lady Thatcher's presence on the night the media outside were speculating vigor-ously about Lamont's future. Another school chum, talking to Plowman when Lady Thatcher hove into view, recalls that 'John saw her, and decided he'd go over and ask her if she'd accept the offer of the vacancy at Number Eleven. Just as he set off, Michael saw what was happening out of the corner of his eye, and moved at a speed of which I never thought him capable to intervene.' Scenting trouble, Portillo had moved to avoid embarrassment. 'Michael got to them just after John had asked his question. She told him one should never go back, and before he could make any more mischief Michael steered her away.'

Plowman was not the only guest to take advantage of the social mix to nobble the powerful. Clive Anderson's wife, a consultant at Bart's AIDS unit, lobbied every minister she could find to try to save the hospital from closure.

Portillo, proud of his range of friends and addicted to being at the centre of things since his schooldays, was in his element, but the most pleasurable, and embarrassing, moment was still to come. Well into the second hour of the evening, as guests were looking at their watches and preparing to move on to dinner, Lady Thatcher asked for silence – she was going to give a speech.

One guest believes, 'She had clearly had more than she ought – there was an unmistakable glassy look to her eye – but her voice was clear.' And so was her message. Looking at Portillo – who, a little nervously, said, 'Please don't think you have to' – she invoked the royal 'we' and proclaimed her heir: 'We brought you up, we expect great things of you, you will not disappoint us.'

Shortly after she spoke, the party broke up – the revellers to their next appointments, Lamont to his last night in Downing Street, and Michael and Carolyn Portillo back to their flat for dinner.

The Portillos had invited twenty of their friends to join them. With the care of a true politician they were not the twenty closest, but a judicious mix of the entertaining and those to whom an obligation was owed. Two schoolfriends were invited, including the mischievous Plowman, along with the odd MP and one of Portillo's civil servants. Portillo was unfazed by the events earlier that evening, a relaxed and congenial host.

In the months that followed Portillo sought to live up to the benediction he had been given. And, in trying to be true to his inheritance, he found himself travelling ever more dangerously along a path he had so far trodden only with the greatest of care.

CHAPTER THIRTEEN

Clear Blue Water

The British people are not that much concerned about capitalism. They only become enthusiastic for it when it is presented in a patriotic context.

T. E. Utley

It would be fatal for us to stand just where we are now. What would be our slogan for the 1990s if we did that? Would 'consolidate' be the word that we stitch on our banners? Whose blood would run faster at the prospect of five years of consolidation?

Margaret Thatcher, speech to the Conservative party conference, 1987

The knowledge that he was safe, albeit under suspicion, allowed Portillo to strike out over the next two years to delineate a distinctive position. He did so with a series of speeches, articles and interviews that were designed to raise his profile and make the case for the Right, within the party and across the country – playing on Thatcherite themes arranged for a nineties audience.

Portillo had made deliberately provocative speeches before, but those speeches were either the interesting first foray into the front rank of politics by a promising young minister or the dramatic but direct exposition of a problem recognised by the whole Cabinet. From autumn 1993 he was speaking as a 'Bastard'. Although every word was cleared by the Cabinet Office, few other members of the Cabinet would have expressed themselves as Portillo did. While many Tories openly questioned the future of their leader and the party's sense of direction, Portillo sought to provide clarity and purpose.

The most significant, and certainly the most widely reported, speeches were delivered during the political season which ran from autumn 1993 to 1994, starting with an address to a religious conference in September 1993, followed by speeches to the Tory conference fringe, a dinner of Conservative Way Forward and then Fife

Conservatives, before culminating in Portillo's speech to the full party conference in 1994. This chapter will examine these speeches in detail for insights into his ethical and political thinking.

Portillo's first speech in the series, to 'The Church at Work in London' conference on 15 September 1993, pre-empted the theme that was to dominate the 1993 Tory party conference. It was an attempt by Portillo, in his own way, to go back to basics by providing an analysis of the moral and ethical underpinning of his brand of Toryism. Although the speech was quite ambitious, he still did not want to be seen to be straying too far from his brief as chief secretary, so the address was entitled 'Ethics and Public Finance'. Intended to address the assumption that 'caring' Conservatism meant an interventionist role for an ever-bigger state, and ever-greater taxation, it sought to make the case for low taxation on a moral and not just a political basis.

Portillo's starting-point was, curiously enough for one raised as a Roman Catholic, the moral importance of the individual securing his own salvation by making his own moral choices. It was a theme perhaps more in tune with Protestant theology, but Portillo chose to avoid those distinctions by rooting his analysis in no particular Church but within the broader Judaeo-Christian tradition:

Like the Judaism which lies in its origins, it [Christianity] is about individual responsibility. The Christian message concerns the salvation of souls – individual souls.

The call to do good that lies at the heart of Christianity demands an individual response. You can't do good by proxy. There's no virtue in paying big taxes if you have no part in the decisions about how they are to be used, or – as so often in bureaucracies – you don't even know where they go.

The fact is, though, that for many people the role of government has sapped from them – one might almost say confiscated – their sense of responsibility towards other people.

There were echoes of Margaret Thatcher's 1988 address to the General Assembly of the Church of Scotland in Portillo's theology and phraseology. She had argued then that salvation was a matter of individual exertion, quoting from the hymn 'I Vow to Thee, My Country', and pointing out that heaven's bounds increased 'soul by soul' – in other words, one by one – and not by collective effort. The echoes were not accidental: they were designed to reawaken something of the passion that had driven the Thatcherites to take political risks.

Most postwar politicians have been reluctant to make any explicitly religious justification for their action, leaving confessional politics for Northern Ireland. There have, however, been numerous attempts to appropriate quasi-Christian language by politicians. Labour's post-1945 project was portrayed as an attempt to build a 'New Jerusalem', and Quintin Hogg in the sixties tried to make 'The Case for Conservatism' in a series of Penguin pamphlets with reference to original sin.

Since then, as society has become more secular, politicians have become less keen to justify their actions with reference to religious doctrine. The majestic Anglican indignation of Gladstone deployed during the Bulgarian massacres, the deep Christian pessimism of Salisbury that made him so fearful of mass democracy, the Quaker fervour of Bright and other nineteenth-century radicals, the enlightened Tory altruism of Shaftesbury, all flowed from deep religious faith in a country overwhelmingly church-going, if not entirely God-fearing. Now politicians are more reluctant to use explicitly Christian rhetoric. But, even as Christian observance has fallen, a sense that our leaders should have a moral purpose to their conduct has persisted. Even now the prurient interest in our politicians' private lives suggests an expectation that they should still exercise explicitly moral leadership.

The Left – dedicated to expanding state power to alleviate suffering, helping the poor and eliminating want – had found it easier to present their agenda as morally driven than had the Tories, whose language speaks of pragmatism and efficiency. Margaret Thatcher changed all that. In a manner not so much Conservative as radically reactionary, she sought to take back the language of moral conviction from the Left and use it to energise her followers.

Portillo, according to one of his speech-writing coterie, thought it was important to reintroduce the sense of purpose and enthusiasm that Thatcher had brought to politics, commenting, 'We wanted to excite people again.' But, in making religion the starting-point for his series of speeches, Portillo was not only exploiting the Thatcher inheritance: he was also acknowledging a debt to another influence – Maurice Cowling.

Religion is not as central to Portillo's politics as it is to Cowling's. Portillo is not a regular church-goer and describes himself as a 'bad Catholic', but, nevertheless, Cowling's position has influenced Portillo's thinking. In choosing to make explicitly moral the first of a series of speeches he was to give, and rooting that morality in religion, Portillo was acknowledging that politics had to be about more than exposing that the opposition's sums do not add up. He realised that when it came to inspiring an audience he had to appeal beyond their pocketbook and penetrate deeper. In Cowling's own words, 'the eloquence of Hayek and Adam Smith is not enough'.

Portillo's recognition of the importance of a moral underpinning for policy – even the most economically efficient of policies – reflects an affinity with Churchill's insights into the needs of voters in the late twentieth century, quoted in Cowling's *Religion and Public Doctrine in Modern England*: 'Their hearts will ache . . . their lives will be barren if they have not a vision above material things.'

Significantly, the injection of religion into politics, as an influence on thinking if not an automatic guide to action, has been the hallmark of another forty-something politician who sees himself as an heir of Margaret Thatcher – Tony Blair.

Like Portillo, Blair was influenced by an older man with a deep religious sense and a talent to amuse. Where Portillo had Cowling, Blair enjoyed the influence of an Australian theologian called Peter Thomson. Thomson introduced Blair to the writings of ethical and Christian-socialist thinkers – most notably the Scots philosopher John MacMurray – in much the same way that Cowling and Shirley Letwin introduced Portillo to a Tory tradition of thinkers, from Hobbes to Hayek.

Blair has been given credit for the recognition that the electorate of the nineties does not want to lose the material gains that most made in the eighties but wants to see politicians address deeper questions of security, belonging and self-belief. His instinct that voters now want to hear as much about responsibilities as rights and his interest in using the arguments of 'communitarian' thinkers like Amitai Etzioni and Alasdair MacIntyre to develop those points has been innovative, and effective. But many of those same insights are reflected in the speeches Portillo made in the year before Blair became Labour leader. The conclusions Portillo draws are often very different from Blair's, the intellectual influences are usually opposed, but many of the preoccupations are similar, and the sense of a new, less liberal, mood in the country is shared.

One specific example, raised in the 'Ethics and Public Finance' speech, is family policy, and, in particular, the increase in the number of teenage pregnancies and single parents. Portillo drew attention to the fact that 8,000 girls aged below sixteen became pregnant every year in England and Wales and pointed out that payments to lone mothers were the fastest growing item in the £80 billion Social Security budget. He argued that, whatever the effect on the exchequer, the increase meant that more young women faced a life with fewer opportunities as a result of their condition: 'Teenage pregnancy often leads to a whole life of state dependence, with few luxuries. The teenage mother is rarely able to gain a full education or develop a career.'

He sought to stimulate the debate on why the number of teenage pregnancies should be so on the increase, comparing the UK with another advanced, predominantly Protestant, but increasingly secularised Northern European state: 'Our rate of teenage pregnancies is seven times higher than Holland's – and not, I think, because the British teenager is more likely to have pre-marital sex than her Dutch counterpart. Our rate of abortion is much higher too.'

Portillo did not make the automatic assumption that young women were becoming pregnant solely to receive state benefit, but he was trying to raise the issue of what part benefits might play in influencing behaviour.

Portillo's ideological ally Peter Lilley has also explored how the dispersal of earnings in the eighties has affected the attitudes of working-class women. With technological and economic change now rewarding 'brain' much more relative to 'brawn', the traditional role of the working-class man as breadwinner is under threat. With fathers no longer able to provide as they once were, is it surprising that some women prefer to turn to the state as a more reliable provider?

Indeed, according to some thinkers on the Left, along with the disappearance of the traditional patterns of work that bolstered family life there has been an erosion of the traditional values that encouraged young men to assume a responsible role as fathers.

The ethical socialists Norman Dennis and George Erdos have attributed the rise of single parenthood, at least in part, to a decline in respect for the once unquestioned working-class values of self-reliance, family loyalty and social solidarity.

The causes of family breakdown are complex, the reasons for the rise in single parenthood difficult to pin down. But, while there is still doubt about the causes, the increase in the number of single parents is now accepted as legitimate cause for concern across the political spectrum. Tony Blair, in an interview with Brian Walden, made clear his preference for children to be raised in a two-parent family wherever possible. Frank Field, the Labour MP for Birkenhead and chairman of the Commons Social Security Committee, has signalled his wider concern at the 'growing armies of claimants hooked on the dependency culture'.

By raising the matter in a speech concerned explicitly with the ethical basis of politics, Portillo sought to reconnect an issue associated in the minds of some with simple parsimony towards the poor with a broader debate on the values and attitudes involved. Of course, as chief secretary to the Treasury, he was concerned with the crude question of trying to reduce state spending. But he was also trying to do something more – to advance the debate on how to deal with a society becoming less stable.

Did he succeed? In the eyes of dead-centre Conservative opinion he seemed to. The *Sunday Express*, the most cloyingly loyal of all the Tory tabloids, never normally as radical as the *Mail*, or even the *Sun*, applauded the speech. Its leader on 19 September was remarkably warm. Under the headline 'At last a man with vision', it rhapsodised:

There has seldom been such a dearth of political vision as there is now. We have a team of Ministers and Shadow Ministers who rush around talking constantly. But they are saying nothing. The contrast between them and Mr Portillo could not be more stark. His speech on Thursday demonstrated that, in him at least, John Major's government has someone with a point of view, an ideology . . . a vision.

Among commentators on the centre-Left the response was a little less warm. In the *New Statesman*, Ian Aitken, an old Tribunite who nevertheless had a soft spot for thoughtful Tories, homed in on Portillo's assertion that increasing state spending undermined the ability of individuals to make moral choices for themselves: 'This, he says, is why the government stopped paying benefits to 16 and 17 year-olds. Never mind that, more than anything, this condemned so many teenagers to live in cardboard boxes. It gave them the opportunity to make a soul-enhancing choice between starvation and prostitution.'

Aitken's spirited attack was one of the first hostile press responses to Portillo's project of setting new compass bearings for his party, but it would soon seem milk-and-water stuff compared to the bilious reaction Portillo was to inspire in other commentators, many of them writing in Tory-supporting papers.

The next speech to attract significant notice, and criticism, was one delivered to a fringe meeting at the 1993 Tory party conference, held by the Centre for Policy Studies on 7 October. 'The Blue Horizon,' like 'Ethics and Public Finance', dealt with the size of government, and questioned the morality of believing that 'the state could cure all our woes by throwing taxpayers' money at our problems'. But Portillo went beyond simply arguing for a smaller state, to attempt to explore what a government's proper function was, and where political leaders should flex their muscles more vigorously.

Portillo did not argue for the eventual erosion of the politician's role as the functions of the state reduced, not even as the most distant ideal to steer towards. He argued that a withdrawal from wasteful effort should allow for a strengthening of the politician's real role: the defence and maintenance of civil society, the safeguarding of shared virtues and the provision of leadership.

He went on to insist that a Conservative government should seek to embody recognisably Tory principles in the implementation of policy, and in so doing he identified a new battleground where the Left were launching an assault – political correctness:

The state has slipped into an attitude of studied amorality. Our benefit system takes little account of whether people have come to need state help as a result of behaviour that was reasonable or unreasonable, responsible or irresponsible. To talk today of the deserving and undeserving poor is guaranteed to make people wince – a mark of the triumph of political correctness.

Portillo was attempting to re-educate his audience in their

assumptions about what politicians were for. In his previous assaults on the size of the state he had argued that politicians were less effective at spending money and doing genuine good than were individuals or voluntary associations. He wanted politicians to be statesmen, not managers:

In the 1990s people are looking for more from politicians than good administration. They are concerned about the condition of our society and its values. We must throw away decades of claptrap served up by sociologists. It is time to return to plain speaking and traditional values.

In asserting that the electorate of the nineties wanted direction more than dry competence, Portillo was again touching on a theme to be developed by Tony Blair during his leadership. But more, perhaps, than pre-empting a Blair theme, Portillo was adapting a Thatcher lesson. One of the main criticisms of Margaret Thatcher's governments, and indeed of most Tory administrations, was the perceived tension between the 'libertarian' and 'authoritarian' strains in her character and the party's ideology. How could she simultaneously wish to roll back the frontiers of the state and enlarge individual freedom while taking up 'illiberal' positions on, say, capital punishment, a core curriculum, police powers or immigration?

To argue that she, and Tories generally, are inconsistent is to miss the point. Of course the mix of prejudice and principle does not fit any rational template exactly, but Tories are Tories because they reject simple systems that explain everything and programmes of political action that smooth out the rough and complex edges of human character. Thatcher's position may be inconsistent, but it is *coherent*, in the sense that when she outlines her views she is easily and immediately understood. She effectively articulated a supreme moral populism.

In recognising that it was core values that came first, Portillo was learning from The Lady. But he was also, in 'The Blue Horizon', reiterating an important Thatcherite lesson: Tories should want strong government, but within a limited scope. There is nothing contradictory in asking politicians to do less but to do it better, and in urging them to sacrifice responsibility but to recover real power.

Portillo's speech was temporarily eclipsed by an attempt by the

prime minister and the Cabinet to put Maastricht behind them
and unite the Tories on a populist platform, with the emphasis on
an anti-crime, pro-traditional-values, anti-permissive thrust to a
programme of domestic legislation. The prime minister summed
up the new approach as 'Back to Basics'.

A tub-thumping speech on the conference floor from the new
home secretary, Michael Howard, was complemented by social-
security secretary Peter Lilley's crowd-pleasing digs at foreign
fraudsters. These speeches, along with a crude attack on European
Commission president Jacques Delors from previously passionately
pro-European employment secretary David Hunt, were seen as
evidence of a shift to the Right, designed to reassure activists after
the trauma of Maastricht.

At the end of the week, as commentators began to assess the
significance of the conference, it was the Labour-supporting Peter
Kellner on the Tory-supporting *Sunday Times* who sought to play
up the importance of Portillo's speech. Linking it with Howard's
contribution, he observed that Portillo was 'trying to drive British
politics further to the Right under John Major than it ever travelled
under Margaret Thatcher'. In fact Portillo was not attempting to
forge relentlessly forward, uprooting any evidence of the established order he could find on his Long March to a free-market
paradise. He was reviving a Tory tradition – right-wing, but not
especially radical – and attempting to refurbish it for the nineties.

The clearest evidence that Portillo was not attempting to con-
struct a programme of restless, radical, free-wheeling, economically
driven reform came in the most controversial of his speeches of the
period – the President's Lecture to a dinner of Conservative Way
Forward in London on 14 January 1994. Entitled 'The New British
Disease', it was delivered at a depressing time for the Tory party.

'Back to Basics' had become identified in the public mind with a
new moralism in government, particularly directed towards single
mothers. It was an approach popular with the Tory grass-roots,
who, according to recent academic studies by Patrick Seyd and
Paul Whiteley of Sheffield University, remain very socially conservative. However, if there was one place where 'Back to Basics'
was more popular than in the Conservative Clubs it was in Wap-
ping newsrooms. Politicians' urging a return to traditional values
– and, in particular, urging sexual restraint on young women –

made it much easier to justify investigation into the morality of the men laying down the law.

When the *News of the World* revealed that Tory minister Tim Yeo had fathered a child by his mistress, so doing his bit to fuel the worrying growth in single-parent families, the rally in Tory fortunes promised by 'Back to Basics' turned into a humiliating reverse. After the event, the inventor of the phrase, Sarah Hogg, head of the Number Ten Policy Unit, was to claim that it had meant no more than a return to best practice in the public sector, but its identification in the public mind with a restoration of traditional values had not been challenged before the Yeo scandal by Tories anxious to benefit from any apparent revival, however slight, whatever the cause.

Against this background, Portillo's CWF speech was trailed by his advisers beforehand as a defence of 'Back to Basics', a demonstration that the policy was still on track and remained valid despite the frailty of some ministerial flesh. It was intended to support a prime-ministerial initiative, but its tone and nuance contained some subtle, and not so subtle, coded criticism of Tory policy in previous years.

In effect the speech was intended as a warning. In language some thought exaggerated, and which was certainly not understated, Portillo tried to arrest his audience's attention by examining 'one of the greatest threats that has ever confronted the British nation'. That threat – the New British Disease – was 'the self-destructive sickness of national cynicism':

It is spread by so-called opinion-formers within the British élite, the people who think they know what's best for all of us.

The disease shows itself in a readiness to denigrate our country and praise others; to devalue our achievements and envy others; to hold our national institutions in contempt and to look with approval on other people's; to deride every one of our national figures.

The complaint Portillo was making has been made by other Tories – most notably Douglas Hurd, who has deprecated the 'culture of denigration' which makes the British too quick to criticise and insufficiently ready to applaud achievement. But few politicians would have expressed themselves as forcefully as Portillo in attacking the so-called denigrators.

Having identified the problem as a 'disease', he developed the medical metaphor in a manner that to some appeared tasteless: 'A poison has been spread by pessimists. Too many politicians, churchmen, authors, commentators and journalists exhibit the full-blown symptoms of this New British Disease.'

He then went on not only to defend the ambitious from the envious, but to defend institutions that Conservative politicians have often shied away from praising since the sixties, but which were once the essential Tory Trinity – Church, Queen and Parliament.

The monarchy, Portillo argued, was 'an institution vital to our national well-being', the established Church a 'moral and moderate' independent institution of worth, and the House of Commons, despite being 'rowdy . . . adversarial and confrontational', was central to the survival of the world's most successful democracy, which was why:

it's much more important than a zoo and far too important to be treated as a joke. In half the world people would be willing to die for such an institution and for such democratic safeguards – literally. Even within the developed world very few countries have systems which produce national government of such incorruptibility. That's something to be proud of, something to hang on to.

Portillo deplored the acquiescence of these institutions in processes that undermined their innate dignity:

Those who advised the royal family to become more populist and more ordinary probably played into the hands of those who wanted to make them soap opera or farce. Parliament was, I think, ill-advised to let in the TV cameras. The Church has been rushing to reform in a way that seemed to owe more to late-twentieth-century political correctness than to the apostolic tradition or to universal truths.

After discussing its institutions, Portillo turned to the nation itself, identifying new threats to the integrity of the state. Taking head-on the argument that Euro-sceptics like himself were the real pessimists because they lacked the confidence to believe Britain could compete within the EU and wanted to withdraw, in sullen isolation, to the sidelines, he tried to turn the argument round by attacking the federalists and their supporters:

On the latter it seems to me that those who wish to give up national sovereignty and see Britain absorbed into a trans-European political body show the ultimate symptoms of national self-doubt, even defeatism. The European Superstate is a serious proposition on the agenda of some of the bureaucracies of Europe, and you find it too on the agenda of those who regard Britain's institutions as élitist, effete or merely risible.

The standard Tory attack on European federalism had generally been based on economic arguments – the opt-outs from the single currency and the social chapter protected the pound, and industry, from costly entanglements in Continental projects. Having got rid of socialism in Britain, the Tories were anti-Brussels because they did not want it coming back by the 'back-Delors'. Here, however, Portillo, no slouch when it came to attacking Brussels on economic grounds, was choosing to argue from a nationalist point of view, defending from Brussels' expansionist ambitions the ancient British constitution rather than Thatcherism's recent gains.

The speech was remarkable. Why was the eighties radical now so keen to appear a nostalgic in the nineties?

In a full-page editorial entitled 'It's time to grow up, Mr Portillo', the London *Evening Standard* took Portillo to task, arguing that the cost-cutting, cheese-paring, candle-end-counting Thatcherite in the Treasury could not be taken seriously posing as the guardian of established institutions which 'he, in so brutally wielding the axe on public spending, has done so much to destroy'. It went on:

Mr Portillo cannot be expected to be taken seriously when he asks for respect for British institutions when his policies are leading to the closure of St Bartholomew's Hospital ... He speaks for institutions and yet happily stands by as our great universities go into decline, as do our orchestras, our theatres and our libraries.

It also attacked Portillo's hyperbole, complaining that his description of cynicism as 'one of the greatest threats that has ever confronted the British nation' might offend readers who had lived through the Battle of Britain.

Less personally abusive, but no less pointed in its way, was the criticism in a *Times* editorial. The leader-writer found Portillo's analysis 'flawed', coming from a man associated with the 'angry pessimism of the radical right'. The leader argued that 'Mr Portillo has not yet proved himself a populist', and attacked what it saw as a central inconsistency in the case of a minister apparently, through his Fundamental Expenditure Review, engaged in a tireless search for economy and efficiency:

The difficulty for Mr Portillo is that the Conservative Government of the last 14 years cannot escape responsibility for the change. With its ethos of competition and comparison – epitomised by public service league tables – politicians have encouraged citizens to scrutinise the institutions that serve them. The effect is paradoxical. Standards rise but so too do knowledge, expectations, dissatisfaction and disappointment.

Robin Cook, at that point Labour's Industry spokesman and an opposition politician who had admired Portillo's competence in committee as a junior minister, found the sentiments 'nothing more than a bankrupt demonstration of saloon-bar prejudice'.

The feeling that Portillo's message was incoherent, and all the more incongruous coming from a man with his form as a radical right-winger, was encapsulated most crisply by Andrew Marr in the *Independent*, who asked, 'Who, after all, is Mr Portillo, if not an élite opinion-former, a pillar of the new establishment, and a Thatcherite hammerer of institutions?'

Most commentators united to condemn the speech, but then were they likely to welcome an attack on their trade? Would the Amalgamated Union of Opinion-Formers, Commentators, Columnists, Critics and Associated Wordsmiths be likely to clasp this upstart to its collective bosom? The fiercely critical, and disparaging, reaction from *bien-pensant* metropolitan opinion played to the prejudices of Portillo's main audience as effectively as the original speech had done. The squeals showed he had hit home.

The audience Portillo was addressing was not the editorial-writers but the bewildered mass of his party – angered at having seen their assumptions overturned on everything from the management of the currency to the value of their houses, from the treatment of the criminal to the conduct of their leaders. Andrew Marr realised the speech's appeal even as he disagreed with its content: 'For most Conservatives these words are true, raw and timely.' Assessing the speech in tactical terms, as a piece of political positioning, he acknowledged its effectiveness, but was Portillo doing any more than crudely recycling his audience's prejudices in an effort to ingratiate himself?

Among Tory MPs who know Portillo – whatever their position in the party or their view of aspects of the speech – there is a broad consensus that it was a sincere expression of deeply felt anger, and in tune with Tory activists' concerns in a way a calculated pitch could never have been. One member of the 1992 intake, normally a Portillo fan, had his doubts about the speech, and told Portillo in the lobby that he thought its tone exaggerated – in particular the passage about cynicism being the greatest-ever threat: 'I asked him, "What about Hitler, or Communism?" and he swore at me. There was real passion there. There's no doubt it was sincerely meant. It was a cry from the heart.'

Older voices, from other parts of the party, now think, with the benefit of hindsight, that the speech was a helpful contribution to the debate. Tristan Garel-Jones commented, 'I had a lot of sympathy with a great deal of what he was saying.' Robert Key goes, if anything, further in his assessment of the effectiveness of the speech: 'He believes passionately in trying to reflect the views of supporters in the country at large, and I am in absolutely no doubt from my own constituency that an awful lot of people look to him at some point in the future.'

Most of the speech was written by Portillo himself. He has pressed a variety of figures into service to come up with ideas, develop themes and polish phrases for speeches, but this particular effort was, according to his most energetic speech-writer, David Hart, nearly all his own work.

Portillo sometimes writes the first draft of his own speeches; often he leaves the early structural work to his special adviser, Alison Broom. Broom also acts as a filter for contributions from a variety of sources. In the past Portillo has been helped by, among others, Jonathan Aitken's former special adviser John Bercow, Tory student leader Conor Burns, Conservative Way Forward organisers, scholarly journalists and TV script-writers. But the biggest influence, bypassing Broom and working directly with Portillo, is Hart. One former Treasury official recalls Hart injecting humour and invective into dry civil-service drafts for Commons speeches: 'He came up with a hilarious series of jokes at poor Harriet Harman's expense, comparing her to Joan Collins, a big spender who wants the best of everything, that sort of thing. Not award-winning stuff, but it goes down brilliantly with the back-benchers.'

Hart concedes that Portillo's CWF speech may have been strong stuff, but he believes the style was appropriate to the subject, and the occasion: 'He used words to grab people's attention. Speeches on occasions like that are theatrical. People paid attention to what he said. He opened up a debate and demonstrated he had bedrock beliefs and a clear political agenda.'

Portillo's tone was dramatic for several reasons. He needed, by his language, to prove that he was expressing beliefs that were deeply felt, rather than coolly considered. His choice of words betrayed the anger of an individual who feels deeply about his country seeing it sold short by those who love it less. Additionally, he had to demonstrate to a broader audience, more acquainted with him as a 'Thatcherite hammerer of institutions', that his Conservatism ran deeper. Thirdly, and perhaps most importantly, he had to show that the Tory party of the nineties was prepared to take on the Left on the new battleground they had chosen – which was cultural, not economic.

It is because of his background – both family and educational – that Portillo cares, perhaps more deeply than many Britons, for the historic continuity of British institutions. He has been compared to the Irish prime minister Eamon De Valera, a politician of Spanish background whose affection for his new homeland developed into a narrow nationalism and a suspicion of neighbours. But the influence of Portillo's family background is more complex than that. As the son of a refugee who spent childhood holidays in an authoritarian state, he cherishes the good fortune the British have had in seeing, admittedly imperfect, institutions preserve their liberties for so long.

Like so many with backgrounds that place them outside, or at least athwart, the mainstream currents of British life, Portillo can see more clearly the advantages of institutions that the British take for granted. Edmund Burke, an Irishman, John Buchan, a Scot, Disraeli, the son of a Jewish immigrant, and Labour's Bryan Gould, a New Zealander, were all keener supporters of British democracy in its rickety, unreformed, but persistent and unassuming state than many whose family came over with the Conqueror.

Lord Beloff has written movingly of the pride generations of immigrants have taken in becoming British citizens and living in a
nation where liberties are safeguarded by the rule of law and parliamentary democracy. For millions like him, who would never consider themselves wholly 'English', being British is both natural
and a source of pride.

So, for personal reasons, it is not surprising that Portillo spoke
with the passion he did. However, there was also a political imperative for using language that seemed exaggerated.

During the 1992 general election, John Major had warned the
electorate, 'Wake up, wake up, the United Kingdom is in peril.'
Despite the doubts of some of his colleagues – including Chris
Patten – Major felt it was appropriate to use strong language to
alert voters to one of the most dangerous aspects of the Labour
Party's plans: their devolution proposals. It is now a commonplace
that Major's constitutional counter-attack won votes across the
UK, and seats in Scotland, for the Tories. But Major made the
point not just to win votes, but to win an important argument.

He recognised that, having lost the economic argument, and
having accepted that they could not win elections by promising to
renationalise, roll forward the frontiers of the state and squeeze
the rich until the pips squeaked, the Left were now trying to win
power by fighting on other ground. During the election, as well as
arguing for devolution for Scotland and Wales, Neil Kinnock flirted
with proportional representation and made clear his enthusiasm
for ceding power from Westminster to Brussels and Strasburg.

Major saw that Labour were trying to channel the perennial
discontent with flawed, fallen politicians into an appetite for institutional reform which could be used to rewrite the rules in the
party's favour. Labour-voting areas would be strengthened, and
the nation-state – a pragmatic bulwark against idealistic, univer-
salising ideologies like socialism – would lose its potency. It was
a point that had not been lost on Portillo either. In 1985 he had
told the Commons that 'the Labour Party's first instinct when
faced with a problem is to turn to constitutional reform'.

Tony Blair has been at pains to neutralise many of the potentially unpopular parts of the Labour platform he inherited, including some of the more extravagant constitutional proposals, but
Labour remain committed to massaging the electoral process to

increase female representation, introducing assemblies for Scotland, Wales and London, to be followed in due course by some
English regions, reforming the House of Lords, and playing a more
positive role in developing European institutions. The reforms are
intended to make Britain a more plural, inclusive, participatory
and open democracy, as well as capitalising on the feeling that
Westminster has 'failed' and that a Victorian Parliament is unsuitable for the next millennium.

It may seem ironic that the answer to the failure of politicians
is to have more of them, and it may seem narrowly rationalist to
believe that a 'modern' constitution is a precondition for economic
success when the world's two biggest economies, those in the USA
and Japan, are run, respectively, by rules laid down by white,
middle-class slave-owners in the eighteenth century and by an
emperor, but Labour's proposals have proved popular.

As a student of Hobbes and Richard Hooker, Portillo recognised,
in the words of the latter's *Of the Laws of Ecclesiastical Politie*, that
'He that goeth about to persuade a multitude, that they are not
so well governed as they ought to be, shall never want attentive
and favourable hearers.' Acknowledging that Labour's assault had
to be met with all the force he could muster, he served notice with
his CWF speech that he was prepared to defend Conservatism on
cultural and constitutional grounds, as well as on the economic,
efficient and moral grounds fought on before. It was a considered
response, by Portillo and his advisers, to what they saw as a new
mood abroad in the country.

David Hart believes that the eighties may have been dominated
by economic debate, but in the nineties a different tone needs to
be struck: 'The theme we wanted to develop was sovereignty – a
sovereign nation, governing itself; sovereign institutions people can
respect; and sovereign individuals making their own decisions, free
of government interference. Ultimately, it's an appeal to pride and
patriotism.' Hart's analysis draws on some of the prime minister's
own insights from the 1992 election campaign.

However, the dangers of Portillo's appeal to national pride, and
the ease with which a carefully presented, but deeply felt defence
of patriotism could be obscured by comments construing it as
swaggering nationalist superiority, were exposed a few weeks later.
In a speech to the Southampton University Conservative Associ-

ation on 4 February, Portillo made comments about 'abroad' that prompted the *Daily Mirror* to call him the 'World's most hated Tory'. Following up his theme of a month before, that Britain had much to be proud of, he slipped from the positive celebration of British achievement to the negative criticism of others, commenting:

If any of you have got an A-level it is because you worked to get it. Go to any other country and when you have got an A-level you have bought it.

When you go into business you will win contracts because you are good at what you do. Go to a number of other countries and you would win contracts because your cousin was a minister or because you had lined the pocket of some public official.

Portillo's remarks reflected the feeling of many Tories that the sleaze alleged to tarnish British public life paled into insignificance compared with that in other nations. Britain did not have ministers in league with the Mafia, as in Italy, or embroiled in bribery scandals, as in Belgium, France, Germany, Japan or Spain. However, by choosing to defend standards in public life in such a crude way, Portillo had made a mistake, and he knew it.

He moved swiftly to try to repair the damage, asking a reporter from the Southampton *Evening Echo* to amend his words, almost as though it were a Hansard record he was trying to correct. The reporter refused, knowing he had a story, and perhaps, given Portillo's theme, anxious to ensure that the British reputation for incorruptibility extended to the press.

Once the story hit London, Portillo was forced to trail from TV studio to TV studio, eating huge helpings of humble pie in each one. He told Channel 4 News:

On the spur of the moment I chose my words poorly. I didn't say Britain was the only honest country in the world. But I certainly did say more than I intended because I was speaking off the cuff and I exaggerated.

As soon as I finished my speech I moved to set the record straight. I said more than I intended. I am sorry if anyone was insulted by it.

The apology did not stop the criticism. The suggestion that the sentiments expressed had been exaggerated because Portillo was speaking off the cuff were undermined when it was revealed, in the *Sunday Telegraph*, that a similar speech had been delivered to Eton's Political Society just a few days before the Southampton fiasco. Commentators concluded that Portillo had done his career terminal damage, and rushed to finish off the job. The *Sunday Express* concluded that 'Michael Portillo's chances of succeeding John Major lay in tatters.' In the *Observer*, Andrew Rawnsley believed 'it was a silly speech, which has pricked the speculative bubble around the Thatcherite darling'.

On the Right of his own party the reaction was rather different. One member of the 1922 Committee executive thinks the comments did Portillo no end of good: 'He said what we all know to be true. Anywhere south of Beachy Head you can't get anything done without greasing palms. He shouldn't have apologised.' This view is shared by David Hart: 'The only mistake he made was to withdraw. It looks irresolute. He should have defended the speech.' Some aides hint that the decision to apologise was not made by Portillo alone.

His special adviser, Alison Broom, accepts that there was one obvious slip: she argues Portillo did not mean to say that A-levels could be bought in 'any' other country – only in some. Even with that change, however, and without any apology, the speech would still have struck a sour note after the CWF lecture. It was an unnecessary hostage to fortune, and sat ill next to his previous statements deploring denigration. Whatever his anger at seeing Britain adversely compared with countries he thought much more corrupt, was it altogether wise to be seen lashing out in this way?

Genuinely repentant, or not, Portillo showed he was not going to be diverted by the furore a few weeks later, when he chose to deliver another, widely trailed, set-piece speech. Speaking to the North-East Fife Conservative Association, in the East Neuk town of Freuchie on 22 April 1994, Portillo delivered a speech, 'The Conservative Agenda', which sought to reconnect the Tory party with the supporters it had gained in the eighties but seemed to have lost in the nineties. He tried, as he had before, but more explicitly, to argue that Conservative values were the values of a 'quiet majority' shut out by the mendicant clamour of the groups gathered on the Left.

North-East Fife had been a Tory seat until 1987, and Portillo was invited to speak by Mary Scanlan, the right-wing candidate

who had failed to win it back in 1992. She had been impressed by
him at the 1993 party conference.

Portillo set out to explain why a government that was doing its
job should expect voluble criticism and unpopularity:

We understand that it is our first duty to govern for the nation as a
whole, not for partisan interests, to take decisions which will be judged
wise in the long term, not just popular in the short term, to pursue the
difficult virtues of thrift and prudence rather than the easy option of
satisfying every immediate demand.

A usual-enough Tory apologia had extra point when the party
was trailing Labour by more than thirty percentage points in the
polls, but Portillo sought to turn a fact of life – unpopularity – into
a positive virtue. He started by looking at a natural Tory Aunt
Sally, the allegedly unsympathetic media, and invited his audience
to look beyond the chorus of criticism to examine why it was
necessary to endure attacks:

We have a free press in Britain. Despite the many occasions when we
politicians find it intensely irritating, it is our good fortune that it is free.
It keeps politicians honest, and helps prevent corruption.

But a free press also provides the means for vested interests to trumpet
their causes. Governments are vulnerable to pressure from the groups
that attract media and public sympathy. We must always hear them,
but not always pay them heed, for in the clamour of vociferous minorities
we must listen to the still small voice of Britain's quiet majority.

It has become a cliché of current political chatter to say that
the mass parties are dinosaurs, already overtaken by the more
adaptable, and popular, pressure groups, like Greenpeace or the
League Against Cruel Sports, which wield real power and are
more representative. The membership of many of these groups,
particularly those with environmental concerns, is a challenge to
the main parties, but in Portillo's analysis their energy and apparent popularity lead to the overlooking of the needs and wishes of
those who feel no need to join a pressure group. The Conservative
Party should seek to speak for those who do not see themselves as
'political' at all, those who do not look to government intervention
to improve their lot, those whom he characterised as 'the responsible parent, the law-abiding citizen . . . the people who believe in

self-improvement and self-reliance'. Portillo argued that, 'quiet' though they might be, they too had concerns, which the Tories understood, and would address:

The quiet majority is dismayed by much of what goes on around it – standing in the post office queue watching handouts going to people who seem capable of work, reading of yobbos sent on sailing cruises, being told that competition in schools is divisive and demoralising.

Unlike the noisy lobbyists they issue no press releases, they organise no rallies and no marches. They look to government for support. They look to the Conservative Party to articulate their point of view, and through its policies and legislation to validate their way of life and under-pin their beliefs.

Again, as throughout this period, Portillo was trying to argue for a Conservatism rooted in core values rather than trying to convince purely on competence. Arguably this approach was a practical necessity. After Black Wednesday, competence was a dif-ficult card to play. The best way Portillo saw to rally voters was to remind all those attracted by Thatcher and enthused by Major in 1992 that their values were embodied in the Tories in a way they could never be with the Labour Party. If the Tories outlined positions that were popular, but incapable of adoption by Labour, they would succeed, in the overworked phrase of the time, in put-ting 'clear blue water' between the parties.

Portillo became closely associated with that phrase. It adorned the cover of a collection of extracts from his recent speeches which was published by Conservative Way Forward during the 1994 party conference. It was the title of an address he gave at that conference. It is code for a strategy the Right believe needs to be pursued if victory is to be achieved – not victory for them in a struggle within the party, though that would be a by-product, but victory at future general elections.

Critics of 'clear blue water' argued it meant electoral oblivion in the end, as the Tories became more 'extreme' in their efforts to distance themselves from a Labour Party moving to the political centre. This is an understandable concern. Traditionally Left Tories have been anxious not to cede what are seen as 'moderate' positions to the opposition. However, apologists for the policy argue that history tells a different story.

The Tories were seldom more 'moderate' than in 1974, when Edward Heath even offered to lead a government, committed to wage and price controls, with members of other parties and none. He was defeated in two general elections within eight months of each other.

The Tories were seldom more radical than in 1983 and 1987, when they promised large-scale privatisations and union reform, but they won 100-plus majorities. Even in 1979, when the manifesto was cautious, Margaret Thatcher was popularly seen as a shrill, unrepresentative right-winger pitched against moderate, reassuring Jim Callaghan. She won.

In the USA, moderate conservative George Bush lost in 1992. In 1994 extremist Newt Gingrich delivered a Republican landslide in Congress. In 1980 and 1984 Ronald Reagan swept to power as the most right-wing candidate for president since Barry Goldwater.

Why? It seems, according to strategists on the Right, as though electors prefer parties that are proud of their positions, and can evangelise enthusiastically. If Heath did not have enough faith in his own party to govern in 1974, why vote for it? If you are apologetic about aspects of your party's platform, why bother?

In one sense, 'clear blue water' is about occupying a position uncompromisingly distant from the opposition, and being proud of the difference. It is intended to inspire supporters to fight all the harder and to communicate their enthusiasm to the electorate.

Also, more than enthusiasm, there seems to be a premium on intellectual vitality. In the same way that Margaret Thatcher was certainly more extreme than Jim Callaghan in 1979, Clement Attlee, for all his moderation of manner, had proposed a much more extreme programme than Winston Churchill in 1945. What both Thatcher and Attlee seemed to have, however, were the ideas appropriate for their age. In contrast to their exhausted, though experienced, opponents, they offered convincing answers to the challenges of the new eras.

One area where Portillo felt the Tories were more at home than Labour, and had colonised first, was the 'community'. A concept often so woolly as to be meaningless, it has been used by Tony Blair as a reproach to what he sees as the aggressive individualism fostered by the Tory Right and rejected by New Labour. However, the Right argue that their enemy is not the community but the overweening state, and that empowering and freeing the individual makes communities stronger.

David Willetts's Social Market Foundation pamphlet *Civic Conservatism* argues that the state has usurped the functions of communities and weakened the fabric of civil society. A still more vigorous assault on the state was launched in *Saturn's Children*, by Alan Duncan MP and Dominic Hobson, a former Tory researcher who collaborated with Lord Lawson on the latter's memoirs. The authors argued that state agencies and confiscatory taxation have eroded the spirit of voluntarism vital to the health of natural communities.

Portillo used part of his Freuchie speech to advance the case that the community depended for its health on the power of the individual, in a defence of putting the individual first that echoed one of the themes in his speech to 'The Church at Work in London'.

Conservatism begins with the individual but it doesn't end there. We defend the rights of every individual, but we emphasise the importance of personal responsibility – and personal responsibility includes duties towards others. Rights and duties are inseparably linked. Conservatism can be seen in practice through the association of individuals of course, but also in the activities of groups and associations. Personal responsibility is shown through action in the family, in the community, in business and in the work of voluntary organisations.

The natural organisations for giving help and support are the family and our community. We supplant them at our peril. We cannot wash our hands of the problems and distress we see around us, in the belief that the state will solve and provide. We cannot be compassionate at second hand. We cannot allow all our personal responsibilities to be discharged remotely.

This speech, less ambitious in scope and more moderate in tone, was, generally, more warmly received.

The *Guardian* was critical, repeating the accusation of incoherence that had been made by the *Evening Standard* against the CWF lecture. Its leader thought that a Thatcherite had a cheek seeking to speak for the majority and the community, advancing a theme subsequently picked up by Blair and others on the Left: 'the Conservatives abandoned such principles when they took a conscious decision to celebrate possessive individualism above the solidarity of tradition and community'.

However, among the Tory press the welcome was universally warm. The speech was extensively puffed and sympathetically reported on the front page of the *Daily Express* – most Majorite of all the tabloids. *The Times*, critical of some of the CWF speech, was enthusiastic, and dignified Portillo's thoughts by placing them in distinguished intellectual company:

The credibility of Mr Portillo's attempt lay in his emphasis upon the difficulty of regeneration. Following the lead of thinkers on the right such as the late Shirley Robin Letwin, he praised the 'difficult virtues' – thrift, providence, self-reliance – to which high taxation and over-mighty government are naturally hostile.

Having recovered something of the momentum lost by his South-ampton gaffe, and something of the bottom put at risk by the extravagance of the language and strength of view expressed in his CWF speech, Portillo tried to be a little less visible over the coming months.

He had laid out his stall, been 'anointed' as the natural candidate of the Right, shown he could soak up criticism, impressed activists and even appealed to some on his party's centre-Left. He had shown he was more than a Thatcherite radical – he was a politician who saw the responsibilities of office extending beyond proving one's skill as a Treasury bean-counter.

He had also exposed himself to ridicule and hatred. He had tried to make the running as a shaper of his party's future and had incurred the envy and dislike of some less well-publicised colleagues. Several thoughtful colleagues were even worried that it was not just his career that Portillo was taking risks with, but his party too. One left-wing Cabinet minister – open-minded, engaging, unsectarian and socially liberal – thought the series of speeches a dangerous departure, commenting at the time, 'I think our party faces a greater risk of factionalism than at any time I can remember. There is every danger we could repeat the mistakes of Labour in the seventies and cripple ourselves with infighting and a search for ideological purity. Ministers have a responsibility not to encourage that development with intemperate comments.'

The series of speeches was inevitably seen as preparation for a leadership challenge. The reporting of every speech was accompanied with references to Portillo's position in the jockeying for the succession to Major. Such speculation was almost more damaging than the speeches to Portillo's reputation within Westminster.

The assumption that Portillo was preparing for a leadership bid was widespread, and not without foundation. Early in 1994 he played host at a series of dinners in his London flat for a variety of 'thinkers'. The brain-storming sessions were intended to provide material for a manifesto for the future. Portillo did not anticipate launching a challenge against John Major, but, if Major fell, Portillo wanted to be primed to succeed.

With the help of David Hart, Portillo arranged several suppers, each devoted to discussion of a different policy area. It was an attempt to broaden the base of Portillo's knowledge, and to reinforce his strengths in some areas. One dinner was spent discussing foreign affairs and defence, with Gerald Frost, director of the Centre for Policy Studies, among several guests brought together by Hart, whose expertise in the area helped inform Portillo's thinking. Another dinner, on economic policy and the size of the state, brought together the usual right-wing suspects, such as Lord Harris of High Cross, and genuinely independent experts. One of the non-aligned guests recalls, 'It was a pleasant evening – nice catered food, and a good discussion. Some of the others were ideologues who just wouldn't see sense, but Portillo was more open and impressive. He's a practical politician, and he grasped the limits of the possible.'

One of the most intriguing guests, at a dinner organised to explore thinking on education, was John McIntosh, headmaster of the Oratory School, in Fulham, south-west London. McIntosh had advised Margaret Thatcher when she was prime minister, but he is also the headmaster of the school Labour leader Tony Blair has chosen for his son, Euan. It is ironic that Blair should choose a school for his son run by a man who has dined with Michael Portillo to discuss education policy.

Dinners were chosen in preference to anything more formal or austere, such as seminars, because it was felt to be a more British way of doing things – exchanging ideas over the dining-table rather than having dry discussions in a strip-lit conference room. The evenings were not devoted to plotting: they were simply to equip

Portillo for the future. They were private, rather than secret, but the discretion deployed by Portillo and Hart was wise given the embarrassment that had ensued when they were too open with two opportunists.

In January 1993 Portillo, Hart, and Alison Broom met two young right-wingers, Michael Romain and Andrew Wigmore, who were keen to 'help' Portillo and outlined a remarkable plan.

Broom was at that point acting as an 'unofficial' special adviser to Portillo. Denied the chance to appoint his own government-sponsored adviser by Lamont's insistence that the Treasury could only support advisers to the chancellor, Portillo had kept Broom on at his own expense. She worked out of the offices of Hart's company, Arcadia Land, on the fifth floor of 23 Buckingham Gate. However, on 14 January 1993 she was in Portillo's office in the Treasury, with Hart, when Romain and Wigmore explained that they wanted to set up a think-tank designed to prepare for a Portillo leadership bid. Portillo listened politely while Romain and Wigmore explained that the think-tank – to be named Independent Policy Research – would have no formal links to him, to avoid the suggestion it was a 'vanity tank', but it would be dedicated to his advancement.

Hart, who was suspicious about the two from the start, and thought them 'spivvy', acknowledged that Major's leadership was in trouble and made it clear he had the money to back a think-tank, but he was dismissive of their plans. Broom had not been impressed by the pair's initial approach, but she had been charged by Portillo to encourage young enthusiasts with ideas to submit them for possible inclusion in speeches, and had not wanted to put them off.

Once Romain and Wigmore advanced their scheme, it became clear that it was a non-starter. If Portillo wanted ideas, would he risk setting up his own think-tank? If he did, would he entrust it to two men in their twenties?

No one at the meeting accused Portillo of plotting Major's downfall. He took time to make it clear he thought Major would survive longer than Romain and Wigmore imagined, but, nevertheless, was it wise for Portillo to have seen them? And to have three meetings with them arranged in his diary? Would a more careful minister not have immediately shown them the door?

Following the meeting, Wigmore sent a memo which outlined his and Romain's thinking:

There would naturally be an off-the-record understanding that you would use IPR as a personal political resource, but that you would not be visibly identified as its focal point or *raison d'être* – otherwise it will be immediately perceived as a launch pad for an eventual leadership bid and consequently disparaged in both the party and the Press, thus damaging your chances.

When Portillo discovered the memo sandwiched between official papers in his red box he was more than a little annoyed. He contacted Broom, and she immediately ordered Wigmore to destroy it, all copies, and any trace of it on file. Unfortunately for her, Wigmore kept a copy.

After the memo, contact was cut off, but that was not the last of it.

In December 1993 Wigmore, who was trying to raise money for a UK edition of the conservative American magazine *National Review*, was on the front page of the *Sunday Mirror*. It was not a successful publicity stunt: he had been exposed as a gigolo, offering clients his services for £1,000 a night. He had taken up the work after finding political research insufficiently rewarding, in the hope that acting as an escort would tide him over while the magazine was established. It was not a great money-spinner; he was caught out within days of starting.

After his exposure, all plans for the magazine were dropped, and Romain had nothing more to do with him. Political work dried up – except for one curious act of charity.

Malcolm Tyndall, Portillo's agent, took pity on Wigmore, whom mutual acquaintances had described as being well-disposed towards Portillo, and offered him some work as an assistant in the constituency office. At that point Tyndall did not know of the Treasury meeting, the mooted think-tank or the rogue memo. He soon found out. On 8 May the *Mail on Sunday* published details of what they called 'a campaign to secure the leadership of the Tory party for Michael Portillo'.

Quoting from the memo, and revealing details of the January 1993 meeting, the article was clearly well-sourced. The source was Wigmore. Desperate for money, disgraced, and having lost any prospect of a political career, he had cynically sold his last asset, evidence of contact with Portillo. The *Mail on Sunday* paid Wigmore a five-figure sum for his story, led with it on the front page, and devoted a leader to questioning Portillo's judgement. Wigmore used the money to leave the country, and now lives in Monte Carlo as a presenter with Riviera Radio.

There was no evidence to indict Portillo as a plotter, but the story stuck because his other actions suggested all too clearly where his ambitions led. As well as giving concrete expression to the unspoken assumption that he was an undeclared future candidate for the leadership, the incident again called his judgement into question. One MP, otherwise well-disposed to Portillo, commented, 'What was he doing seeing them? I'm not surprised to see Hart involved. Associating with him can only harm Michael.' Others were disposed to take a more charitable view, accepting that Portillo could not control all those who sought to act in his name, and deploring the stitch-up. But, with a reshuffle coming up, it was publicity Portillo could have done without.

So angry had Major become by whispering and plotting on the Right that, at a private dinner for journalists, planned to say farewell to his press secretary, Gus O'Donnell, he had promised to 'fucking crucify them'.

Major's suspicion was, on one level, well-founded. The rhetorical and political positions Portillo occupied, to the Right of the Major administration, inevitably made him more attractive to those anxious to see the certainties of the eighties return. However, in another way, this suspicion could be construed as a misjudgement. Support for Portillo was symptomatic of the problem Major had in leading a party still riven by unresolved tensions from the Thatcher premiership. It was certainly encouraged by Portillo's public statements. It was cultivated and exaggerated by Portillo's admirers. But Portillo himself was at pains to assure supporters he never intended to launch a challenge to a sitting prime minister. Whether out of simple prudence or honourable honesty, he told friends that it was his view that the British people chose John Major, as they chose Margaret Thatcher, and the decision as to whether or not the prime minister should remain in office should be theirs.

Some of Portillo's closest supporters, not least Hart, had urged the advantages of resigning from the Cabinet and having a tilt at the leadership. A group of those closest to him – more advisers and journalists than parliamentary colleagues – have argued that association with the current administration hurts him, and he should have stood down in 1994 to prepare himself for a future bid. But Portillo is not a natural resigner. His addiction to the inside track makes him averse to placing himself, wilfully, in the wilderness.

His desire to be loyal to established institutions – in particular the Tory Party and the Queen's government – inclines him further against resignation. Moreover, his practical experience of concrete, albeit limited, achievement – even under colleagues who are not natural allies – binds him to office, where real work can be done and real power be wielded.

Portillo's resolve not to resign was to be sorely strained, but, before then, his careful strategy of shifting the party to the Right was to be upset by the actions of some of those whom he had trusted most.

CHAPTER FOURTEEN

Party Games

I am very sorry that I am unable to join the Association to
mark Michael's tenth anniversary as Member of Parliament
for Enfield Southgate. I well remember the tragic circumstances which led to the by-election which brought Michael
into Parliament. He and I understand each other well!

It is much to his credit that he has won the support of so
many in the party for his views and not least his courage in
expressing them. I wish him a happy evening and every success
in the important political future he deserves.

Norman Tebbit, in a letter to Malcolm Tyndall, Tory agent
for Enfield Southgate

Reading the *Sunday Telegraph* has seldom been a chore for Michael
Portillo. Since his admirer Conrad Black acquired the Telegraph
Group in 1986, the Sunday's 'Comment' section has been in impeccably right-wing hands. However, on 7 August 1994 Portillo found,
on its front page, one of the most irritating, and embarrassing,
articles he had ever read.

The paper's political diarist had a scoop. Petronella Wyatt, editor of the 'Mandrake' column and daughter of the Thatcher-loving
Lord Wyatt of Weeford, revealed that Portillo was planning
another anniversary party. But this was no intimate gathering for
friends in a small room of a London club to mark his birthday.
Alexandra Palace, the north-London Victorian 'People's Palace',
rebuilt at embarrassing expense by Labour-controlled Haringey
Council after being burnt down in 1980, had been booked on Friday 2 December, fireworks had been bought, Lady Thatcher, Lord
Tebbit and Gyles Brandreth had been invited, and a video had
been commissioned to tell the story of Portillo's life and times –
all to mark the tenth anniversary of his election as MP for Enfield
Southgate. North London would not have seen a celebration like
it since Arsenal won the double – and all for a man barely forty
and only two years in the Cabinet. What had he done to deserve
it?

Portillo apparently asked himself the same question. He subsequently told friends that the story came as a surprise to him. Earlier that year Portillo had been approached by his constituency agent, Malcolm Tyndall, with sketchy plans for a fund-raising event to mark Portillo's ten years in Parliament. Portillo gave his blessing, but, according to Tyndall and others close to Portillo, he was not informed about the details, because the actual scale of the event was meant to be a 'surprise'.

Portillo's friends say he was genuinely shocked by what had been planned in his name. But is it possible that the MP with a reputation for assiduously scrutinising seating plans to smooth social events would not have known that his own constituency association was planning to hire the Ally Pally and invite Lady Thatcher and hundreds more to mark his first decade in Parliament?

Tyndall maintains Portillo trusts him to run the association, and does not interfere or fuss unduly. The agent is a party professional, employed by the association, not the member, to keep the constituency organisation in good repair. But, even though Portillo did not choose Tyndall, they have worked harmoniously since his appointment.

Tyndall runs a large and efficient operation, has kept association membership near 2,000 during a difficult time for the party, and has made good use of the generosity of some of the wealthier members in the stockbroker belt of Hadley Wood. He has also maintained Portillo's majority in the face of a Labour encroachment in the less salubrious south of the seat, where creeping demographic trends have worked against the Tories.

Given his overall efficiency, and the energy he showed during the 1992 campaign, Portillo was inclined to allow Tyndall a good deal of leeway. He turned a blind eye to Tyndall's support for a referendum on Maastricht, a position he, personally, has consistently opposed. He also forgave him the eccentric decision to employ Andrew Wigmore before Wigmore's betrayal. So, it is possible that Portillo did simply let him get on with his plans, unaware of the details. But why was Tyndall planning something so ambitious?

Tyndall claims his motives were mixed: a desire to reflect the regard in which Portillo was held in Southgate, and a wish to maximise fund-raising for the association by capitalising on Portillo's wider popularity in the party. 'We wanted to make as much money as possible, knowing there'd be a big demand for tickets for an event like this, and the opportunity to secure sponsorship. It's part of my job as agent to raise money for the party.'

There was also a personal element. Tyndall's admiration for Portillo goes beyond the ordinary amiable, but strictly professional, relationship between MP and agent. Tyndall is typical of several Southgate figures deeply loyal to Portillo as a consequence of having worked closely with him: 'Michael is capable of extraordinary generosity and thoughtfulness. Just weeks after I was appointed in Southgate I had to go back to my previous constituency, Shipley, to do a sponsored speech for charity. I went up for the weekend. I was nearing the end on Sunday when I got the surprise of my life. Michael and Carolyn, who'd been in Scotland over the weekend, walked in with a cheque for charity from them and from the people they'd been staying with. It was extraordinarily thoughtful.'

Tyndall has also appreciated trips to the Portillos' Buckinghamshire home for convivial suppers, and occasional bottles of champagne for conspicuous effort in the MP's service. All this makes his ambitions for the event a little easier to understand. But, whatever Tyndall's thinking, after a year when Portillo had taken risks to raise his profile, but all the time contriving never to appear too openly ambitious, this celebration seemed spectacularly ill-judged.

After Portillo's series of speeches, even his supporters, like Iain Duncan-Smith, had wondered if he had not gone just a touch too far. But the speeches, at least, could be seen as contributions to an ongoing debate. Private suppers with supporters could be presented as nothing more than the legitimate exploring of ideas by an intellectually engaged politician. Indiscreet memos from over-enthusiastic fans could be written off as the intemperate behaviour of people over whom Portillo had no control. The Ally Pally extravaganza was different. Portillo's own people were responsible for an event which looked, at best, like a gauche transatlantic import, at worst like a badly misconceived launch pad for the leadership.

Immediately the article appeared, Tyndall rushed out a statement to the Press Association stressing the party had been planned in secret. How, then, did the story get out?

Outside Southgate, Tyndall had planned to approach several

businessmen to supply sponsorship, but had so far written only to David Rigg, communications director of Camelot, the National Lottery firm, whose first draw would have been made a few days before the party. It was not a happy choice. The Treasury in general, and Portillo in particular, had been associated with opposition to the lottery.

The Treasury was traditionally suspicious about the raising of government revenue which it could not control. Margaret Thatcher was known to be vigorously opposed to the extension of state power which the lottery – a nationalisation of gambling – would inevitably involve. She was also instinctively opposed to wealth acquired without work. Portillo was known to combine the Treasury suspicion towards the lottery with Thatcherite distaste.

Under the circumstances, Rigg was disinclined to support the event, and, slightly surprised that he had been approached, he passed Tyndall's letter on to a Tory acquaintance. His contact then passed on the letter to the *Sunday Telegraph*, where Wyatt realised its contents would guarantee front-page coverage, given Portillo's profile.

Portillo hoped Tyndall's statement stressing the party was a constituency initiative would close the issue down, but the damage had been done. And the difficulties did not end there. Portillo was, as he told an acquaintance later, to have 'litters of kittens' as the months passed before the party was held.

When the story had broken, Portillo was still trying to find his balance in a new post. On 20 July Major had promoted him to head his own department. After two years at the Treasury he was appointed secretary of state for employment. However, within a week he was dogged by unfinished business at the Treasury, and within a month he was embroiled in a war on two fronts, against the disabled and Brussels. The last thing he needed in the middle was to be embarrassed by his own supporters.

The Treasury trouble came just eleven days into his new job, when the *Guardian* published a leaked letter, written by Portillo as chief secretary to Heseltine as president of the Board of Trade. The letter was part of the ritual spring exchange of correspondence between the chief secretary and spending ministers, but it was more than a provocative tweaking of the lion's tail: it was a deliberate attempt to clip his claws and draw his teeth.

Drafted in response to a DTI list of potential economies, the letter ran through a far more extensive range of cuts that could be contemplated. The tone, however, was not that of a respectful junior and former deputy petitioning for a rethink but that of a superior whose patience had been tried once too often by a difficult subordinate. The magisterial tone of Portillo's correspondence while chief secretary once prompted his Cabinet colleague John Gummer to complain to the prime minister about Portillo's 'student beer hall' manner, but the tone of Portillo's letter to Heseltine was particularly pointed. Overall, he attacked the lack of radicalism in the DTI's response to his Fundamental Expenditure Review, writing, 'Nowhere in your department's report is it suggested that the best help we can give to our business is to get taxes down or control public spending. Nowhere is the assumption that it is government's proper task to intervene in the functioning of the free markets actually questioned.'

The *Guardian* described the letter as 'scathing', and its leaking unleashed a war of claim and counter-claim as sources in the Treasury deplored DTI tactics in trying to defend its budget by breaching confidentiality and DTI sources attacked the Treasury for trying to bully cuts out of it in public. Attention focused on the tone, but Portillo's private secretary at the Treasury, Peter Wanless, thought it typical of many pieces of correspondence that would have crossed Portillo's desk at that point: 'Most such letters are actually written by officials. I rewrote that one. Some letters he'd write himself, but the point to remember is that it's the chief secretary's job to ask difficult questions, and everyone in the Treasury knows that.'

The no-nonsense tone of the letter, and the fact that it was sent to Heseltine, the Right's bogeyman, meant the Westminster consensus soon settled on Portillo as the leaker. It was assumed he had done it to bolster his standing with his natural supporters. But would Portillo, still circumspect in his dealings with the press, risk leaking – and to, of all papers, the *Guardian*? Wanless dismisses the idea: 'He wouldn't have leaked it. He actually often asked me to redraft things because he was worried that it might get into the press.'

The suspicion that Portillo was the culprit certainly played into the hands of his internal opponents. They could point to the ideological content and the swaggering style, and use them as evidence of the young pup's unfitness for the highest office – in stark contrast so, say, Industry's True Protector. The sense that Portillo was teetering on the edge of unwarranted arrogance was scarcely diminished by the Ally Pally anniversary revelations, and was then given greater momentum by a row that broke out over the fate of a hitherto obscure scheme to help the disabled.

The Priority Suppliers' Scheme allowed companies which employed a high proportion of disabled people the right to submit second bids for government contracts if their first bids were undercut by rivals. One of Michael Portillo's first acts as employment secretary was to scrap it. He did so not out of free-market purism but because Brussels told him to. A European directive intended to create the same conditions throughout the Union for the award of public-service contracts made the scheme illegal. The directive, agreed in 1992 and effective from June 1994, made it an offence for the state to privilege the disabled over other groups when bids were received for government work.

Government lawyers told Portillo, on his arrival at Employment, that the scheme had to go. Coming three months after the government had conspired to talk out legislation to give the disabled equal rights, it was unfortunate timing, but it seemed there was no alternative. In Portillo's own words, the advice was 'unambiguous'. The Francovich ruling in the European Court of Justice meant EU citizens had the right to sue national governments if they had suffered as a consequence of the government's failure to implement directives. In effect, any contractor who lost out to a rival who benefited from the Priority Suppliers' Scheme could sue the government. A welter of complex and costly litigation would almost certainly ensue if the scheme was not abolished.

These legal niceties were, however lost on the disabled workers affected, the press and public.

When news of the scheme's abolition crept out, Portillo was on holiday, as was his private secretary, Peter Wanless, whom he had taken with him from the Treasury. The officials responsible for the scheme had not prepared an appropriate explanation of the need to end it, and, without the secretary of state there to fight his corner, the squall blew up into a political storm. Portillo was painted as a heartless Scrooge hurling ranks of Tiny Tims on to the scrap-heap.

He returned home to try to calm matters down, only to find that the European Commission had contrived to make matters worse. After initially confirming that Portillo had simply complied with the directive, the single-market commissioner, Raniero Vanni d'Archirafi, claimed the directive could be 'adapted' to save the scheme.

Portillo's first public appearance on his return from holiday was a press conference at the IBM factory in Leeds, designed to trumpet the good news of another fall in unemployment. *En route* to the factory, Portillo was waylaid by four disabled protesters in wheelchairs. Employees of Remploy, the country's biggest employer of disabled workers, with 9,000 on its staff, they demanded a U-turn. Unabashed Portillo declared that the best news for disabled people was the continuing fall in the jobless total overall. He was unrepentant about abolishing the Priority Suppliers' Scheme, but did promise help for those affected, commenting, 'I do not think that the abolition of the scheme will have a very important effect, but I certainly pledge that if it does have any effect we are going to step in and help any disabled people who are affected by the abolition of this scheme.'

But by this point the affair had become more than a dispute on the best way to help the disabled: it had become another occasion for the playing-out of the seemingly unending struggle between the party's pro- and anti-European wings. Sir Edward Heath suggested Portillo's behaviour was designed to convince the British of the merits of withdrawal from the EU. Sir Teddy Taylor stung back, 'They are all going for Mr Portillo, who is a superb minister. It's just silly to go around attacking government ministers in this way when all they are doing is telling the truth.' Explaining the background to the affair did, however, provide Portillo with an opportunity to develop a persistent theme: the superiority, and resilience, of British institutions – in this case the rule of law.

Portillo launched his counter-attack on the BBC, and in the pages of the *Daily Express*. He sought to limit the political damage by explaining that subsidies to firms that employed disabled workers would continue. He expressed his regret that the PSS scheme would go, but pledged that anyone who lost their job as a consequence could be helped in other ways. And he then sought to dismiss the suggestion from the Commission that a way could be found round the law. Writing in the *Express* on 16 August, he argued:

What we cannot do is ignore the law. Even if the law was not intended to have this effect, ministers must obey laws once made. Even the European Commission cannot unmake European law.

We in Britain take laws seriously, even if they are not always convenient to follow. We would be on a very slippery slope if ministers could pick and choose what laws to follow, or if bureaucrats could wish away laws that ministers in Europe have made.

It was an argument backed up by Oxford politics don Michael Pinto-Duschinsky, writing in *The Times* the next day: 'The case is symptomatic of a conflict between British and continental political cultures. To British civil servants, regardless of ideological sympathies, the law is the law, is the law. To apply it selectively is to tread the path to despotism.'

By posing as the defender of democracy against despotism and of the rule of law against arbitrary decision-making, Portillo did not defuse the row completely, but he did extract advantage from it. He took an adverse political situation, which could have left him looking simultaneously powerless and heartless, and used it to forward his own agenda – defending British institutions and pointing out one of the dangers of the European project by pointing up the consequences for democracy of further integration.

Of course, Portillo would rather have avoided the row altogether, and Wanless ruefully drew certain conclusions: 'We shouldn't all have been on holiday at the same time. We should have insisted on better advice. It was just unfortunate.' But, after the dust had settled, once the Commission had backed down, Portillo had made his point. He had also impressed admirers on the Right – Iain Duncan-Smith among them: 'He's had the most impossible brief and carried it out rather well.'

Employment secretary was never going to be a plum post. It was the job in which Norman Tebbit had made his reputation, and from which David Hunt had just been promoted to become Major's *chef de Cabinet* as chancellor of the duchy of Lancaster. But it had become progressively less important throughout the eighties as the power of organised labour had been broken and persistently high levels of unemployment became more a general cause for concern and less a goad to anger.

Although it was promotion, some on the Right felt that Portillo had been shunted into a siding. The Department of Employment's functions had shrunk over time. With the unions tamed, all the secretary of state did was collect the unemployment statistics, act as overseer for the nation's suppliers of training, and fly to Brussels to say no to other 'social-affairs' ministers. Portillo sat on several Cabinet committees which dealt with economic issues, but his friends felt he had been marginalised.

Sceptical back-benchers like Bernard Jenkin thought Portillo might be attacked by some for an 'uncooperative' attitude towards other European social-affairs ministers and then be found even more wanting when, as with the PSS affair, he was powerless to protect the UK from the effects of European legislation. Jenkin commented, 'The social-chapter opt-out is supposed to stop all this stuff, but the Commission smuggle all sorts of directives through in other ways, by invoking their competence in competition or health and safety.' He thought the expectations aroused by the fanfare that had greeted the social-chapter opt-out could only make Portillo's task more difficult.

Whether or not Jenkin's fears were justified, Portillo soon showed that he could turn his responsibilities decisively to his advantage. When the incorrigibly wet Peter Walker had been sent to Wales in 1987, he proved himself a skilled politician by turning internal exile into an opportunity to experiment. Chris Patten, by his prestige and skill, enhanced the status of the post of Tory party chairman after 1990, whereas John Gummer diminished it, and himself, in his tenure in 1983–4. Enemies of Portillo on the Tory Left were reportedly delighted he had been pitchforked into a department simultaneously obscure and difficult, but he soon proved himself a sufficiently skilled politician to make the most of the post, and two months after the PSS débâcle he proved his mettle.

It is no privilege to be the first speaker on the second day of a Tory party conference. It is the morning after the night before for many representatives who have been keener to make their quota of the round of receptions rather than tuck themselves up early for the next day's debates.

For the younger representatives, early rising is always difficult. Plotting, dreaming, drinking, arguing, networking and even flirting are all higher priorities than catching what conference thinks of the Citizens' Charter. Snatching a half-hour with a glass of warm champagne and a Central Office secretary after the Saatchi reception is the focus of far more effort than bagging a good seat for a right honourable member's early-morning roll-call of cones removed and wayside halts erected.

So, one older representative was a little surprised, just after eight o'clock on the morning of Wednesday 12 October 1994, the second day of that year's conference, to see a queue outside the conference centre. He was even more intrigued to see that most of those queuing were the young activists he had left in the hotel bar the night before, just as their faces were becoming a little shinier than their suits. Bound early for London, and business, his curiosity got the better of him. He followed the posse into the conference hall and saw the group, most of whom seemed to know each other, fan out. Rather than cluster together like a party of friends at a rock concert, they moved to spread themselves right across the hall, in ones or twos. Bewildered by their behaviour, he looked at the programme for that day, and noticed the name of the chief speaker in the first debate – Michael Portillo, the secretary of state for employment.

Were these young people looking for reassurance in an increasingly insecure market? Had the prospect of growing up faced with fiercer competition than ever before prompted them to seek security? Was it that that drove them to master their headaches and prepare themselves for the employment secretary's speech?

In a way, yes. The reassurance they wanted was not that they had a future – most were prosperous, or at least had prospects. The market-place in which they wanted to find security was not primarily economic. The reassurance they wanted was that the romance and adventure in politics that had made them Tories had not disappeared. The market they thought insecure was the arena where ideas competed. Would the certainties they had grown up with over the last decade survive? They were looking for Michael Portillo to give them the answer.

As the 9.30 opening of the debate approached, the hall began to fill. Normally the conference hall does not reach capacity until the traditional top billing, in the hour just before lunch when even the latest risers feel the need of some preprandial rhetoric. But that morning the conference centre was full, and ready to applaud enthusiastically, when the secretary of state was introduced. Smart in a single-breasted blue suit, his tie thickly knotted and the waves of his hair framing a face dominated by a strong nose and rich lips, he acknowledged the kind introduction with his familiar grin, teetering just this side of arrogance. Also on the platform were his wife, Carolyn, his ministerial team, and two old friends, Neil and Christine Hamilton. Pointedly, no other Cabinet ministers were there.

The representatives sat politely through most of the debate. There was polite applause when the appropriate buttons were pressed by right-wingers like former Newham candidate Jackie Foster, but no particular warmth. The atmosphere remained just a little morning-afterish. Then came the final speaker from the floor, John Bercow: a former chairman of the Federation of Conservative Students when they were Thatcherism's revolutionary guards, and the defeated candidate in Bristol South in 1992.

Bercow is a small, almost swarthy figure – not a naturally dominant presence – but he is a skilled platform performer. His speech was calculated carefully, sailing close to the wind with the odd provocative phrase thrown out to get the audience in the mood for more. Using mimicry and mockery, and pushing a passionately Thatcherite message, he warmed them up perfectly.

For some in John Major's entourage the words had an uncomfortably familiar ring. It was not that Mr Major would ever express himself in that way – no, the danger was that Mr Portillo might have. Some of the phrases in Bercow's speech had been excised from a previous draft by the party hierarchy – but the draft had not been Bercow's, it had been Portillo's own speech. The uncompromisingly Euro-sceptic message had been one the conference wanted to hear, and Portillo had, through his ally, made sure it heard it. When he got to his feet the representatives' early torpor had been replaced by a sense of incipient excitement.

His start was a little downbeat. He has never been a good speaker first thing in the morning, and his dry mouth and an almost hesitant early delivery meant his projection suffered and words were swallowed. He made the noises expected from an employment minister about the miseries of the dole, though he ended with a restatement of a central tenet from the Thatcherite catechism: 'Politicians don't create jobs. Businessmen do.'

He went on, with growing fluency, his voice occasionally straying nervously near the top of his register, to make the case for wealth-creation. He deployed the tested conference technique of alliterative lists to ram home his argument. As he seemed to grow in confidence, so the conference seemed to respond to him, applauding and laughing at a gentle jibe at those who knock quality goods made in Britain which might have foreign-sounding names: 'Many of the world's household names are British. Rolls-Royce, British Aerospace, Burger King, Calvin Klein, Haägen Dazs and even Moët et Chandon. All British.'

He was making an important point. Patriotism and openness to the influences of international capital were complementary. And, he might have added, names don't matter – belonging does.

Having stoked up a pride in country, Portillo then moved to the heart of his speech – Europe. In a brief, staccato passage he hit the conference's G-spot:

Europe isn't working. We've got to get Europe back to work.

At Maastricht, John Major negotiated our opt-out from the social chapter, because it threatened more regulation, more bureaucracy and more job losses. He told Brussels we wanted no part of it. We still want no part of it. We will have no part of it.

Sometimes you have to tell Brussels when to stop.

Stop telling us how many hours we're allowed to work.

Stop telling kids they can't earn pocket money from doing their paper rounds.

Stop telling small businesses they must give three months' paternity leave.

Stop the rot from Brussels.

The conference signalled its approval with raucous applause. The same body that had been split on Maastricht two years before by agonised trauma over whether to support its heart, and Norman Tebbit, or its head, and Douglas Hurd, had come a long way since then. Bruised by the parliamentary battles, battered by a recession they associated with the German occupation of the Bank of England, and tired of reading that the Belgian empire's writ ran daily over more of British life, it was ready to applaud the man who understood, and articulated, its anger. The threat to paperboys may have been a phantom, the prospect of paternity leave an unlikely imposition, but the details did not matter. The sense that a distant bureaucracy was encroaching on the British way of doing things was as widespread in the hall as the need to see bedrock Tory beliefs spelt out without qualification or apology.

Building on his assault on Europe, Portillo turned on Labour. Where Brussels was malevolent, Blair was merely empty: in Portillo's phrase, empty of philosophy, inspiration and beliefs. But, though more time was devoted to attacking Labour than Europe, and there was a side-swipe at Labour's hostility to wealth-creation, it was across the clear blue water of the Channel and not at Her Majesty's Loyal Opposition that the fervour in Portillo's speech was directed.

Portillo's peroration was a restatement, in bolder form, of the patriotic themes he had played on earlier. The swelling crescendo included tributes to the Tory touchstones – the armed forces, Disraeli and Churchill, privatization – all of them formed in 'the greatest parliamentary democracy on earth'. His final triple-list, designed to trigger applause as surely as the list of complaints against Brussels had done, was hardly elegant, but brutally effective in its unapologetic directness: 'Never did I feel more certain of being a Conservative. Never was it more important to be a Conservative. Never have I felt more proud to be a Conservative.'

As he finished, the men and women who had queued early to get into the hall rose, clapped and cheered. They were joined by an audience who had wanted their Toryism as blue and raw as bloody beef. For activists tired of apologising, here was a man who could make them feel good about their basic instincts. In the far from spontaneous, but still sincere, standing ovation even the most docile representative was swept along.

It went on, and on, and on. The clapping hands seen on TV sent a simple signal to the Cabinet ministers watching their most junior colleague acknowledge the applause. The conference had a new darling. It might still love John Major, but it wanted more of Michael Portillo.

Commentating on the speech on BBC TV, the former minister

Alan Clark called it 'by far the most effective attack on Tony Blair' he had seen and 'as clear a bid to put himself in the ranking for the succession as I've ever seen. The audience were lapping it up.'

At the back of the hall, a journalist looked on in faint disgust at the display. Noticing a Tory of leftish hue next to him, he was quite surprised to see him join in the applause as enthusiastically as any, and even more astonished to hear the moderate proclaim that he could happily follow wherever Portillo led.

As the applause died down, the hall settled for the next debate and the TV cameras turned their attention to knots of activists outside. One, Mark Allatt, of the Thatcherite Conservative Way Forward, pressed the claims of Portillo as a future leader. Another, Robert Walter, of the Heathite Conservative Group for Europe, deprecated the idea. The BBC's careful balance was preserved, but the reaction from the conference hall suggested where the truth behind the balance might lie.

Four hours after the first queues had formed outside the confer-ence hall another cluster of representatives began to form outside a nearby hotel. It was not lunch that had brought them to the Connaught Suite in the New Connaught Hotel on the brow of a hill a few hundred yards above the beach-side Bournemouth hall. Hundreds of representatives who had heard him only a few hours earlier were crowding into an inadequate ballroom to listen to Michael Portillo again.

The speech was a more considered, leisurely, even philosophical, effort than the main conference address. It was given the title 'Clear Blue Water' – a phrase that was to become the conference cliché, embodying as it did the Right's drive to make the Conserva-tive Party more Conservative. As a metaphor it hardly ranked with 'the wind of change', but as a rallying-point it was effective. For many Tories the problem with their party was that it was not Tory enough.

The audience craved ideological certainty, and Portillo hoped to supply it. The speech was designed to remind them what it was that made them Tories, and why they would always oppose Labour, whatever guise the party chose to adopt to make itself more electable.

It was an uncompromising speech. It attacked inflation, and

cited Enoch Powell in preference to the more moderate commentators who might have illustrated the same point.

It was a speech with definite philosophical echoes. In his attack on Labour's inability to understand the Tory view of human nature there was a metaphor borrowed from Plato:

We applaud success, knowing that its spirit is infectious. We celebrate human ingenuity and enterprise as the foundation of a prosperous and cohesive society. Labour has a dim sense that this is so. It sees the shadows of Conservative belief flickering on the wall of its cave. But it cannot quite share them.

It was a provocative speech. Opt-outs negotiated at Maastricht to propitiate Tory sceptics and designed to maintain flexibility in the future were painted as positions of principle – nos not maybes. The tone was clear: 'We are, with reason, a nation confident enough to take a distinctive position on the social chapter and European Monetary Union – and to stick by it.'

The audience loved it. The applause was as long and, in the uncomfortable acoustics, as loud as a few hours before. Apart from a few journalists, the only group to stay silent was a small, and unhappy, section of Tories in their late twenties and early thirties, wearing suits of a slightly better cut than most of those around them.

Sue and Martin Woodroffe and Jane Ellison were all members of the Tory Reform Group, the progressive caucus that had championed economic intervention, higher spending and greater European integration throughout the eighties. Traditional Tories to some, social-democrat entryists to others, they were unamused by Portillo's speech, or its welcome. They were there not to applaud but to warn. They wanted to see who were the Portillistas, to gauge their strength, and to ensure that the microphones that would afterwards be thrust under noses found voices prepared to play down the Portillo phenomenon. They were engaged in a war for the future of their party, and they could not afford any battle to go by default. But this week, it seemed, the war was not going their way.

During his speech Portillo had been flanked by his wife, Carolyn, and Sir George Gardiner, of Conservative Way Forward, the organisers of the meeting. That same day Sir George had produced a pamphlet under the CWF imprint with the same title, *Clear Blue Water*, bringing together thoughts from interviews and speeches given by Portillo over the previous year. Its forty-eight pages of large print cost £4.95. The only new thing in it was the introduction from Cecil Parkinson. It was the fastest-selling item at the conference bookstall. That afternoon Portillo's bold signature decorated the forewords of scores of copies placed in front of him by representatives, from teenagers to old men with a military bearing, all of them fans for that day.

That night Portillo allowed himself to relax. Seldom seen out of a suit, he changed into a blazer and chinos for the British Airways reception. An old friend of the former chairman, Lord King, and a former transport minister who had done much to liberalise the skies, he laughed and joked with the other guests. By his side, as they had been that morning, were his wife and their friends Neil and Christine Hamilton. Others at the party noted an exultant glint in the Portillos' eyes.

Any politician might have allowed himself some quiet satisfaction that night after a day crowned with such success but some noticed not so much satisfaction as smugness – a sense that Portillo thought he could walk on Clear Blue Water.

It was most apparent in his new attitude to the anniversary party his association still hoped to hold on 2 December. Portillo had tried that summer to cancel the event, feeling it would only damage him if it went ahead, but the preparations were so far advanced that his constituency association had to tell him that cancellation could bankrupt the association. Following his conference coup, Portillo's attitude changed: he told his constituency supporters to scatter invitations to the party 'like confetti'. It was a remarkable volte-face. Prudence had given way to hubris. The enthusiasm was short-lived. When the afterglow of conference success faded, cooler calculation prompted Portillo to beat a messy retreat.

He instructed his agent, Malcolm Tyndall, to ask Thatcher and Tebbit not to turn up. Both had been invited months before, and both had agreed to attend. Neither was entirely happy at being told the event no longer required their attendance. Alternative engagements were found for them, excuses were made, and embarrassment was covered, but neither hid their annoyance from their closest associates.

The Tebbit and Thatcher invitations were not the only treats withdrawn late. Tyndall had planned to show a short film, *The Life and Times of Michael Portillo*, as an affectionate tribute just before dinner. The video had been made by Laurence Marks, one half of the writing partnership with Maurice Gran responsible for successful TV comedies such as *Shine on Harvey Moon*, *Birds of a Feather* and *The New Statesman*.

Marks, originally from Enfield, had got to know Portillo when he had been taken on a tour of the Commons by the MP as part of his research for *The New Statesman*. He had been charmed by Portillo, and they remain friends, occasionally dining together. At one dinner David Hart asked Marks, a gifted comic writer, if he could come up with some jokes for Portillo's speeches. Marks politely pointed out that he was a Labour supporter. Nevertheless, he agreed to help Tyndall put together an affectionate, light-hearted video. They spent months collecting archive material, and thousands of pounds on editing.

On the morning of the party, Portillo demanded they pull it. A mocking report on that day's *Today* programme had presented the video as the last word in vanity. Portillo was adamant: no video – it would seem 'too presidential'. Reluctantly, and regretfully, Tyndall agreed. Marks was philosophical. He had wasted thousands, but, as he told a reporter, 'I'm not worried. I'm loaded.'

Portillo has insisted that the master-tape remain safe in Marks's hands, and the video has never been publicly screened. But, despite the drama, the video is innocent and inoffensive. A montage of clips from Portillo's by-election campaign, his early Ribena Kid appearances and other shots from his progress upwards in the eighties are cut together to accompany a simple soundtrack – 'It had to be you', followed by a speeded-up sequence to a Latin, lambada-style rhythm, and ending with 'You saved the best to last'.

Portillo may have thought pulling the video would save him some embarrassment, but there was embarrassment aplenty anyway. In the week before the party the *Evening Standard* had run a series of satirical features asking, 'Who's going to the party of the

Decade?' On the day itself, every quality paper save for the *FT* had some gently ragging article on the event.

That night the revellers – 400 or so: some 200 less than hoped for – had to run the gauntlet of protesters from the Socialist Workers Party and other assorted revolutionaries. When they arrived, they had smoked salmon, beef and baked Alaska to console them, and a warm-up routine from Chester Tory MP and former breakfast-television presenter Gyles Brandreth to entertain them – including a joke about Lord Curzon.

Portillo's speech was a little more relevant. After a series of prepared jokes he relaxed a little and gave a speech far short of his conference best but decent enough to pass muster among his fans. The guests – some from as far afield as St Andrew's – applauded enthusiastically.

The speech over, Portillo mingled with the crowds but deftly avoided the invitations to dance to Tuxedo Class, the jazz band booked by the association, delighted to be off the bar-mitzvah circuit for one Friday night. After the raffle, he gently melted into the background, drawing strength from a glass of champagne and the company of a few friends in a small room off the main hall.

It had been a difficult day. One of Lady Thatcher's staff, who had turned up despite her mistress's absence, had laid into Portillo's indecision about the party: 'All this shilly-shallying. Imagine if she'd been like that with the *Belgrano* – "Sink it, no don't, yes do." Hmm!' Portillo was simply glad it was over. An event he had never wanted, planned in a way he would never have done it himself, had dominated his press that autumn, overshadowing all his efforts to set a serious agenda. At the end of the evening money had been raised for the constituency and there had been no single catastrophe to attract the press's continued attention, but what damage had already been done to his reputation?

Portillo entered 1995 determined to efface memories of the party. In the first week of the new year he managed to attract attention for the right reasons: applause for a thoughtful speech delivered in Liverpool Cathedral.

The lecture, on 6 January, was designed to echo some of the themes of the campaign just run by Newt Gingrich in America. Gingrich had masterminded a Republican clean sweep of Congress and Senate with a ten-point 'Contract with America' that reinvigorated the Right after six years when a party that had been growing ever more conservative had been led by moderates.

Most of Portillo's content was the mixture as before – a plea for a smaller state, a declaration that individuals spend their money more wisely than the state ever could, a defence of institutions, and a plea for a government animated by clear values. What was new was the scholarship – quotations from Sir Isaiah Berlin and references to colonialism, echoes of Thomas Carlyle – and the explicit links to Gingrich's success with a simple rallying call to further reform on the Right: 'Today's political leaders must not abdicate their responsibility to continue improving the quality of government. All over the world – not least in America – there is clear evidence that the public expects further reform of the state.'

Portillo deliberately invoked the central message of Gingrich's contract: the need to win back the voters' trust by returning power to them. 'One reason that politicians are held in such low esteem in our time is that government has claimed to be able to do too much. It has led people to believe that they themselves can do too little.'

Gingrich's pollster, Frank Luntz, visited England in April to talk to Portillo, and David Hart confirms that he and Portillo have drawn inspiration from Gingrich: 'He's worked from first principles, seen that there's been a shift since the eighties, and identified the new issues that matter.' Others on the Right – including some close to Redwood and Thatcher – believe the Tories can renew themselves, Gingrich-style, only in opposition. It is not a view Hart and Portillo share.

A month after Portillo's speech in Liverpool, Kenneth Clarke addressed the European Movement in London and declared war on the sceptics who were trying to tie his hands on a single currency. He listed some of the benefits of currency union, and some of the drawbacks, all the while making it clear he thought the balance tilted towards the benefits. But, more provocatively than that, he argued that, 'It is quite possible to have monetary union without political union. It is a mistake to believe that monetary union need be a huge step on the path to a federal Europe.'

By arguing that monetary union had no significant constitutional ramifications, Clarke was cavalierly ignoring the careful Cabinet compromise on a single currency: in essence, 'It's so complicated, so unlikely, so silly and also so important that we can't make up our minds.' By asserting that it was all so simple – indeed possibly so desirable – Clarke was deliberately provoking the sceptics. Portillo knew it, and his aides set about ringing BBC studios the next day to secure the platform for him to say it. Portillo slapped Clarke down for straying from the collective Cabinet line and putting a single currency back on the agenda. It was an outrageously cheeky performance.

Portillo sought to paint Clarke as a disruptive influence, arguing that the Cabinet had agreed to postpone any discussion of the merits of a hypothetical single currency until concrete proposals were on the table for its creation. However, he himself had played fast and loose with collective responsibility with his candour about the consequences of a single currency, a single central bank and a single federal government in a television interview in the run-up to the European elections just twelve months before, when he had told GMTV's Mike Morris, 'A [single currency] would mean giving up the government of the UK. No British government can give up the government of the UK. That's impossible.'

Rebuking Clarke may have been cheeky, but it was effective – Portillo had proved himself the minister prepared to take on all comers in defence of the sceptics.

Clarke and Portillo were to clash again. Both spoke on the first day of the Scottish Tory conference in May.

Clarke was in unapologetic form – sniping from the Right on taxes and Europe brought a defiant response: 'I'm not a chancellor who ever has been or ever will be driven off the right Conservative economic course because of short-term political pressures.' For his pains he was attacked from the floor, with one representative attacking plans to tax mortgage insurance payments with the words: 'These are socialist policies, not worthy of a Tory.'

In stark contrast, Portillo received a rapturous reception. In a direct rebuff to Clarke, he attempted to reach out to natural Tory voters bruised by current policies, such as tax rises, and also attempted to rally the faithful with the simple theme of sovereignty, developed by him and Hart:

At the next election there will be a stark choice for the British people. The fundamental issue will be sovereignty: sovereignty of the nation and

sovereignty of the individual. Britons can vote to lose it or defend it . . .
that is clear blue water.

He won a standing ovation.

Watching the two wings of his party travelling in different direc-
tions could only exasperate the prime minister. He would have to
act. Would he move to embrace the populist agenda outlined by
Portillo, or try to crush it? Or would an altogether more delicate
finesse be attempted? Within weeks, the world would find out.

CHAPTER FIFTEEN

Friends of Michael Portillo

The prime minister is my candidate.

Michael Portillo

Every MP who is going to vote is going to vote for John.

John Redwood

Portillo is cold, sensual and superior and smart enough to know that those qualities can work for him. The Castilian stallion excites men with the smack of firm government and has every woman in the land reaching for the basque separates.

Allison Pearson, *Independent on Sunday*

Saturday 24 June was the longest day of 1995, not least for the coming men of John Major's Cabinet. Two of Major's ministers spent much of that weekend taking calls from two millionaires urging them to stand against the prime minister they had hitherto supported.

John Redwood listened sympathetically to the urgings of David Evans, the former professional footballer and MP for Welwyn Hatfield who had served as his parliamentary aide, sat on the executive of the 1922 Committee, and was now pressing him to stake his claim for the Tory leadership with characteristically pungent brevity, simply saying, 'Go for it.'

Michael Portillo was also under pressure from an old friend. The employment secretary faced – not for the first time – a persuasive presentation of the case for resigning and running for leader from one of his staunchest allies, David Hart. Hart outlined again to Portillo the advantages of boldness.

Both Redwood and Portillo were in their early forties; both had won their political spurs under Margaret Thatcher but had survived, and risen, under John Major through sheer competence and not a little chutzpah. Both had voted for Major during the last leadership election, in 1990. Both would rather Thatcher had survived – and Portillo had risked telling her so beyond the point when it was obvious to most of his colleagues that she was finished. Now both were presented with a difficult decision by a leader whom, as loyal members of a Conservative Cabinet, they were bound to support.

Dare they raise the banner of revolt and risk defying the old Tory saw that he who wields the dagger never wears the crown? Should they put unease with the direction of policy ahead of the ties of loyalty necessary for the smooth working of any collective endeavour, especially Cabinet government? Above all, how best could not just a Tory government but true Thatcherite principles be advanced and secured? By an impetuous cavalry charge? Or by keeping one's powder dry?

The tough decisions had been forced on the two men by an audacious tactical manœuvre from John Major.

Almost on the stroke of five on the afternoon of Thursday 22 June, a little after England's Rugby Union team had fallen to France in the third-place play-off of the World Cup, and while the country's cricketers still battled against the West Indies at Lord's, Major had abandoned his usual interest in the progress of the nation's sportsmen to announce a contest that would have the country's political class convulsed for the next ten days. Addressing a hastily assembled audience of lobby correspondents in the garden of Number Ten, watched nervously by his wife and a cluster of aides, he sought to end speculation about his future by resigning the leadership of the Conservative Party, triggering an election for the post, and putting himself forward as a candidate.

The week before he had been barracked at a meeting of nearly 100 MPs. Members of the Euro-sceptical Fresh Start Group, chaired by Michael Spicer, had allowed their criticisms of the prime minister's European policy to descend from the robust to the downright rude. Major's exposition of his reluctance to rule out a single currency lest Britain lose its influence over the economic destiny of the rest of the EU had been interrupted by one passionately sceptical new boy, Bernard Jenkin. The prime minister's attempt to defuse the incendiary electoral potential of Europe was flatly contradicted by Sir Ivan Lawrence, once Major's candidate for solicitor-general, who argued for an aggressively nationalist assault on the opposition.

Following that, Major had spent an almost unendurable weekend in Nova Scotia at the G7 summit, in which his performance had been overshadowed by reports of plotting in preparation for a November challenge to his leadership. The *Sun* and the *Sunday Times*, two of the biggest-selling titles in the Murdoch stable, openly questioned the wisdom of Major going on.

Convinced he could not continue to govern while daily undermined by internal critics, Major sought to end speculation by daring his critics within the parliamentary Tory party to 'put up or shut up'.

Only a few members of the Cabinet, including his nascent campaign team, knew what Major's intentions were when they met that Thursday morning. Before making his announcement on the Thursday afternoon, however, he had made arrangements for Cabinet members to be informed and their loyalty secured. Even though he wanted a contest, the prime minister wanted to ensure it was against, at best, a second-rank figure who could be seen off easily.

Michael Portillo, in particular, thought the tactic misguided. He was convinced the speculation about a challenge would, as so often before, have come to nothing. Now, by provoking a challenge, John Major risked providing a focus for all the varied discontents rumbling within the party, which could fatally destabilise him and even see the leadership lurch further to the Left, under the corporatist, interventionist and federalist Michael Heseltine. But, faced with a simple request to proclaim his loyalty, Portillo did not demur. One MP close to him recalls why: 'He was worried Major had made a fatal mistake, but he wasn't going to run against him. Michael thought the whole basis on which Cabinet government works would be destroyed if ministers who had sat, apparently happily, in the government for months just resigned to pick a fight, instead of on a matter of principle.' Portillo himself told aides who raised the prospect of resigning that it would be 'naff'.

The weekend of 24–5 June, after a flurry of phone calls, Portillo and his wife stayed with Hart at his Suffolk home, Chadacre. Hart was convinced that in a straight fight between the heavyweights of the Tory Left and Right – Michaels Heseltine and Portillo – the Right would win: just. Victory for Portillo would be followed first by an appeal for unity and then the 'bringing of weight to bear' on a party grown used to rebellion, as well as an all-out attack on Blair.

Hart believed Portillo was more than a match for Blair: young, ideologically self-confident and charismatic, he would have the advantage of running more naturally with the 'radical, yet reassuring tag' Blair had tried to make his own. If Blair thought the best way to win over waverers who had voted Tory in the past four elections was to portray himself as Thatcher's heir, the best riposte was to allow the voters to elect the man she had actually anointed.

Since their first meeting Hart has been a consistent champion of Portillo, and Portillo, despite the misgivings of more cautious friends, has been a staunch ally of Hart. But for all Hart's charm, his experience in intrigue and his influence over Portillo, he could not persuade him of the advantages of an early entry into the field. Portillo listened, but remained convinced that discretion was the better part of valour.

At that point Portillo hoped Major might still win, but feared he would be wounded. Portillo was convinced, however, that he should not resign. It was not in his nature.

Portillo believed it would be dishonourable to stand against Major, but he also believed it would be imprudent. He thought it might mean a reverse for the Right, if they allowed themselves to fight on ground, and at a time, not of their choosing. He accepted that the growing strength of the Right in the party might allow him to win in a second round, if Major was terminally damaged, but he believed that as the years passed, the arguments were made, and a younger generation made its influence more strongly felt, the Right's position would strengthen. Striking now risked replacing the pragmatic Major, who had some sympathy with right-wing reservations on issues like education, the economy and even Europe, with the thoroughly left-wing Heseltine.

Portillo had never been afraid to stick his neck out before, and it was tempting to try it this time, but he told his supporters that weekend that to challenge Major would be wrong in principle and wrong in practice. Events during the next seventy-two hours were to give him cause to think again, and he moved to take steps to prepare for any eventuality, but he never wavered from his first, instinctive, reaction – running against the man in whose Cabinet he had been happy to serve for so long was wrong.

John Redwood took a rather different view. The prime minister had not regarded him as a threat in the same way as Portillo, or Michael Heseltine. As Welsh secretary, with just two years in the Cabinet, the Vulcan – so called by *Times* sketch-writer Matthew Parris because of his detached manner and distant intellect – was not considered a political heavyweight.

Lord Cranborne, the lord privy seal, had been asked to secure Redwood's loyalty. The most right-wing Cabinet minister on the Major campaign team, it was thought he would be on the same wavelength as Redwood.

Robert Cranborne is a unicorn in the squawking, scratching Conservative menagerie: noble, rare, romantic – almost too pure, in Tory terms, for our times. The Old Etonian grandson of 'Bobbety' Salisbury, the quixotic defender of colonialism in Macmillan's Cabinet, Cranborne had once used precious parliamentary time, while MP for Dorset South, to try, unsuccessfully, to restore separate representation in the Commons for the country's ancient universities and so reverse the tide of the previous one hundred and fifty years in favour of uniform suffrage. The idea that he was the man best-placed to reassure a minister of modest birth, grammar-school education and impeccably liberal economic views might seem eccentric, but the strength of the Conservative Party, and indeed its right wing, has been the range of individuals who have come to share its prejudices.

Cranborne might have been able to persuade Redwood of the wisdom of Major's course – possibly by appealing to the need to see off any challenge now to prevent a shift to the Left under Heseltine – but it will never be known for sure, because Cranborne never talked to Redwood. Instead, he delegated the job to Michael Howard, a fellow right-winger who had worked with Redwood at the Department of the Environment. It was a tactical error.

Even though Redwood had been Howard's number two at Environment for a year, from 1992 to 1993, the two men had not got on famously well. Howard had a reputation as a right-winger, but many on the Right suspected him of inauthentic populism. Redwood had served him loyally, but there was little warmth between them. Howard was an instinctive loyalist, one of those on the Right most dismissive of resignation talk at the time of Maastricht. Cranborne, a man who had resigned from the government on a point of principle and whose right-wing instincts were impeccable, might have been better placed to appeal to Redwood.

Howard eventually tracked down Redwood at 3.30 that afternoon, after Prime Minister's Question Time, and with only an hour to go before Major was due to make his resignation statement. He intercepted him on his way out of the Commons as Redwood was *en route* to the BBC studios in Millbank for a TV interview.

When Howard explained what Major planned, Redwood simply said, 'It's a mistake,' before going off. He was fuming.

According to one of those who worked on the Redwood campaign, it was the final straw in a series of humiliations for the Welsh secretary: 'John was probably the cleverest man in the Cabinet, and certainly the most underrated. He had come up with a string of ideas in office which were overlooked by Major. On the Wednesday before Major's resignation John had tried to present a policy blueprint for revival. Once again he was ignored. That night Major told Winston Churchill – a far from consistently loyal back-bencher – that he was planning something dramatic, but during a private chat with a member of his own Cabinet he didn't say a thing.'

Redwood's special adviser, Hywel Williams, in conversation with another Redwood supporter compared his master's position to that of Sir Geoffrey Howe under Margaret Thatcher – a naturally loyal minister driven to disloyalty by being ignored, snubbed and sidelined.

Redwood was uncertain what action to take. Resignation was risky, but he might never have another chance to set out his stall. Unless he acted now, he faced the permanent eclipse of his ambitions, but if he miscalculated he could become another Enoch Powell or Randolph Churchill, captain of a rebel band, dependent on future Tory troubles if his star was ever to rise again.

That Monday Redwood had endured an uncomfortable forty minutes watching a BBC *Panorama* profile of Portillo, teasingly entitled *The Right Stuff?* It was a pretty sympathetic portrait. It ran through evidence of Portillo's past misjudgements but painted him as a natural leader of the future and, most tellingly, showed a focus group of wavering Tory voters rallying to the patriotic, robustly anti-criminal, low-taxation, minimal-state message he had been arguing for during the previous two years. Redwood decided that, unless he struck now, he would never have a chance of catching up with the progress Portillo had made in establishing himself as the natural voice of the Right.

At first, Redwood's discontent eluded detection. In the maelstrom that followed Major's announcement, few thought to question the position of the Welsh secretary. Speculation on a possible opponent centred on the former chancellor, Norman Lamont, or one of the nine Euro-rebels from whom the party whip had been withdrawn earlier in the year. It was only on Friday lunchtime that a BBC correspondent caught up with Redwood and invited him to join the list of Cabinet ministers ritually pledging loyalty. He declined.

When news of Redwood's reticence reached the rest of the world, Hywel Williams found himself besieged. After a hurried telephone conversation with his boss, Williams issued a statement, attributed to an anonymous 'spokesman'. It was significant more for how it was issued than for what it said: 'John Redwood has been a consistent support of John Major since he became leader. He continues to be a supporter of the prime minister.'

The statement was not issued in Redwood's own name. It was issued only under duress. It lacked any expression of confidence either in the wisdom of the prime minister's calling the contest or in his winning it. When it was put to Williams that it would do nothing to dispel speculation that Redwood would stand, he would only reply, 'The secretary of state will issue a full statement on Monday. He's just behaving in his normal, cool, calm, laconic fashion.' The dry, and firm, delivery of these words by the Welsh parson's son could not be faulted, but he did not convince the doubters.

Over the weekend the Redwood home was surrounded by the world's media, waiting for an answer. Throughout, Redwood would say only that he would make his intentions clear on Monday.

Williams was genuinely uncertain about his boss's intentions, but he knew the balance was tilting firmly in favour of a contest. On the evening of Major's announcement Redwood had rung his constituency chairwoman to prepare his association activists for a challenge.

According to one former minister, known to have a policy grudge against Major's leadership, Redwood supporters had been discreetly canvassing support for their man weeks beforehand. A dual process of advertising his virtues and gently rubbishing the allegedly flashier Portillo had been going on in the Palace of Westminster's precincts that spring: 'His people had been at work for some time. A core of supporters was already in place.'

Redwood may have been preparing the ground for a challenge but was the time right now? That weekend he weighed up the arguments. David Evans, a man who has won most of his battles by brute force, seldom by tactical subtlety, was in no doubt. He had been irritated by the claim by Sir Marcus Fox, chairman of the 1922 Committee, that all the members of the committee's executive backed John Major's decision to stand down. Evans, the most recent addition to the executive, had not been consulted.

Redwood had appointed Evans his PPS after the 1992 election in the hope that the populist charm of this bit of back-bench rough might rub off. Evans, who had made his millions from his own cleaning company, was a natural NCO to Redwood's staff officer. He has the voice and values of a regimental sergeant-major, and a face that could have made him wealthy playing innumerable East End villains, which masks a shrewd political instinct.

Evans believed Redwood had to stand. Though by nature a loyalist, he saw a Redwood candidature as a chance to revitalise the party, and advance his own career, at a stroke.

He did his bit to push Redwood on to the battlefield. On the Saturday he gave an interview to BBC's *On the Record*. Framed by his luxurious home, he gave a hint of the attitude that had helped him make the money to buy it. He revealed his objection to being automatically enlisted as one of John Major's supporters without so much as a by-your-leave in tones that would once have given slow payers a shiver: 'I don't like people putting my name on bits of paper without asking me.' Asked if Major could, in any case, count on his support, Evans replied that he most certainly could not.

Even as Evans was pushing him, Redwood's own family were expressing reluctance. His wife, Gail, a successful barrister who had risen fast in business to become company secretary of British Airways, before scaling down her commitments to spend more time with her family, was inclined against her husband running, but promised to support him whole-heartedly whatever he chose to do.

By Saturday evening Redwood was pretty much decided, but, teasingly, he decided to stick to his plan of saying nothing until Monday morning and tantalised journalists by spending his Sunday afternoon playing village cricket.

As time wore on, without a word being said, a Redwood candidature moved from being a possibility, to a probability, to a racing certainty. Irritable sources in the Major camp speculated that his refusal to end the uncertainty over his intentions made his continuing in the Cabinet impossible, whether he ran or not. What, then, had he to lose?

Sensing that the last thing to do was force Redwood into a corner, without a get-out, the Major campaign team deputed the Major biographer and *Sunday Express* columnist Bruce Anderson, in the Major HQ in 1995 as he had been in 1990, to ring Redwood direct and assure him his future was safe, even as late as Sunday evening, if only he would endorse the PM. Anderson, like Cranborne, was a right-winger to his marrow, but a Major loyalist. He tried, repeatedly, to wring a loyalty pledge out of Redwood, forecasting a glittering future if only he would relent. It was no use: Redwood was sayin' nuthin'.

At seven o'clock on Sunday evening Redwood at last rang Hywel Williams at the latter's Pimlico flat to confirm he would stand.

Williams had spent his Sunday morning, as was his custom, worshipping at St Mary's, Bourne Street, an inordinately High Anglican church on the borders of Belgravia and Chelsea.

A cultured man in his late thirties, a fluent Welsh speaker with a wicked laugh and a broad mind, Williams is unlike most other special advisers. Usually drawn from a pool of Central Office researchers, they can range from natural politicians undergoing a necessary apprenticeship in power, like Portillo, or Michael Howard's former aide David Cameron, to make-weight bag-carriers. Few have the range of experience, or learning, that Williams brought to his job. A former history master at Rugby, he had also written scholarly journalism and enjoyed the patronage of Portillo's old tutor, Maurice Cowling.

Williams was determined to enjoy his last hours of peace before what he expected would be ten turbulent days, and after church he had spent an agreeable hour at lunch with one or two fellow-worshippers, including David Ruffley, Kenneth Clarke's special adviser. He delicately dodged their cross-examination about his boss's intentions before excusing himself early in the afternoon to go home and await instruction.

When Redwood rang, Williams was enthused but unsurprised, and he immediately set about making arrangements for the launch of the campaign. As well as sketching out the policy points of the leadership bid and thinking through logistical problems, he also rang his mentor, Maurice Cowling, in his Swansea home, to discuss the constitutional niceties.

David Evans had also been on the phone, marshalling the support of several MPs on the Right who he knew were sympathetic to a Redwood challenge. The final decision had been taken late in the day, but the Redwood camp had been making provision for just such an announcement.

When, on Monday afternoon, Redwood launched his campaign in the Commons' Jubilee Room, the cameras caught, framing the challenger, the turquoise bosom of Teresa Gorman and the stripes of Tony Marlow's Old Wellingtonian blazer. But what escaped obvious notice was the number of other Redwood supporters scattered round the room. Gorman and Marlow, the Baader and Meinhof of back-benchers, were the usual suspects for any revolt. What was more surprising was the presence of previously loyal MPs like Julian Brazier, Matthew Carrington, Paul Marland and Andrew Hargreaves. Their presence bespoke a degree of planning behind the campaign, a gentle wooing over time of disgruntled colleagues, which belied the colourful chaos of the launch.

On the same Sunday afternoon that Redwood was fielding reporters' questions and Williams was enjoying his lunch, another group on the Right had met. Under the auspices of Alan Duncan, the MP for Rutland and now PPS to Brian Mawhinney, several figures from Conservative Way Forward met to discuss what action, if any, to take. Like Tristan Garel-Jones's drink for friends in his Catherine Place home on the November night in 1990 when Margaret Thatcher had failed to win her first ballot outright, it was not meant to be a cabal – certainly not yet. It was simply an opportunity for the like-minded to meet.

Most of those there, including CWF's main organiser, Mark McGregor, came to the same conclusion that Portillo had, though independently of him. Although there was admiration for Redwood, and an expectation that he would stand, there was a strong feeling that his challenge could too easily prove a mistake. They thought Redwood was unlikely to win on the first ballot, and his challenge could leave Major in place, with the Right tarnished as the party's trouble-makers. Or he might so wound Major as to clear the way for Heseltine. As one of those there put it, 'A Redwood challenge was a gift for Heseltine. All Major's fire would have to be directed at the Right – they'd get the reputation as the wreckers, as disloyal. Then all the Heselteenies could vote for Redwood, get rid of Major, and urge us to rally round the "unity" candidate who'd stayed loyal all along.'

Several MPs on the Right, fearful of the consequences of a Heseltine premiership and anxious that the Right's influence should not suffer further by association with rebellion, had already volunteered their services to the Major HQ. Alan Duncan, Bernard Jenkin, James Cran, Archie Hamilton, Michael Brown and Michael Forsyth – Euro-sceptics all – had individually joined up. They had made their decision in the expectation of a stalking-horse, like Norman Lamont, gathering enough protest votes to let Hezza in on a second ballot. Redwood's candidature threw those calculations into doubt – he was a Cabinet minister who saw himself as a much more serious challenger.

Some of those at Alan Duncan's house that Sunday were tempted by the Redwood challenge, but the majority felt they should still support Major. Some of the younger activists present were impatient to be rid of him, but older heads reminded them of his virtues.

Several there were admirers of Portillo, and their loyalty was placed under strain by Redwood's actions. However, after a vigorous discussion, a consensus emerged that the only way the Right could win a second round was if its candidate could rally centre-Right loyalists. They needed a figure of greater weight than Redwood – someone who would also have supported Major throughout. Their judgement at the end of the afternoon tallied with their instincts at the beginning: they would stick with Portillo. Some there had cause to question the wisdom of the decision during the next ten days, but most remain convinced it was the only course they could have taken.

Although the Redwood campaign launch had brio, and some

surprising supporters, it was flawed from the start. The prominence of Gorman, Marlow and some of the more spirited sceptics – such as Bill 'Biggles' Walker and Chris 'Butcher of Ludlow' Gill – prompted one Major campaign worker to characterise the Redwood team as 'Ward 8 from Broadmoor'. It was a jibe that stuck: later that week Evans was to complain that the launch had been overtaken by the 'loony element'.

Redwood himself benefited from his hitherto low profile, joking about his Vulcan image by remarking that he had not hired a 'spaceship for this enterprise' and providing an attractively traditionalist ring to a key sceptic demand by pledging, if elected, never to bring forward any plans to 'abolish the pound sterling'. But the early promise was not sustained. As he revealed more of his manifesto, bit by bit, in a dance of the seven veils, it was seen to be a threadbare thing of sceptic shreds and populist patches.

He pledged to cut £5 billion from public expenditure to make room for tax cuts, trumpeting the existence of a 'mechanism' that would allow him to succeed where others had failed, but came up only with exhortation and a commitment to wage war on waste. Wars on waste – like crackdowns on crime – are the traditional refuge of Tory politicians when all originality is exhausted. He also promised to save the royal yacht, preserve the present strength of the armed forces, save small hospitals and schools, and safeguard teachers and doctors – as well as taking steps to buttress the family and protect home-owners.

Of course, Redwood was trying to draw as many disgruntled colleagues as possible into a broad coalition for change, but the lack of specifics, the shirking of hard choices, impressed neither mainstream commentators nor the more rigorous thinkers of the Right. Peter Riddell, the *Times*'s political columnist, found the Redwood manifesto a deeply unserious response to the challenges of the nineties and compared it unfavourably with Tony Blair's realism. In the *Independent*, Dominic Hobson, the libertarian thinker who had collaborated with Lord Lawson on his memoirs and with Alan Duncan on the polemically anti-statist *Saturn's Children*, thought it did not go nearly far enough in tackling the inevitable accretion of power, and money, to the government.

Behind the scenes, the lack of clarity in campaign organisation matched the lack of candour in the manifesto. There was no shortage of enthusiasm, or of volunteers, but none of the cool and measured strategic planning required to avoid the inevitable squalls. The first twenty-four hours of the campaign passed without a proper HQ. When one was found – the Victoria flat of Euro-sceptic baronet Sir Benjamin Slade, handed over to Chris Gill – it had to be vacated within days following complaints of lease-infringement from neighbours. A hasty decamping to an empty Buckingham Gate office was presented as 'a move closer to Number Ten', and an expansion of efforts, but Redwood's team were simply trying to make a virtue out of a necessity.

The campaign team were of variable quality. Although some of the Tory party's brightest youngsters, including Saatchi executive Steve Hilton, pitched in to help, there were also, in the words of one worker, 'several flakes'. Another campaigner commented, 'It was a shambles. Hywel was overworked. No one seemed to be in charge. The best use wasn't made of what talent was available.'

The amateurism extended to some of the canvassing carried out by pro-Redwood MPs. With fewer open supporters than the prime minister and without the experience and resources of a bank of serving and former whips to draw on, their appeals for support seemed clumsy. One MP recalls, 'I was very pleasant to them, and they may even suspect they had my vote, but they were nowhere near as professional, or persistent, as the Major people.'

Nevertheless, there were converts, attracted by the apparent audacity of Redwood's bid, and their names and number gave Portillo supporters some cause for concern.

Redwood enjoyed an early endorsement from the former Tory party treasurer, Lord McAlpine, and warm words from Lady Thatcher – a significant boost, even though neither had a vote. As well as the initial gaggle of back-bench supporters, a few bigger-hitters among MPs weighed in, including Sir Tom Arnold, a former party vice-chairman, John Butcher, a former Industry minister, and Iain Duncan-Smith, a dogged and meticulous opponent of the Maastricht Treaty.

Duncan-Smith's defection caused a degree of heart-searching among his friends in the 1992 intake who shared his scepticism. Bernard Jenkin, Alan Duncan and John Whittingdale had admired his analysis in the past, but there was a feeling among others on the Right that he was inclined to take too purist a stance. They considered that intellectual attraction to the Redwood agenda was not enough: a cooler look at the landscape demanded a different response.

One other adherent to the Redwood flag caused a flutter. He was another man naturally suspicious of anything that smelt of compromise – Duncan-Smith's predecessor as MP for Chingford, Norman Tebbit. Tebbit had been at Redwood's launch – but, he had stressed, only in his capacity as a disinterested *Sun* columnist. Just how disinterested became clear the next day, when he praised Redwood's 'electric' performance. It was no surprise when, four days later, he declared for the rebel.

Despite having been party chairman, Tebbit is a natural outsider. He first made his mark in Parliament with his attacks on Heath from the back benches, was never happier in the government than when fighting to overcome the wets in the early eighties, but grew estranged from Margaret Thatcher during her heyday. He returned to type in the late eighties, leading the revolt against greater immigration from Hong Kong. Entry into the Lords in 1992 did not mellow him: he put himself at the head of the anti-Maastricht revolt at that year's Tory conference, and later objected to the release of prisoners as part of the IRA peace process.

A natural insurgent, Tebbit's anti-immigration, anti-Brussels, anti-Dublin stance confirms him as one of the purest Powellites in politics, and, like Powell, at heart he remains happier scenting betrayal than reconciling himself to the way the world is.

Tebbit, Duncan-Smith and McAlpine were all useful figures, but why was there not more momentum for Redwood on the Right? Inevitably the weaknesses of the campaign, in organisation and ideas, played a part; but, more than that, there was a sense that the battle between Redwood and Major was at best a shadow contest, at worst an unnecessary one.

Throughout the contest the press, progressively detaching itself from Major, coalesced around a consensus in favour of a second round. As Major's campaign manager, Ian Lang, pointed out, they had a vested interest in manufacturing as much news as possible. A resounding victory for the incumbent would be the dullest result of all. However, several titles – particularly *The Times* and the *Sun*, but also on occasions the *Daily Mail* – expressed a clear preference for the sort of second round they wanted – John versus John had to be followed by the battle of the Michaels. *The Times* characterised such a titanic struggle as the battle the Tory party 'needs to have'. The *Sun* showed warmth to Redwood, but declared that Portillo was its favoured candidate:

Unless the farcical first round election is opened up to all comers, it will settle nothing. What Britain needs is a man who speaks the language of the people. A man who articulates forcefully their hopes and fears. A man who will stand up to Europe, cut taxes and, above all, reduce the size of government, ease the stranglehold of the bureaucracy and give more freedom and choice to the people. In short, a leader. That man is Michael Portillo. He must not be kept waiting in the wings.

Redwood recognised the dissatisfaction felt by some with the stark choice, and at his penultimate press conference, on the Friday before voting, he reinforced his simple message of 'No Change equals No Chance' by inviting those MPs with 'other agendas' to cast their votes for him as the only candidate who could trigger change. One significant late convert to Redwood's cause even declared that his support was intended solely to open up the contest. Sir George Gardiner, chairman of the 92 Group, the main caucus on the Right of the parliamentary Tory Party, declared for Redwood on the eve of the contest, explicitly arguing for a wider choice. There was no doubt whom he wanted – anyone uncertain of his real motives need only have looked at his introduction to Michael Portillo's speech at a Conservative Way Forward dinner in 1994. Sir George had referred then to the lure of Number Ten, and had promised 'We hope we can help you when and if you apply.'

Although there was a groundswell of support for Portillo – the result of months spent painstakingly consolidating friendships, visiting constituencies and staking out a distinctively right-wing position on carefully chosen platforms – he did not endear himself anew to many during the leadership crisis. He was caught between two stools – loyalty to the prime minister and admiration for Redwood's 'intelligence, instincts and ideology' – but his balancing act might have been better managed.

Doubt was cast on Portillo's commitment to John Major – the man he always referred to as 'my candidate'. The first public question mark came with the disclosure that Portillo had met Redwood on the Monday of the latter's declaration. Portillo spent forty minutes in Redwood's office, during which time he spelt out his concerns – his fear that the Right could split, and his concern that only Heseltine could benefit. He asked Redwood bluntly, 'Why have you done this?'

Redwood, of course, had stood to steal a march on his younger and, so far, stronger rival. After anger on both sides had subsided, Portillo assured Redwood he would not stand in the first round, and confirmed he would support Major for as long as the prime minister remained in the race. Both were anxious that the campaign should not descend to the personal – Redwood's 'ultra-right-wing' position had already been attacked by Kenneth Clarke – and an agreement was made not to resort to negative campaigning. It did not last. The next day, Tuesday, Portillo supporters did not disguise how unimpressed they were by the Redwood manifesto. One dismissed it as 'pathetic'.

The Redwood team, worried they were not picking up momentum, operated a two-track strategy to detach support from Portillo. Publicly they praised him, and dangled the prospect of promotion. Walter Sweeney, the Redwood-supporting MP for the Vale of Glamorgan, told the BBC that Portillo would be chancellor or foreign secretary in a Redwood administration. Privately they sought to paint Portillo as a second-rater. Redwood had had the 'balls', or 'bottle', to challenge; Portillo, by implication, had not.

An associate of, of all people, Norman Lamont dismissed Portillo as a 'salon Conservative', more at home in fashionable metropolitan circles than Redwood, who, despite his years as an Oxford postgraduate at All Souls and a merchant banker at N. M. Rothschild's, was presented as a man of the people. One MP contrasted Portillo's Spanish surname and 'thick lips' with the homely Englishness of Redwood. One Redwood supporter even tried to exploit the Portillos' childlessness by arguing that MPs should support the man with the superior understanding of the problems of raising a family.

The whispering campaign did not ruffle Portillo's composure, but he was aware of the dangers of being left behind in the starting-blocks if a second round began.

On the evening of the Monday he declared his challenge, Redwood had gone to a meeting of the No Turning Back Group, the self-selecting Thatcherite cadre that saw itself keeping the radical momentum going within the government. It had been agreed that he should not speak, because there were supporters of both his and Major's candidature present. However, on entry he had been greeted by a warm ovation from sympathisers, including the guest speaker, Norman Tebbit. Significantly, several of Portillo's friends who were Major supporters, including Ian Twinn and Michael Forsyth, sat on their hands.

Portillo had not been there – a rare absence. That same night a potential supporter asked if he had regretted not throwing his hat in the ring, but Portillo was certain he had done the right thing. He recognised there were dangers, but said, simply, 'I'm quite relaxed.'

At that point Portillo believed Major would win the first round, but he feared he would be so wounded that he would have to step down – if not immediately, then in the autumn. Portillo also believed that he was the only candidate on the Right who could be sure of defeating a Heseltine challenge. If the battle went to a second round he thought he could join the contest, with new supporters and more momentum, peeling off some Redwood adherents and eventually overtaking Heseltine in the third round. It was a view he shared the next day, Tuesday 27 June, with two journalists, Mark Mardell and Jon Sopel, both BBC political correspondents. Over lunch, with his special adviser Alison Broom also in attendance, Portillo outlined his analysis and confirmed his determination to enter the race in the event of a Major withdrawal.

It may have appeared like a statement of the obvious, but, in retrospect, many MPs were to see it as a damaging miscalculation. That night's *Newsnight* led with the revelation that Portillo thought he could be leader in six months. It was a legitimate gloss on his words, but it did not seem to help John Major that one of his ministers was so privately pessimistic about his candidature.

At the same time as Portillo was acquainting Mardell and Sopel with his thinking, two of his most trusted lieutenants were also letting it be known that Portillo was ready to enter the lists. Alan Duncan and John Whittingdale emphasised that Portillo would, as they would, vote for Major, but if the way were clear he would definitely enter the second round.

The impression that a concerted undermining of Major's position was in progress was reinforced by another chance discovery in the early hours of Tuesday. Journalists were surprised to see British Telecom engineers working outside 11 Lord North Street, an elegant terraced house halfway between the Commons and Conservative Central Office. When asked what they were up to, they revealed that they were installing forty phone and fax lines. For whom? They declined to say.

Suspicions were aroused, and assumptions were quickly jumped to when the education minister and NTB member Eric Forth was sighted popping in to 11 Lord North Street late one night with his PPS, John Whittingdale, one of Portillo's oldest political friends.

The owner of the house was discovered to be Greville Howard, a former private secretary to Enoch Powell, who was chairman of the electrical group Arlen. Howard was a friend of John Aspinall, Sir James Goldsmith and their set of wealthy, raffish right-wingers. Through that set, Howard was also an acquaintance of his near-neighbour in Lord North Street, Jonathan Aitken. Aitken – at that point Treasury chief secretary – had once harboured hopes of leading the Tories himself, but was now loyally supporting Major. He, however, like many on the Right, had his own preference in the event of a Major withdrawal. He was ready to throw his weight behind Portillo.

Aitken was an old school chum of Portillo's adviser David Hart. Hart was a long-time admirer of Aitken – they had worked together at the Ministry of Defence, where Hart had been co-opted as an adviser by the secretary of state, Malcolm Rifkind, and their relationship had been strengthened by the part Hart had played in trying to save Aitken from a series of newspaper allegations about his personal life and business dealings.

The web of links leading from Greville Howard back to Hart and then to Portillo could mean only one thing: if there were to be a Portillo campaign, this would be its HQ. Portillo was not going to risk the faulty start that had dogged the Redwood challenge – he would be ready.

Alan Duncan had told one journalist, very early in the campaign, that it was important, in case there was a second round, that Portillo's supporters were seen to be more loyal than Heseltine's. So far, with prominent Portillistas speaking up for Major while the Heselteenies kept their own counsel, this seemed to be happen-

ing. But to set up a rival campaign HQ before there was any formal
rivalry sent a very different message.

Why had Portillo allowed this to happen? The answer seems to
lie in Suffolk. David Hart, the man who had done so much in the
name of 'The Lady' during the miners' strike – usually without
her knowledge – had decided, again, to act in what he perceived
to be the best interests of his candidate.

Hart's success in organising a network of working miners in
1984 had undoubtedly played a part in Scargill's defeat, but his
activities – using a *Daily Express* photographer to serve a writ on
Scargill, dangling cheques in front of the nascent UDM, posing as
a journalist himself to secure access to meetings from which he
might otherwise have been excluded – were not those which could
ever have been happily sanctioned by Number Ten. That had not
mattered to Hart, he knew he was acting in The Lady's interests,
and she had smiled on him. That was enough for him.

Hart's relationship with Portillo was closer than anything he
had enjoyed with Thatcher, his commitment all the greater, but
his judgement remained idiosyncratic.

Early in the spring of 1995, when Portillo was resisting a particular course of action urged on him by Hart, Hart had told him,
'Look, it's my job to look after your future. Summon me and I'll
explain what you should do.' The same self-confidence seems to
have prompted Hart to order the installation of the phone lines.
Greville Howard's home had been offered after a meeting, again
much earlier in the year, when a group of businessmen had indicated to Hart and Portillo that they wished to be of assistance in
the event of any future leadership crisis. None had foreseen a direct
challenge to Major, but the prospect of defeat at the looming general election had concentrated minds.

Apart from Howard, Portillo's admirers included Algy Cluff, a
former proprietor of the *Spectator* and owner of Cluff Oil, whom
Portillo had first met when he worked in the oil industry in the
early eighties; Lord King, who had taken a keen interest in Portillo's political progress from the mid-eighties; and a businessman
who had more recently been alerted to Portillo's merits: Sir James
Goldsmith, the Anglo-French billionaire who had formed his own
party in France at the last Euro-elections, securing the election of
thirteen MEPs, including himself. Although nominally committed

to setting up another new party in the UK to campaign for a referendum on further European integration, Goldsmith had been attracted by what he had been told of Portillo by acquaintances, including his PR adviser Patrick Robertson and one of Major's more sceptical cabinet ministers.

All these expressions of interest were, nevertheless, conditional. No matter how qualified the support from outside Westminster, though, what mattered most during the leadership crisis were the perceptions of MPs. The installation of forty phone lines did not impress them. One Major loyalist on the Right recalls, 'It was certainly damaging to Portillo. If he'd authorised it, it looked like he was already plotting to knife Major. If it was Hart who was responsible then you had to ask what Portillo was doing associating with a maverick like that.'

The impression that Portillo's support for Major was decidedly equivocal was not helped by his performance on the *Today* programme on the morning of Thursday 29 June. The day before, Michael Heseltine had jousted magnificently with John Humphrys, ruling out a referendum as a way of wooing the Right and proclaiming his loyalty in extravagant terms but with the tiniest let-out clause possible. Heseltine declared he would not stand against John Major 'in this contest' – leaving, despite his protestations, a tantalising opening for an entry into a second round, or a later contest.

Portillo had agreed to appear on the programme nominally to discuss his work at a meeting of EU employment ministers, but his real task was to impress, demonstrate his loyalty, but also hint at his availability. After dealing in a straightforwardly sceptical fashion with the first questions on Euro-business, he found himself on the defensive when questioned about the forty phone lines. He refused to 'confirm or deny' that he had a headquarters in preparation in Lord North Street, deprecated the appearance of a 'rumour a day', declared he would do nothing to encourage more rumour-mongering, and affected anger that BT technicians 'could not go about their work in SW1' without being constantly harassed.

If it was Portillo's intention to ensure he had nothing he need disavow in any future contest, his refusal to be drawn might have been a defensible tactic. But Major loyalists were unimpressed. One source close to Michael Howard commented, 'He should have disassociated himself from the forty-phone-line nonsense. If his tactic was to seem more loyal than Hezza, it didn't work.'

Why would a politician as apparently adept as Portillo – the favoured candidate of a master intriguer like Sir George Gardiner, the considered preference of the Murdoch press, and the natural choice of the Right within the ranks of the government – allow himself to appear so clumsy? A glimpse into the Portillo camp's thinking was given in the *Mail on Sunday* on 2 July. Under the headline 'Portillo's Cunning Blunder', the paper's political correspondents, Joe Murphy and Adrian Lithgow, took the reader through the Portillista 'spin' on the week's events. It may have been their work, but there was more than a whiff of David Hart's *modus operandi* about the story.

The establishment of a Portillo HQ in Lord North Street, and the sighting of known Portillo supporters stealing in, was presented as a deliberate tactic on Portillo's part to obstruct the Redwood challenge. Described as a 'calculated move of which Machiavelli himself would have been proud', it was argued that the Portillo camp had decided he should wait for Major to leave the stage before challenging for the top job, but 'what had to be avoided at all costs was to allow the Redwood bandwagon to build up an unstoppable momentum'. The BBC briefing, the phone lines, John Whittingdale's late-night journey: all part of a ruse to keep pro-Portillo centrists and right-wingers out of the Redwood camp, by signalling that their man was willing to stand when the time was right.

The *Mail on Sunday* quoted a 'furious' Redwood aide's view that Portillo 'did it to show his own supporters he was standing in earnest and to split our vote down the middle', and it was argued that Portillo's intervention had indeed prevented any haemorrhage of support to Redwood.

That intervention was presented as more than just a reminder to Redwood of Portillo's power: it was also argued that it had helped the man Portillo was backing – John Major. The *Mail on Sunday* reported, 'The failure of any grander figure to emerge presented a gift to John Major's campaign team. "Redwood's bandwagon is falling apart," sneered a Major aide to MPs in the Commons . . . "Where are all the big guns he claimed to have behind him? No one will believe anything he says from now on."'

So, was the impression of disloyalty in fact the most signal service Portillo could have rendered? Was the impression he was ready to stand, and its allegedly destabilising effect on the Redwood camp, worth more than any number of passionate protestations of loyalty to John Major?

It was certainly true that Portillo could not have kept his credibility with the Right if he had, point by point, rebutted Redwood's arguments on the risks of a European single currency and joined in the general Major-camp rubbishing of Redwood's 'extremist' agenda. When Michael Forsyth – a prominent Portillo supporter, if anything further to the Right than Redwood – defended Major against the challenger on *Channel 4 News*, one other Portillo supporter was not impressed: 'He risked making himself look ridiculous.'

So, if following Forsyth would have been unconvincing, and unimpressive in the eyes of many of his supporters, was Portillo actually pursuing the only course that was credible, and yet also helpful to Major? For David Hart, a student of Machiavelli and Clausewitz, there would have been a delicious irony in executing a manoeuvre that helped Major by appearing unhelpful and harmed a natural ally by appearing to shoot oneself in the foot. However, whatever satisfaction Hart might have derived from that, and however persuasive the *Mail On Sunday*'s view of events, to many on the Tory back benches and beyond Portillo's position did not seem stronger that Sunday.

Redwood's supporters believed it was Portillo, and not their man, who was risking a split on the Right. Several of Major's team simply saw a minister on the make fail to show the required loyalty to his leader. At the time, however, many of these judgements were provisional. If Major was fatally wounded then all bets would be off and everything could depend on the candidates' performance in the field. Even after all the HQ hullabaloo there was evidence that the centre-Right still saw Portillo as their most credible candidate. On Sunday 2 July Sir Archie Hamilton, a former defence minister and a natural loyalist, told the BBC's *On The Record* that he hoped Major would win but that he would definitely back Portillo in any second round.

The uncertainty of the eventual outcome of their first ballot made most MPs reluctant to venture any definite statement of intention for the first vote, never mind for a second ballot, and during that weekend the feel of the party was still relatively fluid. If there was any movement, it seemed to be a rallying back to the Major camp – a process which seemed to gather momentum on Monday, with support for Major coming from some previously undeclared figures on the Euro-sceptic Right, such as Vivian Bendall, the member for Ilford North, who is, supremely appropriately, the representative of the taxi trade in the Commons.

On Monday 3 July – the day before the first ballot – there was furious speculation that most of the supporters of Portillo, and of Heseltine, would abstain – depriving Major of a winning margin but also denying Redwood an unstoppable momentum. Gardiner's declaration in support of Redwood that evening was intended to serve a double purpose: to give Redwood's faltering challenge a late boost, in the hope he would attract enough votes to provoke a second contest, and also to ensure that, come a second round, there was a visible erosion in Redwood's support as defectors went over to Portillo. One Portillo supporter explained, 'George wasn't the only Portillo supporter to vote for Redwood – if there'd been a second round several of Redwood's supporters, including some of his campaign team, would have come over.'

These calculations, however finely calibrated, were set at naught by manœuvrings that took place on the morning of the first ballot, on Tuesday 4 July, not between undecided MPs, rival factions or even telephone engineers, but between the prime minister and the self-styled president.

John Major spent three hours deep in discussion with Michael Heseltine that morning. Afterwards, Heseltine claimed they were discussing the competitiveness of the British economy. Not since *Private Eye* caught *in flagrante* a diplomat who claimed to be just 'discussing Uganda', has an excuse been so bare-faced. Would two politicians, on the day that would decide their fates, with the biggest prize in British politics on offer, which one was determined to hold on to and the other had coveted since university, really waste their time discussing productivity ratios?

It soon became clear, as the dust settled following the leadership election, that Major had reached an 'arrangement' with Heseltine. In the post-election reshuffle Heseltine was given the title 'deputy prime minister', and was promised access, status, and a rejigging of committees in his favour.

John Major's negotiations got him off the hook. Heseltine followed his chat with a trip to the Commons' committee room where MPs were casting their votes. There he ostentatiously ticked the box beside Major's name. Later that day ticks in Major's favour were recorded by a series of Heseltine admirers, including Peter Temple-Morris – Clarendon to George Gardiner's Cromwell – and Keith Hampson. They, and others, had been expected to abstain in the hope of seeing Heseltine enter a second round. Their firepower had been held in reserve until late in the day, but, following the Major–Hezza summit, their favourite had ordered his tanks off the Downing Street lawn.

There was almost as much uncertainty about what would constitute an authoritative majority for the prime minister as there was about the intentions of individual members. The newspapers, anxious as ever to prolong his agony, presented anything over 100 votes against Major as the danger zone. It was a view shared by some MPs. The independent back-bencher David Wilshire told the BBC that 100–110 votes against the prime minister would put a question mark over his future.

However, when, at almost twenty past five, Sir Marcus Fox, the chairman of the 1922 Committee, announced the result – 218 votes for John Major, 89 for John Redwood and 20 votes for neither candidate – it was greeted as a triumph. From ministers poised by radio microphones and TV cameras to the BBC's political editor, Robin Oakley, there was near unanimity that Major had pulled it off. No dissenting voices were raised, and, shortly after the announcement, Redwood emerged from his campaign HQ to concede defeat gracefully. He had earlier said, 'If either of us wins by just one vote under the rules it will be enough.' He was as good as his word.

Over the next seventy-two hours Major set about reconstructing his government, and shifting it firmly to the Left. The assumption of Heseltine and the promotion of old wets such as Stephen Dorrell, Sir George Young and Douglas Hogg was reinforced by the consolidation of the power of centre-Left ministers, with Malcolm Rifkind taking over at the Foreign Office following Douglas Hurd's decision to resign on 23 June and William Waldegrave recalled from the

Cabinet's departure lounge to take charge of spending as chief secretary to the Treasury.

Major had not planned to move his government quite so firmly to the Left. He had hoped to promote David Maclean, the right-wing Home Office minister, to the Cabinet, but was surprised to find Maclean determined to stay where he was, in a job he enjoyed. He had flirted with elevating the sceptically inclined Michael Howard to the Foreign Office, only to back down in the face of a majestic Rifkind huff.

He had also planned to make the centre-Right William Hague – as fiscally rigorous a Yorkshireman as ever wandered out of the West Riding – chief secretary and send William Waldegrave across the Severn, reasoning that a Bristol MP would be the perfect Welsh secretary. But the veto of the chancellor, Kenneth Clarke, torpedoed that scheme and forced Major into an inelegant last-minute swop, sending a Yorkshireman to Cardiff and putting a wet in charge of spending cuts.

If everything had gone according to his original plans Major might have had a more balanced Cabinet, but the tilt, while less pronounced, would still have been decidedly to port.

Some Major backers on the Right were disturbed at how the battle for his survival was being exploited by some – in particular the former deputy chief whip Tristan Garel-Jones – to do down the Right, rather than bring the party together. One MP on the Right who supported Major complains that 'The Major campaign was supposed to be a unity campaign. Garel-Jones tried to run it as a factional thing. He saw it as an opportunity to shaft the Euro-sceptics, and the Redwood campaign played into his hands.'

The association of the Right with rebellion made it easier for Major to shift his government to the centre-Left, and he was encouraged to do so by several of his oldest advisers who had long encouraged him to end the delicate balancing act between the two wings of the party and follow his liberal instincts.

When the list of new appointments was announced two of the happiest men in the House were MPs whose positions had not changed: Garel-Jones, still in retirement on the back benches, and the Hon. Nicholas Soames, kept in place as armed-forces minister. The two thoroughgoing wets – proud pro-Europeans throughout their careers – were sighted on the Commons Terrace roaring with laughter at the relentless advance of 'their' candidates through the ranks of the government. With delicate disingenuousness, Garel-Jones, for whom few of the names could really have come as a surprise, remarked, 'I couldn't have done it better myself.'

The advance of the Left in the ranks of the government obscured another story: division within the ranks of the Right had denied a numerically more powerful faction the influence it might have wielded.

Many on the Right were convinced that in any second, or even third, round their candidate would have won. They argued that a second round was avoided only because Heseltine shirked the challenge. According to Graham Riddick, who supported Redwood, 'Heseltine calculated that in any future contest he didn't have the numbers to beat the Right, so he ducked it and cut a deal with Major.'

Other theories have been advanced to explain Heseltine's decision – his heart stopped him; his wife prevented him; he thought a second round would fatally damage the Tories' chances of re-election and did not want to lead his party to annihilation; he was bored; his admiration for Major meant he could not contemplate a challenge. But is it credible that a man who had built his life around becoming prime minister would withdraw at the last minute if he thought the prize was his?

If there had been a second ballot, Portillo would have entered the fray with a properly prepared manifesto, commitments costed, and policies spelled out in some detail. He would have had the support of the main right-wingers in the Cabinet, most notably the economic liberal Peter Lilley and the High Tory sceptic Jonathan Aitken. He would have a swathe of support from middle-ranking ministers and back-benchers charmed over the years by a politician with a personality cultivated since schooldays. He would also have had a variety of MPs visibly defecting from Redwood, arguing that their allegiance had been only tactical. The number might not have been large, but the effect of the momentum would have been in one direction.

If Redwood had stayed in the race he would certainly have denied any candidate a clear-cut victory, but a third round would then have followed. In that contest the top two from the second round would have faced each other in a head-to-head. As such an election would inevitably have polarised on European lines, Heseltine might well have reflected on the pendulum swing in favour of scepticism in his party since Margaret Thatcher's fall and concluded that his time had passed.

The result of any second ballot is, of course, unknowable; speculating on it is an exercise in the hypothetical all politicians would publicly abjure, but privately adore. Calculations about the consequences of a second ballot had influenced the thinking of MPs throughout the contest, and post-mortems on the actual result colour the prospects of all the main players. For weeks after the election MPs were still fascinated by the actions and motivations of their colleagues during those difficult ten days, and continued to play the what-if games that had been such a delicious, but confusing, part of making their minds up.

Because no second ballot ever occurred Michael Portillo's preparations for one appeared to most observers neither smart tactics nor simple prudence. Bruce Anderson, an acquaintance of Portillo's from the seventies, argued on the night of Major's victory that Portillo had been a loser, because 'he showed himself willing to wound but afraid to strike'. In the same breath he predicted a glittering future for Jonathan Aitken, who was to resign from the Cabinet within hours.

But Anderson's impression that Portillo had suffered was shared by several other commentators. In the *Spectator*, Boris Johnson felt that Portillo had not had 'a good war'. Peter Riddell, in *The Times*, felt Portillo had shown he needed to study more carefully the practice of 'high politics' anatomised so effectively by his old university tutor, Maurice Cowling. Journalism demands instant judgements, but there is little doubt the chattering-class consensus was that Portillo had been found wanting – in loyalty and in judgement.

But Portillo, more than most politicians, has grown used to seeing his career cut short by commentators. From his apparently overeager defence of the poll tax, through his allegedly ill-advised hints of cuts to come in the NHS, to supposed gaffes directed at a populist royal family, foreigners and the disabled, he has piled up almost as many premature obituaries as John Major.

Privately, Portillo was reassured by the result. One supporter commented, 'Michael stopped Redwood supplanting him as the automatic leader of the Right. He'd shown he could command the loyalty of a bloc of MPs big enough to deny Redwood the momentum he needed.' And Portillo had the simple satisfaction, at the end of the crisis, of remaining in office, while his rival was on the back benches.

He also had the grimmer satisfaction of knowing that his initial calculation that a premature challenge from the Right risked playing into the hands of the Tory Left had been proved correct.

Office gives Portillo power, patronage and a platform. It remains easier to win the Tory Party if you are running on the inside track.

In the early sixties the Tory current was running in a liberal direction, but the most outspoken liberal, Iain Macleod, never became leader after he refused to serve under the aristocratic Alec Douglas-Home.

In the late sixties, after years in opposition, the Tory current swung to the Right, culminating in the creation of 'Selsdon Man', a Wilsonian caricature of the free-market Tory policies in the 1970 election. But the drift to the Right did not benefit the most eloquent right-wing voice which had been crying in the wilderness – Enoch Powell. His ejection from the shadow Cabinet for challenging the line on race relations turned him from prophet to pariah, for just long enough to deny him the leadership for ever.

From Joseph Chamberlain to Michael Heseltine, the Tory Party has shown it does not reward the radicals who resign to launch crusades.

Portillo is the most senior right-winger in the Cabinet, responsible for the policy areas – defence and security – central to the next round of negotiations on the future shape of the EU, the 1996 Inter-Governmental Conference. He continues to have a direct influence on policy in other areas, and he has the platform of the party conference as well as ministerial duties to allow him to make his mark.

Inevitably he suffers if the government is seen to falter, but Portillo has in the past distanced himself, delicately and not so delicately, from Tory problems. This is a tactic that has impressed some on the Right, who feel he can prosper if he uses office to push forward the barriers of the sayable without rocking the boat. Alan Clark has always admired Portillo's use of office to advance his ideas: 'He doesn't make gaffes – it's just that he speaks outside the usual perimeters all the time. It is a good tactic. If you are seriously ambitious you don't want to be tainted by the general Cabinet torpor.'

Portillo was one of the few on the Right to receive promotion in the post-election reshuffle. His old department, Employment, where he had been conspicuously underemployed, was divided between Education and the DTI. Secretary of state for defence is a post which has lost something of its prestige with the end of the Cold War, but it is still a useful place for any Tory – especially one with an urban, professional background – to broaden his appeal to more traditional Tory constituencies, as previous defence secretaries Heseltine and Rifkind have proven.

A few weeks after the leadership election Portillo was entertaining a few friends at home for supper. The crisis in Bosnia was absorbing much of his attention, but he had snatched some time to relax. One of the guests was Michael Brown, an old friend who had played a prominent part in the Major campaign. In the course of the evening, the conversation turned to the importance of loyalty.

Portillo was gently chided for his loyalty to David Hart, when Hart's actions had allowed Portillo to appear disloyal to Major. Many of the guests had had reason to be grateful to Portillo in the past for his loyalty to them, and it was felt that one of his most conspicuous political assets, his sense of honour, had been sold cheap. Portillo defended Hart vigorously. He maintained that loyalty was indivisible – he would not let down a friend.

Even those who felt the maverick millionaire was unworthy of the respect Portillo accorded him accepted that Portillo's reaction was all too typical. In a manner that may have seemed cold, that was certainly not attuned to compromise, Portillo was reminding his guests that, having adopted a person, or a principle, he sticks by them. It was that knowledge which had made them stick by him during the last difficult months, and that convinced them that their own loyalty would be rewarded in the years to come.

Index